14 95

S0-BNJ-643

INTERPRETING FILMS

No Longer Property of
Fr. Leonard Alvey Library
Brescia University

INTERPRETING FILMS

STUDIES IN THE
HISTORICAL RECEPTION OF
AMERICAN CINEMA

Janet Staiger

PRINCETON UNIVERSITY PRESS   PRINCETON, NEW JERSEY

BRESCIA COLLEGE LIBRARY
OWENSBORO, KENTUCKY

791.4301
5782

Copyright © 1992 by Princeton University Press
Published by Princeton University Press, 41 William Street,
Princeton, New Jersey 08540
In the United Kingdom: Princeton University Press, Oxford
All Rights Reserved

Library of Congress Cataloging-in-Publication Data
Staiger, Janet.
Interpreting films : studies in the historical reception of
American cinema / Janet Staiger.
p.   cm.
Includes bibliographical references and index.
ISBN 0-691-04797-9 — ISBN 0-691-00616-4 (pbk.)
1. Motion pictures—Aesthetics.   2. Reader-response criticism.
3. Motion pictures—United States.   I. Title.
PN1995.S6735   1992
791.43'01—dc20   91-22248   CIP

This book has been composed in Linotron Galliard

Princeton University Press books are printed
on acid-free paper, and meet the guidelines
for permanence and durability of the Committee
on Production Guidelines for Book Longevity
of the Council on Library Resources

Printed in the United States of America

1   3   5   7   9   10   8   6   4   2

(Pbk.)
1   3   5   7   9   10   8   6   4   2

For Peter Staiger and
Iryl and Don Voelte

86923

Contents

List of Figures and Sources   ix

Preface   xi

PART ONE: THEORETICAL CONCERNS   1

Chapter One
The Use-Value of Reception Studies   3

Chapter Two
Reception Studies in Other Disciplines   16

Chapter Three
Reception Studies in Film and Television   49

Chapter Four
Toward a Historical Materialist Approach to Reception Studies   79

PART TWO: STUDIES IN THE HISTORY OF THE
RECEPTION OF AMERICAN FILMS   99

Chapter Five
Rethinking "Primitive" Cinema: Intertextuality, the Middle-Class
Audience, and Reception Studies   101

Chapter Six
"The Handmaiden of Villainy": *Foolish Wives*, Politics,
Gender Orientation, and the Other   124

Chapter Seven
The Birth of a Nation: Reconsidering Its Reception   139

Chapter Eight
The Logic of Alternative Readings: A Star Is Born   154

Chapter Nine
With the Compliments of the Auteur: Art Cinema and the
Complexities of Its Reading Strategies   178

Chapter Ten
Chameleon in the Film, Chameleons in the Audience;
or, Where Is Parody? The Case of *Zelig*   196

Epilogue 210

Notes 213

Select Bibliography 259

Index 271

List of Figures and Sources

Figures

5.1 *Uncle Tom's Cabin*: The dramatic and the film versions.   106

5.2 Uncle Tom's Cabin: Handbill from C. W. Lang's dramatic version.   111

5.3 Eliza pleads with Tom to run away: Scene 1 of the film.   111

5.4 The Escape of Eliza: Poster from Jay Rial's Ideal *Uncle Tom's Cabin* dramatic version.   112

5.5 The Escape of Eliza: Scene 3 of the film.   112

5.6 Tom and Eva in the Garden: Poster from Jay Rial's Ideal *Uncle Tom's Cabin*.   113

5.7 Tom and Eva in the Garden: Scene 8 of the film.   113

5.8 The Death of Eva: Handbill from C. W. Lang's *Uncle Tom's Cabin*.   114

5.9 The Death of Eva: Scene 9 of the film.   114

5.10 The Death of Eva: Handbill from Kathleen Kirkwood's *Uncle Tom's Cabin*.   115

5.11 The Death of Eva: Scene 9 of the film.   115

5.12 Death of Tom: Handbill from C. W. Lang's *Uncle Tom's Cabin*.   116

5.13 Death of Tom: Scene 14 of the film.   116

6.1 "She was batty"   129

6.2 "The Count's brand"   130

6.3 "For some unknown reason"   130

6.4 "A Song of Hate"   134

Sources

5.2, 5.4, 5.6, 5.8, 5.10, 5.12: *Uncle Tom's Cabin* (Edison, 1903)

5.3, 5.5, 5.7, 5.9, 5.11, 5.13: New York Public Library—Lincoln Center Posters and Handbills for *Uncle Tom's Cabin*

6.1, 6.2, 6.3, 6.4: *Photoplay* (1922)

A COMMONPLACE assumption in criticism today is the notion that the reader of a text, the viewer of an art piece, or the spectator of a film ought to be a focal point of study. While that notion guides this project, my argument is that describing *historical* interpretative strategies and explaining the causes for those specific strategies can make valuable contributions to the history, criticism, and philosophy of these cultural products. Such a proposition assumes that cultural artifacts are not containers with immanent meanings, that variations among interpretations have historical bases for their differences, and that differences and change are not idiosyncratic but due to social, political, and economic conditions, as well as to constructed identities such as gender, sexual preference, race, ethnicity, class, and nationality.

Thus, this project distinguishes itself among much current reader-response criticism or reception aesthetics work. As a materialist historiography, *Interpreting Films* takes a neo-Marxist stance, stressing contextual factors rather than textual materials or reader psychologies as most important in illuminating the reading process or interpretation. It also argues for attempting to describe and explain the *relations* among texts and historical readers. This book asks, What contributions to cultural studies can be made through the study of historical spectators of films?

To answer this question, the book offers both general theory and an application to American film. Part One sets out the value of a comparative historical approach to the problem of interpretation. It argues that most current reader-response research or reception aesthetics (i.e., approaches derived from textual poetics, affective stylistics, phenomenology, transactive criticism, subjective criticism, and literary conventions) tend to represent readers ahistorically. In fact, the so-called reader may be more a fiction of the critical approach than an actuality.

After surveying the critical approaches dominant in literary studies, Part One considers specific paradigms informing film scholarship in this area: contemporary linguistics, cognitive psychology, and British cultural studies. It then proposes an alternative: a contextual and materialist approach to the study of historical spectators and interpretative strategies. Thus, my approach to reception studies might best be understood as having connections with points of view, besides historical materialism, of post-structuralism, new historicism, and cultural studies.

Part Two provides six case studies in the history of American cinema, seeking to show the possibilities, validity, and value of the approach. The studies span the time frame of moving pictures (i.e., from the 1903 *Uncle Tom's Cabin* to the 1983 *Zelig*). Additionally, the studies treat various familiar critical questions: the appearance of the classical Hollywood cinema (chapter 5), affective responses (chapter 6), evaluative debates about technique and subject matter (chapter 7), processes of identifying with narrative stories or stars (chapter 8), the construction and reading of genres or modes of film practice (chapter 9), and judgments about voice, tone, and parody (chapter 10). Each case makes its argument through providing historical evidence about interpretative strategies rather than speculating about interpretations solely or primarily on the basis of the films being considered.

In my previous book, *The Classical Hollywood Cinema: Film Style and Mode of Production*, coauthored with David Bordwell and Kristin Thompson, we pointed out that a history of the consumption of American cinema also needed to be written but that such a history would be another book. This book is not that other book, but it is my view about the directions research might take in order to begin to illuminate what have been the interpretive meanings and affective experiences of the diverse individuals who have watched movies for nearly one hundred years. I hope that we will someday know enough to write that book.

As should be obvious already in this Preface, I have a very specific political position. As a woman from a working-class family, my subjectivity informs my history. Indeed, I would not wish it otherwise. This book is an argument in a conflict that I perceive as having significant pedagogical and political consequences. The issue of "agency" is continually raised by those who are concerned by some directions of new theory. I personally do not see the theoretical frameworks I am employing as ruling out consciousness and an ability to act as a result. Rather, those frameworks do argue that limits exist to consciousness—including limits to knowledges of history. Thus, for me, these limitations compel me all the more to turn my attention to issues of how knowledges are produced so that my agency is as responsible as possible within its historical context.

Parts of this historical context are the numerous institutions and individuals who helped me produce this book. Chapter 6 is revised from original publication in *Wide Angle* 8, no. 1 (January 1986): 19–28. Some original methodological issues have been deleted, while a bit of new historical information and analysis from a feminist perspective has been added. In particular, work by Miriam Hansen on Rudolph Valentino appeared between the original publication and this book, and her research proves very suggestive for starting analyses of female spectators' reception of male stars in the 1920s. My thanks to The Johns Hopkins University Press, *Wide Angle*, and the Athens Center for Film and Video for permission to reprint. Additionally, comments from Janice Welsch, Diane Carsen, and Linda Dittmar on a draft of the chapter were very helpful. Part of chapter 3 was originally published in *The Centennial Review*.

Although this project began during my work on my doctoral dissertation, its first concerted development occurred while I was teaching at New York University. There, I was fortunate to have the support of David Oppenheim, Dean of the Tisch School of the Arts, and Brian Winston, Chair of the Department of Cinema Studies. Their assistance helped me to receive a New York University Presidential Fellowship for Junior Faculty that permitted a semester of intensive reading. Also at New York University, I appreciated the help of my research assistant, Harald Stadler, and the students in several seminars that addressed issues about reception studies. Their debate and disagreements with me contributed in the most fruitful ways to this project. Parts of their research appear with acknowledgments in the text. I thank Ann Harris for her continuing companionship.

Also helpful have been audiences whose interpretations of my arguments made me wonder what I had said and what I wanted to say. I thank the auditors of my papers at the 1983, 1986, and 1989 Society for Cinema Studies Conferences, the 1984 Ohio University Conference, the 1984 Modern Language Association Conference, Yale University, and the Annenberg School of Communication at the University of Pennsylvania. Libraries to be congratulated for their assistance are the New York Public Library and libraries of the University of Texas at Austin.

My colleagues at the University of Texas at Austin have particularly been supportive in the recent three years while I wrote the book. I thank Horace Newcomb, Tom Schatz, Doug Kellner, Penny Marcus, Dina Shertzer, David Prindle, and Joe Slate, who responded to various parts of the book. I also thank the University of Texas Scholars' Project in honor of the Silver Anniversary of the Founding of the College of Communication for being another recent audience to this work.

Good readers from Princeton University Press improved this work significantly. I thank Charles Maland and my anonymous reader very much for their time and effort. I hope they will be proud of their contributions. My editors at Princeton University Press have been particularly helpful and gracious in their suggestions. Authors are extremely fortunate to work with people such as Joanna Hitchcock, Valerie Jablow, and Lauren Lepow.

Acknowledgments for this book could be endless in terms of the number of people with whom I have discussed the project over the years. Each and every one has some trace in what appears here. I want, however, to pay special thanks to David Bordwell and Kristin Thompson, whose confidence in my work has sustained me, and pushed me, throughout my academic life. Their standards of scholarship and their friendship are models I am proud to emulate.

My special thanks also goes to Peter Staiger, who has had to deal with late dinners and distracted conversations far more than he ought to have. This book is dedicated to him and to my parents, who have always told me to do what I think is right.

Part One

THEORETICAL CONCERNS

CHAPTER ONE

The Use-Value of Reception Studies

... consumption is not only the concluding act
through which the product becomes a product,
but also the one through which the producer
becomes a producer.
(*Karl Marx, 1857*)

THE PLEASURES and power of being the reader of a text or the spectator
of a film are expressed in Karl Marx's views about consuming products.[1]
For without an audience, some would argue, no text or maker of that text
exists. This intuitive dialectic is a commonplace assumption in scholarship
today: the reader of a text or the spectator of a film ought to be a focal
point of study. Over twenty years ago Roland Barthes published "The
Death of the Author," while forty years earlier I. A. Richards examined
student interpretative strategies in *Practical Criticism*. Worried about "misreadings," Richards subtitled his book *A Study of Literary Judgment*.
Whether you take the position of Richards, that a hierarchy of appropriate
interpretative activities exists, or that of Barthes, that a celebration
"restor[ing] the place of the reader" is due, hardly anyone familiar with
twentieth-century scholarly trends doubts the considerable theoretical implications of "reader-response" or "reception studies" work.[2]

Yet a trend can also be trendy. Consequently, I believe that it is important to start a book investigating the problems and value of applying reception studies to the history of moving pictures by suggesting the overall
difference such an approach makes to the field of film studies. More particularly, I want to establish the use-value of this type of research.

In a rather simple dichotomy, reception studies might be placed in an-
tithesis to a hermeneutics based on the authority of production (authorship). In fact, some individuals have gone so far as to claim that reception
studies eliminates the need to examine production since, they believe,
meaning*[3] is produced by the reader. As will become apparent, I find such
a proposition dangerous not merely for the reason that any radical historian might (it elides the incontestable force of the historical real to affect
the reader) but because that inference only inverts fallacious binary oppositions: producer/consumer, author/reader. In his dialectical observation

about constituting positions in the social order, Marx proposes that the act of consumption is an event constituting the product *and* the producer. In the case of art, an equivalent achievement occurs: an individual, in taking an object to be art, constitutes through that act the object, the individual as perceiver, and other individuals as producers. To declare that the reader is the site of the production of meaning is to miss the theoretical reverberations of that act of constituting meaning. Arthur Danto neatly summarizes this in his "The Artworld," where he contends that something's being an artwork requires a theory of what art "is": "It is the role of artistic theories, these days as always, to make the artworld, and art, possible."[4] Such a proposition, however, can become a utopian fantasy of free will no longer grounded in material conditions if the question of how and why readers hold theory X, Y, or Z is not also part of the equation. Danto acknowledges this, as he includes not only a theory of the "artworld" but the "artworld's history" as necessary conditions for the perception of an object as art.

The use-value of reception studies, it seems to me, is not to overthrow the author in favor of the reader. The event of the production of meaning is more complicated than a mere reversal of terms would imply. Reception studies raises questions of ontology and epistemology, just as Marx's and Danto's theses imply profound theories of existence, knowledge, and their interrelationships. However, while these questions will be raised, they will not be answered. Rather I intend to aim at proposing answers involving more concrete use-values than those of a fundamental philosophical nature, but those philosophical issues still subtend this research. Despite this disclaimer, the use-value of reception studies does include some weighty business for film philosophy, criticism, and history, and for political and social change.

"DOUBLE-ENTENDRE" AND THE MEANING OF THE FRENCH REVOLUTION

In a 1984 review of the film *Danton*[5] (directed by Andrzej Wajda), Robert Darnton constructs what I consider to be an exemplary analysis of the historical reception of a moving picture.[6] Darnton begins his inquiry, "Danton and Double-Entendre," by noting that François Mitterrand had selected as the starter course for his fall 1983 political menu a criticism of the French educational system. As Darnton writes, "No doubt the president had other worries. But the crisis that he placed at the top of his agenda was the inability of the electorate to sort out the themes of its past,"[7] which Mitterrand and his colleagues attributed to the impoverished state of the French curriculum. As a social and cultural historian, Darnton connects this event with a controversy then raging among French politicians over *Danton*'s representation of the central figures of the French Revolution. The previous year witnessed French leftists, including Mitterrand, disapproving of the film's version of Danton, while French Gaullists "gloated." Darnton astutely observes,

> Such vehemence may seem puzzling to the American viewers of *Danton*. We know that the French take their history seriously and that it doesn't do to tamper with their Revolution. But why should the Socialists disavow a version of the feud between Danton and Robespierre that puts Danton in a favorable light? Could not Danton's attempts to stop the Terror be seen as a heroic foreshadowing of the resistance to Stalinism? Is not Wajda a hero of Solidarity? And shouldn't Wajda's *Danton* be expected to appeal to the moderate left in France, the champions of socialism with a human face, the party that covered billboards during Mitterrand's campaign with pictures of a rose extending from a fist?[8]

In fact, Darnton ponders, what would Wajda's Polish audience have assumed the message of the film to be?

Darnton answers his questions by drawing astutely upon the histories of both countries and statements of participants in the debates. However, Darnton is also careful to point out that disputes over the appropriate interpretation of the historical individuals and the French Revolution were certainly not settled by appeal to any facts, nor were the dialogues value-free. Instead, Darnton foregrounds the political implications of the differing positions: "To control the myth [of the French Revolution] is to exert political power, to stake out a position as the authentic representative of the left."[9]

Although Darnton's observations are more fully developed, much of the controversy can be narrowed down to how Danton is characterized. In particular, "Danton" might produce various connotations, depending on how the viewer understands the body movements of the actor (Gérard Depardieu), the character's activities, and other characters responding to or being compared with him. What is already known about events of the French Revolution and believed about its cast of heroes and villains is also important. For the Polish people, Darnton speculates that *Danton* would be loosely read as an allegory about thought control and Stalinist indoctrination and historiography, with Danton a substitute for the Polish people and Walesa against a repressive Robespierre (the Polish government and Jaruzelski). The point of the film comes down to attacking those who assert the dogma that the means justify the ends, that "tyranny in the service of democracy" is acceptable. In fact, Darnton observes that reading a film as an allegory is a significant tradition in a country in which "the Poles have learned to live with veiled meanings and ambiguous protests."[10]

For the French, the representation of the Revolution has taken a different tack. Rather than emphasize political questions about pragmatism and ethics, French historians and educators have produced interpretations of the Revolution that concentrate on and evaluate people and actions based upon who and what permitted "in the year of the Terror, a republican France [to stand up] against the combined forces of a feudal Europe and [defeat] them."[11] A leftist orthodoxy credits the causality to Robespierre. Consequently, even if Robespierre is not a hero in any popular sense, invoking claim to succession in his policies is a symbolic act referencing what is France and French. (Apparently, this is something equivalent to an American's choosing Washington over King George III.) In Darnton's view, everyone seems to believe that the film comes out in favor of Danton, hence the uproar among French intellectuals: for French socialists, Robespierre, the savior of France, was being discredited.*[12] The interpretive conflict was not about the denotative meaning of *Danton*; it was about what *Danton* implied about history, and French history in particular.

On the one hand, you might argue that this study of the reception of *Danton* in Poland and France could be easily settled by reference to some set of facts internal or external to the film. But, on the other hand, although facts were marshaled by the multiple discussants, facts failed to settle the disputes. For it was the *meaning* of those facts over which debates occurred. Darnton's "double-entendre" is signally appropriate for underlining the flexible, ambiguous, but *political* nature of language in social use.

In theorizing communication, V. N. Vološinov suggests that language and "the ideological sign" are central to historical processes.[13] Just as Ferdinand de Saussure recognizes the social life of language,[14] Vološinov insists that *"the sign may not be divorced from the concrete forms of social intercourse."*[15] Taking this observation further, Vološinov theorizes that the centrality of signs, their "accent," is a region not only for ideological debate but, consequently, for class struggle:

> Various different classes will use one and the same language. As a result, differently oriented accents intersect in every ideological sign. Sign becomes an arena of the class struggle.
>
> This social multiaccentuality of the ideological sign is a very crucial aspect. By and large, it is thanks to this intersecting of accents that a sign maintains its vitality and dynamism and the capacity for further development. . . .
>
> The very same thing that makes the ideological sign vital and mutable is also, however, that which makes it a refracting and distorting medium. The ruling class strives to impart a supraclass, eternal character to the ideological sign, to extinguish or drive inward the struggle between social value judgments which occurs in it, to make the sign uniaccentual.

In actual fact, each living ideological sign has two faces, like Janus. Any current curse word can become a word of praise, any current truth must inevitably sound to many other people as the greatest lie. This *inner dialectic quality* of the sign comes out fully in the open only in times of social crises or revolutionary change.[16]

For example, in African-American language, "bad" can be accented so as to mean the opposite of what it means in hegemonic language.

Although Darnton does not directly explore the *Danton* debates as displacements from other social troubles, he provides information that suggests he makes a connection between a discursive struggle and the social formation. He writes that Mitterrand chose knowledge of French history and curriculum reform as an alternative agenda to "a declining franc, an escalating arms race, a crisis in the Middle East, and trouble everywhere on the home front."[17] Thus, "Danton" and "history" become ideological signs that Mitterand's party wishes to preserve as uniaccentual, the past becomes eternal, while attention to present problems is averted. Obviously, however, what may serve the interests of one opponent does not insure that the foes will acquiesce, as they apparently did not in this case.

The value to me of Darnton's essay is multiple and implies the use-value of reception studies to the history of moving pictures. Darnton does not consider the film as a container, holding immanent meaning. He recognizes the multiaccentuality of ideological signs. He locates variations in reception to individuals actively constituting *Danton*'s meaning. He constructs a comparative historical analysis that illuminates reception by contrast. Finally, he assumes a complex cultural, social, and political context structuring what specific groups of people did. In recognizing variation, he also remembers ideology.

SOME QUALIFICATIONS

Although intellectual focus on the reader has a history as long as that on the author, several scholarly pursuits have been foregrounded recently under the tags of reader-response criticism, reception aesthetics, and reception theory. I am choosing to use the label "reception studies" for this area of research in part to link it to, but also to disengage it from, certain features of these other groups. In the next chapters I will try to survey some of the significant characteristics and contributions of writers grouped within those approaches. Thus, here I want only to define briefly what "reception studies" is and is not. I should indicate as well that this definition will be motivated and is not derived from abstracting properties of other works which might also call themselves reception studies.

First of all, reception studies has as its object researching the history of the interactions between real readers and texts, actual spectators and films. Consequently, it is not a philosophy of reception, although it would need to consider various philosophical propositions about readers and texts in its analyses. Yet, as history, it does have implicit and explicit propositions, which should certainly be considered as theoretical as any philosophy.

As history, and not philosophy, reception studies is interested in what has actually occurred in the material world. Reception studies might speculate about what did not happen, and why that was; in fact, part of its project is to explain the appearance and disappearance of various forms of interaction. But, overall, reception studies does not attempt to construct a generalized, systematic explanation of how individuals might have comprehended texts, and possibly someday will, but rather how they actually have understood them. Additionally, and consequently, reception studies criticizes the notion of the ideal reader as ahistorical.

Related as it is to reader-response criticism, reception aesthetics, and reception theory, reception studies is engaged in understanding the relations between readers/viewers and texts/ films. Since chapters 2 and 3 will survey some of this research, I want only to foreshadow it here. Because of reception studies' stress on the reader as having a privileged relation with the cultural object, philosophical assertions about meaning, knowledge, and effect (ontologies, epistemologies, and effectivities) are in the process of a major paradigmatic transformation.*[18] Various writers hold differing schemas of the reader-text dynamic, but a binding thread among the scholars is overthrowing the notion that the producer-text dynamic determines (in the strong sense) critical conclusions about meaning. Such a position does not deny, and, in fact, may incorporate, the historical reality of production as a factor in a reader's interpretation of a text. What the position does reject is that the production-text relation, or knowledge of it, is a necessary or sufficient condition for ascertaining meaning. For example, in Darnton's case study of *Danton*, the validity of various interpretations of the film was not judged on the basis of some supposed immanent meaning in the text, a residual of the specific production processes of Polish filmmaking or Wajda as an established director with numerous prior credits. Darnton does not regard one interpretation of *Danton* or the French Revolution as better than another. Rather, he considers the range of interpretations and the responses they provoked, speculates about and argues for certain possible conditions for the production of those interpretations, and places those interpretations within historical, cultural, social, and political contexts.

Among the various researchers, all sorts of ranges of positions regarding "meaning," "sense," "interpretation," "readers," "texts," and so forth can be charted. In chapter 2 I shall discuss a number of these, but I shall particularly focus on the researchers' location of primary determinacy: the text, the reader, or the historical context of the event of interpretation. What is consistent, however, in all reception work is replacing the production-text relation as the research field with that of the text-reader.

Consequently, reception studies is not textual interpretation. Instead, it seeks to understand textual interpretations as they are produced historically. As Jonathan Culler characterizes research in reception, it "is not a way of interpreting works but an attempt to understand their changing intelligibility by identifying the codes and interpretative assumptions that give them meaning for different audiences at different periods."[19] Another way of putting it is that reception studies tries to explain an event (the interpretation of a film), while textual studies is working toward elucidating an object (the film). Both activities are useful in the process of knowledge, but they explore different aspects of the hermeneutics of cultural studies. This does not mean, however, that the reception studies worker escapes the difficulties of interpretation, for studying interpretations will, necessarily, involve interpretation on the part of the researcher. Thus, reception studies does not elude the hermeneutic circle even though its work includes investigating its dialectic.

While reception studies considers the process of producing interpretations rather than providing them, Culler and Jane Tompkins point out that studying culture, literature, and art has never been confined only to offering studies of textual meaning. Among other areas of textual research included by Culler are (1) "[accounting for] the role or function of literature in society or social consciousness"; (2) developing "histories of literature as an institution"; (3) "[exploring literature's] historical relation to the other forms of discourse"; (4) understanding "the role of literature in the psychological economies of both writers and readers," particularly "the effects of *fictional* discourse"; and (5) contributing "a typology of discourse and a theory of the relations (both mimetic and nonmimetic) between literature and the other modes of discourse which make up the text of intersubjective experience."[20] Reception studies can contribute to all of these research areas.

Tompkins provides another powerful argument for reception studies. She suggests that emphasizing aesthetics or the text as autonomous from context is actually a historical, rather than essential, approach in the field of criticism. Surveying earlier rhetorical and literary textual methods, Tompkins points out that eighteenth- and nineteenth-century criticism emphasized the functions of speeches and literature instead of their meanings. In particular, analysts attempted to discover how socially and politically significant reader effects were achieved. The twentieth-century's emphasis on determining an essential meaning for a text is only the way criticism has been done lately.[21]

However, unlike some of those earlier rhetorical analyses, and unlike empirical "effects" research, reception studies does not speculate about the relation between interpretation and behavior. What a viewer does about the images, information, values, and ideas she or he takes to be the import of a film or television show is certainly significant. Yet even if you assume significant effect by the images on the viewer's subsequent assessment of and activities in the world, reception studies does not claim to cover the domain of knowledge that might consider this, although the field of research which would study such relations could surely benefit from conclusions drawn in the area of reception studies.

Reception studies encourages a plurality of philosophical and critical observations that might illuminate a historical case study. Perhaps sometime in the future reception studies will have a standard procedure to apply to every instance of reception, but just as historical researchers still debate their procedures,[22] students of the history of reception need to draw upon every sound method for analysis. Promoting plurality of methods does not, however, imply slipshod thinking. To be guarded against are all the traditional fallacies of logic, rhetoric, and evidence.

Someday reception studies may become reception history. Although attention to what "the reader" does has occupied researchers for some time, studying what readers do is fairly new. Reasons exist, however, to account for this new interest in actual readers. A significant one, I believe, is constituted by the activities of groups of individuals seeking the opportunity to escape the oppression and repression of the dominant class. Additionally, contemporary theories of language as social utterance have participated in permitting focuses on sociologies of taste, conventions of interpretation, and struggles to make sense of cultural products. Some of these hypotheses and approaches will be surveyed in chapter 2.

Although many observations in reception studies might logically imply that everyone reads in individual ways, as a research area, reception studies seeks generalizations which, while applying to the individual situation, provide knowledge about larger-scale processes. Consequently, reception studies is no more interested in great readers than it is in ideal ones.

Nor does it accept the proposition that apparent uniqueness among readings implies freedom for readers. Scholars who suggest that potentials for resisting readings exist may be correct philosophically, but history has shown the weight of evidence supports the conclusion that controlling conventions, linked to ideologies, win out over illusionary variety. Not everything is possible at every time—although this potential has signal import for everyone concerned about the social and political future.

In fact, it is this potential that suggests *why* reception studies matters as more than merely another trend in scholarship. As Etienne Balibar and Pierre Macherey express it: "The least one can ask of a Marxist theory is that it begin to produce real transformations, practical effects, either in the means of production of literary texts and art works, or in the manner in which they are *socially* consumed."[23] As I have set out the parameters of reception studies, I have tried to cast the characteristics of this type of re-search so that it meets criteria acceptable to those interested in radical, materialist approaches to cultural history. The emphasis on *history*, on a dialectic of *evidence and theory*, and on *critical* distance from the *relations* being investigated has been intentional as prerequisite to such a marxist historiography. Reception studies is a radical attempt to understand how texts and artworks are consumed in order to act with more knowledge in political situations, to change, where necessary, or where possible, the consumption of cultural products. At a less grandiose and more politically neutral level, however, reception studies has implications for many of the typical areas of research in art and textual studies. While I shall focus on implications for film, connections to other media should be apparent.

THE USE-VALUES OF RECEPTION STUDIES FOR THE PHILOSOPHY, CRITICISM, AND HISTORY OF FILM

Reception studies' use-value for traditional areas of film research in philos-ophy, criticism, and history is important in the setting out of its domain. Philosophical questions about the nature and function of cultural prod-ucts, and cinema in particular, will not be solved by reception studies, but perhaps some common assumptions can be fruitfully questioned. Certainly propositions forwarded by philosophers of the ontology, epistemology, and effectivity of moving images need to be tested by confrontation with historical spectators. Among the various time-honored issues are notions of the impression, or illusion, of the reality of the images; spectators' sus-pension of disbelief; the universality or variety of spectators' relations to the images; spectators' attributions of referentiality to real-life events when viewing nonnarrative and narrative fiction and nonfiction; the stability or nonstability of groupings of films such as genres, modes, styles, and au-thorial sources; the specificity of various moving image media, such as pro-jected images versus electronic ones, or films versus literature or drama; the import of sexual difference or sexual preference; the effectivities of var-ious manipulations of mise-en-scène (such as the narrative-versus-spectacle debates); the significance of memory, the unconscious, and cognitive ac-tivities; and concerns of ideology. I cannot promise that all of these issues will surface in the case studies in Part Two, but many of them will, while the rest will subtend them or follow as interesting lines for further research.

Even if reception studies is not textual analysis, it has a use-value for that. Most important, I believe that many interpretations of texts operate from questionable assumptions about spectators and what they do. Part of this derives from the rhetorical strategy of employing the pronoun *we* to stand in for *I*, whereby disagreement with the critic's interpretation implies inadequacy. Additionally, whether such a possibility as a "misreading" can occur is a discussion that affects some critical positions, as well as having far-reaching consequences as to how interpretations and texts are evaluated.

If reception studies has implications for procedures of criticism as well as judgment of the objects of analysis, it also has purport for the typical questions I would ask of a critical procedure. These include the following: (1) What are minimal criteria for accepting the method? Does it have to be repeatable? Generalizable? What scope does it have? Does it have to be internally coherent? (2) What are the analyst's assumptions about the selection of texts that will be analyzed? (3) What are the assumptions about the analysis process? How does it proceed to segment the text or to relate parts of the text? (4) How does the analyst group texts? By authors? genres? styles? ideological form or subject matter? motifs? (5) Does the analyst hold notions about the autonomy of the text? (6) How does the critic substantiate findings? (7) How does an analyst evaluate the text? As with philosophical questions, some of the answers to these types of critical questions will become foregrounded in subsequent chapters; others will merely be implied.

Finally, I would argue (and will) that the history of cinema might very well be radically rewritten if you pursue it, not solely from the perspective of the production of films, but equally from their reception. Unfortunately, almost all of the work done to date on film audiences and the reception of movies has relied on inferring effects from textual analysis or social behavior. Now if post-structuralism, new historicism and cultural studies teach anything, it is that audience response cannot be derived through examination, exclusively, of texts. Yet to date theses about what has happened in cinema history, even those supposedly concerned with the reception of texts, have often been argued by each historian's producing his or her hermeneutics of the text and then inferring conclusions following from those observations.

Additionally, when historians do examine audiences, often other less than felicitous activities occur: these I call the interpretive strategies of coherence-inference, the ideal-spectator, and the free-reader. In the coherence-inference interpretative strategy, the historian assumes that because his or her textual procedure for reading films or other cultural representations has (a degree of) coherency, the audience or viewer proceeds with the same measure of rigor. No theoretical or historical evidence exists to warrant such a belief, and scholars may get further in analyses once they stop assuming that individuals have one, logical relation to the movies.

In the ideal-spectator interpretative strategy, the historian assumes homogeneity among spectators, perhaps even via "new historicism" by which people are segmented into smaller categorical groups such as "women," "blacks," or "Jewish immigrants." Such an act still universalizes audiences and experiences.[24] Now, although the group may be smaller, the audience category is, nonetheless, assumed to be homogeneous in constituency and thus uniform in response. As Martin Allor writes, "By taking the abstract totality of audience . . . as a starting point, these critical approaches have tended to reproduce alternative abstractions that pivot around single planes of contradiction, such as gender, class, or subjectivity in general, rather than multiple determinations."[25] Audiences are still being "idealized"—even if at a "smaller" level. What might be more useful, although still inadequate, is a multiple intersection of variables, based on the recognition that each spectator is a complex and contradictory construction of such self-identities as gender, sexual preference, class, race, and ethnicity. The pertinence of each self-identity might at times dominate the others, perhaps overdetermine or contradict as well.

Finally, in the recent flurry to give weight to the subject's consciousness, historians may walk close to the edge of duplicating what Louis Althusser fought so hard to resist: believing that because subjects have some degree of volition, they are thus "free" readers. As Terry Eagleton reminds us, "The notion that the text is simply a ceaseless self-signifying practice, without source or object, stands four square with the bourgeois mythology of individual freedom."[26] To think any reader or group of readers can do anything—accept, negotiate, resist—is to lose the very real power of the contributions of cultural and structural marxisms to understanding *constructed* economic, political, social, and psychological identities such as gender, sexual preference, class, ethnicity, and race. Thus, keeping handy the dialectics of data and abstraction, of individual and social formation, and of historical events and general historical processes might improve historiography. I shall return to these fallacies in chapter 2.

The use-value of reception studies includes, then, a foregrounding of differences, of institutions and ideology, and of implicit (and not eternal) systems of cognition, emotion, and judgment. For film history, reception studies asks, What types of interpretive and emotional strategies are mobilized by various spectators? How did these strategies get in place? How might other strategies, perhaps of a progressive nature, replace them? How can radical scholars participate in encouraging what Judith Fetterley calls "resisting readers"?[27]

The use-value of reception studies is not limited to revisionary historiography, however. It also implies an expansion, or reevaluation, of pleasurable objects for the film scholar. Once you abandon the thesis of immanent meanings, once you reconsider the validity of accepting authority figures as mediators between you and a text, once you recognize the variability of responsible readings, texts are no longer frozen in the time of their production or the hierarchy of someone else's value system. Temporal and spatial portability improves. As Marc Silberman constructs the chain of logic:

> Reception theory specifically displaces the focus from the literary work of art to the reader, to the receiver who constitutes the text in a historically mediated process of reading. . . . By defining the reader as the source of meaning, reception theory reformulates the problematic relationship between past and present, and between literary history and extra-literary or pragmatic history. In short, it opens the door to rewriting literary history and to redefining the literary canon.[28]

The political implications of judgments and canons have already received attention, as well as a backlash attempting to preserve the contemporary caste system.[29] For as Barbara Herrnstein Smith explains it, "Institutions of evaluative authority will be called upon repeatedly to devise arguments and procedures that validate the community's established tastes and preferences, thereby warding off barbarism and the constant apparition of an imminent collapse of standards and also justifying the exercise of their own normative authority."[30] This reassertion of authority is achieved through particular strategies of representation:

> The particular *subjects* who compose the members of the [authoritive] group are of sound mind and body, duly trained and informed, and generally competent, all other subjects being defective, deficient, or deprived—suffering from crudenesses of sensibility, diseases and distortions of perception, weaknesses of character, impoverishment of background-and-education, cultural or historical biases, ideological or personal prejudices, and/or undeveloped, corrupted, or jaded tastes.[31]

Gerald Graff, sketching the battle, terms these challenges "questions of cultural politics: for example, is the norm of objective interpretation a critical or pedagogical counterpart of technocratic social control?"[32] Walter Benjamin sees the debate more unfavorably than that, inverting (or correcting) aspersions of barbarism:

> Whoever has emerged victorious participates to this day in the triumphal procession in which the present rulers step over those who are lying prostrate. According to traditional practice, the spoils are carried along in the procession. They are called cultural treasures, and a historical materialist views them with cautious detachment. For without exception the cultural treasures he surveys have an origin which he cannot contemplate without horror. They owe their existence not only to the efforts of the great minds

and talents who have created them, but also to the anonymous spoil of their contemporaries. There is no document of civilization which is not at the same time a document of barbarism.[33]

I realize that much of this last section remains a series of assertions. It will be the job of the rest of the book to prove these. Yet it seems to me that if reception studies can contribute to the understanding of how culture and politics interweave and affect each other, then this type of research will have important use-values. As Vološinov would approve, Darnton's analysis of *Danton*'s reception did not confine itself to an autonomous study of film and viewers, but it foregrounded significant observations about French educational systems, historiography, and the current political behavior of its state leaders. Reception studies, then, has a use-value for understanding historical processes and the struggle over the meaning of signs.

CHAPTER TWO

Reception Studies in Other Disciplines

RECEPTION STUDIES does not start off helpless. On the contrary, an impressive history of discussion requires a sorting out of terms, ideas, and methods that have potential value for the researcher. The lineage of current research in readers' interpretation of texts extends back not only as far as I. A. Richards but certainly also to Aristotle and Plato. However, several contemporary scholarly arenas provide especially useful tidbits of data or wide-ranging theses about readers.

One of these is the revised and renewed interest in sociocultural histories that explore the everyday life of eras, cultures, and collective *mentalités*.[1] Some of this information can be enlightening, particularly when case studies of readers are provided. One such instance is Robert Darnton's investigation of the incredible emotional reaction after 1761 over Jean-Jacques Rousseau's novel, *La Nouvelle Héloïse*. Correspondents to Rousseau describe crying passionately, people traveled some distance to see the author, and some readers seem to have identified with the characters to the point of confusing fiction with reality.[2] Such data are valuable in tracking the historical existence of types of readerly phenomena. Also of importance has been the work of Michel Foucault and others on the historical trajectories of discourses in their function of providing structures for interpretation.

Another research area that intersects with reception studies is the sociology of tastes and cultures. How have ranges of evaluations and aesthetics developed? What explains groups of people's "liking" or "disliking" cultural products? Examples here include the research of people such as Herbert Gans and Pierre Bourdieu, or Peter Bürger, who describes the institution of art during the last one hundred years or so as necessarily (for bourgeois society) operating as though art were autonomous; however, this proposition of autonomy has simultaneously been attacked by some avant-garde movements. Bürger's sociology of art would "define the epochal framework with which the production and reception of literature occurs."[3]

Linked to sociology are Claude Lévi-Strauss, Clifford Geertz, and Mary Douglas in anthropology and ethnography. These individuals have helped redefine their fields using structuralist and semiotic methods. These methods assume communication models that imply the participation of societal

members in constructing cultural meaning. Patterns of behavior and beliefs function conventionally, structuring perception, cognition, and affective practices.[4] Obviously, linguistics has also traditionally concerned itself
with reader comprehension, but recent contributions by sociology and
cognitive psychology have provided some important potential models of
reading.[*5] Furthermore, psychoanalysis, of whatever variety, considers the
emotional effects of individuals' symbolically interpreting events.

History, sociology, ethnography, psychology, and linguistics—each is
contributing to developments in reception studies. Yet immediate and extended discussions of readers have also occurred in literary, fine arts, and
communication fields. A number of immediate influences for these current
investigations of readers have been suggested by various writers. Because
of the prominence of the Constance School theorists, the heritage of German hermeneutics and phenomenology often becomes central to histories
of reception studies. Here Fr. D. E. Schleiermacher, Roman Ingarden,
and Hans-Georg Gadamer are fathers to Wolfgang Iser and Hans Robert
Jauss.[6] Additionally, Robert Weimann considers the publication of Bertolt
Brecht's writings in the 1960s as contributing to a revitalized focus on
readers. Weimann argues that Brecht defined "realism" in terms of a textual effect on the audience (identification versus distanciation), in contrast
to the formalism of Georg Lukács (who defines "realism" via stylistic and
narrative characteristics). An unforeseen consequence of the altered definition was its attention to at least a theoretical, if not empirical, audience
affect.[*7]

As influences, certainly semiotic studies of the 1960s participated. The
study of codes of textuality joined the exploration of conventions of reading and rhetorics of reader-effect. Textual poetics extended its repertoire of
tools and consistency of procedures so that its findings conveyed as much
scholarly authority and precision as had empirical mass communication
studies of effect. Furthermore, once linguistic models of communication
evoked the figure of a message's receiver, readers proliferated. "Ideal,"
"implied," "competent," and "real" readers began showing up. The arrival
of the reader has also promoted historical investigations of how and when
the "reader" as a character in a text appeared.[*8]

Another source for interest in readers has been post-structuralism. The
jolt of Jacques Derrida's philosophical analyses of Western assumptions
and theses about textuality and signifying practices has contributed to
reader-response criticism in the United States in part by implying a "negative hermeneutics."[*9] The proposition of indeterminate meaning now has
an extensive history of debate.

This chapter will not, however, try to catalog all of these genetic
strands. Nor will it cover all of the possible debates among participants.
Rather I want to consider briefly four very specific issues and then survey

86923   791.4301
S782

Brescia College Library
Owensboro, Kentucky

some contributions of several writers in the fields of literary and cultural studies. In particular, the four issues I believe need some sorting out are (1) the range of relations between the terms *reading* and *interpreting*; (2) the difficulties with defining "meaning"; (3) various notions of "readers"; and (4) the philosophical possibility of "misreadings." These explorations will take me into several convoluted philosophical arguments about hermeneutical procedures. However, each of these issues requires some discussion so as to provide a rationale for the thesis that interpreting texts or films is a historical reality determined by context, not an inherent or automatic act due to some essential human process. For once interpretation becomes historical rather than universal, then claims for privileging some interpretations can be refuted. Interpretations-in-history become politicized since they relate to historical social struggles, not to essences. Consequently, these discussions will be an attempt to cut through terminological disputes in order to provide a basis for a historical and contextual view of several common questions in reader theory. Following that, I will compare and contrast a number of writers on several bases, but most of all on their representations of the text-and-reader interaction.

READING AND INTERPRETING

Up to this point I have been using the words *reading*, *comprehending*, and *interpreting* more or less as though they were synonyms. In fact, my thesaurus treats them as such. However, given their connotative force and the fact that individuals make distinctions among the terms, sorting out features of their semantics seems beneficial. Furthermore, debates about the causal *order* of interpretive activities pivot around the group of terms comprising these and *meaning*. Consequently, one must at least be sensitive to the reasons for a variety of distinctions made by some writers, despite the fact that the words are occasionally used interchangeably.

Most writers tend to consider "interpreting" as a subactivity of a larger process, "reading."*[10] Any contentions center on what it means to "interpret" and how "interpretation" fits into its context. Gerald Prince provides a good starting point: "Reading is an activity that presupposes a text (a set of visually presented linguistic symbols from which meaning can be extracted), a reader (an agent capable of extracting meaning from that text), and an interaction between the text and reader."[11] Now, Prince is supposing that meaning is "in" the text—a point which is quite debatable, as I shall discuss below—but his definition provides an otherwise commonsense notion of "reading." Furthermore, as he continues, Prince provides criteria for "reading": (1) knowing the language of the text, and (2) being able to ask and answer relevant questions about its meaning. To do that, he continues, would imply competence in and knowledge of not only linguistic information but also cultural, proairetic, hermeneutic, and symbolic systems.*[12] Variables in ability to accomplish these activities would involve the reader's "physiological, psychological, and sociological conditioning, his predispositions, feelings, and needs . . . , his knowledge, his interests, and his aims,"[13] and so forth. But these variables are normally factored out when "reading" processes are considered in the abstract.

If this is a general notion of "reading," what is "interpretation"? Here differences arise. One clear position is that of George L. Dillon. Dillon begins his book, *Language Processing and the Reading of Literature*, with this seemingly simple proposition: "Reading has at least three levels, which we will call *perception, comprehension*, and *interpretation*."*[14] *Perception* involves general identifications of words but this process, he notes, would also require inferences about words and sentences. *Comprehension* is the placing of materials into some kind of "frame." (Since Dillon draws extensively on psycholinguistic literature, the notion of "frame" is equivalent to that of "schema" for him. Depending on the theories invoked, "codes" or "conventions" might be substitute explanatory models.) Dillon believes that frames may, in return, constrain the perception of new sentences. Finally, *interpretation* "is the most abstract level where we relate the sense of what is going on to the author's constructive intention." This is in any instance of discourse; for literature, literary conventions aid the reader. Dillon further refines this by noting the interplay among the three "levels" of reading: "Interpretation governs comprehension and perception in that we tend to see what we have inferred the writer wants us to see."[15]

What has been achieved in Dillon's definition? In one way, not much, since his discussion provides few stable theses about sequentiality and hierarchies of processes among the three levels. In fact, his final comments about interpretation suggest that, although interpretation may be the most "abstract," or "outer-directed," activity, it could also determine perception and comprehension, thus preceding and dominating them. Consequently, reading means already making an inference from an interpretive hypothesis. But in another way, Dillon has separated out three activities that, if they are separable only by definition and are not yet organized into a functional model of the reading process, are reasonable distinctions about common endeavors in reading.

Dillon's definition of "interpretation" requires further discussion. He suggests that interpretation is developing a hypothesized textual meaning from an inference about an "author's constructive intention." This is an acceptable statement, some would say, *if* it is understood that the statement is a descriptive, not prescriptive, definition; that is, what Dillon is defining as a feature of "interpretation" is what people tend to do, not what they *must* do when interpreting. In other words, when interpreting, a reader might "relate the sense of what is going on to the author's constructive intention," but a reader might also (or otherwise) "relate the sense of what is going on" to something else—say, the reader's notions about reality, or ideas about metaphysics, or views of textual and social processes. Making this adjustment to Dillon's definition, however, results in blurring the distinction between "interpretation" and "comprehension." In fact, as Dillon sets out his three levels, "interpretation" might be argued to be a subset of comprehension: the comprehension "frame" for interpretation is the convention of an "author's constructive intention." Yet as Dillon studies "comprehension," he does tend to discuss what could be considered textual features. Comprehension, for him, seems to involve inferences about the internal world of the reading material.

Although I shall later question what is "in" the text, perhaps it is acceptable at this point to decide, somewhat unilaterally, that "comprehension" involves using frames (or codes or conventions) to make inferences about textual meanings, while "interpretation" involves using frames to make inferences about extratextual meanings, with one possible extratext that of an inferred "author" and his or her "constructive intention." Furthermore, I want to stress, as Dillon suggests, that interpretive frames and inferences influence, and perhaps determine, perception and comprehension.*[16] This causal claim about sequences of influences is important since I am arguing for a contextual approach to understanding interpretation. Thus, inferences established prior to any specific act of reading are determinants to the perception, comprehension, and interpretation that occurs during reading.

This notion of the interconnections among reading activities is common in theorizing about literary reception. As Steven Mailloux surveys the work of Norman Holland and Stanley Fish, he characterizes their positions: "We interpret as we perceive, or rather perception *is* an interpretation."[17] Robert Crosman and Dillon (as well as William Empson before them) note that words in context can be ambiguous so that extratextual (interpretive) assumptions and prior experiences lead readers to whatever perceptual choices they make.[18] Dillon's book is particularly exciting for its array of hypotheses about what may be normative strategies in reading both typical and atypical writing styles.

The proposition about the interpenetration of the acts of perceiving, comprehending, and interpreting may be disturbing for those who claim that they wish to avoid interpreting texts; they only desire to describe textual features. It does not help to argue that a scholar can maintain distinctions about these in critical activities, that the critical act can remain at the level of comprehension. In a set of closely reasoned essays, Michael Baxandall examines the effort to use only so-called descriptive language in art criticism. He points out that phrases are employed that involve "cause" words (how the painting was done), "comparison" words (how the painting relates to other paintings), and "effect" words (how the painting affects the critic). Consequently, Baxandall claims, a picture discussed is not an "unmediated picture but the picture as considered under a partially interpretative description" since description is "a representation of thinking about having seen the picture."*[19] Theoretically, of course, it might be possible to write a critical essay that remains in *phrasing* at the levels of perception and comprehension, but that ex post facto act has still been mediated by the prior reading event, which, as discussed above, has already been influenced, if not determined by, interpretation.*[20]

Where is evaluation in all of this? Certainly it is contingent upon interpretation, no matter what frames of interpretation are involved. Mailloux describes this in a discussion of the strategies of evaluation used by British and U.S. critics in reviewing *Moby Dick*. After charting out traditional literary conventions, reviewers turned those conventions into prescriptions and evaluated the novel against them.[21] Drawing upon the line of logic I have developed so far, I might rephrase this in terms of the reviewers interpreting *Moby Dick* through the frame of hypothesized general textual conventions and evaluating in relation to inferred similarities and differences. These similarities and differences would, necessarily, have involved perception and comprehension, also mediated by the interpretative frame. Mailloux summarizes it nicely:

> Here the act of evaluation reveals itself as a consequence of interpretation. Evaluation follows from the translation of the work from one context (the analyzed specifics of a text's dynamics) to another context (the text in relation to a valued set of traditional conventions); and interpretative work is clearly involved in both the analysis of the text and in the placement of the analyzed work in the context of literary history. Thus, in the British reviews of *The Whale* [*Moby Dick*], evaluation becomes a complex extension of interpretation.[22]

These definitions and discussions of reading and interpreting reveal that while several levels of activity may be parceled out to semantical categories, the causal order suggests the interpenetration of the terms when they are used to describe any actual event of a reader processing a text. Furthermore, the influence of extratextual or interpretive frames on perception and comprehension is widely accepted among writers in reading theory as well as reception theory. Thus, a reader interpreting any work of literature or film will be drawing upon interpretive frames historically available to him or her, and these frames will be influential even in the act of perception or the process of comprehension and evaluation.

MEANING IN READING

Although the mincing of definitions for reading and interpreting may seem tenuous, distinctions among connotations are not when questions of "meaning" are posed. M. H. Abrams considers establishing "meaning" as the key to "interpreting": interpretation for him is "an activity that 'undertakes to determine what an author meant.'"[23] Consequently, Abrams's definition of interpretation implies the extratextual frame of an "author's constructed intention."

Abrams's view is not that of many reception theorists. One of the attributes used to differentiate reader-response criticism from earlier hermeneutical methods is the declaration by most reader-response writers that "meaning" is not "in" the text, put there by an agency of authorship, but originates in the event of reading: "reading is not the discovery of meaning but the creation of it."[24] For some more militant believers, even studying the genesis of a work is fallacious. The production of meaning should only consider what readers make of it.

While theoretically studying readers exclusively might be appropriate, this view seems to me potentially dangerously ahistorical, as though readers were tabula rasa, without knowledge of the physical production of a text (or representations about the physical production of the text), or uninfluenced by the typical interpretative strategy to which Abrams refers: a book "means" what an author "meant" it to "mean." If, in fact, that is what readers make of the text, then reception studies needs to acknowledge the frame of production circumstances as historically pertinent. If an audience member believes that Hitchcock directed *The Birds* or Bela Lugosi died during the filming of *Plan Nine from Outer Space*, the interpretive frame may be part of the pleasure of the film's meaning for that viewer. This said, however, the meaning of "meaning" still requires additional discussion to expand its value for a historical approach to interpretation. Abrams's connections among "meaning," "interpretation," and "intention" are common; I am sure that he expresses the beliefs of many individuals, academic and lay. Yet Abrams's approach must be distinguished from that of New Criticism, and both views from those of reception studies.

Although New Criticism does assume authorial genesis of a text, it argues that a critic can determine "meaning" from the object itself without reference to the biographical study Abrams calls for. New Criticism considers a poem (or any other literary text) "an autonomous whole"; the critic's function is interpretive, considering, as Jonathan Culler expresses it, "thematic operators" of "*ambivalence, ambiguity, tension, irony, paradox*," which allow unification of the text as an expression about the world.*[25] This expression does have a source, the author, but in a case of conflicting interpretations, New Criticism eschews knowledge about authorial intent as the criterion for choosing among meanings. Rather, evidence of authorial intent is objective and public, for it is "in" the text. Important and subtle differences exist between the two propositions of sources of meaning and determination of that meaning.

It is common to associate with New Criticism the notion of the "intentional fallacy" as implying that a critic should not derive textual meaning from knowledge about authorial intent. However, W. K. Wimsatt and M. C. Beardsley's original formulation in 1946 suggests something slightly different: "The design or intention of the author is neither available nor desirable as a standard for judging the success of a work of literary art."[26] Although Wimsatt revised this in 1968, replacing "the success" with "either the meaning or the value,"[27] neither formulation denies that authorial expressivity creates meaning or that the critic's function is to find that authorial meaning. What the formulations do deny is the validity of using knowledge derived from extratextual sources as determinant in cases of disagreement. The 1946 version suggests that causality should not be the basis for evaluation (not interpretation); the 1968 thesis revises this, asserting that inferred authorial intention is inadequate for both interpretation and evaluation. However, neither the 1946 nor the 1968 proposition rejects authorial expressivity as the *cause* of meaning or its definition.*[28]

Thus, what distinguishes Abrams from the New Critic is how each posits that the critic knows intention. For New Critics, knowledge of (authorial) meaning is available to the critic from textual evidence alone. For New Critics, no amount of contextual information could provide evidence whereby a specific interpretation of a text could be validated as correct; evidence of meaning comes from inside the text, and that evidence is public knowledge and objective. In dealing with a text's meaning, then, New Criticism does assume "the author's constructive intention" as its interpretative frame. It infers "the author" (not reader) as genesis, but the evidence for this meaning is "in" the text. Abrams is saying something different. For him, interpretation "'undertakes to determine what an author meant.'" Here the object of investigation is related to something "outside" the text (authorial purpose—conscious or otherwise), as contrasted with New Criticism's use of the end result (the poem).

In the case of either Abrams's formulation or that of the New Critics, reception theorists, deconstructionists, and post-structuralists will all argue that any inferred meaning is the product of interpretation and interpretative frames (the author-as-historical-body, the author-in-the-poem). A reading act's origin and end is the reader.

An attempt to resolve the so-called crisis provoked by the denial that authorial intention or immanent meaning constitutes "meaning" is to create two separate terms, *meaning* and *significance*. Here *meaning* refers to what is "immanent to the system of the text" while *significance* is "designating a relation to facts and ideas outside that system."*[29] Not only is this distinction suggested in the work of Wolfgang Iser, but E. D. Hirsch, Janet Wolff, and Culler supply variations.[30] Thus, *significance* refers to what an individual believes to be pertinent about the text in relation to extratextual concerns or values about a text, while *meaning* is reserved for "authorial constructive intention."

Robert Crosman refutes the distinction's value, arguing that in such a parceling out of connotations, "meaning" is actually a subset of "significance": "The act of understanding a poet's words by placing them in the context of his intentions is only one of a number of possible ways of understanding them." Other meaning/significance-making procedures by readers, a reader-response theorist would argue, are "equally, contextualizing procedures. . . . Thus, I hope to show that the statement 'authors make meanings,' though not of course untrue, is merely a special case of the more universal truth that readers make meaning."[31]

Although, with Crosman, I would disagree with the notion that any meaning is "immanent" in the text and relates to authorial intention, I can make use of the distinction between a reader's conception of what she or he *assumes* is the intent of the text (i.e., meaning) and what she or he sees as that text's relation to extratextual events or discourses (i.e., significance). *How* readers make meaning and significance while interpreting a text is another problem, however.

READERS

In the secondary literature, I have found the following kinds of readers (in alphabetical order): actual, authorial, coherent, competent, ideal, implied, mock, narratee, necessary, programmed, real, resisting, super, virtual, zero-degree. Others probably exist.*[32] Depending upon what you might want to know, certain of these various readers may be useful theoretical notions. However, given the aim of this project (to determine how a historical materialist study of interpretation might be written), I want to focus on three of those readers—the ideal, coherent, and competent readers—as indicators of theses about "texts," "meaning," and "reading."

Ideal Readers

What is the ideal reader? Two connotations emitted by the term *ideal* are "exemplary" and "representative." In either case, when confronted by a text, the ideal reader behaves in an established manner, depending upon the critic's hypotheses about texts, meaning, and reading. Robert De-Maria, Jr. points out the historical variability of the ideal reader. In his "The Ideal Reader: A Critical Fiction," he surveys characteristics that four major literary critics (Johnson, Dryden, Coleridge, and Frye) impute to their readers. DeMaria describes Johnson's reader as the "common reader," something of an archetypical individual, who, while ordinary, is also "the perfect representative of all mankind."[33] Johnson's ideal reader turns out not to be very competent, for he (and it is a he) knows nothing about literary conventions, details of occupations, or facts of places and times.*[34] However, those failures permit the reader to be "common" or universal, to read and judge without the restraints of historical specificity. What such a reader implies is revelatory for Johnson's critical procedures and evaluative criteria. The text should supply whatever pertinent data the reader needs. Basic sense-data input should produce in the nearly tabula rasa reader what is required for the reading. Moreover, the best texts should be universal, appealing to all individuals without consideration of mundane temporal and spatial constraints.

Dryden's ideal reader is not only representative but also exemplary. He is of a particular class: "the best of men" or "'the most judicious'" who "are cultivated enough to learn from conversation; they are open and skeptical rather than positive or magisterial." Dryden recognizes at least two other groups of readers, the "mob" and the "middle."[35] Suggestive in Dryden's triad is the possibility of variable procedures of reading depending upon competency, but a hierarchy of evaluation for those readings supposes more appropriate or socially more conscientious interactions with texts. That judicious readers are also skeptical may imply that resisting textual meanings is not only possible but, for some texts, desirable.

Coleridge and Frye also accept variation among readers, but, like Dryden, assume that ideal readers are exemplary, whether or not they are representative. Coleridge's "'Great Mogul's diamond,'" his best type of reader, is the individual who learns about the self while reading, "surrender[ing] his right to evaluate as he enters into a kind of collaboration with the poet."[36] Reading is something of an inhabitation of the author's soul through the vehicle of the text (and I would point out that such an ideal reader is common among twentieth-century critics who posit the reader from textual evidence*[37]). Finally, Frye's notion of the reader reposits moral responsibility as brought by the reader to the text. However, rather than evaluating the text, Frye judges the reader.

Several lessons may be drawn from DeMaria's observations. For one thing, the characteristics of an ideal reader not only are hypothetical, but they are likely symptomatic of fundamental epistemological and ethical assumptions held by the individual proposing them. Whatever is postulated as the ideal reader reveals more about the critic and the critical method than about the activities of readers. Or at least as far as is known. For none of these critics provides evidence beyond assertion and common sense that readers perform as the critics describe or prescribe. Of course, "exemplary" is precisely one meaning of *ideal*. But what I want to note here is that what is projected outward as "ideal" ought instead to be turned backward toward the critic, for the critic's projection of what is "ideal" is also a sign of ideology at work. The apparent naturalness or commonsensical recognition of any set of characteristics is, as Vološinov observes, a clue that the strategy of the ruling class to make signs uniaccentual is working. The ideal reader is really the reader that the critic, as a representative of a class, gender, race, ethnicity, or sexual preference, has reason to favor for some cause. The motives may be social or political; most likely they are not conscious, but they also are not innocent since they may have effects such as promoting certain types of reading as appropriate or correct.*38

From this, I would point out that ideal readers are nearly all unrepresentative in significant ways. In my reading of the literature on ideal readers, not surprisingly, gender (e.g., male) is presumed irrelevant, sexual preference (e.g., heterosexual) is undescribed, race and ethnicity (e.g., Anglo, west European) are unnamed, and so on. Patrocinio P. Schweickart provides a good current example of this elision in her essay "Reading Ourselves: Toward a Feminist Theory of Reading," where she notes the literal deletion of pertinent historical references to Malcolm X's race by Wayne Booth. Booth uses Malcolm X as an exemplar of "a boy who fell in love with books" but in so doing eliminates Malcolm X's frames for interpretation, which included "'Mr. Muhammad's teachings, my correspondence, my visitors—especially Ella and Reginald.'"39

Furthermore—a legacy perhaps of Johnson, Coleridge, and other great male critics—political and ethical beliefs are rendered as biases. As others have suggested, this procedure is disingenuous, for it disguises the writers' politics and ethics as universals and everyone else's as local opinion.40

Theoretically, I could construct an alternative ideal reader that might display my politics and ethics to counter the other ideal readers offered.*41 However, it is not in my interest to do so. In the political struggle through language described by Vološinov, an ideal reader used in the attempt to render language uniaccentual works as a tool of domination. To posit another "other" ideal reader is merely to repeat an ideological strategy that I oppose.

Consequently, I am concerned that new historicism,*42 despite recognizing the fallacy of ideal readers, might end up reconstructing them. For smaller groups (women, gays, people of color) may acquire characterizations that can become equally ideal—described or prescribed as representative or exemplary of another constructed identity. This has occasionally occurred in film studies. Although this field of research has begun to accommodate the complexities of dealing with sexual difference among movie viewers, the female spectator is often treated as the ideal (male) spectator has been: as unitary. An attempt to provide a more complicated representation is made in chapter 6, where some variety among male and female responses to the film *Foolish Wives* is examined.

Another lesson from DeMaria's essay might be that historical characterizations of ideal readers have varied. Not surprisingly, as Johnson's reader is representative of Johnson's criticism, Johnson's criticism can generally be considered representative of his time, or at least of the hegemonic view. Thus, the discrepancies among critics exhibit the nonuniversal nature of Johnson's common reader, and of the readers of Dryden, Coleridge, and Frye.

Finally, however, prescriptions disguised as descriptions might reveal to reception studies scholars the canonical procedures of reading for a historical period. Thus, while in one way the notion of an ideal reader may be considered a debit in the effort to understand any actual textual reception, in another way the ideal reader might become an asset. If one used the historical period's version of the ideal reader as a backboard and imagined alternative reading practices, the places or ways nondominant readers reconfigured texts could be hypothesized in advance of research. For example, Dagmar Barnouw, in reviewing Wolfgang Iser's books, points out that Iser believes blanks (or gaps) exist in texts. Iser assumes that, when confronted by these, readers either reassemble information to produce meaning or change denotations into connotations. Barnouw counters, remarking that readers could do anything with a blank, and that most likely they do something.[43] As I shall discuss in chapter 8 concerning gays' readings of Garland films in the 1950s, alternative reading strategies by gays may reproduce Iser's ideal reader by finding blanks, but they also produce oppositional meanings and connotations, finding blanks that Iser's reader would not see. Thus, although ideal readers seem to be ahistorical, the scholar who chooses to research reception can find in those ideal readers and their proponents evidence useful for reconstructing the history of readings.

Coherent Readers

Scholars who propose ideal readers do not *necessarily* assert that meaning is immanent in the text, but they do presuppose that either a representative or exemplary meaning results from reading. The same might be said for "coherent readers," who, along with the "competent reader," might be considered a particular variation of the ideal reader. What the notion of the "coherent reader" assumes is that a reader reads so as to pull all of the parts of a text into a single or unified meaning or experience. Immediately, you will notice that such a proposition assumes that a text can be ordered into a coherency and that the controlling activity or purpose of reading is to accomplish this.

Let me consider this supposition from the perspective of both texts and readers. Post-structuralism and deconstructionism have disagreed strongly with the premise that a text is coherent (i.e., noncontradictory). I will not rehearse here the philosophical reasoning that permits such a view, since the proponents' contentions are widely known. What I will do is suggest what these ontological positions imply for the notion of coherent readers. As James R. Kincaid discusses in "Coherent Readers, Incoherent Texts," one way to take the debates of traditional scholars such as Abrams and Wayne C. Booth versus deconstructionists like Hillis Miller is to move away from asking whether or not texts are coherent and have a single meaning, and toward inquiring, instead, what readers do.[44] In Kincaid's summary, Abrams and Booth conclude that deconstruction ends up holding the position Abrams and Booth hold: that texts can be bounded off so as to have a determinant core meaning. That may be the case, Kincaid notes, but what Abrams and Booth do not prove is that the "center exists in any way *within* the text."[45] Instead, Kincaid believes that the texts are not necessarily coherent; readers just try to make texts cohere. Thus, deconstructionists such as Miller are correct that texts and language are contradictory, but Abrams and Booth may be right if readers are the object of the discussion.

Kincaid does resort to a treatment of the reader as ideal. Readers have a "fear" of logical contradiction: "The reading of literature is in large part a search for the organizing patterns . . . that will make coherent all the numerous details or signals we pick up along the way. Readers proceed with the assumption that there must be a single dominant structuring principle and that it is absurd to imagine more than one such dominant principle." Kincaid then proceeds to postulate that most texts "are, in fact, demonstrably incoherent, presenting us not only with multiple organizing patterns but organizing patterns that are competing, logically inconsistent."[46] They "defamiliarize" readers, encouraging readers to see the insufficiency of trying to work out a single pattern.

John Rutherford, in "Structuralism," takes a similar stance. Summarizing structuralist views of the reader as "programmed by his experience of 'classical' literature to fit a text together like some kind of superior mental jig-saw puzzle," Rutherford thinks that "there is in all literature an element of 'unreadability,' a core of resistance to the mind's longing for precise patterns, soothing symmetry, absolute order, and clear meaning; the principle of resistance has been intensified rather than invented by modern writers."[47] In other words, contemporary literature may be heightening inherent contradictory aspects of language and logic.

Kincaid's and Rutherford's distinctions between the fact of incoherent texts and attempts by readers to construct logical interpretations are quite suggestive, and Kincaid takes them further. For one thing, Kincaid examines his own assertion that readers "fear" incoherency. For if he is correct, you might wonder why readers are so resilient or stubborn, refusing to learn that texts are not coherent, continuing to try to make all the parts fit every time they pick up a book or watch a movie. In answering, Kincaid considers Ralph Rader's hypothesis that readers have an evolutionary need to make decisions when confronted by ambiguities.[48] Kincaid does not debate the issue of whether some part of our genetic makeup demands resolution of contradictions. Instead, he queries whether the literary experience stimulates such perceptual and cognitive responses. For Kincaid points out that the act of reading should not be simply equated with everyday life. In this special encounter, it is uncertain that for their own security readers need to interpret literature "accurately." In fact, literature may check the reflexive desire to resolve all crises, thus making individuals more "flexible." Literature as literature may be "playful," improving our "critical spirit" and "imagination"; furthermore, "our perceptions necessary to survival might be complex and contradictory rather than single and harmonious."[49]

Thus, not only does Kincaid call into question the assumption that perceptual and cognitive processes insist upon finding one essential interpretation, but he also seems aware that what is postulated as a coherent reading may actually be what some critical methods offer as the appropriate etiquette for responding to great books. Yet Kincaid does present several common strategies he believes readers use when they do try to resolve contradictory experiences with a possible unified interpretation. These tactics include naturalizing the event (i.e., finding a "higher meaning" to resolve the problem), considering one interpretation subordinate to the other, eliminating one of the solutions as unacceptable for some reason, or considering the experience as a reflexive textual moment. Kincaid also points out that texts might be much more exciting if they were seen as more complex, with multiple genres (promoting varied reading responses) coexisting in them. For instance, he finds in Dickens's and Trollope's novels all four of Frye's genres (tragedy, comedy, irony, and romance). In chapter 9, Kincaid's hypotheses about readers' tactics for unifying contradictory textual experiences will be proven in the case of readers' interpretation of post–World War II art films.

Kincaid's remarks provide insights into protocols for proper reading if one criterion for a good interpretation is resolving contradiction. But two other approaches are to wonder if desires for *textual* coherency are that strong and if they are the only activity in reading. Perhaps, for instance, a reader may wish to construct himself or herself, not the text, as coherent. In sorting out all types of possible readers, Walter Gibson notes the common phenomenon of rejecting the obvious position a text offers the reader. In particular, Gibson describes refusing to become the "mock reader" that advertising and propaganda wish him to be.[50] Such a procedure, assuming that intent to resist produces the effect, may be quite satisfying from the standpoint of the reader's ego, providing the illusion of coherency of the self.

Or perhaps the self takes pleasure in contradiction. In reviewing some of the theoretically possible readers, Jonathan Culler remarks that readers might enjoy the "interaction of contradictory engagements" among the possible subject positions offered by metamorphosing from a real reader into a mock reader into an implied reader, and so on.[51]

Both of these latter reactions to the idea of a coherent reader imply the view of the subject as heterogenous, contradictory, in process. This stance happens to be the one I view as appropriate. Yet even the proposition of coherent readers suggests that a drive for coherency may be more the act of a schooled reader than a necessary result of experiencing a text. Thus, as was the case with the ideal reader, the notion of a coherent reader can illuminate something about interpretation: several common procedures may be used by some readers. However, those procedures should be understood not as inherent but historical (and likely specific to a particular group—scholars). Unless strong evidence is supplied that finding coherency is the dominant or only activity a reader carries out, I would submit that coherency of interpretation is a common, but not universal, tendency. In fact, throughout the historical studies in Part Two, I will present instances of readings in which only the most perverse distortions of the information could conclude that a coherent reading had been attempted or occurred.

The sources for the notion of a coherent reader are multiple. They derive from assuming something about texts (e.g., that texts are coherent), from confusing what might be "in" a text with what a reader might do with the details of a text, and from believing that the primary obligation of readers is creating a logical interpretation rather than, for instance, developing a coherent self in opposition to the text or finding pleasure in dispersion and contradiction. These latter possibilities are more in line with a historical materialist perspective about readers.

Competent Readers

Competent readers, like coherent readers, seem another significant variation of ideal readers. The notion of competency does not assume that a text or a reader is coherent, but it does assume that some readings are better than others. This proposition, thus, implicitly or accidentally acknowledges variations among interpretations, and if variations can occur, the text cannot totally determine or control what the reader does.

An incidental proof of variation among readers, however, is not very important (no one takes the position that "real" readers all do the same thing). Instead, the question here is, competency by what or whose standards? As I suggested with the notion of a coherent reader (in one sense, one type of competent reader), the determination of what standard is competency seems more a consequence of history or evaluation systems than a matter susceptible to proof by any scholar.

One solution to this problem of standards, however, echoes the discussion about interpretation and meaning. As Dagmar Barnouw explains, the ideal reader is "the fully competent reader in the sense of the speech act theory: the reader who is clearly intended by the author and whose 'competence' fully coincides with the author's."[52] This answer is tautological. For if I do not accept meaning as immanent in the text and if I have to interpret what the author intended, including what reader was implied, how would I know if I had a competent conclusion? The only proof would be my interpretation's matching my own or the critic's assumption of what the author intended—which is what I wanted to know.

What "competency" is really about is the possibility of ranking or dismissing interpretations. In *Structuralist Poetics*, Jonathan Culler reveals this:

> None would deny that literary works, like most other objects of human attention, can be enjoyed for reasons that have little [to] do with understanding and mastery—that texts can be quite blatantly misunderstood and still be appreciated for a variety of personal reasons. But to reject the notion of misunderstanding as a legislative imposition is to leave unexplained the common experience of being shown where one went wrong, of grasping a mistake and seeing why it was a mistake.[53]

Two comments are necessary here. Culler is choosing meaning (probably defined as author's intent) over significance as an appropriate hierarchy for evaluating interpretations. Additionally, he appeals to common sense to naturalize that judgment. That is, if a social formation has a set of conventions and protocols for promoting some types of interpretations, then the "obviousness" of making a mistake should be recognized as ideological. Thus, Culler's answer to the question of the standard of competency turns out to hinge on historical variations—current norms and conventions for understanding the text. Readers may be able to judge a competent reading but only within their own systems of interpretation.

The researcher who assumes that ideal, coherent, and competent readers are historical readers falls prey to various of the fallacies that I discussed in chapter 1: the coherence-inference fallacy (assuming readers read coherently), the ideal-spectator fallacy (assuming all readers in a group do the same thing), and the free-reader fallacy (assuming readers have complete freedom). While such propositions about readers may have value for philosophical or critical speculation, a historical materialist study of reception needs, as far as possible, to avoid generalizations that ignore the diversity and variety of interpretative acts by readers.

MISREADING

Culler has changed his position about interpretations. Part of his description of literary competency included the contention that the idea of competency was necessary: "If the distinction between understanding and misunderstanding were irrelevant . . . there would be little point to discussing and arguing about literary works and still less to writing about them."[54] Now Culler writes,

> Since no reading can escape correction, all readings are misreadings; but this leaves not a monism but a double movement. Against the claim that, if there are only misreadings, then anything goes, one affirms that misreadings are errors; but against the positivist claim that they are errors because they strive toward but fail to attain a true reading, one maintains that true readings are only particular misreadings: misreadings whose misses have been missed.

For deconstructionism, misreading is a logical necessity, since the notion of misreading "retains the trace of truth" that a true reading is possible.[55]

My stance on this is that since I wish to write a historical materialist account of interpreting, I want to set aside the philosophical question of whether misreadings are or are not possible. Instead, I want to ask, what counts as a misreading? What situations, methods, procedures, or interpretations are judged by whom to be erroneous? Within that historical context, I want to know, why is a meaning or significance deemed less "true" than another? Here I am responding to Barbara Herrnstein Smith's comments in "Contingencies of Value," that judgments are never value-free, but they are part and parcel of struggles among individuals.[56]

Another part of the reason for my decision to ask what counts as a misreading connects to comments made by Michael Riffaterre in a discussion on the "referential fallacy." By his definition, the "referential fallacy" occurs when a reader "mistakenly substitutes the reality for its representation, and tends mistakenly to substitute the representation for the interpretation we are supposed to make of it."[57] Riffaterre is dealing with one of the difficulties of significance: a reader may inappropriately (by the standards of semiotics as a critical method, not as a communication theory) fail to isolate the interpretation derived during the textual experience from those experiences that are in everyday life. For instance, some viewers of afternoon television dramas write to the actors and actresses of the program, giving them advice about the plot events, as well as using story situations as positive or negative lessons to be applied to their own lives.

Riffaterre points out that "we cannot, however, simply correct the mistake and ignore its effects, for the fallacy is part of the literary phenomenon, being an illusion of the reader's. The fallacy is thus a valid process in our experiencing of literature."[58] If one of the goals of semiotics (or reception studies) is description, rather than prescription, then every act, even an error, is an important datum in evidence gathering and hypothesis making.

Furthermore, I would assert that every so-called error is a sign of, perhaps, the reader's "mistake" but also of the judge's system. John Paul Russo provides an example. Reviewing the evaluative standards of I. A. Richards, Russo describes how Richards's list of ten types of "obstacles in reading" implies a thesis about what is artistic in a text. Among Richards's obstacles are "stock responses, irrelevant associations, doctrinal adhesion, inhibition, sentimentality, and so on." As Russo puts it: "Some of the terminology that defined mental responses and misinterpretation inevitably got into the discussion of the work of art: wholeness, tension, doctrine."[59] In another example, Peter Uwe Hohendahl examines Theodor Adorno's criticism of the type of "impact" studies done by Paul Lazarsfeld. Hohendahl argues that Adorno's rejection of Lazarsfeld's work is aimed in part at the positivism of assuming that reported subject experiences are "primary and indisputable data."[60] Adorno's reaction, however, also presumes the wholeness, autonomy, and integrity of the work of art. Adorno's ideal readers are competent; interpretation is obvious.

> The reader, spectator or listener does not appear as an independent category determining the work because Adorno never questions the hermeneutic act of understanding. . . . the recipient is always an ideal construction which thus cannot violate the text. If this is not the case—as in the relationship between avant-garde art and the mass public—then the blame for this incompatibility lies with the public.[61]

The consequence of this is an ideal reader much like Richards's or New Criticism's views of a reader's interpretive act: meaning is immanent, texts have essences, mistakes are the fault of the reader. It is also, ironically for Adorno, not historical materialism, for his assumptions make meanings ahistorical.

When confronted by the notion that what is defined as "misreading" is actually a symptom of the critical method, some individuals retaliate by stretching that position to a reductio ad absurdum. If misreadings do not exist (except as prescriptions), then any reading is possible. You could, for example, interpret the film *2001: A Space Odyssey* as meaning the same, or having the same significance, as *The Birth of a Nation*. Indeed, one consequence of eliminating the criterion of truth for an interpretation is opening up reading to a polysemy and pluralism that even the most radical scholar might fear.

A possible response to this quandary is to make a distinction between, on the one hand, the *philosophical possibility* of reading anything any way and, on the other, the *historical fact* that the range of interpretations is constrained by numerous factors such as language, ideologies, personal goals for the experience, conditions of reception, self-identities related to class, gender, race, age, and ethnicity, and so forth—including the contemporary critical methods readers have been taught. As Terry Eagleton has already reminded us, "The notion that the text is simply a ceaselessly self-signifying practice, without source or object, stands four square with the bourgeois mythology of individual freedom."[62] In fact, this is what seems most pertinent to me. Reading formations—the variety of procedures or protocols historically available—are a domain of tremendous importance for materialist scholars of interpretation. They are also one of vital political significance, for once "misreading" is considered as a historical variable, then activating alternative reading strategies becomes a political weapon. "Misreadings" may be cultivated as oppositional gambits in battle against hegemonic etiquette. The idea of "resisting readers" seems grounded in just such a fundamental and intentional contrariness.

Political reverberations aside, the notion of historical reading formations still demands attention. In fact, if you believe that you hold a merely curiosity-oriented value system, then you might agree with Culler: "In general, divergence of readings is more interesting than convergence." Culler has preceded this remark by making what I take to be the facetious suggestion that we legislate the grounds for finding a textual meaning. Such grounds might be: (1) "what its author meant by it"; (2) "what it would have meant to an ideal audience of its day"; or (3) "what accounts for its every detail without violating the historical norms of the genre."[63] Prohibition, however, generally fails as perfect prevention. For a historical materialist description of reading, those criminal acts are as much within the range of analysis as law-abiding ones.

TEXTS, READERS, CONTEXTS

The I that approaches the text is itself already
a plurality of other texts, of infinite or, more
precisely, lost codes (whose origins are lost).
(*Roland Barthes, 1970*)

> They reinvent the reader as an energetic creature
> who by turns accommodates and victimizes his
> texts; thus they also reconstitute the reading act as
> not so much a peaceful taking in of information as
> an at times violent appropriation.
> (*Barry C. Chabot, 1975*)

> Reading is as much an act of appropriation
> as a gesture of surrender.
> (*David Coward, 1977*)

Despite the ahistoricism and idealism of a number of reception theorists, comments they make about texts and readers can be useful jumping-off points so long as later the historical variability of these ideas is reasserted.[64] I will discuss several of the major writers in this area of research, making a gross generalization by dividing their work into three groups. These groups are constituted in response to three major questions: What is the ontological status of the text? What is the ontological status of the reader? Where "is" meaning or significance? The three groups I will label "text-activated," "reader-activated," and "context-activated" because the answers to the questions lead to such propositions. Each of the three groups then produces different corollary secondary questions. Given that I have (somewhat) arbitrarily asked the three questions, I would point out that if I asked different questions, the writers might end up grouped in another way.[*65]

Among the approaches that I will associate with the text-activated group are the theories of textual poetics proposed by Roland Barthes, Jonathan Culler (in *Structuralist Poetics*), Umberto Eco, Gerard Genette, Michael Riffaterre, and Meir Sternberg; the affective stylistics and interpretative strategies work of Stanley Fish; and the phenomenology of Wolfgang Iser. All of these theories suggest that the text exists and will set up what the reader will do, that the reader is constituted by the text or by social and literary conventions, and that meaning or significance is "in" the text for the reader to interpret. In comparison, the reader-activated group includes the transactive reading of Norman Holland, the subjective criticism of David Bleich, and the later Culler (in *The Pursuit of Signs*). This group argues that the text exists, but the reader, as an individual, can greatly redo or appropriate that text, that the reader is constituted by social or literary conventions or psychologies, and that the meaning or significance is "in" the reader's interpretation. Finally, those constituting the context-activated group would include theories such as the phenomenology of Hans Robert Jauss, the sociology of Jacques Leenhardt, and the dialectical and historical materialism of Manfred Naumann and of British cultural studies scholars such as Tony Bennett. These writers assume that the text and the reader are equally significant in creating meaning, that historical context is very significant for the interaction, and that meaning or significance is "in" that contextual intersection.

My interest here is not in validating these groupings; instead, I use them only as a device to draw out certain themes and remarks that might be useful in consideration of the historical reception of texts. You will notice as well that I am referring to theorists who focus on literary texts. In the next chapter I will return to these groupings to organize similar work in film and television studies.

Text-Activated Theories

Text-activated theories assume or imply that the text controls or provides information for the reader's routine, although perhaps learned, activities. Even if the reader's engagement is proposed as constructed by social or literary conventions, once the reader knows the conventions, the response is automatic. Only the texts vary, and, hence, the model tends to stress the features of the text that supposedly produce readers' responses. The dynamic of the experience is text-activated. Because of this, the stress in discussion for text-activated theories is answering two corollary questions: what are the specific features of the text? what will the ideal or competent reader do when encountering those features?

What, then, are some theories of textual specificity, and what do readers do as a consequence? Several writers conceive of texts as sets of structures. That is, the parts of a text are in some abstract interrelation, with the sets of structures copresent, usually in parallel. For example, in his *The Role of the Reader*, Eco posits nine structures producing reader activity.*[66] These are: (1) utterance structures (i.e., information about what kind of speech act the text is); (2) bracketed extension structures (information about the possible world of the text); (3) discursive structures (information for basic denotative meanings); (4) semantic disclosure structures (information for thematics); (5) narrative structures (plot and story information); (6) forecast and inferential-walk structures (information that produces hypotheses about textual outcome; such information may require intertextual frames); (7) actantial structures (character information); (8) elementary ideological structures (information about textual ideologies such as what the text counts as good or bad, true or false); and (9) world structures (information for referencing reality frames). Obviously at any point, more than one structure may be cuing readers' activities.

In *S/Z*, Barthes has five "codes" for readers: the proairetic (plot actions), the hermeneutic (propositions of interpretive truth), the cultural (references to world frames), the semic (features of characters), and the symbolic (connotative or metaphoric themes). Although Riffaterre does not delineate possible structures, he does assume them in his discussion of Roman Jakobson and Claude Lǂi-Strauss's analysis of "Les Chats."[67] There his quarrel consists of debating how the critic determines which structures are perceptible to the reader *for poetic effect*, constructing his superreader as the judge and shifting pertinence of data to a (very specific ideal) reader's response.

The structuralist version of a text, particularly the detail supplied by Eco and Barthes, suggests the importance of constantly recognizing the multitude of activities in which a reader might be involved at any moment. The lists may not be complete, but they are surely rich. They are suggestive, for example, of the complexity of any actual interpretative act. Furthermore, they give reception studies numerous areas in which to comprehend the possibilities of variation in historical readings. Additionally, they indicate textual factors that might promote possible contradiction and ambiguity for readers. Several of the studies in Part Two will return to these sets of possible activities.

In its representation of the text as a set of copresent structures, structuralism tends to consider interpretation (but not necessarily reading) as a "holistic" rather than "sequential" experience. Steven Mailloux defines a holistic interpretation as determining how parts "'cohere into a total meaningful pattern.'"[68] Since texts supply the variations for what a reader will do, holistic text-activated theory concentrates on describing how the reader either decodes the structures or uses social or literary codes or conventions to make an integral pattern. Consequently, rules or procedures of interpretation are presented as normative: they describe how the reader confronts textual contradiction, incoherency, or ambiguity, possibly caused by the copresent structures.

For example, Culler provides rules for "naturalization" of texts: "To naturalize a text is to bring it into relation with a type of discourse or model which is already, in some sense, natural and legible."[69] An instance in film studies might be the interpretive tendency to assume that "illogical" texts such as avant-garde films are attempts to represent dreams: the unconventional is naturalized into an acceptable frame.

While Culler does not assume an essential core pattern in a text, his notion of a reader informed by (current) literary conventions produces a guideline for reader competency; thus, in conjunction, the data supplied by the text and the standard of competency permit Culler to know when a coherent reading for a text exists. Conventions he offers as common include "the rule of significance" (a reader should "read the poem as expressing a significant attitude to some problem concerning man and/or his relation to the universe"), "metaphorical coherence" ("one should attempt through semantic transformations to produce coherence on the levels of both tenor and vehicle"), and "thematic unity."*[70] Since what Culler presents is the usually intuited procedures for academic interpretations, his comments are useful for analyzing neither ideal nor competent readers but historical ones: those people trained in literary protocols. Still, because many published accounts of responses are informed by these rules, they become widely disseminated in our culture. In this sense, Stanley Fish's claim that "critical controversies become disguised reports of what readers uniformly do" is central to a text-activated model. With his theory of the interpretive community, Fish does underline that interpretive strategies are historical and learned: he assumes that competent readings are those that are pertinent for scholars in judging among interpretations for a given text.[71]

One aspect of a structural view of the text is how information is encoded so as to insure a corresponding decoding. Thus, while Culler describes general interpretive practices, as features of the structured text change, so might readers' activities. Susan Rubin Suleiman discusses redundancy within and among structures as important. In structuralism, redundancies are systems of repetition of textual data that increase the possibility of agreement among interpreters. Such repetitions involve verbal ones, recurrence of narrative structures, "doubling" of characters, and thematic equivalences.[72] Obviously, looking for redundancies can also be considered a historical and learned literary convention.

Expanding on the idea of relations of data among structures, Christine Brooke-Rose proposes a thesis about effects on a reader depending upon the degree, type, or existence of redundancy.[73] She describes a text as *overdetermined* when information is too clear, too repetitious. Using Barthes's codes, she suggests as an example that proairetic and hermeneutical structures are commonly in sync. Consequently, a reader has an easy time guessing the direction of a plot. When this happens, the reader may shift interest to semic, cultural, or symbolic structures, depending upon the textual material. *Underdetermined* texts (without intense redundancies) exist in various forms: a nouveau roman, for instance, or a detective story (in which overdetermined data are usually false leads but underdetermined ones are the true clues). Finally, *nondetermined* texts are those in which the reader "feels free to read everything, anything, and therefore also nothing, into the text."[74] Suleiman approaches this question from the perspective of intertextuality, defined as "the coexistence of 'several discourses' in a single (inter) textual space."[75] Depending on whether and how the discourses are redundant, texts are conflictual, negative, or affirmative.

Brooke-Rose's and Suleiman's remarks, like the others, hold value in that they describe common reading practices for those tutored in literature studies. Yet they also are suggestive of causes for deviations by nontutored or resisting readers. If the structuralist representation of textual features has validity, then the possibilities for alternative readings statistically become nearly infinite. Since post-structuralism argues for even greater variability (semantics are continually in process), this version of textuality and reading, ironically, provides a powerful argument for individual difference. For instance, in discussing the *roman à thèse*, Suleiman describes characters' semic material as involved in textual ideologies.[76] What matters is how combinations are made. As a character is developed, numerous generic facets are attached to its proper name: religion, ethnicity, political beliefs, gender, and so on. These associations take on ramifications as stereotypes and biases are asserted or denied. Are immigrants communists or anarchists? Do black males threaten white females? Both the hermeneutical conclusions and ideological effects may be produced from the relations among these structures. But what the reader notices, accepts, or rejects as pertinent conjunctions or redundancies matters as well. Which semic features are believed to be pertinent could differ tremendously among various readers. Hence image studies need to look at readers as well as texts.

Suleiman's remarks are directed toward a specific type of text. Another direction holistic text-activated reception theory has taken is to assert not only different interpretative practices depending upon textual structures but also specific aesthetic or affective responses for readers. In *The Delights of Terror*, Terry Heller rewrites Tzvetan Todorov's study of fantastic stories into a reader-response schema producing three groups of texts depending on aesthetic effect. For example, "uncanny horror stories offer the reader the opportunity to pretend to experience extreme mental and physical states by identifying with characters who undergo such experiences." In contrast, "horror thrillers offer the reader the thrill of horror mainly by creating supernatural images, usually monsters, that in various ways and with careful qualifications embody or make concrete unconscious fears that a reader brings to the texts."[77] As with the notion of interpretations, affects may also be considered as historically constructed rather than universal or essential.

Reception theory observations by holistic text-activated writings are one group of valuable thoughts about reading. Another text-activated position is that held by individuals stressing sequential readings. The scholars might traditionally be labeled structuralists, phenomenologists, or formalists, and for them the features of a text are also materials in structures or systems. However, while the materials may have copresent and multiple motivations and functions, the pertinent textual feature is that the textual materials themselves are (necessarily) discrete and sequential. Thus, such reception theory stresses describing the process of encountering the materials and the arrival at a final conclusion, rather than emphasizing an overall, general experience. Furthermore, by stressing the discreteness and order of the materials, these writers often consider the most pertinent feature of texts to be their temporary or permanent gaps or blanks—something holistic text-activated writers deal with only indirectly.

Sequential text-activated writers like to have readers change ideas, and they deal with that possibility. However, as with those theories which emphasize holistic results, readers in these theories operate as they do either solely because of the text's materials or also because of social and literary conventions that produce ideal or competent responses. Thus, given an idealist construction of the reader's character, the variability of the text is what matters. This emphasis produces a "text-activated" model of reading. Meaning or significance is caused by the encounter with the specificity of the text (since the reading activities are a given).*[78] As Fish argues it in his affective stylistics phase, sequence matters: "It is impossible to mean the same thing in two (or more) different ways"*[79] because order of experience is crucial to meaning.

An early notion that the text is a set of specific materials is proposed by the Russian formalists during the late teens and early 1920s. Successors include Czech structuralists such as Jan Mukařovský, as well as numerous later structuralists and formalists including Genette and Sternberg. Among their interests are analyzing the relations among the textual parts and the effect those relations have on literary experience. Perhaps a cause for this concentration is that Russian formalists define literature in part on the basis of the textual effect on the reader, and they also stress aesthetic evaluations which privilege perceptual encounters. They like textual devices that jar or disrupt conventional perceptional strategies. Thus, their critical apparatus includes many terms and propositions that imply reading consecutively.

For example, retardation is observed. How a text is organized to prevent resolution is considered a principal formal prospect—otherwise, the story would be over right away. Victor Shklovsky suggests that retardation can be achieved in various ways, such as stringing together problems to be solved (as in fairy tales and adventure novels), setting stories within stories (framing narratives), and paralleling several plots (common in the nineteenth-century novel).[80] The notion of retardation encourages consideration of the seriality of the materials.

Another textual expectation with similar repercussions is motivation. Mukařovský describes motivation as "a basic requirement of plot construction." Motivation is the reason for the appearance of a material in a text. "Every motif [material element of the text] . . . should be related to another or several others, and [motifs] should . . . determine one another semantically."[81] Furthermore,

> when the initial member of a motivational bond appears, it evokes an expectation in the perceiver; the next then directs the perceiver's attention back-

wards to what has already been perceived. . . . The effectiveness of motivation increases with the distance between the motifs which are bound by it into the contextual sequence. The longer the connection of a certain motif with the others remains hidden from the reader, the more the reader's expectation contributes to the "tension," and the more strongly the action is bound into semantic unity by means of motivation.[82]

You will notice that Mukařovský does not shy away from assuming a final coherent interpretation, but he does pay special attention to "contextual sequence." Additionally, he postulates a reader who reflects backward to previous materials and who projects forward, making (and revising) hypotheses about the materials yet to come.

A third, and extremely prominent, textual attribute described by formalists is the distinction between *fabula* and *sujet*. *Fabula* is generally translated as "story" and *sujet* as "plot," a tradition I will maintain. Plot is the actual sequence of materials in a text. Story exists in the reader's mind: it is the mental rearrangement of the materials into a chronology. The work of Genette and Sternberg has greatly expanded original ideas of the Russian formalists on story and plot. In his study of Proust's *Remembrance of Things Past* (one of the most entangled textual organizations of temporality), Genette sets up numerous categories for considering the varying relation between plot and story.[83] Additionally, he considers the factors in the relations of narrators and characters to plot data, which further complicate possible permutations. Sternberg supplements Genette's work by stressing the gaps among the ordered parts that a reader must negotiate. For Sternberg, these gaps can be filled (insofar as the textual materials are available). The reader manages this by posing and answering questions such as these: "What is happening or has happened, and why? What is the connection between this event and the previous one? What is the motivation of this or that character? To what extent does the logic of cause and effect correspond to that of everyday life? and so on."*[84]

What do readers do as a result in this theory of textuality? As with holistic theories of reading, a dominant activity is proposing, verifying, and revising hypotheses. For example, Fish writes that what occurs is "the making and revising of assumptions, the rendering and regretting of judgments, the coming to and abandoning of conclusions, the giving and withdrawing of approval, the specifying of causes, the asking of questions, the supplying of answers, the solving of puzzles."[85] Also as with holistic theories, the sequential text-activated models sometimes distinguish among texts on the basis of their effect on a reader. Sternberg suggests that the number and significance of gaps varies by genre: gaps are fewer in number and less central to a novel of manners or a picaresque tale than to a detective story. Additionally, affect is produced from the relations among the textual parts. When gaps are emphasized, affective reactions often include curiosity, suspense, surprise, disappointment, or pride in solving the puzzle.

Perhaps not surprisingly, sequential theories tend to describe readers spending their response time trying to link up parts of the text, whereas holistic-theory readers attempt to compare or reconcile structures. A result of this difference, I think, is that sequential theories incline toward treating texts as puzzles to be solved, but holistic theories stress deriving interpretive generalizations. Sequential theories often use language that has the text and reader in a game in which one or the other wins. Holistic theories seem to promote searching for truth. Of course, these two activities can be connected, and often the text is metamorphosed into a trickster, manipulating readers as they seek their goals.*[86]

It might seem surprising that I have included the phenomenologist Iser among the text-activated theorists, since phenomenology as a philosophy asserts a dyadic exchange between object and subject. In one of the most quoted phrases in reception aesthetics, Iser insinuates great reader flexibility: "The stars in a literary text are fixed; the lines that join them are variable."[87] Most reviewers of Iser's work, however, believe that by constructing the text as having "appellative structures" and the activity of the reader as being "ahistorical, abstract and normative,"[88] Iser produces criticism in which the text restrains the (fairly tabula rasa) reader. Thus, in practice for Iser as for the others, the features of the individual text dominate the literary experience.

What does make Iser's slightly different from the other text-activated theories is that the gaps with which he is most engaged are not "in" the text but are intersubjective—between the text's world and the reader's.

> The reader discovers the meaning of the text, taking negation as his starting point; he discovers a new reality through a fiction which, at least in part, is different from the world he himself is used to; and he discovers the deficiencies inherent in prevalent norms and in his own restricted behavior.[89]

Artistic texts offer "schematised views" that readers "realize" (*konkretisation*). While Iser tends to treat reading as a sequential, negating process, and since he assumes a reader's overall objective is learning something about possible worlds, he also offers comments about holistic interpretations: readers form a "gestalt" of the text, unifying the experience. Iser's model, like others in this group, depicts the features of a text activating readers' generalized reactions. Since what Iser describes is likely a well-developed social and literary convention and possibly one of the common goals of many readers, his work can contribute to the understanding of customary activities in historical readers.

Reader-Activated Theories

Text-activated theories perhaps tend toward spotlighting textual features, not out of theoretical necessity, but because the complexities of considering variety among readers would significantly complicate making generalizations. Nearly every one of the writers implicitly brackets his or her work as not referring to "real" or "empirical" readers. In contrast, reader-activated theories flip the coin over. Where text-activated theories focus on features of texts and the effects they produce, reader-activated theories examine features of readers and those features' consequences for the reading experience. Thus, the corollary question for reader-activated theories becomes, what are the causes for the variety of readers? Writings by three individuals will serve as examples of the potential contributions of this approach: Norman Holland's transactive criticism, David Bleich's subjective criticism, and Jonathan Culler's work on literary conventions.

That they approach the issues from the point of view of readers' features may explain the propensity of these theories to start with affective descriptions of reading experiences rather than to tack on affect as almost an afterthought, as seems to occur in text-activated reception criticism. This is, I stress, a propensity, but not inherent in the reader-activated approach (as Culler's work exemplifies and Holland's approach implies).

Both Holland and Bleich appeal strongly to psychological theory for their paradigms of the reading event. Individuals' personalities inform their interpretation of texts. Holland has labeled his approach "transactive," drawing from cognitive, information-theory, and some personality psychology. In a finely argued criticism of text-activated theories, Holland writes that they assume normative responses and posit variations as local phenomena.[90] However, study of human perception shows that "perception is a constructive act in which we impose schemata from our minds on the data of our senses."[91] Thus, readers do not come after the fact to a text, but they constitute a valuable part of a "feedback loop." Holland believes that schemata come from literary, biological, cultural, and economic sources and build an individual's psychology and "identity theme." Thus, variation among readers is normal. In his most fully worked out discussion of types of readers, he describes four modalities, using the acronym DEFT, to tally pertinent psychological dimensions that form an individual's core identity. These modalities are: D—defenses; E—expectations; F—fantasies; and T—transformations (shaping textual data into a meaningful totality). Mailloux points out that Holland's model accounts very well for variety; if sociological and historical dimensions were factored in, then reoccurrence of interpretations among readers could also be explained.[92]

Bleich's model is less formalized than Holland's but also assumes psychological causes for variation and similarity among readings. Perception, affect, and association are its main components. For Bleich, interpretation comes after the reading experience as something of an attempt to assimilate the personal with projections of what might constitute objective evaluation.[93]

Although Culler's early work suggests a text-activated approach, in his *Pursuit of Signs*, Culler begins to historicize his comments, shifting away from general claims of reading competency. Culler becomes intrigued by the historical variation among interpretive conventions. He accepts the idea that perhaps periods of varying literary conventions exist which would explain differences among readers. For example, Culler synopsizes a study by Ivor Indyk of the interpretations of *Tom Jones*. Using codes such as those described by Barthes, Indyk outlines four eras in which critics foreground different hierarchies for the codes. The earliest opinions emphasized plot (proairetic sequences); characters were constituents of the plot. Later an "inversion" occurs: "Incident is interpreted as a revelation of character."[94] In the twentieth century, criticism that seeks unified visions of textual worlds emphasizes thematic codes to produce cohering interpretations. Finally, contemporary criticism may also assume that artistic texts account for themselves, in which case codes of irony or self-referentiality become the integrative device. What Indyk and Culler present is a reader-activated theory in which historical literary conventions account for variations among readings. Readers are different because the academy has changed its methods of producing competent readings.*[95]

As this is described, it would seem that each period seeks a dominant code or has an approved protocol to handle awkward or ambiguous situations. For instance, Culler repeats Indyk's experiment by analyzing interpretations of Blake's "London." He finds four procedures for unifying the poem: noting the particulars of individuals as implying classes that can then be compared; exploiting shifts in meaning to argue that what precedes the shift is false, what comes afterward is true; using local materials to argue parallel, connotative, or ironic semantics; and arguing that closings are what count the most.[96]

Culler's assumption that each era tries to integrate all textual structures or materials, however, needs investigating. As has been noted, different periods have diverged as to the functions of scholarly criticism. Not every era has seen its task as explicating how a text is coherent or unified. Additionally, scholars are only one group of readers. Along with others who are beginning to consider the history of literary conventions informing academic criticism, what Indyk and Culler point out is significant as, likely, a widely disseminated etiquette for reading. However, nonacademic readers are notably resistant to adopting scholarly prescriptions. I would ask as well, What are the literary conventions of the "mass reader"? Why assume coherency as a reader's goal? What are the varieties of nonacademic reading procedures? Are there differences between reading texts and viewing films? And, more broadly, beside psychological and academic features of readers, what else accounts for variety (and similarity) among interpreters of texts?

Certainly a post-structuralist view of individuals confirms the value of such questions. As one theorist sets it out, modern semiotics permits consideration of individuals as constructed selves: "We can only know the self as a sign."[97] As texts vary and are polysemous because of their historical determination and the process of language, individuals are complex productions of historical contexts and discourses. Consequently, accounting for this variety of selves (even within the same individual) is important in theorizing reading experiences and interpretations. A reader-activated theory needs to avoid assumptions that reassert false idealizations of readers.

Despite my reservation that current reader-activated theories tend to reposit unfortunate generalizations about its groups of readers, what reader-activated theories do offer is an important emphasis on the power of the individual—within his or her circumstances—to appropriate (or choose to surrender to) a text. As Walter Benn Michaels describes it, "The most we can say is that we can choose our interpretations but we can't choose our range of choices."[98] Furthermore, at least two categories of causes have been proposed by reader-activated theories as viable for explaining variations among readers: psychologies and literary conventions. Both surely influence the complex makeup of any reader's perception, comprehension, and interpretation.

Context-Activated Theories

The third set of theories I have labeled "context-activated." Neither text-activated nor reader-activated theories assert the irrelevancy of the other. But all the relevant questions cannot be asked at once, and the insights that they contribute come from their perceptual focus. Context-activated theories differ from the first two by looking at contexts for reading experiences. Obviously, this means that historical circumstances become central to the account. Which historical factors matter, however, depends upon the writer's model of causality as well as the event being studied. Thus, the corollary question for context-activated theories is, What contextual factors account for the interpretation?

One context that counts a great deal for any reading is the context of the communication act. A reader's hypotheses about the type of text or speech act and its source narrow the range of semantical choices and participate in limiting the plurality of connotations for a text. In taking a hypothetical case of the phrase "private members only," Fish concludes that "it does not have a literal meaning in the sense of some irreducible content which survives the sea change of situations; but in each of those situations one meaning (even if it is plural) will seem so obvious that one cannot see how it could be otherwise, and that meaning will be literal."[99] This is something like Barthes's declaration that "denotation is not the first meaning . . . it is ultimately no more than the *last* of the connotations (the one which seems both to establish and to close the reading)."[100]

All sorts of data might be used by a reader to hypothesize the appropriate communicative process into which a specific instance fits. As Tony Bennett suggests, the material features of a text contribute to this. Different typefaces, cloth versus paper coverings, blurbs, jacket designs—these are among the most apparent material conditions that "before it is opened, [inscribe the text] within a specific ideology of consumption."[101] But eventually Bennett considers every context as potentially contributing.

Related to the immediate context of the communication act is a text's aesthetic or textual history. Here the reception theory of Hans Robert Jauss offers the notion of "horizons of expectation": the successive interpretations through which a text has been perceived becomes a "horizon" or background that sets up assumptions about a text's meaning and thus influences its current interpretation.*[102] As Bennett cites Pierre Macherey, a work becomes "encrusted" with its previous reception: "'. . . everything which has been written *about* it, everything which has been collected on it, become [*sic*] attached to it—like shells on a rock by the seashore forming a whole incrustation. At which point the idea of a 'work' loses all meaning.'"[103] An example of this situation will be studied in chapter 7's analysis of the reception of *The Birth of a Nation*.

Jauss's critics believe that he emphasizes aesthetic horizons to the practical neglect of discursive, social, political, and economic contexts.[104] Thus, these conditions are also set forth as integral to a text's reception. For example, Jacques Leenhardt calls for a "sociology of reading."*[105] In one study he takes the variable of nationality as his comparative measure. Two novels (one Polish, the other French) were read by five hundred Polish and French individuals from different social backgrounds. Surveys indicated what the participants had read elsewhere, and open-ended questions derived information about this reading experience. Leenhardt concludes that, on the one hand, French readers of the Polish novel sought coherency, trying to tie parts into a thematic logic. On the other hand, Polish readers sought ethical *verities*. Parts of the novel were judged via moral propositions. Both French and Polish readers favored scenes that fit their interpretive procedures. Leenhardt concludes that specific cultural factors related to conditions of nationality (e.g., educational systems and scholarly judgments, political situtions) explain the variation between the two groups of readers.

In a similar vein and using ethnographic methods, Janice Radway approaches one group of romance novel readers. These women, as Radway underlines, "cannot be thought of as a scientifically designed random sample," but they do constitute a case study that might be compared with other groups. The readers' preferences for certain types of romances, their justifications for spending time reading, and their means of explaining the disparities between the lives of the female protagonists and their own—Radway connects these phenomena to several variables, the most significant being the readers' gender, the existence in this culture of patriarchy, and the psychological development of sexual preference. In one summarizing statement, Radway concludes:

> Through the use of rigid socializing procedures, instructional habits, and formal and informal sanctions against deviance, the culture pursuades women to view femininity solely in terms of a social and institutional role that is essential to the maintenance of the current organization of life. Therefore, while the act of romance reading is used by women as a means of partial protest against the role prescribed for them by the culture, the discourse itself actively insists on the desirability, naturalness, and benefits of that role by portraying it not as the imposed necessity that it is but as a freely designed, personally controlled, individual choice.[106]

Radway's and Leenhardt's contextual reading denies neither the existence of specific textual features nor variability of readers. The focus, however, is on the determining force of the specific exchange's context. As Manfred Naumann phrases it, readers and texts "mutually permeate each other." "The concrete individual reception of the work is always a social process mediated by many factors."[107] The factors Naumann mentions include membership in classes, stratums, or groups; material conditions of livelihood and environment; education; age; and gender. I would add others, such as circulating discursive propositions and ideologies, nationality, race, age, sexual preference, life-style, and political beliefs. In every case, the self-images and personal associations constructed by the reader in the reading event and the relation of those self-images and associations to abstract categories of determinations matter more than any theoretical array within which a researcher might be inclined to posit the reader. I shall discuss this issue of precategorizing variables of the reader further in chapter 3.

Context-activated theories of reading assert that meaning is "in" the contextual event of each reading, not "in" one reading event rather than another. Bennett appeals to post-structuralism to support his historical materialism: "We know also, principally through Derrida, that the text is totally iterable; that, as a set of material notations, it may be inscribed within different contexts and that no context—including that in which it originated—can enclose it by specifying or fixing its meaning or effect for all time and in all contexts."[108] As Bennett goes on to stress, post-structuralism does not deny the existence of texts; it denies that of "a text hidden behind the material surface of the empirically given text, somehow *there* but unreachable."[109] Such a proposition does not reject the notion of protocols of interpretation that might determine readings of the textual materials. That proposition, though, implies history. Furthermore, such a proposition does not judge among interpretations. "'Untutored' readings are just as real and material in their effects as 'tutored' ones and may, indeed, be considerably more influential."[110]

As should be apparent, the grounding assumptions of the context-activated theorists are most compatible with my beliefs: if we are to understand the interpretation of moving images, it is crucial that we study historical determinants. Thus, while I shall take a contextual approach, I do not argue that texts are not material or real; they provide sense-data to individuals. However, readers do not just "decode" hegemonic texts; readers are complex historical individuals capable of acting within the contradictions of their own construction as selves and as reading selves. Readers are developed historically, and the interpretive event occurs at the intersection of multiple determinations. Thus, the *interpretation is contradictory* and not coherent.*[111]

In the next chapter, I will discuss reception studies from the perspective of work on moving images. Yet the work of literary and other theorists of reading and interpreting the meaning and significance of culturally produced texts offers valuable contributions toward thinking about how subjects experience textuality. Cognitive, cultural, psychological, psychoanalytic, political, and other differences constitute a conjunction of abstract explanations that can help to account for the real phenomena of interpretative deviations and correspondences. Once the historical nature of interpretation is privileged, the essentialism or timeless nature of remarks by text-activated and reader-activated theorists can be turned to the advantage and use of context-activated studies of interpretation; they become specific instances of contextual protocols for reading among those individuals who have learned frameworks for making meaning from materially inscribed sense-data.

CHAPTER THREE

Reception Studies in Film and Television

GIVEN that cinema studies in the United States has had strong ties to literary traditions, it could be anticipated that reception theories in film and television*[1] would tend toward the text-activated approach described in chapter 2. This predilection has not gone unobserved, although two areas of research—feminism and recent television studies—may have stimulated a recognition of the bias. For example, in "Women's Genres," Annette Kuhn describes the difference between thinking about a film spectator and thinking about a cinematic social audience when trying to understand gendered forms of address.[2] For the former, film studies has recently tended to consider the individual as constituted by psychic relations; in the latter case, the expectations of pleasure transform individuals into audiences in which social subjects choose whether to enter into the position offered by that experience. As Kuhn points out, the notion of the context—psychological versus social—changes the event into two different situations. "Spectators" and "social audiences" have different theoretical and actual circumstances and, thus, varied relations to textual representations. When the idea of what is the context changes, so do the salient determinants of the individual-as-a-subject. Consequently, also altered are what count as data to study and pertinent methods for handling those data. For the spectator, research has focused on hypothesizing from textual characteristics; for the social audience, evidence is gathered and organized around predetermined categories such as sex, age, education, class, and race.

In her essay, Kuhn introduces as well the historical anomaly of film scholars' focusing on spectators while early television research emphasized social audience studies. Thus, when film scholars took up television studies, one initial activity was to treat apparent formal characteristics of broadcast TV as determining the subject. Patrice Petro believes that certain of these textual features have been described in opposition to fictional narrative ("realist") film.[3] Television is characterized as discontinous, direct address, self-conscious, and parodic—thus, "modernist." Petro cautions against such a simple dichotomy. She also rejects the assumption that formal characteristics are determining for the spectator (and the social audience).

Both Kuhn and Petro include calls for research that I would consider to be reception studies. The current observation of a use-value for this type of work, however, might lead to the erroneous assumption that reception theory has only recently arrived in film studies. As I noted about the history of literary theory, questions of reader response have informed film philosophies from the inception of the medium. It seems important to me that genealogies of discourses about film and television viewers be undertaken. I will not attempt that here, but I do want to open up such a project with several thoughts about pre-1960s philosophies and current film and television research, because surprising continuities exist between them. I will then consider three dominant contemporary paradigms for studying spectators, relating them to both the considerations raised in chapter 2 and the history of film philosophy.

CLASSICAL FILM PHILOSOPHY AND THE
FILM SPECTATOR

The neglect of the spectator in film philosophies prior to the 1960s is only apparent. It is a matter, I believe, of how classical film philosophy is ordered. This is the point that André Bazin proposed in connection to the coming of mechanically synchronized sound. Bazin argued that film history should not be split between the pre- and postsynchronized sound eras but rather between films having and not having "faith in the image." Bazin is suggesting that how a field of discourses is split can affect what is foregrounded to perception. Thus, perhaps the habits of our interpretive community's view that the spectator has been neglected in early film philosophy derive from classical expositions of the field, rather than from the philosophies themselves.

One of the standard expositions is Dudley Andrew's *The Major Film Theories*.*4 This book functions as a significant supplementary reading for many of the undergraduate and graduate courses in the United States and is a synopsis and representation of what is regarded as a central opposition within classical film theory: formalist versus realist philosophies of cinema. Of interest is how Andrew organizes this split. He writes that formalist film philosophies arose first because of their historical situation. Cinema was not yet considered an art, so the problem was to define cinema aesthetically and thus as distinct from reality. This act followed nineteenth-century aesthetics, which also sought to make such distinctions. Thus, philosophical discourses written by Münsterberg, Arnheim, Eisenstein, Lindsay, Canudo, Delluc, Kuleshov, Pudovkin, and others emphasized how cinema as an art form changed the world from chaos and meaninglessness into a self-sustaining structure and rhythm. Cinema as art was a process of transformation. Turning to the realist philosophies, which appeared later, Andrew notes that these considered how people could be brought into harmony with nature via the cinema through a reinsured perception, also the product of cinema's specificity. Kracauer, Bazin, British documentarists, and Vertov provide Andrew with realist philosophies.

What is important to me in this split is that, as presented by Andrew, the same presumption regarding the spectator's relation to the object is implicit in both formalist and realist tenets. For each, the spectator is relatively passive while cinema does something. For formalist theory, cinema organizes the world; for the realist, it brings the spectator back into touch with physical reality. Both types of theoretical discourse produce text-activated approaches to the film-spectator relation.

What I would also stress here is that the question asked of the film philosophies determines the discursive field's organization. In Andrew's case, the primary question for his overall split is, what is cinema's function? It may seem trite in this day of metatheory to point out that the question the researcher elects to ask will dramatically affect the answer, but I think it does not hurt to be reminded occasionally of such truisms. Raising originating questions to consciousness helps make some assumptions explicit rather than natural. I point out the artificiality of this structure for classical film philosophy because other questions can be the originating query.*5

Let me propose, then, that another initial question of film theories be considered. The question I ask has to do with reception studies (and has been given to me by current concerns). Let me propose that the question asked is, *What is the film philosophy's conception of what determines the spectator's relation to the cinematic text?* In some sense, this question is contained within, but not equal to, the initial question asked by Andrew. As I already pointed out, for Andrew, cinema's function has something to do with the spectator. The difference between formalist and realist philosophies is not in the possibility of affecting the spectator but in what the cinema *ought* to do, its prescriptive work. Cinema either organizes the world or duplicates the experience of perceiving of it for the spectator. Both formalist and realist propositions represent the spectator as essentially worked on by the text. The difference in philosophy is in the prescriptive work of the medium.*6

Thus, if I ask my question (what is the spectator's relation to the cinematic text?), it seems that all classical philosophies have the same answer: the cinematic text works on an essentially receptive and ideal spectator. The reception of the film by the spectator is determined by the object, not the spectator. With a couple of exceptions that I will raise below, all classical philosophies take a text-activated position. Furthermore, as I will argue in the next section, most post-1960s theories offer the same thesis.

What I am suggesting is that in the discursive domain of film philosophy, text-activated theories far outweigh spectator-activated or context-activated ones. Perhaps this is because the writers, as in the field of litera-

ture, have used the received critical approaches discussed in chapter 2—
formalism and phenomenology, and, later, structuralism, semiotics, and
post-structuralism. This does not mean that what has been must be. It
seems possible that certain epistemological positions (such as some variations of phenomenology, but certainly historical and dialectical materialism) would encourage alternative theoretical emphases. In fact, the idea of
"film philosophy" itself may have limited the field's theoretical horizons—
after all, it has been *film* philosophy, not *film-spectator* philosophy.

A point may be raised against this. What good is an initial question that
cannot make discriminations among theories? Let me respond in two
ways. For one thing, the question has already pointed out a valuable fact
about film philosophies. They have been generally similar in how they address the relation of the spectator to the film. That observation may open
the way to new film theorizing.

More important, despite weak attention to the spectator, film philosophies have not been all the same. For while each one posits a moderately
receptive spectator, and certainly an ideal one, individual theories do not
offer the same description or explanation of the relationship between spectator and film. The philosophies differ over the questions of why that spectator is as she or he is and how that spectator responds to various films. I
do not intend to run through all of the dominant philosophies to prove
this, but a quick examination of Eisenstein's and Münsterberg's writings is
worthwhile since both of them suggest some complexity to the reception
situation. Furthermore, both have interesting connections to the post-
1960 paradigms.

Sergei Eisenstein

Sergei Eisenstein writes in "The Fourth Dimension in Cinema" that "the
basic sign of the shot can be taken to be the final sum total of its effect on
the cortex of the brain as a whole, irrespective of the ways in which the
accumulating stimulants have come together."[7] Eisenstein's early theory
works from an assumption that the mind is matter acted upon by external
stimuli. In film, montage is the source of these stimuli that produce perceptive, emotive, and cognitive responses in the spectator. Working from
a mentalist view*[8] of the mind, he believes that individual stimuli can be
calculated and measured. Eisenstein specifically discusses the need to
control the montage-material: "Thus, where a tightly expounded fact is
concerned, the work of the film director . . . requires, in addition to the
mastery of production (planning and acting), a repertoire of montage-cal-
culated angles for the camera to 'capture' these elements."[9] The aim in his

early theory is to maximize the conflict in the shot as a cell so that the tension will produce intensity and an explosion into synthesis. Since film art should consist of such a stimulation of the perceptive, emotive, and cognitive responses of the spectator, the director's selection and construction of material in the film must facilitate that threefold response. "A *work of art . . .* is first and foremost a *tractor ploughing over the audience's psyche in a particular class context.*"[10]

As Philip Rosen has suggested, in this phase of Eisenstein's work, reception becomes pure input of ideology, which is simply equated with complexes of sensation. The problem with this is that intelligibility cannot be reduced to mere sensation; intelligibility is the organization of those sensations. As the mentalist's position acknowledges, minds can mediate those perceptions based on the individuals' personal experiences, developing their own conditioned reflexes to stimuli. Thus, specificity and history could be, and ought to be, factored in.

In fact, I believe that the possibility of variant subjects troubles Eisenstein's philosophy from its start, and that through about 1932 Eisenstein grapples with the tension between wanting to control the spectator and recognizing that spectators are not ideal and tabula rasa receivers. For instance, in discussing organizing filmic material, Eisenstein parenthetically observes, "It is quite clear that for a worker and a former cavalry officer the chain of associations set off by seeing a meeting broken up and the corresponding emotional effect in contrast to the material which frames this incident, will be somewhat different."[11] As a deconstructionist would note, this parenthesis makes all the differance. Added to this is Eisenstein's extremely complicated description of the text, one that admits to contradiction as he theorizes levels of montage.

By 1932, Eisenstein seems to have reconsidered his situation. I believe he is influenced by Soviet psycho- and sociolinguistic theory, particularly the work of A. R. Luria and Lev Vygotsky, to alter his conception of the spectator.*[12] His new epistemological thesis produces a change in how he will control the spectator. "Montage form as structure" at this time "is a reconstruction of the laws of the thought process"[13] as it was before. Only now the laws of thought change from mentalism to a dialectical materialist psycho- and sociolinguistics. In Vygotsky's theory, language is understood as a tool for thinking. As an individual develops intellectually in a social context, concepts become attached to objects and have public meaning. They also, however, accrue a personal sense, a sensuality, for the specific individual.*[14] Such a social and historical theory of individual language development, if applied to film spectators, demands a different textual practice, one that orders materials so that the representations the text provides fuse into images having the appropriate meanings and senses for the spectator. Eisenstein writes: "Consequently, in the actual method of creating images, a work of art must reproduce that process whereby, *in life itself*, new images are built up in the human consciousness and feelings."[15] For instance, the shot as a cell for conflict becomes the locus for an image association whereby "*through aggregation*, every detail is preserved in the sensations and memory *as part of the whole*."[16] Now the shots build up a fused image with the "chain of intervening links" condensing.[17]

Because of this shift in Eisenstein's philosophy of how the spectator's mind works, the actual montage principles change even though their functions remain the same. It is just as essential as before that the material in the film be selected and constructed by its makers. The director "has to determine the selection of *the right people, the right faces, the right objects, the right actions, and the right sequences*, out of all the equally possible selections within the circumstances of a given situation."[18] These choices must yield a harmonious vertical montage that reemphasizes the central dominant of the film. However, a new consideration becomes apparent: a composition should present the author's connotations. Eisenstein counsels, "At once the question arises: with what methods and means must the filmically protrayed fact be handled so that it simultaneously shows not only *what* the fact is, and the character's attitude towards it, but also *how* the author relates to it, and how the author wishes the spectator to receive, sense, and react to the portrayed fact."[19] This new concern develops from the "subjective" nature of associations. Every mind can use individual bits of data to form images, but for the sensual image in the director's mind to be duplicated in the spectator's, the director must replicate the process of how that image is formed. Since the mind receives representations as images are formed, precise sequential organization of the representations that will be sent for spectatorial reception is important.

Eisenstein's later writings admit of more variation among spectators, perhaps because he has a more powerful theory of cognition and affect, one that emphasizes social and historical circumstances. His emphasis on the director's ensuring that the film's structure will construct the right impressions suggests that the spectator could easily use the representations to form alternative images, to experience the film in a manner at variance from Eisenstein's intent. Eisenstein wants to prevent errors in reading, but then he has a sociopolitical purpose in making movies. At any rate, Eisenstein seems to consider the spectator as somewhat active and able to "misread" as well as somewhat historically grounded: the spectator's own associations already formed in social reality might interfere with those Eisenstein wishes to convey. Had Eisenstein explored film spectators more, rather than try to control them, some exciting possibilities for reception studies might have been proposed.

Hugo Münsterberg

In Hugo Münsterberg's writings a more active and historical spectator is posited, although still not without many of the presuppositions existing in most classical film philosophies. In his introduction to *The Photoplay: A Psychological Study*, Münsterberg poses two questions: "What psychological factors are involved when we watch the happenings on the screen?" and "What characterizes the independence of an art?"[20] For the latter question Münsterberg falls into the tradition of analyzing media specificity. For the former question, which is the foundation for his subsequent conclusions about cinema as art, Münsterberg opens the way for a spectator-response theory of cinema. Coming as he does from work in applied psychology, this might be expected.

In Part 1 of Münsterberg's text, he looks at four "means by which the photoplay influences the mind of the spectator." These are (1) the sensation of depth and movement; (2) attention; (3) memory and imagination; and (4) emotions. In his theory of knowledge, Münsterberg makes a distinction between "an object of our knowledge and an object of our impression." Sense-data input will undergo a transformation in the mind so that what is out there (the objective) may be different from an individual's experience of it (the subjective). For example, in the area of the sensation of depth and movement, Münsterberg is careful to specify that certain depth cues may give a sensation of depth, but because spectators know that the object transmitting sense-data is two-dimensional, spectators are never deceived into believing that what is seen is real depth. For the perception of movement, he takes a position surprising for his time: he notes that the impression of movement is not a result of seeing successive stages of the image but "includes a higher mental act." The *"motion which [the spectator] sees appears to be a true motion, and yet it is created by his own mind."* Thus, Münsterberg concludes, *"depth and movement . . . in the moving picture world . . . are present and yet they are not in the things. We invest the impressions with them."*[21] I am not sure that I want to go so far as to suggest that Münsterberg takes the subjective to be the real, but as an idealist, he posits a theory in which, although the mind acts as a result of sense-data, it also organizes and transforms those sense-data.

At this point, Münsterberg may still present the spectator as ideal—without variation and history, primarily because he believes these perceptual activities to be basic for human mental processes. However, when he turns to the areas of attention, memory and imagination, and emotion, he begins to suggest a more individualized and assertive spectator. As he describes the cinema's possibilities, Münsterberg writes,

We must accompany [these filmic] sights with a wealth of ideas. They must have a meaning for us, they must be enriched by our own imagination, they must awaken the remnants of earlier experiences, they must stir up our feelings and emotions, they must play on our suggestibility, they must start ideas and thoughts, they must be linked in our mind with the continuous chain of the play, and they must draw our attention constantly to the important and essential element of the action. An abundance of such inner processes must meet the world of impressions.[22]

While the film as sense-object may supply data, Münsterberg implies that the spectator interacts on an individual basis with it. For instance, as he discusses attention factors, he argues that what creates meaning in the world is attention: "our selection of that which is significant and of consequence." *"The objective world,"* he writes, *"is molded by the interests of the mind."*[23] Furthermore, personal interests, attitudes, and previous experiences will control attention. As Münsterberg works this out, he concludes that while some attention is involuntary (due to certain aspects of the sense-data, such as sudden sounds or a flash of light), other parts of attention are voluntary—people choose to what they will attend. In his analysis of the cinematic medium, then, he works to specify the particular mechanisms by which cinema controls attention (for instance, the close-up). In Münsterberg's discussion of memory, imagination, and emotion, he follows the same logic. While the spectator can supply variable responses to these means of sensing, the art of the photoplay is to organize and control these responses in the most suitable way so as to achieve aesthetic effects from the experience.

What is important in Münsterberg's theory is the moderately active, self-governed, and possibly historical, spectator. He assumes that personal interests, attitudes, and experiences may differ. Unfortunately, he is not interested in pursuing an analysis of those differences. Rather, he wants to determine the means to regulate or unify those responses, standards derived from his views of society and art. Indeed, although he considers censorship as interfering with freedom of expression, he also worries about "the possibilities of psychical infliction and destruction" from the near-hypnotic effect of the flickering images. He advises "remolding and upbuilding of the national soul."[24]

Both Eisenstein's and Münsterberg's theories of the spectator's relation to the cinema offer potential starting points for a film-spectator philosophy. Of the pre-1960 writings about spectators, theirs are the ones edging away from a text-activated approach and toward either a spectator-activated thesis or a context-activated one. This does not mean that the other philosophies of those years are without value for elucidating a spectator-film relation. As I argued in chapter 2, writings leaning toward a text-activated assumption still offer insights if you assume that a material world of texts exists and that the critic describes interpretative conventions that are historical.

Furthermore, even though the ideas of Eisenstein and Münsterberg are "old," perhaps one reason they have so much resonance with today's questions is that they are derived from theories that were predecessors to contemporary models of how humans know. Vygotsky's dialectical materialist psycho- and sociolinguistics has attracted a resurgence of scholarly interest in the last fifteen years, influencing linguistic and cognitive theories;*[25] Münsterberg's psychology is a forerunner to cognitive psychology, a social science theory that informs one of the major paradigms for film reception (i.e., the work of David Bordwell).

Rereading classical film theory through asking new initial questions can be valuable in reordering the discursive field, bringing to our attention observations and propositions useful to current questions. In this case, scholars might remember that it is not just contemporary philosophies which offer theses about spectators.

CURRENT THEORIES OF THE SPECTATOR

Some research done within the past five years might be considered to belong within context-activated or reader-activated models of film and television spectators, but major competing theories still tend toward text-activated models. An example of a well-formulated statement of context-activation is an essay, "Illicit Pleasures: Feminist Spectators and *Personal Best*," by Elizabeth Ellsworth.[26] Ellsworth considers how lesbian feminist film critics interpreted the film *Personal Best*[*27] as against how the distributing company prepared its reception as well as how dominant (male) media reviewed it. Since her hypothesis is that "social groups use cultural forms in the process of defining themselves," she is particularly interested in this situation, for policy-making in feminist and other progressive movements, of creating resisting readers. Ellsworth carefully establishes her model of the reception process:

> Systems of domination (economic, sexual, racial, representational) shared within particular groups (like feminists) generate specific patterns of hope, anxiety and desire. Social actors may experience these patterns initially as private, idiosyncratic, even isolated responses to cultural forms like films. But through material practices like consciousness raising groups, women's studies courses and feminist film reviewing, feminist communities collectively de-

velop interpretative strategies for making sense of these structures of feeling, moving them into the sphere of public discourse by giving social, semantic form to anxieties and desires.[28]

Such a materialist theory assumes a complex interaction between sense-data information and a subject's transformation of those data, but the transformation is tied to specific psychological, social, and historical conditions. Interpretative strategies do not fall from the skies; they are derived in a material context. Discursive strategies for making meaning and significance have an (uneven) relation to the social formation, much as any artistic work does.

For her case example, Ellsworth describes lesbian feminists varying in four ways from dominant interpretative protocols. For one thing, "some resisted the narrative's heterosexist closure and imagined what would happen to the characters in a lesbian future." Additionally, most rejected large parts of the movie that could lead to a heterosexual orientation to the film's meaning. Furthermore, some readers redefined the hierarchy of actors and characters, elevating the lesbian Tory to central narrative focus and identifying with her. Such a move, Ellsworth points out, could lead to a view of the film's end as a validation of lesbianism. Finally, "in a move that points to possibilities of strategizing for pleasure that go beyond reading films 'against the grain,' some reviewers named and illicitly eroticized moments of the film's inadvertent lesbian verisimilitude." Such semic material was not what dominant media saw (e.g., "'bawdiness,' 'fierce combativeness' and 'loyalty' (read: 'clinging')," but "body language, facial expression, use of voice, expression of desire and strength in the face of male heterosexual dominance."[29]

This description of one self-constructed group of readers' strategies suggests that Jonathan Culler's observations (see chapter 2) regarding academic communities' procedures for unifying texts were not only ignored but rejected by these individuals. However, Ellsworth cautions against distorting the situation. She explicitly underlines that "lesbian feminist reviewers stopped short of rearranging the film's chronological order, severing or rearranging cause-effect relationships in the narrative and changing who does what in the narrative."[30] Thus, as a materialist and context-activated theory, the Ellsworth model does not give free rein to its viewing subjects. Yet, as an example of recent theorizing of reception, the model offers much for those interested in historical and materialist approaches to media interpretation.*[31]

In chapters 6 and 8, I will offer additional examples which support Ellsworth's theory that people do not reject all textual data but rather manipulate features of them in relation to what is pertinent for the individual in the specific reading context (here radical lesbian feminists viewing *Per-*

sonal Best). In this section, however, I want to compare three dominant approaches to the question of the spectator's relation to film and television: contemporary linguistic theory (derived from Saussure, informed by Lacan, often channeled through Christian Metz and the journal *Screen*); cognitive psychology theory (derived from current cognitive science, informed by Russian formalism, proposed most notably by David Bordwell); and British cultural studies (derived from Raymond Williams and Althusser, informed by Saussurean linguistics, presented most forcefully by a group of British scholars once gathered at the University of Birmingham Centre for Contemporary Cultural Studies).*[32] In my opinion, all three approaches share similar goals, including wanting to propose a materialist epistemology of the subject. In some ways they are compatible, but in others they are not. For instance, as I shall note below, propositions about how the mind interacts with sense-data differ significantly between the cognitive psychology approach and the other two: cognitive psychology does not assume a linguistic base to perception.

While eventually it would be nice to resolve some of the toss-up questions such as the "word versus thought" debate, and while such debates are significant, with real implications for models of viewing moving images, for the time being I would like to withhold judgment among the three. This is because I believe that in practice—if not theory—all three tend to present text-activated or reader-activated models of reception. I also believe that all three theoretically could offer context-activated models. The point here is to consider how the three paradigms might be useful in a historical materialist approach to the production of meaning and for interpreting moving images. I will briefly characterize each of the positions before contrasting them as well as indicating their practical bias toward the text or reader as determining.

Contemporary Linguistics

The contemporary linguistic theory of relations between the spectator and moving images postulates a complicated model.*[33] First of all, since the theory has historical connections to the structuralist approach that considers literary texts as sets of copresent structures (described in chapter 2), films exhibited on screens in darkened auditoriums*[34] tend to be considered similiarly: they are "read" by spectators who use codes to interpret the texts.

But viewing moving images is different from hearing words, the linguistic medium that Saussure considered when he proposed a theory of signifiers, signifieds, and signs as well as *langue* and *parole*. Since the late 1960s, writers have grappled with the difficulties of converting Saussurean linguistics from the original medium to images, with Christian Metz's attempts the most notable.[35] Metz's solution ultimately is tinged with his phenomenological heritage, but in *Film Language* he proposes that individuals learn five culturally acquired levels of codification which permit them to understand filmic narratives. These are perceptual (structuring space); denotational (recognizing and identifying objects); connotational (understanding connotations and symbolisms attached to objects); narrational (using sequencing of images to link shots temporally and spatially into narratives—the grande syntagmatique);*[36] and filmic (learning medium-specific signs: e.g., in Hollywood films of the 1930s, fades denote a temporal gap).[37] Metz's epistemological philosophy at this point is partially idealist. He assumes at least one innate mental structure: people attempt to narrativize events, "one of the great anthropological forms of *perception*."[38] Additionally, he implicitly attributes universality to the five levels of codification. Otherwise, in a generous reading and with one exception to be noted, Metz's model permits the materialist possibility that differences as well as historical change could produce at least varieties of readings of images. The exception has to do with perceptual codes. There, by some indications, this contemporary linguistic model may offer a thesis that individuals have a universal response to viewing images, particularly in renaissance-perspective images "positioning" the subject. That is, if perspectival and other depth codes are duplicated by the camera lenses, then a subject finds him- or herself centered in the perspectival pyramids. Such a centering offers the individual a (false) impression that he or she is producing meaning (when in fact the images are structuring the response).*[39] Some writers such as Jean-Louis Baudry do seem to make such a claim. However, perception might, indeed, be cultural in a linguistic model. Since a perceiver cannot possibly process every detail that comes into his or her sensory apparatus, selection is normal and based on learned patterns.[40] Hence, context—including development of other interpretive frames, such as the knowledge of the potential effect of a "centered" visual perspective—may be sufficient to contradict the experience. In fact, given the attention paid to the issue of the false consciousness produced by such representations, academic film critics are already resisting readers, constantly pointing out the culturally and ideologically constructed nature of the viewing experience.

Theoretically, then, the linguistic model does not imply the proposition, such as critics have charged, that "the strategies, forms, and techniques of classical narrative cinema lock members of an audience into an epistemic position that makes it impossible for them to criticize either their own habits of perception in film viewing or the modes of perceptual intelligibility that the films themselves display."[41] In a specific instance, the theory implies, culturally specific and competent readers will comprehend the text. But competency in reading does not imply unconsciousness in a communication event. Using culturally acquired codes to perceive and interpret a message insures neither agreement nor, most certainly, hypnotic submission. Academics at least—and likely others—refuse the position of illusion offered. This is not to say either, and on the other hand, that the subject is totally conscious in a communication event. Individuals do not have full access to *langue* or *parole*.

According to this interpretation of Metz, the variation among spectators that is sought for in a context-activated theory of reception becomes possible, although there still exists some need to work out other details. For example, given the variety within any culture, considering what is social (its *langue*) versus what is specific to an individual (*parole*), as well as *how* individual meanings could develop, would be necessary. Perhaps Vološinov's or Vygotsky's linguistics would be of assistance here, since each considers social formations as dialectical and potentially conflictual.*[42] But even current sociolinguistic theory offers ideas, although the ideas are often in a functionalist model. For instance, Pierre Maranda argues that "semantic charters condition our thoughts and emotions. They are culture-specific networks that we internalize as we undergo the process of socialization."[43] Depending on a person's background, some semantic categories are more likely than others to be associated.

What is selected also relates to a person's "emotion and cognitive state at the time."[44] In fact, contemporary linguistic theory in film studies includes another thesis, one related not so much to a semiotics of interpretation as to a trajectory of pleasure. With the addition of Lacan's rewriting of Freud, cinematic linguistic theory discovered a powerful supplement that could consider affective experiences as well, particularly given its emphasis on visual perception. Stressing more of the conflictual process in psychological development than functionalist psychologies do, Lacanian psychoanalysis provides contemporary linguistics with a compatible theory of the subject. Of course, Lacanian theory also recapitulates the idealist bias of phallocentrism.

Lacanian postulates present more of a problem in developing a historical and dialectical materialist theory of understanding film than do the language aspects of the hypotheses, but I believe that returning to historical context is one solution. While Freud's particular interpretation of how individuals are constituted psychically may require revision, what remains useful is Freud's observation that social and familial circumstances are powerful determinants in constructing subjects. As a cultural proposition, Freudian theory is viable even though specific subject conditions (such as the oedipal crisis, penis envy, or sadomasochism) ought to be understood not as universals but as psychic dynamics produced historically and culturally. Revised in such a way, phallocentrism becomes a feature of a social formation, not a biological or even cultural necessity. (I also wonder if, consequently, Lacan's observation that accession to the symbolic is based on the conception of binary opposition as constituting language structuration might also be a historical rather than universal feature of language development.) The difficulty of tying together psychic dynamics with language acquisition is an essential area of continuing research, but many people believe that Freud's model is fundamentally social and historical. What pertains psychoanalytically to some individuals is not universal, and research on psychical configurations, gendering, sexuality, and pleasure can continue in revised form without lapsing into idealism or text-determined propositions.

Such a revision in theories about pleasure (and affect in general) also applies to the standing hypothesis that viewing commercial broadcast television produces circumstances different from those produced by watching films. The conditions of experiencing television, it is argued, have various consequences: perceptional concentration may rely more on hearing than seeing, so people may reduce the gaze to a glance; textual information is particularly discontinuous (commercials interrupt programs or, vice versa, programs interrupt marketing), while textuality is extremely continuous (the "flow" thesis), providing a contradictory tension for the spectator; dominant viewing circumstances in well-lighted family rooms with constant recognition of the social audience, as well as direct address by televisual narrators to the viewers, increase distanciation instead of promoting identification.*[45]

Since a context-activated theory of reception posits just such local considerations as pertinent to reception (although factoring in all the variables to a model of viewing may become complicated), a context-activated approach is not theoretically at odds with the differences broadcast television might imply for reception. In fact, criticisms by feminist and television studies of earlier universalizing claims in contemporary linguistic theory have caused concern on the part of their advocates about their own tendency to universalize and idealize readers. A good instance of movements to reassert the historical foundations of the contemporary linguistic paradigm is a recent survey essay by Janet Bergstrom and Mary Ann Doane delineating the current recognition by feminists of the necessity for theorizing spectators in terms of gender, class, and race. In particular, they describe the failings of earlier theorizing when spectators or audiences have been assumed to have internally consistent features. Yet the various approaches bearing on these issues do not all derive from similar premises. Bergstrom and Doane coin the term "spectatrix" to emphasize "the density and complexity of the matrix (or matrices)" from which scholars derive their intellectual contributions when they work beyond assumptions that the spectator can be simply hypothesized from critical assertions about the text. Again, one solution, I believe, is to reemphasize the historical possibilities of the theses about learning languages in social, public contexts.[46]

Cognitive Psychology

As I mentioned in chapter 2, various theories of reading and interpreting oral and written language have been proposed. Some function from a linguistic premise, but some take the position that perception and cognition do not require, or at least do not rely fully on, words or signs of a natural language (e.g., English, Spanish, Chinese, Arabic) for comprehension. For example, Harry Singer and Robert B. Ruddell offer four possible models of reading in their *Theoretical Models and Processes of Reading*.[47] One that I discussed in chapter 2 is the psycholinguistic approach outlined by George L. Dillon. However, as Singer and Ruddell describe it, another model is an information processing one which proposes that readers go from print to abstract entities, but not by way of speech. Some theories go even further, arguing that natural language, is not required for thinking, that mental processing (thought) may be "deeper" than natural language, involving mental images as distinct entities.[48] In linguistics, the debate may be described as representativism versus constitutivism, where the representativist position posits that language represents thinking, while the constitutivist holds that "cognition is the product of propositionally based, non-visual representations," that language *is* the information in the mind. In cognitive science the positions are labeled pictorialist and descriptionist.*[49]

Consequently, when David Bordwell argues for a constructivist cognitive psychology model of film viewing, he is overtly juxtaposing a representativist (or pictorialist) explanation of what happens when spectators watch moving images against contemporary linguistic theory, which seems to be constitutivist (or descriptionist).*[50] He writes:

> It will come as no surprise that I do not treat the spectator's operations as necessarily modeled upon linguistic activities. I shall not speak of the spectator's "enunciating" the story as the film runs along, nor shall I assume that narrative sense is made according to the principles of metaphor and metonymy. It is by no means clearly established that human perception and cognition are fundamentally determined by the processes of natural language; indeed, much psycholinguistic evidence runs the other way, toward the view that language is an instrument of and guide for mental activity. For such reasons, I do not call the spectator's comprehension "reading" a film. It is, moreover, needlessly equivocal to speak of the spectator's activity as a "read-

ing" when the same word is applied to the abstract propositional arguments characteristic of critical analysis and interpretation. Viewing is synoptic, tied to the time of the text's presentation, and literal; it does not require translation into verbal terms. Interpreting (reading) is dissective, free of the text's temporality, and symbolic; it relies upon propositional language. This chapter and book try to explain viewing.[51]

As should be apparent from chapter 2, I disagree with Bordwell's belief that viewing or perceiving can be separated, except in a most theoretical way, from interpreting or reading. I believe that interpretational propositions inform perception and viewing. However, in deference to Bordwell's representativist proposition, I do want to underscore that the vocabulary of "reading" films should not imply a linguistic model. Regarding representativism versus constitutivism, the jury is still out for me. What matters here is that the model Bordwell proposes starts with a fundamental thesis about what spectators do when they interact with moving images: they do not process the visual images using codes and signs.

What, then, is Bordwell's model? Bordwell combines current research in cognitive sciences with a critical method that resembles the sequential text-activated approaches for literature described in chapter 2. His epistemology of film viewing begins with the assumption that adult people think through "organized clusters of meaning": *schemata*. While sense data are available to individuals, perception and thinking are, as Münsterberg would put it, voluntary as well as involuntary. People are "active, goal-oriented."[52] As children develop within a society, the routines and patterns of that social formation construct internalized sets of expectations and habits which form their schemata. Schemata continue to change through an individual's lifetime, and the cultural basis for those clusters of meaning will be crucial for a reading theory.

A standard example usually helps: the schema for the clusters of meaning associated with "going to a restaurant in the United States."[53] Choosing to eat away from the home establishes a number of options from which derive all sorts of standard subroutines. If you select eating at a "fast food" place, you learn that your menu is posted near a person who takes your order and your money at the same time. Your food comes later. If, however, you select dining at a "sit-down" restaurant, you expect that a host or hostess may seat you, a busperson may offer you water, someone likely will take a predinner drink order while you peruse a booklet listing the foods, your server-for-the-meal might suggest specialties of the day as you give your selections, and only after you have enjoyed the meal will a bill arrive for payment. Of course, within either of these routines (or other "going-out-to-eat" sequences), options exist. Yet the range of activities is delimited by social custom, and the average situation requires nearly no conscious attention to the formalities and procedures. Only if deviance occurs—your bill arrives with the predinner drink—will the schema of eating out be raised to a metaschematic level. The physiological and ecological reasons for an organism's functioning this way include reducing the number of sense variables competing for the body's attention. How could you have that stimulating conversation with your dinner partner if you had to figure out the routine every time?

This example, however, is only of one schema, and Bordwell suggests others in detail. "The mental image of a bird is a schema for visual recognition, and the concept of a well-formed sentence functions as a schema in speech perception. Schemata may be of various kinds—prototypes (the bird image, for instance), or templates (like filing systems), or procedure patterns (a skilled behavior, such as knowing how to ride a bicycle)."[54] The complex "going out to eat" schema includes all three types.

As indicated, the individual is goal-oriented, but sense data do not always fit into schemata. In fact, using the schemata is based on probabilities. In any actual instance, "the perceiver in effect bets on what he or she takes to be the most likely perceptual hypothesis. Like all inferences, perceptual experience tends to be a little risky, capable of being challenged by fresh environmental situations and new schemata. After some interval, a perceptual hypothesis is confirmed or disconfirmed; if necessary, the organism shifts hypotheses or schemata."[55]

How does this relate to watching films and television? Bordwell argues that in the analysis of viewing moving images, three things must be considered. First is the involuntary perception of image and motion (again, see Münsterberg). Thereafter, the film "cues" the spectator to "operate" or "follow" various "protocols" relating to the schemata associated with narration or other types of filmic organization. Thus, second, and assuming a knowledgeable (i.e., competent) spectator, the spectator's available schemata for viewing are pertinent. Some of these might be ideas of what a story is, notions of reality, and experiences or typings of related films or stylistic conventions. Then, third, and assuming a cooperative spectator, the material and structure of the film are applicable. The film "cues and constrains" the spectator. For instance, here Bordwell offers the notions of *fabula* and *sujet* (story and plot as discussed in chapter 2) as mental activities and textual features significant in the viewing experience. Bordwell provides a psychological explanation for what Mukařovský, Genette, and Sternberg describe ad hoc.*[56]

Bordwell explicitly constructs a competent viewer as his spectator: "a hypothetical entity executing the operations relevant to constructing a story out of the film's representations."[57] He excludes affect, not because it is not pertinent, but because he is delimiting his field of research. He also eliminates historical and cultural differences in viewers. As he admits,

Now there comes a methodological choice. On the one hand, the analyst could describe the various schemata that are available to a viewer at a given historical moment. . . . The alternative approach is more diachronic and text-centered. . . . I have chosen the diachronic approach because I am interested in revealing certain formal changes and alternatives within the history of narrative filmmaking.[58]

Thus, as Bordwell lays out the second half of *Narration in the Fiction Film*, he shifts focus to the last part of the triad of considerations for film viewing: the textual materials that cue, channel, and constrain spectators. Furthermore, he associates different dominant schemata activities with each of the four types of narration he describes. Classical narration calls forth detective game motifs: spectators try to guess the direction and conclusion of the narrative plot. (In terms of another system, proairetic and hermeneutic codes are privileged.) Art-cinema narration has a different "game of form": "The art cinema's spectator, then, grasps the film by applying conventions of objective and expressive realism and of authorial address." (This mode emphasizes cultural and symbolic codes.) Historical-materialist narration relies on schemata related to known cultural stories as well as a macrosocial theory of historical causality. Consequently, this mode emphasizes "unusually innovative spatial and temporal construction. . . . At the barest perceptual level, narration will jolt the spectator." The game here is stylistic, and hence perceptual, surprise and "strain." (Symbolic and cultural codes dominate.) Finally, in parametric narration, commonly "the spectator's task becomes one of recognizing stylistic repetition and staying alert for more or less distinct variations."[59] (Hermeneutic search discovering stylistic patterns tops the hierarchy of viewing activities.)

I have taken the space to describe Bordwell's model because its recent appearance makes it much less familiar to scholars of film and television than the contemporary linguistic model. Thus, its assumptions have yet to elicit a received opinion. Consequently, let me underline several propositions for which I prepared in my synopsis. For one thing, Bordwell overtly and knowingly brackets off areas that might serve as starting points for a context-activated approach to the history of viewing. These include the notion that schemata develop from cultural, social, and historical experiences. These possible starting points also involve schemata connected to affectivity. Bordwell writes that perhaps "psychoanalytic models may be well suited for explaining emotion aspects of film viewing."[60] Yet psychobiological research suggests a much less distinct real separation between cognition and emotion than Bordwell makes for the purposes of his book. Bordwell is discussing these issues theoretically—i.e., as conceptual categories. I am suggesting that the research from which he draws does not prevent a linkage or even interpenetration of cognition with emotion.[*61]

However, because he so chooses, Bordwell does not try to supply a theory of pleasure (or other emotions or sensations).

Bordwell considers the text as "cueing and constraining" responses of competent and cooperative viewers. The consequences of that view are descriptive discussions of "normative" viewing, and his spectators become as ideal as those "positioned" in contemporary linguistic theory. Sometimes, however, what is normative becomes nearly prescriptive, at least in his phrasings of ideas, if not by the terms of his theory. For example, he writes that "the artwork is necessarily incomplete, needing to be unified and fleshed out by the active participation of the perceiver."[62]

Finally, the motif of a game overtly appears in two of the four modes of film narration: classical and art cinema. I extended it to the other two in order to maintain consistency, but perhaps the model according to which spectators bet on probabilities in activating relevant schemata provides a primary metaphor that unconsciously appears in descriptions of the modes of narration. I wonder as well if Russian formalism's thesis of literature's autonomy and Bordwell's claim of the "nonpractical."[63] constituency of aesthetic activity cooperate with the game metaphor to influence an unnecessary disassociation of the process of comprehending literary or filmic texts from the very obvious fact that historical spectators do associate textual events with experiences in their everyday lives. Spectators may treat modes of narration as games, as stretching their perceptual-cognitive muscles, but is that all they do in the act of comprehension? I think not.

When proposing a field of inquiry, a scholar has every right to delimit research agendas, and Bordwell is meticulous in stating assumptions and paths-not-taken. However, as he suggests and I reinforce, cognitive psychology can be taken in several directions. One way it can go is, I believe, toward a context-activated history of spectators. As suggested above, the research itself supports this. For instance, Ulric Niesser notes that adults in Western, time-oriented cultures construct events of experience into a temporal framework of sequence; perhaps this explains why Western film viewers reorder plots into stories. Katherine Nelson finds that "although at this point [1981], we have little systematic data, there is considerable evidence that young children's scripts [schemata of temporally and causally related actions such as 'going to the restaurant'] are initially acquired within contexts that are highly structured for them by adults." Also some cognitive theorists who include language in their models propose that schemata are formed into "social realities" through discussion with other individuals. In this regard a major scholar in the field, Michael Cole, believes that cognitive psychology theory is compatible with Vygotsky's psycho- and sociocultural linguistic hypotheses. Research needs to proceed on that possibility, as well as on the connections between schemata and learned *affective* (not just cognitive) responses. Finally, Neisser mentions that all thought is not goal-oriented; dreams and fantasy are "a mode of thinking and remembering quite different from the step-by-step logic of reason."[64]

As Bordwell summarizes, "It is evident, though, that however much the ability to form schemata relies upon innate mental capacities, viewers acquire particular prototypes, templates, and procedures *socially*."*[65] It is that proviso which permits the possibilities of patterned historical variation among spectators.

British Cultural Studies

That term *social* also permits the introduction of ideology. For it is the British cultural studies researchers who emphasize that interpretations and uses of texts connect to ideologies and cultural, social, and political power. Theories of communication and cultural discourses are numerous. Some scholars assume communication is neutral—the transmittal of messages that may or may not hold ideological content (often called the "transportation" model). Such a position is expressed in one strand of communication theory deriving from the work of Paul Lazersfeld, Kurt Lewin, Harold Lasswell, Carl Hovland, and Wilbur Schramm. This model also occurs when aesthetics separates form and content—a fallacy, according to much twentieth-century literary theory. Other scholars of communication and culture, such as James Carey, take the position that communication is a social or cultural ritual, "a sharing, participation, association, fellowship." Horace Newcomb and Paul Hirsch extend and revise that notion by proposing that at least for commercial broadcast television a "cultural forum" provides individuals not merely information but also a process for "understanding who and what we are."[66]

Then some theorists, such as Vygotsky and Vološinov, assume that communication is a tool. Like other means of production, communication is produced by and for its users: communication transforms reality for the benefit of human beings. However, also as with other means of production, not everyone has equal access to that technology. Signs and their signifieds are not neutral but sites of power. Representations are developed in social circumstances and bear the ideological marks of their origins. The class or group that controls meanings has tremendous leverage in organizing existence for people. Thus, as Vološinov writes, the sign "becomes an arena of the class struggle."[67] Controlling representations and meanings is as much a part of the fight for equity as any political battle.

This notion of communication as a tool does not imply a functionalist theory of society, one that would assume a drift toward equilibrium within a social formation. Instead it posits a marxist thesis that social orders are structured in contradiction and overdetermination. Nor, however, does this notion assume conspiratorial repression by the dominant class; indeed, communication systems may function so well for the dominant class that hegemony often exists. Yet as advocates of this understanding of language caution, the very "common sense" or "naturalness" of discourses or meanings is a strong indicator of power at work. It is this theory of communication and cultural discourses that I shall ascribe to those individuals working in British cultural studies.

British cultural studies is a particular version of marxism developed through debates, mainly in Britain, beginning in the mid-1950s. Several histories exist, detailing a sequence of theoretical problematics from orthodox marxism through culturalist marxism (including the work of Raymond Williams and E. P. Thompson) and structuralist marxism (particularly Louis Althusser) to what Richard Johnson calls "ideological-cultural" marxism—a label that never stuck.[68] In actuality, this last problematic is a combination of aspects of cultural and structural marxism and was proposed by scholars at the Centre for Contemporary Cultural Studies at the University of Birmingham. Its tenets have gained considerable following abroad, and while many members of the original group now work elsewhere, the standard phrase "British cultural studies" has held. I would underline that other marxist theories of cultures and their study also exist, as does nonmarxist cultural studies.

Generally, British cultural studies accepts the advancements of structuralist marxism as most notably proposed in Louis Althusser's essay "Ideology and Ideological State Apparatuses" (and in other similar ways by other marxists).[69] The base and superstructure are theorized as distinct concepts, with elements of the superstructure having potential effect but also "relative autonomy" from other determinants. In capitalism (and perhaps other modes of production), the economic aspects of a social formation "in the last instance" are causal, but economic structures are not sufficient to explain many specific features of a social formation. For one thing, development is uneven. The economic base (the mode of production) is contradictory—history moves through class struggle—and superstructural features bear the traces of that fact. Althusser splits the superstructural features into two groups. Repressive state apparatuses (RSAs) include the government, armies, police, courts, prisons. RSAs function primarily on behalf of the dominant class and often through violence or repression; they are public and generally overdetermined in an effort to repress change disadvantageous to the dominant class. Ideological state apparatuses (ISAs) are all sorts of other institutions and groups such as religions, educational systems, families, political parties, and communication and cultural media. ISAs are plural and function primarily by ideology. Consequently, contradictions and overdeterminations proliferate among the competing discourses, with all classes struggling through the ISAs.*[70] Ideology is defined relationally and materially: it "represents the imaginary relationship of individuals to their real conditions of existence."[71] Ideology exists in the RSAs and ISAs; it exists in practices. The structured relations invite or "interpellate" an individual to take up a position as a "subject" in that imaginary relationship: positions of occupation, social status, gender—whatever constructed but imaginary sense of the self that is useful for the reproduction of the mode of production and the maintenance of the dominant class.

Interpellation is a tricky notion, often defined as "hailing" the individual, calling out for the individual to recognize him- or herself as being the subject who belongs in a role. For example, reverently singing "The Star-Spangled Banner" is taking up an ideological position of nationality, that of a U.S. citizen. The song has interpellated, hailed its subject to position him- or herself into that constructed and, hence, imaginary identity.

This much of structuralist marxism is relatively uncontested by British cultural studies. Where disagreement develops concerns whether the human individual has volition or a consciousness that is other than "false." This is significant for marxists' calls for political action and change; the idea of struggle implies a need for conscious actions on the part of people, and the issues of force and consent are significant. Part of the dispute with structuralist marxism over this point derives from Althusser's use of Lacanian psychoanalysis to describe interpellation. British cultural studies scholars argue that Lacan presents a transhistorical and universal theory of the subject's development; furthermore, that as Althusser argues his model, the psychoanalytical unconscious (rather than economics) becomes the primary determinant developing individuals. Such a model is unacceptable to these writers because in their view the model becomes ahistorical and change impossible to explain.[72]

As I indicated in discussing Freud and Lacan for the contemporary linguistic model, I believe that at least some Freudian-based psychologies can offer social and historical models of psychic development. I also do not think Althusser's model conflicts with such a historical reading of Freudian theories. For one thing, in Althusser, ISAs such as family relations (a major determinant in an individual's psychological development in the past century or longer) are *as ISAs* structured in contradiction; their ideologies have some (uneven) relationship to the in-the-last-instance determinant of the mode of production. Family structures are social, historical, and contradictory ideological sites, and some writers—Charlotte Perkins Gilman Stetson, for example—have made strong arguments connecting family structures such as patriarchy to economic situations such as capitalism.[73] Thus, I do not agree that Althusser's use of Freudian psychology produces a transhistorical, universal, or totally determined subject. I would also emphasize that Freudian psychology never perceived the unconscious as constituting all of the subject; in fact, in the model the ego is often in conflict with the id (or the superego) because of social and public contradictions. A somewhat more sympathetic reading of Freud is not at odds with concerns in marxism that, as historical events indicate, the individual must be represented as also having conscious intentions, understandings, and volition. Freudian psychologies just remind scholars that the consciousness is not all of what people as human organisms are and that heterogeneity and conflict are part of people's psychological dynamics. They are a historical theory of the individual as individual and social being.

In this matter, the issue of Lacan is less clear, but while Althusser's original proposition employs Lacanian language, I am not at all sure that his model's viability depends upon that language. Do the notions of "imaginary" and "interpellation" require the Lacanian twist? In summary, the British cultural studies position may be tossing out a powerful theory of the subject, as well as explanations of some types of affect and pleasure. In fact, some members of the group are now considering the possibilities of Freudian psychologies, particularly in relation to narration and subjectivity.[74] I shall return to this issue below.

At any rate, while temporarily eliminating psychoanalytical theory, British cultural studies theorists paid particular attention to Althusser's use of Gramsci's concept of hegemony to account for the reproduction of ideologies without repeating the universally automatic response they perceive the interpellation thesis to assert. Thus, British cultural studies attempts to synthesize Althusser and Gramsci. People are not *tabulae rasae* but exist in contradictory experiences so that while ideological hegemony often exists, opposition—or at least deviation from the dominant—does too. This can happen, they argue, because the base is contradictory and class continues to be the most significant determinant of human action.

Given these broader suppositions, what does British cultural studies offer as a theory of how readers interpret texts or view moving images? David Morley succinctly sets this out in one of the typical case studies of audiences conducted by this group of researchers. In *The "Nationwide" Audience*, he describes, on the one side, media institutions (such as British television) as ISAs and thus not totally directed by the state. Thus, their activities are also not completely those of a dominant class. On the other side, audiences will not always read a message "'straight'": "messages encoded one way can always be read a different way."[75] The reasons for this are twofold. For one thing, as delineated by contemporary linguistic theory, particularly that of Vološinov and Mikhail Bakhtin, messages are complex, a "structured polysemy." Multiple voices, often contradictory, speak in the message, so multiple meanings exist. Polysemy, he cautions, is not equal to pluralism; discourses and codes are not equal, and dominants exist. For another thing, readers are varied.

> The audience must be conceived of as composed of clusters of socially situated individual readers, whose individual readings will be framed by shared cultural formations and practices pre-existent to the individual: shared "orientations" which will in turn be determined by factors derived from the objective position of the individual reader in the class structure.[76]

This is not mechanistic, Morley claims, because people have consciousness. You will note that Morley brings the readings, in the last instance, down to class as determining. In fact, while he believes that "there will always be individual private readings," what is important is

> to investigate the extent to which these individual readings are patterned into cultural structures and clusters. What is needed here is an approach which links differential interpretations back to the socio-economic structure of society, showing how members of different groups and classes, sharing different "cultural codes," will interpret a given message differently, not just at the personal, idiosyncratic level, but in a way "systematically related" to their socio-economic position.[77]

This theoretical perspective was put into a research procedure. An early task of the British cultural studies writers was to use contemporary linguistic theory and structuralist marxism to read texts ideologically. Several of the Centre people cosponsored Charlotte Brunsdon and Morley's analysis of the British television series "Nationwide" in the monograph *Everyday Television*. Using numerous tactics derived from Roland Barthes's work on popular culture and ideology, the writers considered the *Everyday Television* study as a "base line . . . against which differential readings may be posed"[78] once they did fieldwork on actual audiences. The fieldwork was reported in Morley's 1980 *"Nationwide" Audience* study. Referring to F. Parkin's observations in *Class, Inequality and Political Order* that "three broad 'ideal types' of ideological frameworks (dominant, negotiated and oppositional)" exist, Morley criticizes the simplicity of the "number of 'meaning-systems'" and the lack of multiple origins for those three frameworks.[79] Despite that, he adopts those three frameworks to describe the structured patterns of relations he finds in the responses of his audiences to "Nationwide" and connects them to the various socioeconomic classes surveyed. Stuart Hall outlines the three frameworks: (1) the *"dominant-hegemonic position"*—reading as intended; (2) the *"negotiated code or position"*—"decoding" via "exceptions to the rule" of the hegemonic position; and (3) *"oppositional code"*—putting the information into "some alternative framework of reference."*[80] Other case studies follow suit. For instance, in *Subculture* Dick Hebdige studied rock and punk groups as an oppositional production of meaning from an alienated socioeconomic class: the unemployed youth of Britain.

Fallacies in some of the initial formulations of the British cultural studies research procedure have recently produced a few modifications in their approach. One problem exists in categorizing readings into only three frameworks labeled hegemonic, negotiated, and oppositional. As Morley writes, the idea of three types of readings can become as essentialist as any text-activated notion of contemporary linguistic theory.[81] Furthermore, I would note that the terms do little to help describe what readers actually do in any instance of reading as intended, negotiated, or opposed. All the potential descriptive value of text-activated theories is lost. As work has continued, the idea of these three categories of reading strategies has given way to a continuum from hegemonic to oppositional interpretation, but the frameworks have not been altered.*[82]

But more fundamental are two deeper assumptions of the Centre's research strategies. One is that despite appeals to "polysemy," texts are usually treated as unified, reproducing without contradiction hegemonic ideology. This is not, as I take it, a dialectical notion of textuality or the effectivity of the ideological plurality of ISAs. Produced through the class struggle, texts (and their readers) should display the features of competing and contradictory discourses, their polysemic nature. It is the case, of course, that media channels are owned and controlled for the most part by the dominant class, but that fact does not reduce textual materials into hegemonic representations. Agents of capitalism and late monopoly capitalism seek to maximize profits; a firm might choose to market products that, upon analysis, do not necessarily work toward the long-run benefit of the mode of production. Again, the tendency of textual production may appear to be toward hegemony, but cultural products are not always so monological and their contradictions should also be available for analysis. British cultural studies has produced moderately sophisticated analyses of the texts used for its audience studies, but those "base line" texts are assumed to be entities which ought always and totally to be opposed. Thus, theoretical propositions end up essentializing capitalist-produced texts as unified.

The other deep assumption of British cultural studies that is troubling is that readers are reducible to socioeconomic categories. Such a proposition produces ideal readers. Again, *in practice*, the strategy has been, following standard positivist social scientific habits, to use preset data for categorizing audience informants. People are located as belonging to a particular class if they have particular occupations or make a certain amount of money. The obvious question of class consciousness (and possible disparities between assumed categories and consciousness) is not raised. Also not raised is the notion that a socioeconomic class member is not all that a reader might be, according to a structuralist marxist theory of the subject in a capitalist social formation. Johnson notes this: "One of our own recurrent arguments [with Hoggart, Williams and the idea of 'a whole way of life,'] on the other hand, will be to stress the heterogeneity or complexity of 'working-class culture,' fragmented not only by geographical unevenness and parochialisms, but also by the social and sexual divisions of labour and by a whole series of divisions into spheres or sites of existence."[83] Gender, race, ethnicity, and so forth are also identities in which power differentials affect individuals. Furthermore, these identities are produced when individuals are interpellated to position themselves according to historical discursive systems. If texts are contradictory and in an uneven relation to the mode of production, identities that may be represented may be other than that of class. In fact, given the values of disguising class as pertinent, all sorts of other constructed positions may *appear* to be more significant to readers and viewers of texts: gender and race, for instance. Thus, the contextual situation of the viewer's pertinent self-identities—*as constructed historically*—may have greater salience in any specific reading instance. Analysts such as marxists may wish to discuss how those constructed identities are "false consciousness," but they cannot dismiss them as important causes for how people produce interpretations.

The two assumptions—(1) that media texts reproduce hegemonic ideology and (2) that readers are ideal and uncomplicated representatives of socioeconomic categories—have produced an accidental reader-activated model of reception for the Centre researchers. They imply that given the text and given the several categories of ideal and coherent readers (albeit upper- or lower-middle class or working class or unemployed), a certain type of interpretation or use will be made of the interaction with the text. Thus, the readers' class determines the experience. Where Holland and Bleich find psychological identities and Culler finds historical critical procedures, the British cultural studies scholars find socioeconomics.

As I have suggested, neither assumption is necessary in the marxist model of culture and communication that the British cultural studies theorists use. In fact, the strains of precategorizing the audience into classes are evinced by the fact that other categories of readers have recently received some attention. Morley's *Family Television* (1986) looks at fathers', mothers', and children's patterns of using television and videocassette recorders,[84] and Ien Ang's study of viewers experiencing *Dallas* raises many observations pertinent to consideration of readers from perspectives such as gender. Tamar Liebes and Elihu Katz's analysis of how five ethnic and cultural groups interpreted *Dallas* is another instance.[85] Indeed, the subject positions analyzed *may be* the most pertinent for the text(s) in question (the results are certainly fascinating), but a certain predestination in the research guides interpretations of data when categories of individuals are already constituted by the researchers.*[86]

For a context-activated theory of reception, historical determinations are necessary. Not only would the specific textual address of certain subject positions seem an obvious area for research (as opposed to preconstituting the text's address and the type of subject), but intertextual discourses regarding possible subjectivities for that historical time seem relevant. I note this particularly with an example. In the last twenty years, the United States has witnessed an explicit constitution of variation among sexual preferences as a possible self-identity, marking out an open (if not new) regime of perception and meaning of the self. Homosexuality or bisexuality, of course, has long been a possible way of understanding one's self, but I believe that in the United States the notion that heterosexuality is only one of the possible directions of sexual trajectories has just recently penetrated heterosexuals' self-imaging. It was possible to ignore this when non-heterosexuality was defined in hegemonic discourses as deviance. And many people still hold to that definition. What is different is that the sign "homosexuality" has been and is being fought over in cultural discourses: see any number of less devastating images—still unsatisfactory, I will grant—of gays in film and television in the past ten years. Unfortunately, however, and on the other hand, the gains of Stonewall may be fleeting now that advertising statistics have indicated that gays are an excellent group to target for marketing. Capitalism may now be retaking the sign "homosexuality" and reifying it into just another "life-style." A new, if more subtle, condition of repression may be appearing.

More theoretically, then, notions of the self and available subject positions are transformed in historical discursive formations and among specific contextual situations. For instance, watching *Dallas* in one's own home is different from viewing it as part of a classroom assignment. In the first case, subject positions likely to be taken up could relate to socioeconomic class, occupation, nationality, or gender. In the latter case, the subject position would involve one's role in educational institutions. Another example occurs in the case study of *Foolish Wives* (see chapter 6). The inability of readers in the early 1920s to accept female attraction to the central male figure—a male who had attributes socially, culturally, and historically linked to *both* masculinity *and femininity*—was part of what made a hegemonic (if you will) reading of the text hard to achieve. Almost all the males and at least one female were moderately outraged by the film.

The idea of myself as middle-class, female, American, and so forth is a historically determined representation of an imaginary relation of myself to my real (and contradictory) existence, the terms of those subjectivities constituted through contemporary discourses about the "self." These "selves" all have some near or distant relation to my real existence in terms of my material needs (and the current dominant mode of production). British cultural studies needs to foreground an observation that Hall makes in introducing Morley's *Family Television*:

> We are not "viewers" with a single identity, a monolithic set of preferences and repetitive habits of viewing. . . . We are all, in our heads, several different audiences at once, and can be constituted as such by different programmes. We have the capacity to deploy different levels and modes of attention, to mobilise different competencies in our viewing.[87]

Not the least of these levels, modes, and competencies is that logically some readers may have to hold two reading frameworks in their heads at the same time. As Richard Maltby points out, to argue about "potentially subversive readings of Hollywood texts" requires simultaneously comprehending a hegemonic position: "Necessarily, the subversive reading must claim knowledge of a preferred reading."[88] Deconstructionism would counter that the opposite is true as well: to know what is preferred requires knowing what is not.

As British cultural studies proceeds, it may become more difficult to bother with the idea of a continuum of hegemonic to oppositional readings. Furthermore, as mentioned above, that continuum seems to restrict the possibilities of thinking about what readers are doing. Broadening the types of approaches that explain what readers and spectators are doing does not mean abandoning questions about political effectivity. It does make the problem of categorizing texts or readers more difficult, perhaps impossible, since some moments of the historical interaction may be progressive and others may be regressive. Such a complexity will be discussed in the historical study of the 1930s debates over *The Birth of a Nation* (see chapter 7).

Another immediate consideration for British cultural studies may be to consider theories of affect. The tendency in this area has been to focus on the affect of pleasure (or its lack), although other affects might be considered. When dealing with this aspect of a textual experience, the researchers turn to several models, all of which are oriented toward social determinants. For example, Ang uses Pierre Bourdieu's work on the sociology of tastes. If people can identify with, or recognize, a structure of feeling, then pleasure results.*[89] Such a proposition, however, does not encourage deviation from hegemonic tastes; thus it would seem that people only experience pleasure when they agree with the dominant ideology. In a call for class struggle, arguing against achieving pleasure will be difficult. Furthermore, the model, as Ang reports it, suggests isomorphic homologies between texts and preexistent, internalized structures. All sorts of pleasures and affects experienced from lack of correspondence (such as surprise or opposition) are ruled out. Finally, other affects are not addressed in her model.

Another attempt to discuss affect is in *Television Culture*, where Fiske, drawing on theories that influenced British cultural studies, offers three possible explanations of pleasure: a psychoanalytical pleasure related to desire; a physical pleasure experienced in bodily sensations (which Fiske associates with Barthes's notion of *jouissance*); and a social pleasure derived from play. The psychoanalytical pleasure is "the product of accommodation to the dominant ideology"; the latter two "can be associated with resistance and subversion."[90] It is not hard to guess which explanations Fiske prefers, but to make his argument, he neglects information that might lead him to different conclusions. Regarding psychoanalysis, Fiske uses Laura Mulvey's exploratory essay "Visual Pleasure and Narrative Cinema" to outline his thesis: a psychoanalytical theory of pleasure assumes a male spectator repeating a process that reproduces him for patriarchal cinema. Published in 1975, Mulvey's essay has been steadily revised and challenged by many individuals who promote a psychoanalytical framework for understanding aspects of desire and pleasure. To critique the psychoanalytical explanation in 1987,*[91] Fiske ought to have considered the theoretical developments of the intervening years. Additionally, the psychoanalytical theory explains not only accommodation to patriarchy but also pleasure in its negotiation and opposition in moments of fantasy. In fact, it may be better at explaining deviance than conformity. What Fiske seeks (a radical politics) may also be available in the theory he rejects.

In fact, in discussing Barthes's *jouissance*, Fiske ignores that notion's grounding in just such psychoanalytical variations from normative psychology. Within *The Pleasure of the Text*, Barthes writes approvingly of Bataille and Sade, of perversions: "Is not the most erotic portion of a body where the garment gapes? In perversion (which is the realm of textual pleasure) there are no 'erogenous zones' . . . it is intermittence, as psychoanalysis has so rightly stated, which is erotic." And further on: "Text of bliss [*jouissance*]: the text that imposes a state of loss, the text that discomforts . . . unsettles the reader's historical, cultural, psychological assumptions, the consistency of his tastes, values, memories, brings to a crisis his relation with language."[92] Barthes has a theory of the pleasure and bliss of the text that is not one of a reader following the narrative of a traditional story, but his theory still has psychoanalytical roots in Julia Kristeva's work on semanalysis; *jouissance* is not just a "physical" theory of pleasure, as Fiske would have it.

For the third of Fiske's explanations of affect, the social one of play (related to game theory), he describes pleasure derived from both empowerment and resistance. Indeed, such an approach might prove useful in the elucidation of some affective experiences, for it would be unwise to reduce all pleasure to a single determinant, such as a person's psychology. However, again, research in British cultural studies has tended to assume acquiescence as regressive and opposition as progressive. If the text is progressive, then opposition might be undesirable. The problem here is knowing when contradictory texts and contradictory subjects ultimately produce in a process the kind of experience that British cultural studies or Fiske seeks.

This last problem will also plague any context-activated theory of reception that also seeks to evaluate the event studied. In the next chapter, some of the possibilities for a context-activated approach will be discussed, but many of the questions that I have raised about the current three approaches to the interpretation of moving images will remain unresolved. Contemporary linguistic theory, cognitive psychology, and British cultural studies offer many ideas, but a simple meshing together of the three is theoretically unacceptable. Contemporary linguistics and British cultural studies assume a language-based reading process, but the cognitive psychology approach uses schemata that may not be represented through language. Contemporary linguistics and British cultural studies differ on how to explain the affect of pleasure: while contemporary linguistics turns to psychoanalytical theories, British cultural studies has preferred using sociological ones. Cognitive psychology indicates a willingness to allow psychoanalysis to explain affect and emotion, but its metaphor of the game also appears in one of the British cultural studies models of pleasure. Contemporary linguistic theory has recently concentrated its efforts on the issue of pleasure; British cultural studies and cognitive psychology thrive best in areas of cognitive reception.

If these are some of the dissonances among the three models, a similarity also exists. The practical bias of each has been toward a text-activated or reader-activated model. However, I have tried to suggest how each of the three might be modified into a context-activated, historical model. In trying to do this, I hope that I have not distorted the integrity of any of the approaches, each of which holds promise for furthering reception studies research.

CHAPTER FOUR

Toward a Historical Materialist
Approach to Reception Studies

If the reader also remembers that [James] Stewart
[in *Rear Window*] is first the spectator, he can
conclude that the hero "invents his own cinema."
But is that not the very definition of a "voyeur,"
the very core of morose gratification?
(*Jean Douchet, 1960*)

JEAN DOUCHET's comments[1] in the *Cahiers du cinéma* at the start of the 1960s seem strangely current, for Douchet cautions against privileging the spectator's impression that he or she controls interpretations of films (or events). This is the argument made consistently through one strand of contemporary film and television philosophy: a historical materialist epistemology assumes an interaction among context, text, and individual in which a perceiver's socially and historically developed mental concepts and language may be only partially available to self-reflection and are most certainly heterogeneous.

Because of this, a historical materialist reception studies that is self-reflective has to acknowledge a number of limitations. First of all, the researcher who is doing historical materialist reception studies is as susceptible to the subjective contexts of interpretation as are those individuals being studied. This is a common tenet in contemporary scientific research, and I hope that the process of a dialogue or dialectics between theory and sense-data can somewhat control the classical hermeneutic circle. At any rate, I am not yet ready to give up the production of knowledge in the face of a nihilism that may serve the interests of the dominant class. However, the researcher might also be reminded to be somewhat humble before the material of study.

In addition, reception studies research cannot claim to say as much about an actual reading or viewing experience by empirical readers or spectators as it might like. Several factors intervene between the event and any possible sense data available for its study. As any cognitive psychologist would point out, verbalized manifestations by a subject are not equal to the original experience or its memory. Reporting, whether through a crafted ethnographical interview or a published review, is always subject to the problem of retrieval, as well as to language, schemata, or representations of the subject that mediate perception, comprehension, and interpretation.[2] In fact, memory might be considered a constructed representation of the past, an image as liable to manipulation as the photograph that seems to authenticate the android Rachel's existence in *Blade Runner*.

Furthermore, the souvenirs of evidence for interpretations and experiences by readers are tainted with the power struggles, contradictions, and overdeterminations existing in the superstructure. Evidence exists or does not exist partially by the whims of chance but much, much more because of the strategies of dominant ideologies. Recall Walter Benjamin's remarks:

> Whoever has emerged victorious participates to this day in the triumphal procession in which the present rulers step over those who are lying prostrate. According to traditional practice, the spoils are carried along in the procession. They are called cultural treasures, and a historical materialist views them with cautious detachment. For without exception the cultural treasures he surveys have an origin which he cannot contemplate without horror.[3]

Likewise, the policies of museums, archives, and libraries, of publishing houses and media channels, participate in retaining, maintaining, preserving, and foregrounding material culture in less than neutral ways. Historians have been aware of this for decades, but marxist historians recognize the political implications of those institutional choices for attempts to study questions from a radical perspective.

One more problem exists besides those of the researcher's subjectivity, the difficulties of interpreting evidence, and the bias of what evidence remains available for study. While surveying current audiences is an important activity, the meaning of the results requires historicization. Dialectical materialism insists that what is important is not the state in which the object appears, but the rate, direction, and probable outcome of the changes that have taken, and are taking, place as a result of the conflict of forces. To know what it means for a working-class audience to believe itself addressed in particular ways by "Nationwide" television requires a comparative and historical study. If context is an important determinant for the interaction, then what is salient in that context cannot be understood from idealized speculation. History is necessary.

Consequently, to work toward a historical materialist approach to reception studies requires, minimally, tracing as far as possible dominant and marginalized historical interpretive strategies as mediated by language and context. These should be considered as indicators of the range of strategies available in particular social formations. The historical transformation of that range also requires analysis. Furthermore, a historical materialist approach means tracking as far as possible the historically constructed "imaginary selves," the subject positions taken up by individual readers and spectators. Finally, it means, without a doubt, acknowledging that the researcher is imbricated within the analytical results. As I suggested in chapter 1, the reception studies I seek would be historical, would recognize the dialectics of evidence and theory, and would take up a critical distance on the *relations* between spectators and texts. It would not interpret texts but would attempt a historical *explanation* of the event of interpreting a text.

This call for research remains abstract. To make it concrete, in this chapter I want to compare how a historical materialist reception studies would assess a case instance in contrast to the three contemporary approaches described in chapter 3. Following that, I will briefly make some general observations about what reception studies would do with a number of standing questions in the field of film and television studies. But what a historical materialist approach to reception might look like is also suggested in the six case studies that follow this chapter. It is there that I hope to indicate best its use-values to the philosophy, history, and criticism of moving images.

LOOKING THROUGH *REAR WINDOW*

The case instance I will use has been given to me by David Bordwell in his *Narration in the Fiction Film*.[4] To exemplify his cognitive psychology theory of film viewing, Bordwell analyzes *Rear Window*. However, his subtext is not too subtle; he wishes to contrast his commentary on the cognitive activities of viewing with the traditional psychoanalytical readings of the film offered by people such as Jean Douchet, as well as the film's initial reviewers in 1954, and such commentators as Alfred Hitchcock, Robin Wood, Alfred Appel, Jr., Laura Mulvey, Robert Stam and Roberta Pearson, and others.[*5] In brief, Bordwell rereads the film as a dissertation on cognition rather than "the positioning of the spectator within [the cinematic] apparatus" and a "critique of voyeurism."[6]

As Jonathan Culler points out, a deconstructionist might contend that a dispute over two interpretations is a reenactment of the conflict in the text which is being investigated.[7] In this case, the situation is quite twisted, since even the first reviewers thought the film had something of a reflexive turn. *Rear Window* was early on interpreted to be addressing questions about the epistemology of cinema. Consequently, the dispute I am about to examine might be partially attributed to features of textuality, as well as to possible reading strategies of the mid-1950s that have developed as encrustations affecting the transformation of subsequent readings. Ironically, then, debates over interpretations of *Rear Window* have been over interpreting, something of a deconstructionist's paradise.

But I am anticipating what will be part of a historical materialist analysis of the film. Before I turn to that task, I want to review briefly some early analyses of the film. Then I will use a very recent contemporary linguistic interpretation of *Rear Window* to contrast with Bordwell's. Since no British cultural studies approach has been applied to the movie, I will have to speculate about how those scholars would handle the film. Finally, I will suggest what a historical materialist reception studies analysis would take, leave, and add to those three.

In the mid-1950s, psychoanalytical theory was a popularized discourse in the United States, available to explain human psychology, and had been so since the 1940s. So it is not surprising that John McCarten in the chic *New Yorker* writes of Jeff (James Stewart) that "our man, possibly because of the habit pattern induced by his calling [as a photographer], whiles away his immobile hours with a spot of voyeurism." Referring to a line of dialogue in the movie, McCarten also calls Jeff a "Peeping Tom."[8] Additional to the psychoanalytical motif in the first reviews is the reading strategy of authorship. All three period reviews under consideration here place the movie within Hitchcock's oeuvre, with Jesse Zunser calling the director a "grand master of the suspense melodrama."[9]

Several years later (1960), French writer Douchet, quoted in this chapter's epigraph, weaves a modern art discourse of textual reflexivity into the network: "It is [in *Rear Window*] that Hitchcock elaborates his very concept of cinema (that is to say of cinema in cinema), reveals his secrets, unveils his intentions." Furthermore, Jeff becomes a surrogate for the audience:

> James Stewart [*sic*], a newsphotographer, is before everything else a spectator. This is one of the reasons why he is seen bound to his wheelchair. Through him, Hitchcock intends to define the nature of the spectator and, especially, the nature of a Hitchcockian spectator. The latter is a "voyeur." He wants to experience (sexual) pleasure (*jouir*) through the spectacle. What he looks at on the screen (in other words, what Stewart watches in the building on the other side of the courtyard) is the very projection of himself. Only the latter is capable of interesting him. In one way or the other, it is himself that he comes to see. . . . From then on, his understanding is fixed on this idea which becomes an obsession. Reasoning and deduction are subordinated to subjectivity, to feelings of desire and fear. The more he desires or fears, the more his expectation will be rewarded and beyond all his hopes. . . . More than a therapy, cinema, here, is a truly magic art.[10]

When François Truffaut interviews Hitchcock in 1966, Hitchcock is also repeating interpretations using psychoanalytical, authorial, and modernist discourses. Jeff's "a real Peeping Tom"; "Sure, he's a snooper, but aren't we all?" The film "was a possibility of doing a purely cinematic film."[11]

Disagreeing in part with Douchet's analysis, Wood in 1969 adds narrative progress through the film as pertinent to his rereading: *Rear Window* is "the cleanest statement in Hitchcock of what I have called the therapeutic theme." Wood constructs his psychoanalytical version of the reception epistemology: "We tend to select from a film and stress, quite unconsciously, those aspects that are most relevant to us, to our own problems and our own attitude to life, and ignore or minimise the rest; and we tend to use such identification—again, usually unconsciously—as a means of working out our problems in fantasy form."*[12] Wood then offers the thesis that while the spectator identifies with Jeff, the director Hitchcock shows the spectator what Hitchcock wants the spectator to see, producing a confrontation for both Jeff and the spectator with "our unknown, unrecognized 'Under-nature'"[13]—hence, the therapy function.

By the early 1970s, these interpretations were being further elaborated but basically uncontested. In *Film Comment*, Appel expands the film-as-metafilm discourse by suggesting that "each window [in the buildings opposite Jeff's room] reveals (and conceals) a donnée for a feature-film of its own, from Honeymoon Farce to Murder Melodrama." The killer Thorwald asks, "What, indeed, *do* readers and viewers really want?"[14] Appel writes that the answer appears to be in the choice of windows. In 1975, taking a feminist point of view, Mulvey describes the activities of Lisa [Grace Kelly] as exhibitionist, with the consequence that Jeff is more attracted to her.

Later (1983), Wood responds, charging that while misogyny exists in Hitchcock's work, *Rear Window* and others of his films cannot be reduced to that. Furthermore, Hitchcock's movies may be about cinema, but only the idiosyncratic cinema of Hitchcock's own making. For instance, through their reflexivity and contradictions, they call into question "the male drives and fantasies that provide the films' initial impulse." In *Rear Window*, the spectator "inscribed in the film is by no means neutral: It is unambiguously male," but a male who is experiencing castration anxiety. This anxiety, Wood concludes, so troubles *Rear Window* that what the film "ultimately achieves is the calling into question of our culture's concept of 'potency' (masculinity), with the insupportable demands it makes on men and women alike."[15]

Wood's reading departs somewhat from earlier ones by reintroducing a social referentiality, something the critics in 1954 mention but that seems somewhat submerged until the feminist critique by Mulvey. That is, the first critics ask what the film is saying about society (i.e., its significance), providing another discursive dimension to the interpretations. When the reflexivity motif enters, it seems to relocate interest from social questions to the individual: what the film is saying about a person's psychology in experiencing movies.

In the same year as the publication of Wood's 1983 "Fear of Spying" essay, Stam and Pearson's article appeared. Their essay's subtitle is "Reflexivity and the Critique of Voyeurism." Two epigraphs head their discussion: "'I choose this picture of all the films I have made, this to me is the most cinematic'—Alfred Hitchcock" and "'We've become a race of Peeping Toms'—Stella in *Rear Window*." Stam and Pearson take a straightforward contemporary linguistic approach, one that also repeats three of the dominant discourses threaded through the prior interpretations: psychoanalysis, authorship, and reflexivity. What they transform in their interpretation is what has already been altered in contextual theoretical discussions: the psychoanalytical and linguistic models of epistemology in use by the leading film philosophy. That is, their interpretation is the same as Douchet's, Wood's, Mulvey's, and so forth. The film's meaning and significance is as a reflexive text about cinematic epistemology. Their reading strategy is also the same. They seek an essence of the text. The difference is that Stam and Pearson employ the most recent version of psychoanalytical and linguistic film philosophy. *Rear Window* is reflexive about dominant cinema and Hitchcock's (the auteur's) own cinema, with its structures of scopophilia and identification. It is also "a multi-track inquiry concerning the cinematic apparatus, the positioning of the spectator within that apparatus, and the sexual, moral and even political implications of that positioning." Jeffries's function, both as director controlling the spectator's view and as "a relay for the spectator," is described through the authors' drawing comparisons between Jeffries and the immobile, "all-perceiving" film spectator of Jean-Louis Baudry's theses on the ideology and ego-gratification of dominant cinema. Stam and Pearson agree with some earlier writers that the film ultimately criticizes voyeurism through narrative structures, thematic motifs, and point-of-view techniques: Jeffries's "ordeal is also a cure, both social and sexual." They summarize:

> *Rear Window* provides an object lesson in the processes of spectatorship. "Tell me what you see and what you think it means," Lisa tells Jeffries, and her words evoke the constant process of vision and interpretation, inference and intellection, inherent in the "reading" of any fiction film. . . . Jeffries, Lisa, Stella and Doyle collaborate in producing the meaning of the spectacle before them, much as we collaborate in producing the signification of the film. . . .
>
> With its insistent inscription of scenarios of voyeurism, *Rear Window* poses the question that so preoccupies contemporary film theory and analy-

sis: the question of the place of the desiring subject within the cinematic apparatus. This theory and analysis shifts interest from the question "What does the text mean?" to "What do we want from the text?" "What is it you want from me? . . . Tell me what you want!" Thorwald says to Jeffries, and his question, ostensibly addressed to the protagonist, might as well have been addressed to us. What indeed do we want from this film or from film in general?[17]

The answer for that question to Stam and Pearson is in affectivity: from seeing and identifying, "spectators want to experience certain 'subject effects.' They want to find themselves in a heightened state of pleasurable absorption and identification." Ultimately, however, the film "cures" the spectator through catharsis.[18]

What the spectator wants is quite different for Bordwell but also quite predictable: *Rear Window* is an exercise in inferencing. "The pattern is set: this film will encourage us to construct a story on the basis of visual information (objects, behavior) and then confirm or disconfirm that construction through verbal comment." "[Lisa's] remark concisely reiterates the film's strategy of supplying sensory information ([tell me] 'everything you saw') and then forcing Jeff (and us) to interpret it ('and what you think it means')."[19]

Since Bordwell has excluded affective experiences as being explained by his theory, he concentrates on cognitive work, particularly for this film, which he considers "at once typical in the job it hands the spectator and extraordinary in the explicitness with which tasks are spelled out." Bordwell makes the point that these cognitive duties occur for both a suspense and a romance plot. Besides the mission of making the best inferences—ones better than Jeffries's ("Note that Jeff's inferential process does not completely mirror our own"—spectators ought to discover that Jeffries tends to think in rigid binaries. "For example, the spectator must discover the absolute opposition which Jeff creates . . . is a false one; one can find adventure in the most mundane urban milieu"; "Jeff tends to utilize schemata that are strictly homogeneous: Thorwald killed/did not kill his wife; Lisa and Jeff are exactly alike/diametrically opposite."[20] Where Stam and Pearson concentrate on spectators looking and feeling, Bordwell emphasizes them looking and learning.

How would a British cultural studies researcher approach *Rear Window*? In the first phase of the scholarship, an ideological analysis would be done, particularly as to how the film's representations set up preferred readings useful to the dominant class since the film was a product of the Hollywood film industry.*[21] In the case of *Rear Window*, aspects of the film scarcely mentioned in other analyses come forward. For instance, while Lisa's and Jeff's personalities (passive versus active) are described in the dialogue as the source of their conflict, their occupations and living habits are also at odds, making their class allocation different. In fact, the question of class distinctions seems symptomatically repressed, with the film attributing the couple's difficulties to personalities instead. Such an unstated problem surfaces through contradictions and overdeterminations.

Although Lisa works, she does not seem to need her job to support her life-style; she seems already to belong to the upper class. Instead, the work fills her days before she marries. It is truly for her just an occupation. Fortunately for viewers who enjoy spectacle, Lisa's job requires that she dress in high fashion, and Grace Kelly's appearance in the role helps make the watching pleasurable. Thus, the classy woman is both upper-class and an exhibition of feminine high class, doubly desirable in a capitalist and patriarchial social formation.

Lisa might also be defined as part of the "jet set," a common mid-1950s description of the leisured privileged class. That semantical terminology permits her to connect with Jeff, a world traveler and adventurer. Jeff obviously has lived dangerously but successfully, which gives him a strong masculine presence even if that is temporarily under seige through his recent accident and Lisa's marriage assault. Jeff, however, is not upper-class; he is a free-lance action photographer, a job apparently his livelihood. That type of income accounts for Jeff's small New York apartment, certainly not the home of one of Lisa's regular friends. Yet Jeff's rooms might also be considered as merely a stopping place between assignments to foreign and exotic climes. Thus, what Jeff lacks in value in terms of actual financial status is returned in assets of masculinity.

Lisa makes quite clear that Jeff could join her set by becoming a successful fashion photographer, an occupation Jeff considers boring (and castrating). On the one hand, then, their possible alliance represents something of a move upward for Jeff (into high society), which would not compromise Lisa's inherited position or her feminine value. Yet, contradictorily, Jeff's asset validating his entry might be lost. On the other hand, if Lisa were to follow Jeff, then she would have to give up the important pleasures of fine clothing and dinners at Sardi's. The conclusion of the film implies a subtle if uncertain victory by Lisa—perhaps because the terms of the romance have no simple resolution. Jeff is doubly immobile (both legs are broken now); Lisa covertly reads her fashion magazines behind the covers of adventure journals. Somehow or other, though, Jeff's loss seems also his gain. Class wins out. But so does at least one traditional gender role.

I have concentrated on the representations of the class theme as it relates to gender issues because British cultural studies has emphasized segmenting audiences by class and gender. The second phase of the research would be to solicit audience reactions to *Rear Window* and analyze those findings, distributing them into hegemonic, negotiated, and oppositional readings. From the point of view of British cultural studies, ethnographic or other forms of audience-interview research are a valuable source of evidence.

This obviously cannot be done for an older text's period audience, and the problem affects a historical materialist researcher as well. Two solutions exist: one is to attempt to constitute the era's reactions by historical research. The other is to use current audiences. Both solutions have associated problems. For the former, evidence of nondominant readings is likely difficult to find. Thus historians will have extensive work to do, ferreting out information from nonstandard historical sources (such as diaries, letters, small mimeographed newsletters, oral histories, etc.). Case studies may actually develop out of accidental findings of this sort. Likewise, though, many questions may be impossible to answer, even with considerable extrapolation from available information. I fear that will too often be the case.

For the latter (using current audiences), the historical disjunction makes conclusions about a period's audience difficult. How much have social formations changed in the past thirty-five years? How much are extraneous factors (such as changes in codes of masculinity and femininity or lifestyles) distorting reactions? (An attempt to deal with this methodological problem informs the case study in chapter 8 on gays' readings of films in this same period.) Of course, what you could find out is what a current audience does with the text, which might have some value in terms of illuminating the present. Comparisons of reactions over a number of years (e.g., doing a series of studies five years apart) might also prove useful. However, since this is an example broadly comparing possible reception studies methods, I will just offer a hypothetical finding, cautioning that my own research and the studies already done by British cultural studies writers indicate that audiences are much more complicated and contradictory than expected.

A preferred reading of *Rear Window* would be one in which the audience members became involved in the suspense plot, enjoyed the moments of spectacle, identified with Jeff and Lisa, and found the ending satisfying. Negotiated and oppositional readings might have come from several audience categories. Depending on the success of dominant ideologies to forge a hegemonic point of view, lower or working class members, males and females, and other categories might have had degrees of interpellation into the class and gender subject positions offered.

Presumably the suspense plot could intrigue any class, but since a great deal of textual time is given over to the romance plot and its attendant spectacle, those more resistant to an American-dream ideology might have either negotiated or resisted deep identification with Lisa and Jeff. Lisa and Jeff have at least two proairetic figurations: protagonists in the murder investigation and lovers in a courtship. Consequently, negotiating audiences probably endured the flirtation scenes, which emphasize clothes, foods, and activities inaccessible to them, while waiting for the mystery plot to pick back up. Those scenes were probably culturally explained as due to genre conventions: movies always have those kinds of scenes, and the resolution in favor of the dominant class most likely was read as the standard happy ending of a Hollywood film. (Similar negotiations occurred in Ien Ang's study, where audiences used the discourse of U.S. cultural imperialism to justify other people's attraction to "Dallas.")

Findings in the "Nationwide" study suggest that resistance can often appear through disavowal of address. "They were not talking to me"; "It does not have anything to do with me." The romance segments might have so disturbed an audience's pleasure that they overwhelmed any enjoyment of the suspense scenes. Thus, some lower- and working-class viewers might just have sat through the film, if they even went. In a British cultural studies analysis, a fully oppositional reading would look very much like the ideological analysis I provided. Such a reading, while improbable in most situations, might have been possible among marxists who by the mid-1950s commonly did similar ideological studies (although without the semiological and structuralist theories added in the next decades).

A large presumption headed my analysis of audiences categorized by class: that was, that any class might find the suspense plot interesting. That assumption I am simply going to let stand. However, evidence does exist that genders differ in their interest in genres, particularly the two represented in *Rear Window*. In fact, a bit of period research can supply a basis for this part of my speculation. As of about 1950, audience analysis conducted through traditional communications research indicated that women liked love stories and romances but disliked mystery and horror pictures. Men were moderately neutral about mystery and horror pictures but disliked love stories and romances.[*22] Hollywood filmmakers at this point often tried to please mass audiences, and mixing elements of various genres to appeal to possible subgroups within the audience was a common production strategy.

From the perspective of gender, then, I would speculate that in preferred readings, men likely attended to the mystery and suspense portions of the movie, while women were attracted to the romance scenes. In this case, gender identification with individuals of the same sex as the audience member should have occurred, and pleasure would result from watching Lisa (in the case of males) or being watched (in the case of females).[*23] The resolution might have presented some difficulties, even for a preferred reading, but as before, the cultural code of conventions in Hollywood films can explain the heterosexual couple.

Negotiated and oppositional readings by each gender might have existed. In the case of women, dealing with the (probable) disparity between the body of Grace Kelly and the spectator's own physique might have produced some dissonance with identification processes. Women's liberation was yet to emerge as a discursive formation that might help produce oppositional readings (see Elizabeth Ellsworth's thesis in chapter 3) which, like those for class, would critique the textual operations.

Negotiated readings from men might also revolve around the degree to which identification with Jeff was possible or difficulties with the resolution, which seems to favor the woman's point of view. That resolution, of course, participates in the 1950s discursive formation which implied that a man chased a woman until she caught him. In this case, Lisa is particularly aggressive in the pursuit, but then she is also represented as a most desirable woman. Additionally, the romance plot was likely tolerated as conventional Hollywood fare, perhaps made more bearable for men with its spectacle accoutrements.

My speculative presentation of how a British cultural studies researcher might approach *Rear Window* has been necessarily as brief and schematic as the review of the contemporary linguistic and cognitive psychology approaches. I think, however, that an outline of what such research would do with the movie is there.

What would a historical materialist reception study of *Rear Window* look like in comparison? What it would *not* do is combine the three previous approaches. Rather, it would begin nearly at ground zero. As Douchet reminds his readers, if Jeff is a voyeur who believes he makes his own cinema, such a belief is likewise a "morose gratification." Consequently, reception studies would start by considering the contextual reading strategies available to a spectator in the mid-1950s. What were possible and pertinent ways to interpret *Rear Window*? The answer to that question is unknown because histories of reading strategies have not yet been attempted. In fact such case studies as this one are providing the beginnings of data for hypothesizing. In this instance, I want to emphasize the tentative nature of the findings. Three problems exist in this part of the case study. For one thing, I have not attempted to cover fully the range of review responses for *Rear Window*, so my sample is very limited. Additionally, I have not tried to find marginal readings in nondominant media sources. The reading public studied is film reviewers and (later) academic scholars. Finally, the review and scholarly article are genres in themselves; thus, their conventions mediate the results. However, as a starting point I will use three release reviews to initiate the analysis because even they are quite revealing.

As I have partially indicated above, the period reviewers that I surveyed appealed to four major intertextual discourses: psychoanalysis, authorship, generic conventions of Hollywood filmmaking, and current social issues.

These four discourses explain much for the reviewers. Psychoanalysis (or psychology) accounts for character motivation and narrative progression. Referencing of this discourse was likely stimulated by specific lines in the film such as Stella's remark that Jeffries was becoming a "Peeping Tom," but psychoanalysis was also a popular theory of subjectivity that had been widely available to the reading formation for at least a decade.

Authorship illuminates the origin of something of a "stunt" quality to the movie. The reviewers assume that a director makes a difference in what happens in the film, and they perceive Hitchcock as something of an innovator. Two of the three reviewers reference prior movies directed by Hitchcock, such as *Rope*, to prove their point. Apparently, Hitchcock helped them do this. In a study of Hitchcock's reputation, Robert E. Kapsis points out that from the beginning of Hitchcock's career he used "biographical legend and publicity to promote his films."[24] Thus, the reviewers' activities have significant contextual sources motivating their remarks. But they also think the story source is another factor to consider. Bosley Crowther mentions the script writer John Michael Hayes, and Zunser and McCarten reference Cornell Woolrich's original short story. Thus, authorship is dispersed among several individuals, and the hegemonic theory of individuals as sources of texts is not violated.

While the film is considered somewhat different from Hollywood fare (particularly because of the single set location), reviewers also place it in standard Hollywood generic categories. That *Rear Window* is working in a traditional genre is remarked upon as part of the explanation of the film's pleasure. However, which genre it is in depends on the reviewer. Crowther writes that it is melodrama—probably a surprise by today's notions of that genre; Zunser calls it a suspense melodrama as well as a thriller, a pleasant romance, and a bright comedy; McCarten describes it as belonging to the detective genre.

For the fourth discursive intertext, the reviewers consider the film as a possible transporter of social messages. For instance, Crowther remarks, "Mr. Hitchcock's film is not 'significant.' What it has to say about people and human nature is superficial and glib. But it does expose many facets of the loneliness of city life and it tacitly demonstrates the impulse of morbid curiosity."[25] Zunser says it makes an "amusing comment on our neighbors in New York's great backyard."[26] Thus, the early reviewers saw the film's significance as relating to human nature in urban centers, a dominant social issue in the 1950s.

The four intertextual discursive strands are joined by the reviewer's conventional responsibility: evaluation. Two of the reviewers (Crowther and Zunser) praise the film for succeeding in building up suspense and excitement. They seem to have become involved in the plot and had affective responses of which they approved. Furthermore, they evaluate the film on the basis of what they thought the film wanted to achieve. Only McCarten dissents. While he assumes the same intent for the film (producing concurrence among the three on what a preferred reading would be), he negotiates his judgment in a symptomatic way. Recall that McCarten is publishing in the *New Yorker*. He thinks Woolrich is a "popular drugstore author, and Hollywood's affinity for him is easily understandable." Thus, Hitchcock's association with such lowbrow tastes is disappointing to him since he seems to think Hitchcock has some pretensions to creating "art." Contradictorily, however, McCarten also thinks Hitchcock is not Hollywood enough. The director has a "footless ambition to make a movie that stands absolutely still. . . . One of these days he's going to bust out the way he used to, and then we'll have some satisfactory films." What makes the film tolerable for McCarten is Lisa/Kelly. He concludes his review: "If it came to eating fish heads and rice, I can't imagine anyone more likely to make them palatable than Miss Kelly. Indeed, her very presence in this film brings on an uncriticial tolerance of the thing."[27] (If psychoanalytical theories about affectivity and voyeurism are correct, then McCarten's reaction demonstrates them clearly.)

So far, what is different between my historical materialist approach and the other three? For one thing, instead of looking to the film *Rear Window* for hypothetical evidence of what spectators are doing, I have looked at responses—albeit mediated ones. The distinction is a broadening and historicizing of the description of interpretive activities. While the period reviewers definitely looked and felt and looked and learned, what was projected as felt and learned seems somewhat at odds with the hypotheses forwarded by contemporary linguistic and cognitive psychology approaches, both of which assume ideal spectators in their text-activated models. For one thing, none of the reviewers seems to have identified enough with Jeff to have experienced any catharsis eliminating undesirable voyeurism or learned any lessons about inferring. All the reviewers treat the film largely as fiction and messages about other people, not themselves. None of them—at least in their reviews—ask the question, am I, too, a Peeping Tom? (Even McCarten, who obviously is one.) None of them—at least in the reviews—ask, was Jeffries a poor thinker? (In fact, McCarten thinks Jeffries's "intuition" wins out over Doyle's professionalism.*[28] McCarten seems to learn that emotional guessing is better than rational predicting.) While all the reviewers indicate some affective experiences, those emotions are all couched within standard generic terms; that is, the affects are explained through references to cultural codes and schemata such as genres (thrillers and melodrama) and modes (fiction and Hollywood films), and not to an essential meaning of the film as being about cinematic epistemology.

Consequently, and additionally, I have not considered universal linguistic frameworks, schemata, or ideological interpretations to hypothesize about the production of meaning. Rather I have suggested the existence of contextual discourses that might explain the evidence of actual comprehension. For instance, the four specific discourses used by the reviewers were within normative frames of reference for the mid-1950s, and feminism (as an oppositional discursive reading strategy) was not. The history of the deployment of these four discourses—psychoanalysis, authorship, Hollywood generic conventions, and social significances embedded as textual messages—is uneven and for the most part unknown. As I mentioned, psychoanalysis was common parlance in the United States from the mid-1940s, but the historical function of "authorship" discourses goes back at least several centuries. This disjunction among the temporal sources of these discourses in relation to the current 1950s social formation is explainable in the model of historical change marxism provides, for features of textuality in the superstructure have an uneven relation with the base. What is important, then, is to research these discourses and their relation to specific historical formations and the range of reading strategies these formations employ.

Furthermore, in my historical materialist analysis, no assumptions about preference on the basis of class or gender were made. In the case of gender, predictable results did develop: the male reviewers apparently liked watching the movie, in one case only because of Lisa/Grace Kelly. However, hypotheses about class consciousness or ideological sensitivities are not borne out. McCarten writes for the social sphere represented by Lisa. Thus, as a representative for the dominant class, he should have praised the film since ideologically it reconfirms that class. However, McCarten's response was the most negative. His distaste for the movie cannot be attributed to gender (i.e., masculine anxiety) since he finds Lisa the movie's compensating value (unless, of course, this is some type of displacement).

Instead, a possible explanation for his response comes from another aspect of his class configuration. In the mid-1950s, a pervasive discourse was the marking out of tastes in relation to class categories: high-, middle-, and lowbrow. In a particularly influential essay, *Life* magazine outlined this "new U.S. social structure [in which] the high-brows have the whip hand."[29] For entertainment, for instance, a highbrow enjoyed ballet, an upper middlebrow liked the theater, the lower middlebrow took in musical and extravaganza films, while the lowbrow went to western movies. Thus, McCarten's alliance with at least the upper middlebrow (displayed in his snide references to Woolrich and Hollywood) likely derives from contemporary discursive notions of *levels* of aesthetic preferences. His judgment against this "claptrap," however, is then contradicted by his desire for Hitchcock's earlier fast pacing (a narrational technique certainly associated with conventional Hollywood film practices).*[30]

Thus, the failure of McCarten to fit into a British cultural studies prediction highlights the importance of determining address, not as a theoretical feature to be derived from ideological analysis of the text and precharacterization of the subject, but as a contextually and historically variable factor. From the point of view of McCarten, his "imaginary self" as representative of highbrow tastes and his gender conflicted with any textual ideological address to a dominant class for which he may have worked.

Other observations about these three reviews could be made, but I hope the general differences are starting to stand out. As I suggested at the opening of the chapter, a historical materialist approach to reception studies tries to trace possible dominant and marginal interpretive strategies available historically. Both what is and what is not used are important. Additionally, the procedure investigates which subject positions readers consider the text to be offering them and then asks who does and does not take up those positions and at what points in the reading experience.

In the ideal situation, a historical materialist reception studies does not stop, however, at the time of the initial reception of the movie. The reason for this is that such a synchronic vision of the experience is only part of what might be learned. In the best of cases, the picture is widened in every direction—to other films of the same year, across cultures, races, nations. But also into a diachronic analysis. Consequently, the continued rereadings of *Rear Window* by academics (described above) are also part of a possible study. In this case, they continue as encrustations. Furthermore, their interpretations suggest some quite interesting historical shifts in at least the academic community's procedure for interpreting films. Here deconstruction enters, for with the intervention of modernist discourses about art as reflexive, the movie *Rear Window* becomes a prototypical playground for debating theories about the epistemology of cinema. In fact, the reading strategies for interpreting *Rear Window* duplicate the history of approaches to spectators. Thus, what a historical materialist approach could do is to go back and reread each of the interpretations from Douchet on as informed by their contemporary discursive formations, as well as linking those interpretive activities to specific historical situations (e.g., modernism's association with reflexivity, and the value that representation may have had for early 1960s French and American social and economic formations). I am not going to pursue this line of research, but I do want to make four summarizing points about the subsequent interpretations and their reading strategies.

The original reviewers of *Rear Window* assumed that the film's significance might relate to pertinent social issues, specifically human behavior in an alienating urban environment. Although not obliged to provide such an interpretation, the reviewers assumed that an obvious reading strategy was to figure out what the film said about current society. Once Douchet introduces the reflexivity discourse, the reading strategy of finding a film's significance continues, but the arena of that significance shifts to aesthetic and personal epistemological themes. For instance, Douchet's thesis of reflexivity allocates to Jeff not only the function of narrative protagonist but also that of spectatorial "surrogate." Whether the formalism of reflexivity tends toward focusing on the individual rather than the social requires research before the case of *Rear Window* is considered normal.

This weighting of location of significance alters once more. By the mid-1970s, Mulvey's and Wood's essays reassert social implications and effectivities in the epistemological issues: feminism and gender stereotyping studies help transform the film analyses. This reintroduction of the social can be easily explained, since post-1969 ideological analysis linked to linguistic and psychoanalytical theories reemphasized social and historical causes for those (temporarily) personal themes.

Second, as I noted above, deconstruction would argue that the debates over interpretation reenact the conflict in the film. Since historical materialism assumes a text does exist, something must be activating the debates over epistemology and effectivity. However, that the first reviewers do not raise such queries makes me leery of assuming textual materials as the primary source of the dialogues. Additionally, the contradictions within and among the individual interpretations point to the heterogeneity of the interpreting subject. Deconstruction is useful in drawing out ideological assumptions, but in the case of *Rear Window* textual features alone cannot explain the responses. They might be necessary determinants, but this time they are not sufficient.

Third, I have said little here about the affective consequences of the viewing experience. Although cognitive psychology brackets off those questions, contemporary linguistic theory and British cultural studies address them in various ways. It seems to me that historical materialism ought not to ignore the interpenetration of cognition and affect. My readings suggest to me the power of psychoanalytical theories of individuals as constituted socially and historically to explain many features of affectivity. Such a combination is viable for my model, but I do wish to leave this issue more up in the air than others. In the case of *Rear Window*, several factors seemed to influence McCarten's affective response. To explain that mixed review requires some psychoanalytical tenets (features of spectacle, objectification and exhibition of the female, trajectories of anxiety, perhaps sadomasochism). But also involved were current discursive evaluations of taste. Affect derives from unconscious dynamics, I think, but also from intertextual discursive structures.

Fourth, subject address changes depending upon the individual's need to respond (reviewer, academic scholar) and the theory of film. Movies are entertainment, auteur expression, psychological producer of catharsis, patriarchial repression, ideological representation, cognitive playground, social manifestation, or site of the production of meaning. It is the last category that I have taken up as the research imbricated in the interweaving of epistemological theories. Terry Eagleton writes that reception theory is "a social and historical theory of meaning."[31] My interpretation and reading strategy of the other interpretations are as informed contextually and historically as they were. In my case it has been by the theories available to me in the 1980s.

LOOKING BEYOND

Rewriting the history and philosophy of moving images from the point of view of reception studies will take many years, but the transformation produced by asking the question "What is the spectator's relation to the cinematic text?" and trying to answer it through a context-activated, historical materialist approach will result in important reactivations of other questions. For I believe that every aspect of the domain of cinematic and televisual studies could be affected. To give just a brief indication of what might happen, I want to look at three general problems: critical issues as reading strategies, difference as historically constructed and varied, and evaluation as political.

When considered from the perspective of reception studies, a number of traditional approaches to film and television studies take on new life. Specifically, notions such as auteurism, national cinemas, genres, modes, styles, and fiction versus nonfiction become significant historical *reading strategies*. That is, all of those notions, as methods by which to understand a film, have been significant interpretative strategies. Thus, instead of debating whether or not auteurism is a theory of the production of textuality, reception studies considers how auteurism as a theory has informed the reading of movies. Hypothesizing personalities as the origin of the text is a common procedure for giving a source of narration to a text, and—as others, such as Michel Foucault, have suggested—that practice seems to have ideological import for humanist social formations.

Allocating films to other categories besides origin is similarly historical and ideological. Constructing an imaginary community called the nation and then defining a film by its national production circumstances offers viewers as much of a strategy for comprehending the movie as the reading strategy of genre. A reception studies researcher might, for example, investigate how the attribution of nationality or genre determines what salient items are featured in an interpretation. A researcher might consider what happens to schemata or structurations of codes if the readers consider the texts as failing to conform to constructed categorizations. Genres themselves might be redefined, not on the basis of textual features, but by reader activities, with contextual factors producing a historical dimension to generic definition. (If *Rear Window* was a melodrama in the mid-1950s, what was *Written on the Wind*? What were readers observing and not observing in each to categorize them together?)*[32]

Modes such as Hollywood cinema or art cinema or avant-garde, or styles such as "realism" or "reflexive" might be explained historically on the basis of interpretative strategies and the production of meaning rather than ideally by supposed inherent textual features. What is fictional or nonfictional may reside in whether or not spectators use referential codes to presume correspondence between the moving images and the real world. Or a reception studies researcher might produce a historical materialist history of the reception of documentaries. None of these critical issues is fully resolved by reception studies, for, as I have stressed, this is only one type of question useful to ask about moving images. But reception studies does transform those critical issues from essentializing questions about categories to historical reading strategies.

If reception studies changes the way critical issues might be tackled, it emphasizes that difference is historically constructed. The subject is constituted within a social formation, and the range of possible subject positions changes. The taking up of those historical subject positions is an area of research as well, for interpreting a film requires perceiving from some perspective, even if that perspective changes through the film. Thus, what positions are possible and how individuals function in those perspectives matter. Currently, the types of subject positions available to a reader include at least occupation, class, sex, gender, sexual preference, nationality, ethnicity, race, life-style, and political allegiances (radical, feminist, and so forth). Some of these positions are more pertinent than others, however. Thus, reception studies research might ponder a series of questions: Which positions count more than others? When? Why? What difference does subject category make? What happens to an interpretation if dissonance among subject positions occurs? For example, as a student of Hollywood cinema, I find *Raiders of the Lost Ark* a masterpiece of filmmaking, but as a feminist I am appalled.

This last question, like all the others, concerns politics. Deriving from ideological state apparatuses, discourses and meanings are not neutral but the sites of class struggles. Interpretations, reading strategies, and evaluations, thus, are too. One use-value of reception studies is as a tool for understanding meaning as produced historically and socially by individuals. Connected to that are procedures for evaluation. Considering how canons are formed or reformed, how evaluative criteria come and go, how tastes appear and disappear—all these constitute seminal questions for reception studies. Notions of value are not universal. But they can be political weapons.

At the start of Part One, I quoted Marx. He writes in 1857, "Consumption is not only the concluding act through which the product becomes a product, but also the one through which the producer becomes a producer." I might disagree with him only as to whether consumption is the concluding act or part of a process, for what is most important is that consumption is also how a producer becomes a producer. Interpreting films is not an isolated, merely aesthetic act. It is a practice transforming the material world for our use. Researching how this happens can make a difference for the future.

Part Two

STUDIES IN THE HISTORY OF
THE RECEPTION OF AMERICAN FILMS

Rethinking "Primitive" Cinema: Intertextuality, the Middle-Class Audience, and Reception Studies

—On the television screen, an image of five men and two women, smiling; they wave toward the camera and exit right. A close-up of plumes of white clouds exhausting from the bottom of an engine. Long shot of a rocket, hesitating, lifting foot by foot, as if in slow motion. Another long shot of a vapor trail that suddenly splits in two, then five, six, ten streamers tumbling in all directions, a fan of fluffy white lines against a bright blue sky.

—A medium shot of a middle-aged man, a middle-aged woman, and a young woman, looking up with smiles, which then turn to puzzlement. The older woman averts her eyes, places her head on the man's shoulder.

—A schoolroom with girls and boys wearing party hats, cheering, then silence. A slow retreat from the room.

—A still, medium shot of the president speaking toward the camera.

—A shot of a Catholic church, with parents and children hugging stuffed toys, singing, talking, praying.

—The space shuttle administrator, Jesse Moore, speaks into a microphone.

—Shots of ships, with debris piled on the decks.

—A long shot of the other side of the space shuttle *Challenger*, with a small plume flaring, then spreading, before a sudden flash of red-white.

A case of noncontinuous editing? A case of tableau scenic arrangements? Yes. But no—not to a contemporary American audience fully familiar with the tragic story of the *Challenger* flight of January 1986.

I take this set of images from the repertoire of present-day narratives for a specific reason. I assume that despite my imperfect descriptions of these shots, you can bring to mind not only the images but also your feelings as the American populace viewed and re-viewed them. Not only are the story and its sequence accessible to you, but so is its emotional impact.

Let me, however, move a distance—temporally, emotionally, and conceptually—from my first set of images. I would move to the space of early film practice and its history. What I want to discuss in this chapter might already be apparent: to understand early cinema requires not only looking at its films but also analyzing its audiences and their knowledges. I shall be arguing that textual analysis combined with reception studies can change current understandings of this period of film practice.

My thesis is a moderately simple one: that American film did not change its priorities to privilege a continuity narrative form after 1909, but that narrative continuity and clarity were dominant organizing principles from the beginning of filmmaking in the United States. What is evident from around 1909 on is the adoption of certain organizational procedures of movie materials which filmmakers believed would insure that *every* spectator could follow the sequence of events. Thus, and perhaps more controversially, the signifying practices that develop into the classical Hollywood film mode were not due to an attempt to woo a middle-class audience to all-movie theaters, but that *just the reverse* is the case. The textual continuity perceived by later historians is a result of the expansion of the audience to include the working class, immigrants, and rural audiences, to make moving pictures a mass medium rather than one accessible to just a privileged few. What I will be suggesting, then, is a major change in a predominant representation of causality for the history of U.S. film.*[1] The implications of this change in the historical representation of the period spread to questions about bourgeois ideology and spectator-effect.

This argument stems from my attempt to think through the suggestions of recent scholarly work and to underline what that work indicates implicitly and explicitly. In its pursuit, I want to review what are now understood to be the conditions of reception of films in the early years in the United States,*[2] to reconsider the narrative practices of pre-1909 films in terms of these conditions, and, finally, to offer a hypothesis that should revise prior assumptions as to why film practices shift from their early procedures.

WATCHING MOVIES IN THE EARLY YEARS

Of primary concern are the conditions of reception. The recent research of Robert Allen, Charles Musser, and others has shown that between 1895 and at least 1903, although traveling exhibitors were common, the major sites of film exhibition were vaudeville or theater houses that catered to urban and primarily middle-class audiences.[3] Although some contention exists between Allen and Musser as to the continuing popularity of films at these houses, both agree that the organization of exchanges (which could buy films from the producers and then, as distributors, rent them to exhibitors) helped promote the feasibility of low-cost, all-movie houses. Musser also argues that the pleasure produced by fictional narratives was necessary to the growth of movinggoing—something Allen would not deny, although Allen also points out that fictional narratives had certain industrial advantages in terms of meeting a demand for good product.

These low-price houses, the nickelodeons, appear sporadically from the beginnings of cinema but certainly take off in numbers by 1907. Allen's research suggests that around twenty-five hundred nickelodeons existed by early 1907, and the number escalated thereafter. In the midteens, the figure hits a plateau of around fifteen thousand. As a cheap entertainment, nickelodeons particularly attracted a segment of the population somewhat excluded until then from movies because of cost factors. This was the working class, which included native-born Americans, as well as first- and second-generation immigrants. Although much research on audience composition and sociology needs to be done, current representations are that it took several years for middle-class individuals to enter the nickelodeons in any numbers. However, vaudeville houses continued to show films to the middle-class during this period, and entrepreneurs rapidly attempted to entice members of this class into the less expensive, alternative entertainment houses (often offering small-time vaudeville in conjunction with the films and in competition with the major vaudeville houses). Although films were shown in smaller cities from the start, consistent presentation of movies in those towns and in rural areas does not really seem to begin until after 1907 at the earliest, but thereafter those places follow urban trends. By 1909, trade papers were encouraging nickelodeon operators to upgrade their theaters, installing soft chairs, ambient lighting, and circulating fans,[4] and by 1911, many middle-grade movie houses throughout the nation were populated with a mix of classes. Women and children attended regularly although apparently this varied from one neighborhood to the next. In small cities movies showed in the local opera houses, as well as in tiny all-film theaters. Segregation existed in the South, but balconies were open to blacks. By 1915, several picture palaces had been constructed. Hence the transformation in audience composition from 1895 to the early teens was from a predominantly restricted big city urban middle-class to a genuinely "mass" audience.

Yet the conditions of reception include much more than the sites of film screenings and the classes, genders, races, ages, and ethnic origins of audiences. Also salient are the conditions of presentation and the films themselves. Two historically specific aspects of these factors need to be considered. For one thing, Musser observes that the tactics of early exhibition often included a lecturer or at least some oral commentary and positioning of the films within a context. Sound effects and exhibitor-added intertitles might also be used. Musical accompaniment was common. Such an exhibition situation produces a text that goes beyond the boundaries of the celluloid remnants available to historians.*[5]

Additionally, Musser points out that many early films were based on current affairs: recordings of important political or sports events or natural disasters or travelogues to foreign countries. But recordings of vaudeville acts or fictional narratives were likewise chosen on the basis of audience familiarity. Doing this had various effects. He writes, "When films were based on well-known stories, comic strips or popular songs, this meant a different relationship between audience and cultural object than in most contemporaneous literature and theatre, where it was assumed that audiences had no fore-knowledge of the narrative's plot, characters, etc."[6] Early film practice, then, often relied on, or assumed, or worked through intertextual knowledges.

This observation seems critical. One of the major use-values of reception studies may be to reconfigure representations of spectator-text relations. Among such prior images of the film spectator are those discussed in chapters 2 and 3: notions of ideal spectators, of passive or tabula rasa viewers. Moreover, since reception studies questions the idea that texts are autonomous objects, it argues that the production of meanings is a consequence of specific object-spectator contexts. Given this proposition, then, a study of textual features of early cinema without regard to the historical context and the spectator of those films is theoretically and critically fallacious. For a charting of meanings, linking those to the conditions for their production, provides valuable information about social formations, cultural discourses, power struggles, and the meanings of those textual features.

For instance, the 1902 film *Uncle Josh at the Moving Picture Show* has been used to argue that early spectators found the experience of film going to be illusionistic. Since the story of Uncle Josh's visit has him accidentally tearing down the movie screen when he believes that he needs to protect the heroine from the villain's advances, this proposition has a certain logic if you assume that the audience itself is naive and the movie is a documentary of a sort. However, once you consider that the "Uncle Josh" figure is a classic American theatrical and literary figure—the country bumpkin—the tale becomes a comedy, in which case a very knowledgeable audience laughs at the foolishness of taking a film to be real. The significance of *Uncle Josh* for early film practice reverses. This example underlines both the need for contextualizing filmic interpretations within the conditions of their historical relation to their audiences and the value of considering meaning in the interpretive act rather than as immanent within the text.

To explore how the conditions of reception and attention to audience knowledges change prior historical representations of early film practice, I will use a case example, the 1903 film *Uncle Tom's Cabin* (directed by

Edwin S. Porter for the Edison Company). The example will need to be qualified later, but as something of a limit case, it is valuable as a starting point.

EXPERIENCING *UNCLE TOM'S CABIN*

To today's film viewer, the event chain in the 1903 film of *Uncle Tom's Cabin* is somewhat obtuse. (See list of captions from the film in fig. 5.1, right-hand column.)*[7] Fourteen shots separated by fragmentary headline intertitles constitute the celluloid footage. The causal motivation of a number of the actions is unspecified, and certainly little textual information is given to describe the characters' traits and the relations among the individuals.

But for an urban, middle-class audience in 1903 nothing could be more obvious.[8] Harriet Beecher Stowe's novel was published in 1852 and became a best-seller, with more than two million copies sold. Although cheap publishing in the United States begins in the 1840s, making the novel more accessible to potential readers, and lending libraries were common, many Americans became familiar with *Uncle Tom's Cabin* through the stage version. Adapted by George L. Aiken in the same year as the novel's publication, the play would run continuously somewhere in the United States for more than ninety years.

For many people, seeing the dramatic version of *Uncle Tom's Cabin* was their first introduction to the suspect halls of a theater, particularly when abolitionist ministers encouraged attendance for the moral and educational benefits of the plot. When the play moved to New York City in July 1853, it opened at the National Theater, a house previously known for offensive dramas and prostitutes soliciting in the balconies. For this play, women were banned from evening performances unless accompanied by men. The theater did institute a matinee (a relatively uncommon custom then) so that women and children could attend. Designated "The Temple of Moral Drama," the theater attracted church groups lead by their pastors. Working people as well as middle-class people came; and blacks were admitted, but in a segregated area of the theater. Significantly, reviewers described "rough men and boys" moved to shouts and tears, and their subsequent conversion to the antislavery cause.[9]

The excitement and currency of the play might have been expected to slacken after the Civil War, but instead it seems to have taken off even further. Some historians claim that every important American actor and actress of the period performed in *Uncle Tom's Cabin* at some time. Touring companies traveled throughout the United States. In the 1890s, one estimate was that more than five hundred companies were "Tom

5.1 *Uncle Tom's Cabin*: The dramatic and the film versions.

DRAMATIC VERSION	FILM VERSION
Uncle Tom's Cabin [compilation of 1852 version by George L. Aiken and 1934 version by A. E. Thomas	*Uncle Toms* [sic] *Cabin or Slavery Days* [Edison Co., 1903, Edwin S. Porter]

A 1	S 1	Plain Room. George and Eliza talk. George is angry about slavery, and his master is threatening separation from his wife Eliza who lives at Shelby's. George decides to flee to Canada, later to buy Eliza and their son George.	
	S 2	Middle-Class Dining Room. Shelby has to sell Tom to settle debts. Haley wants Harry and Eliza as well.	
	S 3	Uncle Tom's Cabin. Eliza enters, saying Harry's been sold. She plans to flee. Tom refuses to go.	1 Eliza Pleads with Tom to Run Away
	S 4	Tavern Room. Eliza enters with Harry to cross Ohio River. Phineas tells how he fell for a Quaker woman and freed his slaves. Haley enters, following Eliza. Marks volunteers to catch Eliza. Eliza escapes but is seen and chased.	2 Phineas Outwits the Slave Traders
	S 5	Snowy Landscape. Eliza flees onto ice.	3 The Escape of Eliza
	S 6	Ohio River. Eliza flees across ice.	
	S 7	Race between *Robert E. Lee* and *Nachez*.	5 Race between the Lee and Natchez 6 Rescue of Eva
	S 8	St. Clare arrives home with Aunt Ophelia and Eva, and tells Marie of Tom's rescue of Eva.	7 The Welcome Home to St. Clare, Eva, Aunt Ophelia, and Uncle Tom [includes material from A 1, S 9]
	S 9	Garden. Eva and Tom play. St. Clare chastises Ophelia for her prejudices while preaching blacks' freedom. St. Clare gives her Topsy, who steals Ophelia's ribbon.	
	S 10	Tavern by Ohio River. Phineas plans to find husband of Eliza (who is hiding across the river). George enters, disguised (wanted poster for him on wall). Phineas informs him he will take him to Eliza. Haley, Marks, and others arrive, but Phineas traps them in cellar.	
A 2	S 1	Plain Room. Topsy sings and dances about her wickedness. Eva enters and tells she loves her; she asks Topsy to try to be good.	
	S 2	Room. Eliza and George reunited with Haley in pursuit. George says he will fight. Phineas accompanies him.	
	S 3	A Rocky Pass. George, Eliza, and Harry cornered by Haley, et al. Shots exchanged, but family is safe.	4 Reunion of Eliza and George Harris
	S 4	Chamber. St. Clare is drinking and Tom is worried. Ophelia is unable to control Topsy. Eva has a cough.	
	S 5	The Lake. Eva reads the Bible to Tom. Tom sings. Eva foresees her death. St. Clare promises to free Tom when Eva dies.	8 Tom and Eva in the Garden

(5.1 *cont.*)

S 6	Eva's Room. Eva dies with Tom et al. present.	9	Death of Eva

S 6   Eva's Room. Eva dies with Tom et al. present.

S 7   "Gothic Chamber." St. Clare in mourning and doubt, but Tom tries to reactivate his faith. St. Clare plans to free Tom, but Tom says he will stay until St. Clare is out of trouble. Ophelia drags in Topsy who has a lock of Eva's hair and a book that makes her feel and be better.

S 8   Marks introduces Cute to Legree. St. Clare intervenes in fight between Legree and Cute. St. Clare is wounded.

S 9   Handsome Chamber. St. Clare dies before signing Tom's papers of freedom.

S 10   An Auction Mart. Sale of St. Clare's slaves with Emmeline and Tom going to Legree.

A 3 S 1   A "Rude Chamber." Tom in room with curl of Eva's hair. Legree enters with plans for Emmeline, who refuses. Legree instructs Tom to beat her but upon Tom's refusal, has him beaten.

S 2   Dark Shed. Tom lies in shed with Cassy holding water to his lips. Tom refuses to give in.

S 3   Street in New Orleans. Shelby enters with plans to repurchase Tom from St. Clare. Marks agrees to take him to Legree who now owns Tom.

S 4   A "Rough Chamber." Legree enters, but Cassy points out stupidity of harming Tom. Sambo comes in with Tom's hair curl from Eva. Legree recalls his mother whose last note included her lock of hair. He feels bewitched.

S 5   Street. Marks meets Cute. Since only Marks and Cute witnessed Legree's murder of St. Clare, they will take vengeance on Legree's pulling knife on Cute.

S 6   Rough Chamber. Legree calls for Cassy. Sambo reports that Cassy and Emmeline are missing. Legree says to call out dogs. Tom is dragged in and threatened with death if he doesn't tell about Cassy. Legree hits Tom and he is carried off. Shelby, Marks, and Cute enter. Shelby goes after Tom. Marks and Cute show warrant for Legree on murder charge. Legree breaks, Marks fires, and Legree falls. Shelby enters, carrying dying Tom. Tom dies. George covers Tom with cloak. "Clouds work on and conceal them, and then work off."

S 7   "Apotheosis." "Gorgeous clouds, tinted with sunlight. Eva robed in white, is discovered on the back of a milk-white dove, with expanded wings, as if just soaring upward. Her hands are extended in benediction over St. Clare and Uncle Tom, who are kneeling and gazing up at her. Impressive music. Slow curtain." [1852 version]

Right column entries:

9 Death of Eva

10 St. Clare Defends Uncle Tom [events somewhat at odds with dramatic version]

11 Auction Sale of St. Clare's Slaves

12 Tom Refuses to Flog Emal'ine

13 Marks Avenges Death's [*sic*] of St. Clare and Uncle Tom.

14 Tabl'eau. Death of Tom.
—angel in upper corner
—man exiting with child surrounded by guards
—Battlefield of the Civil War
—Lincoln with slave at his feet
—War's conclusion

Troupes," and in 1902 sixteen groups were on the road in addition to any number of repertory and local companies producing the play. One reviewer estimated that in that year alone 1.5 million Americans (or one in every thirty-five) would see the play.

As the plot and characters grew in familiarity to audiences, the size and spectacle increased as companies competed for the title of the best production. In the 1880s, one traveling show had fifty actors, twelve dogs, a mule, and an elephant. An 1891 production added alligators snapping at Eliza as she crossed the icy river. In 1908, a company advertised a thirty-thousand-dollar production including thirty ponies, horses, and donkeys; fifteen "ferocious-man-eating bloodhounds"; and three musical groups. Absent from the original version, dogs were incorporated around 1879 by the Rial and Draper troupe, adding subsequently to the amusement of jaded reviewers. An 1890s Minnesota paper noted: "Thompson's Uncle Tom's Cabin company appeared at the Opera House last night. The dogs were poorly supported."[10]

Beyond multiplying numbers and types of participants, the productions also exploited visual spectacles. In 1888, the Peck and Fursman company inserted a steamboat race between the *Robert E. Lee* and the *Natchez*, using mechanical models and sound effects of steam whistles and bells. Uncle Tom's death provided the potential for a grand finale in an allegorical tableau, a highly popular feature of late nineteenth-century drama. In 1880, one company had the staging for that scene painted in gold tones and illuminated the set with electrical lights—this is cited as the first use of electricity on stage. In an 1897 one,

> three tiers of profile pink and white clouds, edged with gold and silver spangles, were planted on the stage floor. The voices of a celestial choir issued from behind the gauze-covered perforations of the canvas drop, then the floodlights backstage were turned on, and the holes became little golden stars twinkling through the glow—revealing a winged Eva—with a covey of attendant angels suspended as if in a gentle spring breeze. And in the foremost rank of the profile clouds, Uncle Tom knelt with up-lifted arms.[11]

By the 1890s, some productions "ended not with Uncle Tom approaching the gates of heaven but with the Union armies triumphing over the Confederates."[12] A tableau showed Lincoln signing the Emancipation Proclamation, and during the Spanish-American War, the entry of "men in blue" carrying the American flag while singing a patriotic song would be a final, rousing crowd pleaser.

Knowledge of the story by a 1903 film audience, however, was not limited to dramatic exhibition. In 1899, the novel was the most frequently borrowed book from the New York Public Library. Literary people discussed it, with the novel assigned in literature classes at Yale and Harvard in the 1890s. But an American did not need an Ivy League education—or even literacy—to know the story, for its iconography permeated the social formation. By 1857, 500,000 copies of the novel had been sold (the figure equals about 2 percent of the population of the United States at that point), but many of those novels were illustrated, some with up to 150 images. Posters, cards, and programs surrounded the play productions. Visual and aural tie-ins started early: in 1852, at least twenty Uncle Tom songs were published. Entrepreneurs brought out two card games and a puzzle based on the characters.[13] In 1899 the Kleine Optical Company produced a series of twelve slides illustrating the famous scenes; such slide series were common souvenirs for late Victorian parlor entertainment.

Furthermore, the story became the site of two early twentieth-century political battles. According to Harry Birdoff, in the New York City fall 1901 mayoral election, "Seth Low, president of Columbia, had been derisively nicknamed 'Little Eva' by his opponent Devery, and the popular reaction to the light use of the beloved little lady's name resulted in Devery's defeat for mayor." The other incident occurred in 1903—early in the year of the film version's production—and Edison's catalog refers to it in its film description. As sentiment against continuing racism grew in the North, *Uncle Tom's Cabin* was criticized for representing blacks as inherently and biologically inferior. In New York City (a major market for the film), a movement developed to restrict the novel's circulation, but the public Board of Education decided to include it on its list of "60 outstanding books required for every school library."[14]

One unambiguous index of a story's familiarity is its replication in parody, since parody's humor relies on an audience's intertextual knowledge. Vaudeville often parodied *Uncle Tom's Cabin*. For example, a 1901 New York theater played as a farce the story and its production history (in most rural towns generic backdrop curtains were commonly all that were available for scene design): "They used standardized sets, and when Legree and Marks turned up their coat collars and talked of a 'river of ice,' the drop behind them pictured an idyllic summer afternoon in Central Park."[15]

Now, if the people who saw the 1903 film version of *Uncle Tom's Cabin* were primarily an urban, middle-class audience, it is difficult to believe that the film version would have been as opaque to them as it may be to a present-day audience. On the contrary—all sorts of referencing of cultural codes and gap filling would have been operating for those spectators.*[16] To aid this, the film version draws on the familiar iconography in its representation of the scenes. The posters, programs, lithograph cards, and handbills for the play crystallized into a set of prototypical scenes as provocative of their context in the story as my initial example of the images from the *Challenger* catastrophe. Figures 5.2 through 5.13 juxtapose pre-1903 iconography with frames from the film.*[17]

Furthermore, an illuminating comparison can be made between the dramatic and filmic versions of the story. Many aspects of the story not evident from the film's shots are available intertextually. One of these gaps mentioned earlier was the lack in the film of motivation for characters' actions. However, a synopsis of the dramatic version of *Uncle Tom's Cabin* (see figure 5.1, left-hand column) dissipates much of the ambiguity. For example, in film scene 1, Eliza arrives at Uncle Tom's cabin and seems to be encouraging him to run away. In the dramatic version (act 1, scenes 1, 2, and 3) Eliza's decision to flee is well-established through appeal to commonsense psychology. Eliza's husband George has already escaped to Canada, but now she is to be sold before George can earn enough money to buy her from Shelby. Running away is her only obvious solution to the crisis. Film scene 1 starts without this expositional material. Another example is film scene 2, "Phineas Outwits the Slave Traders." Phineas's cooperation with Eliza and George is motivated in the dramatic version by dialogue: his affection for an abolitionist Quaker woman encourages him to help because he thinks his charitable act might convince her to marry him.

Besides character motivations (actantial structures according to Eco, semic codes via Barthes), the dramatic version provides causality for linking together the scenes of the film. For instance, film scene 11 (the auction sale of St. Clare's slaves) does not clearly follow from film scene 10 (St. Clare defends Uncle Tom) unless you know that in the dramatic version (act 2, scene 9) St. Clare has died in debt and without fulfilling his promise to Little Eva to free Tom. Furthermore, the irony and pathos of film scene 11 would be missed by the spectator who lacked that causal information. But as I am suggesting, I believe almost everyone in the 1903 movie audience would be able to fill in those data.

In fact, between the dramatic and filmic versions of *Uncle Tom's Cabin*, only one variation exists in the sequencing of the causal chain—although a significant one for the question of defining this film practice. In the play, the story of George and Eliza is interwoven with the action among St. Clare, Eva, and Uncle Tom. However, the film version follows the George-Eliza plot in film scenes 1 through 4 before going back to pursue the other plot line. Here the "crosscutting" of the dramatic version is shifted through a rearrangement of plot order in the film version.

However, contrary to the view of some historians, this need not mean that a different sense of time and causality operated in early cinema. In drama act 1, scene 8, plot information is also rearranged from a literal chronology, for a similar short "back-step." St. Clare, Eva, and Uncle Tom arrive home and then proceed through expositional dialogue to describe events that happened earlier. Between drama act 1, scene 7 and scene 8,

5.2 Uncle Tom's Cabin: Handbill from C. W. Lang's dramatic version.

5.3 Eliza pleads with Tom to run away: Scene 1 of the film.

5.4 The Escape of Eliza: Poster from Jay Rial's Ideal *Uncle Tom's Cabin* dramatic version.

5.5 The Escape of Eliza: Scene 3 of the film.

5.6 Tom and Eva in the Garden: Poster from Jay Rial's Ideal *Uncle Tom's Cabin*.

5.7 Tom and Eva in the Garden: Scene 8 of the film.

5.8 The Death of Eva: Handbill from C. W. Lang's *Uncle Tom's Cabin*.

5.9 The Death of Eva: Scene 9 of the film.

5.10 The Death of Eva: Handbill from Kathleen Kirkwood's *Uncle Tom's Cabin*.

5.11 The Death of Eva: Scene 9 of the film.

5.12 Death of Tom: Handbill from C. W. Lang's *Uncle Tom's Cabin*.

5.13 Death of Tom: Scene 14 of the film.

Uncle Tom saved Eva from drowning (incidentally, an event *shown* in the film version).

Rearrangement of events from their strict chronology has been a feature of storytelling from the days of Homer's *Odyssey*. In literature and drama, exposition has functioned to inform an audience of prior events, with such exposition scattered throughout a text. Furthermore, among the most complicated genres in terms of such reorderings are the detective story and the gothic novel, both very popular types of narration at the turn of the century. As discussed in chapters 2 and 3, the distinction between plot and story helps analysts account for this structuring of textual narration, and various theories of cultural codes or narrative schemata explain how spectators make sense of this. No good reason exists, then, to assume or claim that a 1903 middle- or working-class audience is unable to recognize and understand the difference between the story order of a chain of events and its sequencing in a textual plot, assuming, of course, that sufficient plot information is provided in some way—internally or externally to the celluloid text. Now, a filmmaker might be clumsy about providing the information, but that proposition differs from suggesting the filmmaker does not have standards of narrative clarity and continuity. If the film practice of the early years assumes audience competency in stories and current events, then that intertextual knowledge can be relied upon for audiences to fill in proairetic, hermeneutic, and semic gaps in the film, constructing a clear story and continuity to the temporal order.

Thus, one assumption of this film practice is that its audiences can reorder plot events into a story. Another assumption is one involving representing simultaneous events by sequencing the events in a text. Recognizing that two events are occurring at the same time but are being represented successively would hardly be an unusual or difficult feat for any early film spectator. In fact, the dramatic version of *Uncle Tom's Cabin* employs some short-range, multiple-occurrence alternating of plot lines, a very common manifestation of the period's narrational tactics, as Sergei Eisenstein points out about Charles Dickens's fictional techniques. The play of *Uncle Tom's Cabin* clearly works on this in its development of a suspenseful climax. In dramatic act 3, scene 2, Tom is lying ill from Legree's beating; shift to scene 3 of Shelby's arrival to repurchase Tom; cut to scene 4, with Legree continuing to pressure Tom; alternate to scene 5, in which Marks and Cute plan revenge on Legree; and progress, finally, to scene 6, with its convergence of the two lines of action. In the case of the film's choice to show the George-Eliza plot in sequence, given the audience's knowledge of the dramatic version, most likely spectators would mentally rearrange the information into the well-known story order.

Emphasizing that audiences at the turn of the century commonly considered successive and alternating representations as "meanwhile" propositions relates to the hypothesis mentioned before: some historians of early cinema argue that pre-1909 filmmakers and audiences had an "ambivalent" or "different" sense of temporality and causality than did producers and viewers of later years. The example for making this case is the 1902 *Life of an American Fireman* in which a fireman rescues a woman and child "twice." First the event is shown from inside of the burning house, and then the action is repeated from the exterior. Although the filmic execution of this action may be clumsy by current norms, the question from the point of view of reception studies is not whether production standards match the conventions of classical Hollywood cinema but how filmmakers and audiences of the period comprehended those shots.

Historians who argue that the norm of narrative continuity and clarity is introduced around 1909 (with material procedures such as matches-on-action, point-of-view shots, and close-ups developing to support this norm) might have a hard time explaining "relapses" into noncontinuous and tableau-style shooting. Such an argument, which is based predominantly on only textual evidence, would imply that the set of images of the *Challenger*'s explosion indicates a regression on the part of present-day filmmakers to a "primitive" cinema. Given the common and normal textual manipulation of story order for centuries prior to the 1900s and the high evaluation by late-1800s audiences of the well-made play and the unified short story, I cannot believe that an audience of 1903 does not already consider narrative continuity and clarity part and parcel of good storytelling and fine entertainment.

Furthermore, neither do I believe narrative continuity and clarity are the only means of pleasure they seek during an evening at the theater or movies. As discussed earlier, the dramatic version of *Uncle Tom's Cabin*, which appealed to both working- and middle-class audiences, interlaced spectacle with a tight crisscrossing of two subplots for a final, if melodramatic, climax. Narrativity and visual spectacle existed as available sites of affective response for all spectators of various classes.

RE-VIEWING *UNCLE TOM'S CABIN*

The introduction of reception studies into the history of filmmaking's early period and this case example of *Uncle Tom's Cabin* produce several new propositions about so-called primitive cinema. Regarding the film, it is difficult to maintain any notion that it is merely a set of tableau shots. For the spectators who likely saw it (an urban, middle-class audience), it must have called up a whole causal chain of events, fully motivated in psychologies of characters, and complexly ordered into a story that involved a simultaneity of events as well as sequentiality. As with the re-viewing of the

Challenger images, using a familiar iconography and plot, the film could have cued not only culturally shared knowledges of events and characterizations but a reminder, if not a replay, of the dramatic version's emotional impact. This film, then, relied on a highly extrareferential, nonredundant, intertextual film practice. In a sense, it could be claimed to be more sophisticated than some later cinema, at least in its assumptions about what its audience could do.

However, the case of *Uncle Tom's Cabin* needs to be qualified. It is an extreme example since the story was most likely the best known of its era—although, as Musser has pointed out, a great many of the early film actualities and narratives were based on contemporary events and familiar stories and characters. However, this film practice was about to encounter a change in the composition of its audience that transformed early cinema. What I believe happens after 1909 is an increasing movement to provide *within the film* causality and motivation supplied earlier either by the audience (through its prior knowledges and intertextual processing) or the lecturer (through the exhibition strategy).

Why would this happen? The explanation is that when the cheap nickelodeons became an economically feasible form of entertainment to all people, native-born and newly arrived immigrant working-class and rural peoples are added to the audience. With this new audience segment—not necessarily adepts of common middle-class narratives or readers of daily English-language newspapers—filmmakers could not count on all of their audience to know the particular story that they would be filming, even if these new audiences were already well-rehearsed in standard storytelling practices such as described above. Although an informed lecturer could perhaps supply exposition, for a nickelodeon operator a live performer was a labor expense that could be avoided if film manufacturers supplied a product that provided the information.

Hence, the cinema of the early years gives way to a cinema more self-contained and redundant, at least in terms of some features of its subject matter, with intratextually supplied causality and character motivation. Intertextuality continues, most prominently through genres and star vehicles but no longer in the areas of presentation of narrative events and characterization. Indicators of sequence, simultaneity, and order are provided through textual information rather than prior audience knowledge or an additional laborer in the theater, and film structure and material practices shift to continue the normative standard of good storytelling: providing narrative continuity and clarity.

Two cautions need to be made as I conclude. First, I am not suggesting that early textual practices are the same as those of the post-1909 era. Certainly they are different. However, I am arguing that a serious reconsideration of various previous assertions is necessary—in particular, the proposition that early cinema indicates a different attitude toward representations of temporal relations and the importance of narrative clarity. Or its follow-up postulation: that post-1909 film practice is due to the sudden imposition of a bourgeois ideology. In fact, what I have shown suggests that although post-1909 film practice is due in part to the opening up of film to the working class, immigrants, and rural populations, the classical Hollywood cinema film practice ought to be connected to a bourgeois ideology for the masses. Yet early film practice ought to be as well. Pre-1909 cinema is no more the proletariat's cinema than the cinema to come. At no time in the history of American film has any so-called proletariat or working-class film practice been dominant, even if certain textual practices do change.

What may have caused the prior historical representation of such a change is the effort to place information into discrete and opposed categories (proletariat-equals-this versus bourgeois-equals-that), thus following older marxist theories of the relations of classes to their cultures. Frank Trommler argues that not all countries' classes and cultures can be separated as neatly as, perhaps, can be done in England, the country whose divisions have served as models for many hypotheses about base and superstructural relations. In his specific study, Trommler believes that before World War I, German working-class culture was strongly indebted to a *Handwerk* tradition which was also, in W. L. Guttsman's words, "'bound up with bourgeois culture and whose attitudes were shaped more by piety, sentiment and a clamouring for education than by politics.'" In Germany, "at no time in history was the culture of the working class independent from the culture of the ruling classes. Concurrent with the advent of a mass-marketed culture of entertainment and information at the turn of the century this interdependence became even stronger and with it the influence of the new aesthetic attitude [by marxists in Germany] toward society and politics."[18]

Trommler's comments are useful as a reminder of structuralist marxism's and British cultural studies' objections to reducing cultural objects to reflecting the ruling class or assuming coherence within classes and ISAs. Perhaps in the United States, as in Germany, the cultures of the classes are overlapping and interweaving. Perhaps as well, the sense of narrative clarity and continuity, of temporal rearrangements from story into plot for cognitive and affective pleasure, does not "belong" to either class but is one of the features of a prior mode of production still functioning hegemonically in the social formation.

My first caution about my argument raised issues of textual analysis and film history: looking just at celluloid texts will no longer do in writing film history; dividing textual practices into those belonging to one class or the other is also unacceptable. The second caution involves the representation of the audiences. I am not suggesting in this study that the working-class, immigrant, or rural audiences were somehow incompetent viewers, unable to employ intertextual processes in experiencing film narration. In fact, quite the contrary: descriptions of their storytelling practices or pleasures reading novels and viewing drama suggest no significant variation from other classes. Rather, the consequences of their impoverished economic status, the transportation to a new nation, or culture's still regional nature at the turn of the century diminished the number of actual texts with which filmmakers could assume these audiences were familiar.

But the need for a sufficient knowledge of actual stories applies as well to the established middle-class audience. Evidence indicates that when those audiences failed to recognize an intertextual reference necessary for the plot, they might evaluate the film as unsuccessful. For example, in discussing current cultural allusions in the 1907 film *The "Teddy" Bears*, Musser believes the conclusion of the film is a satirical reference to Teddy Roosevelt's hunting exploits in which Roosevelt was accused of going after easy targets. Musser points out that a *Variety* critic seems to have missed this joke. The reviewer, "Simi," writes: "The closing pictures showing the pursuit of the *child* by the bear family is [*sic*] spoiled through a hunter appearing on the scene and shooting two. Children will rebel against this position. Considerable comedy is had through a chase in the snow, but the live bears seemed so domesticated that the deliberate murder in an obviously 'faked' series left a wrong taste of the picture as a whole."[19]

Musser continues, however, by arguing that the reviewer takes the film to be addressed to children. Musser concludes: "By judging the film from the viewpoint of a child who could not be expected to grasp a range of contemporary adult references, Simi postulated a relationship between viewer and cultural object that would be applicable to later cinema. In fact, Simi's review indicates that criteria for assessing films were changing and that films relying on a prescient audience were received with less sympathy."[20] However, if Simi's statement indicates that the reviewer missed the intertextual reference, his further statements do not necessarily indicate a changing nature of audience address (from adults to children). Rather, I interpret Simi to fear that any children in the audience might be confused and distressed by the final scene. Thus Simi's concern raises the general problem of parody and intertextuality for any audience member. The criterion of clarity for assessing films is not changing; intertextual references and an assurance of wide knowledge of them apply to middle-class viewers too. What this film lays bare is that much humor depends on cultural knowledge and to miss a reference can provoke interpretations aberrant to (assumed) production intentions as well as attributions to the text of "failure."

Furthermore, filmmakers had a problem once the nickelodeon boom increased demand for product. The range of possible narratives far exceeded those widely known even to their original customers, and the explosion of film going and pressure for story films necessitated reaching further afield than the American middle-class canon of circa-1900 stories. Thus, it is not an issue of differing procedures or abilities to comprehend a film among the various sectors of the audience that becomes a major determinant in film's signifying practices, but economically, culturally, and psychoanalytically based desires for variations from a small set of widely known stories. Once film manufacture went into mass production, as it did after 1907, its film practice was transformed to be accessible to all its potential consumers, even the middle-class.

Nothing I say here should be taken to imply that all of the audiences were the same or that they interpreted films similarly. Viewing a film involves far more pleasures and experiences than sorting out who did what to whom, when, and how, which is what has been at stake regarding the questions of narrative continuity and clarity. It is in such differences that much research about this cinema needs to be done. In "From the Prehistory of Novelistic Discourse," M. M. Bakhtin writes, "Every available style is restricted, there are protocols that must be observed."[21] While much study of early cinema has been to discover such stylistic protocols, I would also ask about the protocols of its film viewing.

For example, what was "ungrammatical" for the period? Was anything nonnormative in early cinema? Or nonnormative within its category? Take, for instance, a five-minute 1905 Biograph film, *Interior N.Y. Subway, 14th Street to 42nd Street*. Angles and movement of the camera result in tricks of depth perception that provide today's viewer with the odd experience of perceiving visual illusions of the depth shifting from three dimensions to two. Since today's view of this has available modernist notions of the surface as meaningful, today's spectator might well wish to place the film within some "visual pleasure" or modernist category. Yet was such a perception possible in 1905? Was it "unperceivable"? Or if perceived, was it considered a "mistake"? Or perceived but understood as within the norms of cinematography's apparatus?*[22]

Every one of these possibilities is different from those available to the current-day spectator who might seek such "avant-garde" moments in early films. From a post-structuralist perspective, of course, none of these possibilities is an "error" in perceiving and interpreting. Yet from a historical post-structuralist perspective, scholars might wish to make distinctions among these possibilities, particularly if they are claiming anything about causality for the development of the set of films known as Hollywood or the centering or decentering of a perceiving subject.

Textual analysis combined with reception studies, then, transforms the representation of early cinema's history. Pre-1909 cinema should not be seen as a working-class film practice erased or submerged when the middle class takes over production of and attendance at films, forcing ideologies of narrative continuity and clarity on a nonlinear film practice; rather, pre-1909 cinema is a middle-class practice assuming narrative continuity and clarity provided by intertextual knowledges or exhibition practices. After 1909, the transformation to the mass audience produces a signifying practice in which the film provides information helping spectators piece together a story from the plot. This condition for the production of meaning, however, is only one determinant, although a salient one, in the transition to classical cinema. Moreover, this textual and production practice is *only part* of what might constitute the interpretations and pleasures for different parts of the mass audience, for the various subjects who view those films within that historical context.[23]

This condition also illuminates my opening set of images. Within the current historical period, these "noncontinuous," misordered, "tableau" images of the *Challenger* tragedy have a powerful cognitive and affective meaning to this society. In years to come, when these images lose their intertextual context, their chronological relations will be forgotten; as merely souvenirs, they may be a "primitive" cinema to another audience.

CHAPTER SIX

"The Handmaiden of Villainy":
Foolish Wives, Politics, Gender
Orientation, and the Other

ERICH VON STROHEIM'S 1922 *Foolish Wives* provoked a reception that can hardly be considered neutral. *Variety* wrote that the film was a "leering insult to Americans in general, and American womanhood in particular," and *Photoplay* agreed, calling it not only "an insult to every American in the audience" but "unfit for the family to see." *Moving Picture World* was perhaps the most incensed, declaring it "a studied and flippant slam at all things American," a "Darwinian Phantasy of Bad Manners and Sneers." In an instance in which one writer pointed out that the "handmaiden of Villainy" was "courtesy," something clearly had gone wrong.[1] Or had it? Despite (or because of) the reviews, *Foolish Wives* went on to gross over $850,000.[*2]

Although atypical because of the vehemence of its reception, *Foolish Wives* strikingly illustrates the problems of determining a film's historical reception and implications of that reception for American film and American history. Through the hyperbole and contradictions surrounding discussion of this film, I hope to indicate something of what is at stake in the consideration of various widely divergent reactions to a moving picture and how discourse surrounding that film can indicate, symptomatically and inadvertently, ideological and hegemonic notions about such concepts as "American," "masculinity," and "propriety." The consequences of the diversity of reaction have both philosophical and historical implications concerning the degrees to which films influence, affect, motivate, or reconfirm representations already active within spectators' repertoire of explanatory systems: representations such as conservative, liberal, or socialist; Anglo-Saxon or Mediterranean; American or European; U.S. citizen or foreigner; male or female; feminine or masculine. For all of these classifications are both constructed and questioned in the historical reception of *Foolish Wives*. Most significantly, the hard-to-detect, but apparent, resistance of women in the early 1920s to patriarchal notions of propriety and alignments of desire are well illustrated in the event of this film's exhibition.

Foolish Wives provoked in the dominant, bourgeois media an expression of outrage. Its scandal seems somehow to revolve around its discourtesy in not playing by some notion of appropriate discourse, and the audience's consternation at its displeasure (and pleasure) throws open submerged questions of expectations, address, and interpretation. In addition, the heightened, and I would say hysterical, discourse allows a slippage onto the surface of contradictions, overdeterminations, gaps, condensations, and displacements. Useful here theoretically is V. N. Vološinov's model of language as social utterance and the importance he attributes to "ideological signs" for cultural and historical analysis. As I noted in chapter 1, Vološinov writes: "Various different classes will use one and the same language. As a result, differently oriented accents intersect in every ideological sign. Sign becomes an arena of the class struggle."[3] He argues that in times of social crisis while the dominant class may assert a traditional meaning for a sign, opposition to that attempt to achieve hegemony may develop: the minority may assert a contrary semantics.

The dominant discourse in the early 1920s at the time of the film's release, along with some indications of an alternative response to the film, suggests the potential conflict within just such an apparently hegemonic coherency when confronted by an Other—a conflict manifested within an attempt to hold onto established interpretations, semantic organizations and definitions, and configurations of eroticism.*[4] This Other appears first in the American husband, Andrew Hughes, but eventually centers on the figure of Count Karamzin (and the actor who plays him, Erich von Stroheim). The count becomes a contested sign, and, as I shall argue, the symptom of several interwoven social crises involving patriotism, gender differences, foreignness, and sexual desire. Furthermore, the plentitude and complexities of readings suggest this despite the struggle by some individuals to declare a fixed and universal understanding for the film, their effort to make the sign "Count Karamzin" uniaccentually villainous. Thus, even within the dominant media, opposition and resistance emanate from several individuals, notably women.

This morass of responses is not easily entered, but let me start with ones related to expectation, moving subsequently into address and interpretation. In all three areas, the conflict revolves around the confrontation of protocols, the insult by this film of assumed courtesies between a film and a spectator, and the decorum of signs having only one, authoritative meaning.

EXPECTATION AND "100% AMERICANISM"

A study of the reviews, letters to the editors, and parodies of *Foolish Wives* indicates that a number of expectations existed, some of which, when confronted by this film, proved contradictory. Hans Robert Jauss, drawing from the Russian formalists' concept of a "background set," argues that scholars might construct from the group of surrounding texts "horizons of expectation" for any given text. However, as Susan Suleiman points out, different segments of society may have varied horizons.[5] Furthermore, I would add that the texts available ought to represent genres other than that of the text examined, particularly if a period's discursive organization is to be mapped. Texts for such a background set for *Foolish Wives* cannot be limited to fictional narrative films of the early 1920s but must include literary and dramatic fictions, as well as historical, political, scientific, and pseudoscientific discourses. This is particularly pertinent for *Foolish Wives* since intertextual and referential codes of verisimilitude are disputed, as is the received understanding of specific cultural and gendered "types."

One of the major debates generated by the scandal of this film concerned the depiction of the American husband, and it was fought out through disagreements about historical accuracy and unspoken norms of "masculinity." The reviewers were by no means sure how well Andrew Hughes came off. While the *New York Times* declared Hughes "adequately forceful" and *Motion Picture Classic* described him as a "good natured boob," the *Moving Picture World* and *Variety* reviewers repeatedly asserted that Hughes was made to appear a "jackass" or a "monkey." Drawing on textual evidence, but using it as a point of contrast to conceptions of actual American ambassadors, these reviewers claimed that the representation of Hughes was disparate from those images, that thus the characterization of Hughes as an American diplomatic agent was unrealistic, and, consequently, that the representation portrayed the American abroad as stupid and unsophisticated. Hence the film was an insult to American ambassadors, American foreign politics, and Americans in general. For example, *Variety* writes:

> What a sap this husband is, and what a conception of an American diplomat, entrusted with an important mission to the Prince of Monaco, von Stroheim has of an American diplomat. Imagine a man of 41, no matter how raised or born in the smallest backwoods town of America, who upon being presented to the Prince, doesn't know what to do with his hands, and who, as Mr. von Stroheim has conceived him, generally suggests a rube storekeeper, rather than a member of the diplomatic corps.

Similarly, *Photoplay* notes, right after its comment about the film's insult:

> Consider: an American, of sufficient prestige and importance to be selected by the President of the United States as a special envoy in charge of a vitally important mission to the Prince of Monaco, is depicted as a man who does not know how to enter a room or wear formal dress!

Already, the reviewers' attention to manners and tastes in clothing seems oddly foregrounded, and this sense of "appropriateness" will haunt every aspect of the reviews.

Not all writers agreed, however, that Hughes was unrealistic, and judgments of the film almost always find as one of their warrants assertions about verisimilitude and its implication for Americans and America: American politics are fought over through Hughes as a contested sign. For example, Frederick James Smith in *Motion Picture Classic* was one of the few reviewers to give credence to the realism of the characterization: "Knowing the calibre of some of our American representatives abroad, we find nothing but realism in this."

Sources for America-philia reach back several decades into the 1800s,*6 but the years 1919 and 1920 were a period of intensification of "Americanism." The post–World War I era witnessed the "Red Scare," debates over the peace treaties and League of Nations, the Palmer raids, the Sacco-Vanzetti trial, the solidification of the American Legion, the resurgence of the Ku Klux Klan, and the formation of the internal intelligence division of the Justice Department (headed by J. Edgar Hoover). This intelligence division's primary obligation was investigating aliens, who were especially marked as likely agents for radical activities.[7] As one historian writes, "In 1919–20, '100% Americanism' was the alternative to deportation."[8]

Although the most evident aspects of the Red Scare and xenophobic hysteria subsided by the end of 1920, through the decade nationalism and American patriotism were dominant ideological discourses reinforced through laws (the 1920 Immigration Act imposed the first quota), educational commissions (foreign-language teaching was reduced and restricted to upper-level studies), company programs to "Americanize" their workers, and civic organizations like the Good Citizen's League joined by the protagonist of *Babbitt* (published the same year as the release of *Foolish Wives*). The ideological state apparatuses constructed a strong hegemonic version of Americans versus (dangerous) foreigners as a major way for U.S. citizens to construct their self-identities.

A counteroffensive by alternative political groups was the attempt to redefine patriotism and loyalties away from nationalism and toward class. For example, Alfred Baker Lewis writes in 1922 in the *New York Call* (a socialist party newspaper), "Too often patriotism has been a mere camouflage for the class interests of the capitalists, especially such patriotism as that of the chambers of commerce or the self-styled '100 per cent Americans' in this country, and the advocates of the 'American plan' for smashing the trade unions."[9] However, Lewis and other socialists of the period failed to significantly alter American legal, political, or ideological direction as Calvin Coolidge began his eight years as president in 1920. Patriotism focused on country of citizenship rather than class.

For *Foolish Wives*, the reviewers, with the exception of Smith, apparently accepted the dominant position on the sign "patriot," equating the "country bumpkin" representation of Hughes with subversive views. It did not help either that the director, von Stroheim, and the producer, Carl Laemmle, could be associated with those suspect foreigners; many of the reviews mentioned Count Karamzin's "Junker physiognomy." Smith found Hughes "realistic" and astutely attributed the negative reaction to "parlor patriots," "100 per cent Americans," "boobery and provincialism," and those desiring a "pale Pollyanna echo of life." The other reviewers, however, declared the film "junk," "tainted chuck steak," "artistically nothing," "gruesome, morbid, unhealthy," "atrocious melodrama," and "not good, wholesome entertainment."

While I hope I have somewhat accounted for part of the negative response, what can explain its intemperate nature? When the protocol of an appropriate representation of Americans was broken, the film *Foolish Wives* was judged villainous. However, the response to Hughes is complex and is not based solely on how he is characterized. The response is also established through a contrast with Karamzin and fear of "foreigners." The reviewers' early impressions of both characters overwhelmingly determined judgments. As *Photoplay* put it, "Your verdict is ready before the end." Despite the conclusion of *Foolish Wives*, in which Hughes may be argued to have been represented as possessing many more desirable features than the courteous and refined Continental Count Karamzin (who is tossed down a sewer with a dead cat), the reviewers' tally was unchanged. In the case of *Foolish Wives*, not only could contemporary semantic orientations not be defied, but judgments based on early portions of the film (the reviewers' primary impressions) overdetermined*[10] any later reevaluation and reinterpretation.*[11] Thus, as suggested in chapter 3, Elizabeth Ellsworth's theory—that people do not reject textual data but do manipulate it where possible—seems only partially borne out in this case, but this event is definitely at odds with notions such as Jonathan Culler's that readers try to unify texts. These reviewers paid attention to the initial representations and, rather than assuming coherency to the text, evaluated the movie as unsuccessful. World structures (per Umberto Eco) or cultural codes (per Roland Barthes) were more pertinent for these readers than proairetic, hermeneutic, or symbolic codes.

As in the debate over the realism of Hughes as an American diplomat, reviewers' attitudes toward Karamzin were constructed by extratextual as well as intratextual evidence. Von Stroheim argued later that he thought that he had sufficiently contrasted Hughes and the count so that the film indicated where the audience's sympathies should lie; he claimed that he had used the device of the count's elongated, effeminate*[12] cigarette

She was batty over the count and a real human
dog when it came to taking abuse

6.1 "She was batty"

holder, as well as his rapacity, to suggest Hughes's masculinity and virtue by contrast. As he said in an interview,

Originally I had had the American ambassador smoke Bull Durham and roll his own. I was told in horrified whispers that I was insulting the American. And yet I had put it in simply as a contrast to the elongated, perfumed cigarets [*sic*] of the Russian count, things no honest-to-god American he-man would smoke! Bull Durham to me is a national trait in America.*13

In fact, in a satire of *Foolish Wives*, "Solving the Million Dollar Mystery," all three sketches illustrating the parody prominently show Karamzin smoking (see figs. 6.1, 6.2, and 6.3). Obviously the device was memorable even if its planned effects did not achieve what von Stroheim claimed he had anticipated.

Further aspects of Karamzin's representation will be considered, but here I want to note that the reviewers not only consistently judge Hughes by a presupposed and intertextual conception of an American emissary, but they assume that traits of savoir faire coincide with diplomacy. Despite intratextual gestures of joining "virtue" and "Hughes," the connection of "American" with "lack of sophistication" *and* the attribution of that fea-

The Count's brand of chin goods was immense, and his
line of attack made Don Juan look like a bush leaguer

6.2 "The Count's brand"

For some unknown reason, the women all fall for his stuff

6.3 "For some unknown reason"

ture to the foreigner were doubly difficult to abide. Thus, textual and intertextual determinations reinforced one another: the semantics of various
textual devices were ambiguous (because they were potentially capable of
multiple connotations), and preestablished expectations from hegemonic
fields of discourse overrode possible configurations of meaning. Thus, the
linkage to the contemporary political context, images of American diplomacy, and preset notions of the American (male) ambassador seem to have
prevented any viewing of the film as an autonomous object within a mode
of discourse distinct from "everyday" discourse. Even if the text's meaning
was pro-Hughes, its significance to reviewers provoked outrage.*[14]

ADDRESS AND "TAKING THE COUNT"

Another reason for the complicated response to *Foolish Wives* may well be
its provocative and contradictory address, and certain disturbing implications of recognizing that address. As suggested in chapter 5, a presupposition of American exhibition by the teens was the mass audience, entertainment and pleasure for the entire family. Reviewers who declared the film
an insult cautioned directly that it was unfit fare for children, adolescents,
and the "family." Indirectly this broken protocol surfaces through displacement. Repeatedly, the film is described in metaphors related to oral
consumption.*[15] It is "goulosh [*sic*]" and has a "bad taste." The most extended version of this is: "Serving a hamburger steak on a gold platter
doesn't make the hamburger quail on toast. But comparing 'Foolish
Wives' to hamburger is a bit tough on the hamburger. Maybe chuck steak
would be better, and tainted chuck steak at that." Von Stroheim countered, "You Americans are living on baby food." One letter writer responded: "I wish your indignant correspondents would avoid asinine mis-
statements such as 'The American man is the ideal lover and husband'—a
statement as sensible as 'Pork and Beans are the perfect food.' So they
are—if you like 'em." The issue of to whom this film was or ought to be
addressed, then, was at stake, with varied opinions as well as attributions
as to the resulting wholesome pleasure or illness from its consumption.

Yet this issue of health obviously is not really about whether children or
"the family" ought to see *Foolish Wives*. That was a subterfuge for the more
disturbing question of female sexual desire. Although clearly a publicity
release, one article queried:

> What kind of men do women adore? Why do women often reject hand-
> some men who would make good husbands only to lavish their love instead
> upon the tyrannical and brutal type of man who treats them roughly? Do all

women stand for this sort of thing, or is it a fact that only some women are influenced by the bruttal [*sic*] side of man's nature. . . .

This picture, built around the character of a fascinating roue, has a peculiar attraction for women. . . .

Are the women who see "Foolish Wives" doing so because they are hypnotized by this type of villain? Or do they go to see "Foolish Wives" because of the enormous satisfaction in seeing a villain who has treated so many women badly, meet a death that is well deserved at the finish?

Why women went to the film, and what they received satisfaction from, is not clear; but as one correspondent noted, despite reviews indicating that *Foolish Wives* was "an especial insult to the womanhood of America," "there were quite as many women in the audience as men. I am just getting over the shock!" "The Man You Loved to Hate" underlines the contradictory and confused representation of von Stroheim's Count Karamzin as well as the relation of women to that image. Knowledge of a writer's gender is available for most of the reviews,*[16] but generalizations are difficult because of the diversity of remarks (nor would I expect consistency, since gender stereotyping is essentialist as well as discriminatory). Male writers repeatedly describe the count in nonwhite or nonhuman tropes: "simian," a "human beast of prey, an unbelievably contemptible animal," a seeker of "blond, brunette, and henna scalps," a "monster." The "hunt" motif abounds.

Women's responses are equally intriguing. Revealing is one woman letter-writer's description of Karamzin as "a cross between a crown prince and a weasel." But another view comes from a female reporter. Although she cautions her readers that von Stroheim the individual does not equal the character he plays, in an interview with von Stroheim, Harriette Underhill continually stresses his courteous responses while noting, "We were lucky that he didn't brain us or throttle us, as he did to people and animals and birds in the picture [*sic*]. At any rate, we were sure we were right and were ready to take the count, if you know what we mean."

The double-entendre of Underhill's remarks suggests perhaps some inability to express desire directly. The historical period surrounding the release of *Foolish Wives* abounds with queries regarding women's sexuality, most resembling the classic "What do women want?" For example, H. H. Van Loan, an advice columnist for amateurs trying to break into writing movies, muses, "In looking over the scripts sent me by aspiring screenwriters, I note that the 'sex' stories are always written by women. Maybe someone can explain this!"[17]

Just what did women want? *Foolish Wives* was released in January 1922, ten months after *Four Horsemen of the Apocalypse* (February 1921) and two months after *The Sheik* (November 1921). The Rudolph Valentino craze was just starting, but in retrospect Valentino is only the most conspicuous of a number of objects of women's attention. Furthermore, that attention, and the movie industry's address to it, preceded World War I. A number of male stars in the twentieth century's second decade antedate the early 1920s' array of male leads to whom women were apparently attracted. The earlier stars included Francis X. Bushman and Maurice Costello—for whom Vitagraph produced in 1912 a delightful satire, *The Picture Idol*, about young girls worshiping movie stars. The plot of this two-reeler is clever: a young girl devotes all of her time to thinking and learning about her picture idol, much to the consternation of her family. The opening shots of the film are shot/reverse shot in which several youngsters are gazing transfixed at a movie starring Costello. At home, the heroine reads about her idol in the *Moving Picture Story Magazine*[*18] and hugs a photograph of him. Her devotion leads to deteriorating attention at school, and Mom and Dad decide a cure is necessary. The idol is invited to dinner, but his faked poor table manners do not hinder her affection. Only after being fooled into thinking that he has a wife does our young woman tear up his picture.

Such movies might have reproduced conventions of female desire (both of what it is and of how it is expressed), but the circulation of cultural rituals is more complex than mere aping of film imagery. When Valentino and von Stroheim arrived on the screen, the desiring woman spectator was an established feature of the commercial and psychic exchange among film producers, the social formation, and sexual identity.

Yet the characterization of that feature was not stable or apparent. In fact, evidence suggests a range of possibilities, including variety among women. Drawing on filmic and other evidence, Miriam Hansen hypothesizes about the attraction of Valentino for (some) 1920s women. Although Valentino films follow and to a certain point accept the patriarchal logic of the gaze as belonging to men, the films are undercut by the "figure of the male as erotic object . . . accompanied—most strikingly in the case of Valentino—by a feminization of the actor's persona. These mechanisms, however, are not naturalized as they are in the representation of a female body. Rather they are foregrounded as aspects of a theatricality that encompasses both viewer and performer."[19] Additionally, variations of sadomasochism occur in the plot: Valentino and the female leads alternate in positions of victim and victimizer.

Valentino was certainly the most prominent example of an object of woman's desire, particularly in the hysteria surrounding his death. Period evidence also indicates something of men's response to Valentino's threat. Dick Dorgan, author and cartoonist of the satire displaying von Stroheim brandishing his cigarette, also produced "A Song of Hate" (July 1922). This short essay and sketch provide something of an awareness of the *Ra-*

A Song of Hate

By Dick Dorgan

As the men see him   *As the women see him*

I hate Valentino! All men hate Valentino.
I hate his oriental optics; I hate his classic
nose; I hate his Roman face; I hate his smile;
I hate his glistening teeth; I hate his patent
leather hair; I hate his Svengali glare; I hate
him because he dances too well; I hate him
because he's a slicker; I hate him because
he's the great lover of the screen; I hate him
because he's an embezzler of hearts; I hate
him because he's too apt in the art of
osculation; I hate him because he's leading
man for Gloria Swanson; I hate him because
he's too good looking.
   Ever since he came galloping in with the
"Four Horsemen" he has been the cause of
more home cooked battle royals than they
can print in the papers. The women are all
dizzy over him. The men have formed a
secret order (of which I am running for
president and chief executioner as you may
notice) to loathe, hate and despise him for
obvious reasons.
   What! Me jealous?—Oh, no—I just
Hate Him.

6.4 "A Song of Hate"

shomon effect. As Dorgan conceives of it, women see Valentino as dash-
ing, but "all men hate Valentino" (see fig. 6.4). They hate him for, among
other things, "his oriental optics," "his classic nose," "his Roman face,"
"his Svengali glare," and because "he's too good looking."[20] Dorgan concludes: "What! Me jealous?—Oh, no—I just Hate Him."
   Hansen's analysis of the psychoanalytical figures provoking women's
desire is excellent, disabusing scholars of hasty assumptions that a masochistic positioning is the explanation for women's response to Hollywood
narrative cinema. Yet by placing significant weight on the Valentino-event
as a "first,"[21] the essay may produce an alternative vision that should not
carelessly be taken as a new explanation for women's sexual desire. For it
is evident that women in the period were also addressed by, and responded
to, other male stars, few of whom (if any) could be said to duplicate the
complex of variables that intersect in Valentino. The theoretical thrust of

Hansen's work is cautioning scholars to avoid essentialist versions of women's desire, and the von Stroheim case bears this out. For reasonable evidence exists that some women's responses to von Stroheim do imply a masochistic positioning (but also something else). And what are we to do with some men's responses such as that by Smith, who rebuts the simple political analysis of his colleagues and summarizes the count as "dissolute, dapper, monocled, a reckless player with passion, drinker of perfume, base student of feminine psychology, unscrupulous thief, scoundrel guilty of all the sins on the calendar; yet fascinating withal." The answer to this question of address and desire is bound into interpretation.

INTERPRETATION AND "THE HANDMAIDEN OF VILLAINY, COURTESY"

As suggested in Part One, interpretation is intricately tied to affective reception, and affective reception may be bound to preconceived and unconscious processes by which individuals produce meaning. A number of writers provide pointers toward reconstructing such interpretative strategies, as well as toward methods of examining the implications of those strategies. Stanley Fish suggests looking at the shape of the readers' perceptual categories, and, as I discussed, Culler and Tompkins both write that the institutionalized rules for appropriate criticism vary historically. Timothy Clark, in a discussion of Manet's *Olympia*, looks at parodies to determine where stress in a received paradigm of expectations is confronted and repressed through satirical devices.[22] Vološinov also contributes, observing struggles over a contested sign. These and other remarks about interpretation may work toward an explanation of the contradictory responses to the figure of the count.

Continually stressed in the published responses is a whole set of categorical binary oppositions: American/un-American; American/foreign; masculine/feminine; hero/villain; mannerly/unmannerly. For *Foolish Wives*, the protocol of the slash between opposites is rudely abandoned, the representations crossing and linking alternatives previously—and externally to the film—taken as givens (or hegemonically assumed as such): hence, I believe, the insult and consternation within the institutionalized response.

This wiping out of the slash is symbolized through the one reviewer's phrase "the handmaiden of Villainy, Courtesy." The count, our villain, contains conventionalized yet exaggerated characteristics of the masculine:*[23] uncontrolled sexual desire and uncivilized brutality and aggression toward women. Yet also striking is his association with the feminine. Not only does he sport an elongated cigarette holder, enjoy perfume, and wear, as one woman noted, "a middy blouse," but his polite and mannerly attentions to the American wife are posited as the source of his attraction, as opposed to Hughes's ineptness, described in one parody as "the American Ambassador eating with his knife, and offering his royal host a quill tooth-pick." This satirical representation is blunt in more ways than one. Fur-thermore, courtesy is defined as a "handmaiden," as feminine. The vio-lence of the abrogation of these oppositions within the single site of the count renders his figure monstrous and alien. Thus, while this disturbs sexual differences, it also unsettles sexual desire and preference. Mrs. Hughes, a representative for American women, is now placed in the posi-tion of desiring a gendered "maleness" at least partially linked to a social-ized femininity. A submerged homosexuality lies barely beneath the textual surface.

Additionally, the expectation that American ambassadors ought, like-wise, to display such mannerly and mannered attributes—so that they are not "jackasses"—simultaneously sets up a standard that would "feminize" them as well. Thus, although Count Karamzin's *body* is not feminized, as is Valentino's, *attributes* of his personality are, and these are represented as provoking women's desires, both internal and external to the film.

As a consequence of the combination of Karamzin as masculine and feminine but also "foreign" and desirable, "foreignness" assumes connota-tions beyond designations related to national origin. Apparently, viewers of the period were interpreting these films such that American women de-sired "non-Americans," a confrontation not only to sexual ruling norms but, then, to political ones as well. In fact, redistributions of the meaning of *foreign* go so far as to delete more obvious definitions. In *Photoplay*'s July 1922 issue, "A Motion Picture Dictionary" satirically defines *foreigner*: "Foreigner, *n*. (1) A villain; a *gonof*; a professional seducer. (2) Anyone who gesticulates excitedly and shrugs his shoulders when talking."[24] In-triguingly, neither definition (1) nor (2) attributes any significance to place of birth. Instead, villainy and trickery practiced against women are treated as synonyms in the first set of connotations. Thus, the definition likely displays subconscious, alternative, but powerful organizations of se-mantic fields, and their revisions relate to contemporary film representa-tions and their historical reception. While secondary movie characters might fit definition (2), surely the protagonists played by von Stroheim and Valentino were sources for connotation (1).

As compelling figures within American discursive fields, these stars may have confused other primary notions operating in political semantics. The American/foreign (European) opposition, associated with a naive/deca-dent combination, is common in turn-of-the-century "high literature," such as in works by Henry James and Edith Wharton. Thus, I am not claiming anything about sources for these arrangements of meaning, but their political and sexual implications for a reception of *Foolish Wives* do seem pertinent for explaining the vehemence of some male reviewers' interpretations and evaluations. Once the sign "foreign" reverses its meaning from "undesirable" to "desirable," then struggle for control (or recontrol) of meaning occurs. Thus, not only is "masculine/feminine" (and "heterosexual/homosexual") under seige but so is "us/other."

Yet defining "foreignness" is further confused when it is connected to the perceived national, ethnic, or racial origin of the two stars. The populace of the period were particularly paranoid about Southern European and East Asian immigration, while Teddy Roosevelt worried about an Anglo-Saxon "race suicide." Writers associate Von Stroheim with a Germanic heritage*25 and consider Valentino as "Latin," "Roman," or even "oriental." Thus, von Stroheim becomes a *undesired* Anglo-Saxon while Valentino is a *desired* Mediterranean. The "proper" distribution of the evaluations to the ethnicities should have been the opposite. Perhaps this is also a factor contributing to the problem of *Foolish Wives*.

Thus, oppositions historically structuring the semantical fields of gender identity, sexual preference, nationality, and ethnicity have been confused by Count Karamazin and textual systems in *Foolish Wives*. All of these semantical fields assume the ability to define reality through a stable arrangement of terms and their values. However, a threat to assuring meaning is the possibility of "theatricality," which places in crisis the meanings of a discursive structure since a signified cannot be read off from its signifier. As Hansen discusses it, Valentino's metaphorical "theatricality" plays a crucial role in some women's identification with Valentino and the protagonists he played. "Theatricality" is slightly different for *Foolish Wives*. Unlike the Valentino films that involve an exchange encompassing the viewer (directly, or via a character in the film with whom a viewer might identify), in *Foolish Wives* the character of Karamzin is literally theatrical. The count may be in some sort of mixed cross-dress (his middy blouse and cigarette holder), but he is also an actor, with his coterie of fake aristocratic female relatives. Significantly, however, in contrast to the Valentino characters, Karamzin's *theatricality* is the site of his villainous threat, not part of what might encourage identification. But the masquerade that he takes on is what lures women to him.

Consequently, variations from the case of Valentino occur, but several tropes (homosexuality, sadism and masochism, theatricality) still provoke desire and scandal. Additionally, the variety of male and female responses to *Foolish Wives* suggests that the attribution or denial of "villainy" to *Foolish Wives* calls out at another level a replay of the threat of a contested sign, one having different meanings for various political groups, and sexual addresses for men and women. For if classes struggle over social value judgments, so do all constructed categories, such as American and foreign, male and female, masculine and feminine, heterosexual and homosexual.

What the case of *Foolish Wives* illustrates for reception studies of American film history is that studying available responses to a particular film requires attention, not only to the film itself, but as much or more so to concurrent texts (both internal and external to the genre), as well as to interpretive strategies. Response is a result of textual and contextual determinants.

Furthermore, the spectator cannot be generalized into some idealized subject, devoid of networks of sexual, cultural, political, ethnic, racial, cognitive, and historical differences. Such versions of idealized readers fall into the fallacy of assuming meaning resides in the text rather than in the relations of spectators and films across history and differences. Although hegemonic notions of what reality is and institutionalized versions of how to produce meaning, as well as widespread constructions of individuals as subjects, may provide some limits, spectators do sometimes resist, producing meaning at least in part at odds with dominant patterns. In fact, some signs may become contested sites of battle over expectation, address, and interpretation. While making generalizations is important in historical and critical work, these must not too readily yoke any features to particular constructed categories of the human person. For *Foolish Wives*, the scandal of the film displays the complexity, and explodes the permanency, of binary oppositions.

CHAPTER SEVEN

The Birth of a Nation:
Reconsidering Its Reception

IN AUGUST 1978, the Ku Klux Klan of Oxnard, California, exhibited *The Birth of a Nation* as a fund-raiser and membership promotion. A militant communist splinter group, the Progressive Labor party, counterdemonstrated. And local Mexican-American and black associations protested against both camps. Tempers were hot and eventually violence broke out.[1] Once again, sixty-three years after its first turbulent showings, the 1915 film *The Birth of a Nation* had precipitated a ferocity and wrath sufficient to provoke men and women into a physical response.

One of my questions about the reception of *The Birth of a Nation* is why this film continues to outrage individuals. While the subject matter itself is probably sufficient as a solution to this problem, I would offer the thesis that *The Birth of a Nation* is encrusted with a history of responses and debates which make it a symbol of more than racist propaganda. At least for two decades, diatribes against it and defenses of its director play out major political battles in leftist politics as well as important debates in the history of film scholarship. Consequently, the continuing history of the reception of *The Birth of a Nation* can be considered as a nodal point for analyzing conditions of reception as they relate to evaluating subject matter and narrational techniques, positing effects of movies, and, ultimately, revealing racial attitudes and political positions of a film's opponents and defenders.

Specifically, although the 1915 reception of *The Birth of a Nation* can be organized around interpretations related to the question of racism—in which one can construct a complex continuum of reactions labeled by Joel Williamson as liberal to radical conservatism,[2] in the late 1930s, another continuum transforms the conditions for the film's subsequent reception. This second continuum can be associated with the contemporary political crisis of the European war for leftist radicals. Here the dynamics shift from, on the one hand, according to Communist party members, accusations of the film's complicity with capitalism's exploitation of workers and blacks to, on the other hand, defenses of the film by some leftists breaking from the party line. These defenses include attacking the film's critics as "totalitarians." Consequently, the race issue per se is reconfigured, intersecting with debates over the political economy and arguments about evaluating films and other cultural products of that political economy. As I suggested in Part One, the popular representation of the reception of a film becomes one of the conditions for its subsequent reception. First, a bit of context before I move to an analysis of the history of the film's reception.

THE HISTORICAL SETTING

Most film scholars are somewhat familiar with events surrounding the initial distribution of *The Birth of a Nation*. Thomas Cripps notes that the film appeared as conditions for African Americans were deteriorating. Despite its progressivism in some areas of social action, Woodrow Wilson's presidency was perceived by blacks as a resurgence of "Southern ideals"; black people were denied the ballot box; Jim Crow laws were expanding; and between 1898 and 1908, race riots occurred in Wilmington (North Carolina), New York City, New Orleans, Atlanta, and Springfield (Illinois). However, African-American leadership and consciousness had also "sharpened."*3 Although from the mid-1890s, Booker T. Washington was assumed by many to represent the voice of African Americans, extensive violence by white racist extremists during the same time provoked alternative strategies. W.E.B. Du Bois specifically began to stand out after 1903, with his published attack on Washington's leadership. In 1905, Du Bois organized the Niagara Falls Conference, assaulting accommodationism and promoting a nascent "black is beautiful" campaign. In 1909, the Niagara movement and northern white liberals formed the National Association for the Advancement of Colored People (NAACP), which by 1914 had six thousand members in various cities.*4

African Americans on the west coast began to protest against *The Birth of a Nation* once they were aware that the film was to be based on Thomas Dixon's play, *The Clansman*.5 In 1905, Dixon combined two of his novels, *The Leopard's Spots* (1902) and *The Clansman* (1905), into dramatic form and began a theatrical road tour. At that time, however, Dixon's extreme racism was not widely acceptable, even in the South. Joel Williamson in *The Crucible of Race* argues that the recent race riots produced repercussions. For various reasons, including public safety, after 1906 few individuals encouraged representing blacks as beasts and advocating their deportation in order to achieve national unity and security—two extremely radical-conservative positions taken by Dixon.6 Williamson argues that from 1880 through 1920, three "mentalities" exist in southern thinking about people of color. The "liberal" believed in the black's possibilities. Perhaps the oldest, the "conservative," presumed inferiority but was willing to permit these people in their "place." The "radical conservative" (which Williamson argues emerges in 1889 and appears through 1915 and in which category Williamson places Dixon) thought that the "'new' negro" was regressing into savagery. For this mentality, the paranoia over interracial sex (through rape or marriage) was a fear of the possible "perverted" offspring. As Thomas Gassett expresses it, "If a black has white intermixture, he is especially dangerous. White intermixture, Dixon thought, improved the intellect of blacks without changing their morals."*[7] Dixon was not, however, unique in his opinions (and many may have held them more quietly). For example, in 1907, Benjamin R. Tillman, a U.S. senator from South Carolina, defended the South's repression of blacks by arguing that the evils of the Reconstruction era proved the inability of people of color to assume public roles, that they were inherently inferior, and that southern men needed to protect their women. Tillman claimed that black militiamen were overheard to say: "The President is our friend. The North is with us. We intend to kill all the white men, take the land, marry the white women, and then these white children will wait on us."[8] Nor was radical-conservative racism confined to the South. In 1916, New York City anthropologist Madison Grant in *The Passing of the Great Race* claimed that racial "hybrids" were suicidal for the American.*[9] Dixon's two novels and play dramatized these beliefs. In 1906 in Philadelphia, blacks rioted over the play, with the effect that public safety claims were used to block some openings.[10] *The Clansman*, however, did continue to tour through the end of the decade.

One month prior to *The Birth of a Nation*'s opening in New York City, the NAACP chose the strategy of a nationwide protest against the film, hoping to prevent its exhibition on similar grounds of threat to the peace. This tactical choice produced conflicts among the NAACP's supporters since many of the association's white backers also tended to oppose censorship.[11] Furthermore, the film's technical virtuosity became a compensating feature to rationalize exhibiting the movie. Thus, any individual (then or now) might have conflicting or overdetermined views about *The Birth of a Nation* depending on that person's attitudes toward and judgments of its representation, its technical presentation, and censorship.

The NAACP did manage to delay several showings of the film, and some film review boards required changes. Although violence—such as throwing eggs at the screen—occurred,*[12] public safety alarmists were disarmed by the protesters' recognizing the long-term disadvantage of violent tactics. In an effort to "soften" the content, the film was edited, several intertitles were added, and the short-lived Hampton Institute epilogue was tacked on. Aggressive defenses by Dixon and D. W. Griffith also blocked opponents.*[13] I will return to these arguments momentarily.

Between 1915 and 1973 the right to screen *The Birth of a Nation* "was challenged at least 120 times."[14] Indeed, the strategy of the NAACP was to continue its opposition to the film anytime someone tried to revive it. In 1921 the NAACP petitioned the Boston mayor not to show it "because it is a malicious misrepresentation of the colored people, depicting them as moral perverts," while five people were arrested for picketing and protesting in New York City.[15] When *The Birth of a Nation* was to be rereleased with a sound track in 1930, the NAACP and others appealed to Will Hays and the Motion Picture Producers and Distributors Association to censor it, as they controlled sexual and criminal content, but no equivalency for racism was made.[16]

A reinforcement to protesters was apparent proof from social scientists that the film created attitudinal changes. When one of the 1933 Payne Fund studies screened *The Birth of a Nation* to 434 middle and high school students in a predominantly white Illinois town, the researchers determined the "largest effect found in any of the experiments we conducted."[17] The children's "favorable" opinion of African Americans dropped from a mean of 7.46 on a scale of 11 to 0 to 5.93, down 1.48 points. Testing five months later suggested only a partial return to the original views.

But it was later in that decade when a radical transformation in the implications of the film's interpretation and evaluation occurred among a political subculture in the United States. One's view of *The Birth of a Nation* became not only a litmus test of one's attitudes or beliefs about races, censorship, and aesthetics but also about the contemporary international political scene. The film became encrusted with debates and accusations exchanged between party-line Communists and anti-Stalinists.

THE INITIAL RECEPTION OF
THE BIRTH OF A NATION

To clarify the complexities and ironies of positions that were to be taken in the late 1930s, when Communists appropriated the film as a symptom of fascist and monopoly capitalist ideologies, I want to summarize the debates of the midteens since they reappear in the later discussions.*[18] The comparison between these periods valuably illuminates the complexities and contradictions that this transformation produces.

When *The Birth of a Nation* was originally exhibited, reviewers uniformly praised the presentation of the subject matter, separating off the narrational techniques (i.e., style) from what was being represented. (This "form/content" split is typical of reviewing of the period and is due most immediately to nineteenth-century aesthetics.) The writers then varied: some thought the representations were accurate; others were neutral; some ignored the issue; and the rest regretted or challenged what they saw. Numerous attacks on the subject matter were marshaled, but for the sake of brevity, five may be delineated as major themes. The most obvious indignity was that the film distorted and consequently falsified the history of the Reconstruction era. Within this theme were subroutines: the facts were inaccurate or the examples were not representative of the whole history. Second, and related to the fabrication of history attack, was the assertion that the film misrepresented the character of blacks both as individual people and as a race. In particular, reviewers noted that the only people of color shown were either bestial or subservient to whites. As the *Crisis* put it, "The Negro [is] represented either as an ignorant fool, a vicious rapist, a venal and unscrupulous politician or a faithful but doddering idiot."*[19]

A third theme was that the film glorified crime, specifically lynching. Writers pointed out ironies and contradictions following from that: pictures showing murder and robbery were routinely censored. Furthermore, whites were willing to suppress by law boxing pictures in which blacks beat whites, but they would not stop the exhibition of *The Birth of a Nation*. Specifically, the 1912 Sims act preventing interstate transportation of boxing films was enacted after the heavyweight champion, John Arthur "Jack" Johnson, who was black, kept beating white contenders. In 1910, when Johnson defeated Jim Jeffries, at least eighteen blacks were killed in the fight's aftermath, which reinforced sentiment for the passage of the federal bill.[20]

Fourth, opponents argued that the film incited prejudices against people of color, having an immoral effect or threatening public peace (as its predecessor *The Clansman* had done). Finally, *The Birth of a Nation* taught the doctrine that African Americans should be removed from the United States, a doctrine undemocratic, unchristian, and unlawful.

Defenders of *The Birth of a Nation* did not directly respond to all of the opponents' themes, and they introduced ones of their own. Griffith and Dixon both argued that the historical representation was accurate. Griffith wrote in 1915 that to show the history of the West one would have to "show the atrocities committed by the Indians against the whites."[21] Dixon appealed to the argument that historical accounts are variable since they are based on perspectives. At another point he claimed historical truth based on popular consensus: the film "expresses the passionate faith of the entire white population of the South. If I am wrong, they are wrong. The number of white people in the South who differ from my views of the history of Reconstruction could be housed on a half-acre lot [*sic*]."[22]

Regarding the accusation of a biased representation of blacks, Dixon, Griffith, and others claimed that the film authentically depicted the character of blacks during the Reconstruction era, if not now. Furthermore, the film not only portrayed bad people of color but also praised good ones who protected their former masters. Thus, the representation was balanced.

Defenders attacked their opponents in three ways. They argued that artistic and dramatic merit justified the film's exhibition, that their opposition was stifling free speech, and that those who wanted the film banned supported interracial marriages. This last theme was particularly promoted by Dixon, but even Griffith writes, "The attack of the organized opponents to this picture is centered upon that feature of it which they deem might become an influence against the intermarriage of blacks and whites."[23]

Among the approximately sixty reviews and articles studied, no extrinsic reasons for alignment with one position or another were discernible; for example, there were no consistencies from a regional perspective. Although Russell Merritt writes, "Most of the audience that came out of the [Boston] Tremont theatre that night in 1915 . . . believed Griffith's story was historically true,"[24] other northerners were not of that opinion, with many of them leading the attack on the film. Dixon claimed he presented "the passionate faith of the entire white population of the South."[25] This view is somewhat supported by John Hammond Moore's survey of South Carolina's reviews. Moore found that the state's papers about-faced from their 1905 denunciation of Dixon's *The Clansman*. When the play toured, reviewers took issue with the historical accuracy of the thesis, chastised the Ku Klux Klan for getting out of hand, and opposed the themes of blacks as beasts and the need to transport them out of the United States. *The Birth of a Nation* received no similar objections, with "almost unanimous approval" of the film.*[26] However, the white arrested for throwing eggs at the New York Liberty Theater presentation claimed, "I am a Southerner and a libertarian, and I believe in the education and uplifting of the negro. It made my blood boil to see the play and I threw the eggs at the screen."[27]

The lack of a coherent regional response is scarcely surprising since racism occurs throughout the United States. While a more systematic analysis of opinions might reveal patterns associated with sectors of the nation, Williamson's observation of at least three southern "mentalities" (liberal, conservative, and radical-conservative) during the 1880–1920s seems reconfirmed by this study although these mentalities may be more national than regional. Furthermore, from today's perspective, even the 1880–1920s liberal mentality is scarcely a nonracist attitude.

For these 1915 spectators of *The Birth of a Nation*, besides the questions of causes or types of racism, it is important to consider the complications of assumptions about the possible effects of watching movies and social responses to that possibility. While turn-of-the-century reformers operated on the assumption that a scientific study of society and humans provided the basis for policy-making, many also steered away from overt censorship. The National Board of Review, the film industry's voluntary self-regulation system, merely advised film companies about subject matter (although local boards with legal powers could require changes). Confronted by this film, many opponents argued that portions of the film could have real behavioral effects, stimulating or changing preexistent attitudes in directions unfavorable to social harmony. On the basis of actual experiences following theatrical productions, they tried to argue that *The Birth of a Nation* was a threat to public peace. While defenders did not disagree with the position that films could be causal forces, they stressed First Amendment rights of free speech—a widely accepted discourse considered an idea fundamental to the preservation of the United States. As a constructed characteristic of the identity of "American," "free speech" serves as a centering notion against which non-American positions are positioned as dangerous. Opponents to *The Birth of a Nation* could only argue, *not* that the defenders were wrong, but that the film threatened public peace, which might be more important than free speech. This prediction of danger, however, was a hard claim to prove since violence was very local and sporadic.

Placing positions of free speech versus public safety in a continuum of political persuasions (liberal to conservative) is impossible, given the historical variations on this debate. Witness, for example, the 1989 U.S. Supreme Court decision that burning the American flag is acceptable as a form of political expression. Judges labeled in 1989 as "liberal" and "conservative" show up on both sides of the judgment, as do individuals in the subsequent furor over amending the Constitution to prohibit such an act. For the analysis of *The Birth of a Nation*, however, the implications of the differing positions need to be stressed, if not labeled. Everyone agreed that films had some type of effect, but not everyone concurred as to the relative merits of solutions in balance with possible compensating values (e.g., free speech and a widely accepted aesthetic quality). Legal actions related to society's needs were in conflict, but everyone recognized that this film pushed the question to a certain limit. That racist (from today's perspective) material was eventually tolerated is not indicative of a social decision that free speech overrides filmic effects. After all, legal and semilegal apparatus (mainstream industry agreements not to compete in subject areas that might provoke the retaliation of pressure groups) did censor subject matter related to certain types of criminal behavior and sexuality. Thus, one conclusion is that either racism was perceived as less menacing than that other subject matter, or it was in the interest of those in positions of authority to permit an amount of racist representation up to the borderline of the tolerable (relative to the counterthreat of suppression of opinion).

However you understand these conditions, a significant factor in the reception of *The Birth of a Nation* in 1915 is the political and racist underpinnings of social policy in relation to the film's representation and effectivity.

Thus, the initial reception of *The Birth of a Nation* constitutes what might be called a generic reaction quite understandable within the contradictions of the period's social formation. While I might draw out numerous other discursive strands within the individual essays relating them to their historical contexts, the dominant points involve an agreement that subject matter and narrational procedures could be judged separately, but differences existed over evaluating subject matter and its potential effects on spectators. Here tacit race attitudes intersect with other beliefs—ones about what constitutes acceptable historiography; whether a film should be judged on the content or effects of its subject matter, narrational procedures, or some combination of them; and whether censorship of certain representations is more important than free speech. All three of these issues still concern scholars and citizens today, making these aspects of the reception of *The Birth of a Nation* constant across a stretch of seventy-five years.

A TRANSFORMATION OF THE RECEPTION OF
THE BIRTH OF A NATION

In the late 1930s, themes from the 1915 period would reoccur, but other revisions are indications of how historical change and political perspectives influence argumentation about films. As events in Europe and the Soviet Union altered the political strategies and alliances of the American radical Left, *The Birth of a Nation* continued to be an exemplary case in film studies for issues of socially acceptable representations of U.S. racial minorities, procedures of response against some subject matter, and systems of evaluating narrational procedures and possible audience effects.

In 1936 Richard Watts published in the leftist journal *New Theatre and Film* a commentary on Griffith that criticized *The Birth of a Nation*'s "cruel unfairness to the Negro." Three years later, Lewis Jacobs published his history *The Rise of the American Film*, concluding that "the film was a passionate and persuasive avowal of the inferiority of the Negro. In viewpoint it was, surely, narrow and prejudiced." But in December 1939, David Platt went further. Writing for the Communist party newspaper, the *Daily Worker*, Platt argued that *The Birth of a Nation*, "by creating racial prejudice, helped create the basis for war [World War I] propaganda." Furthermore, the resurrection of the Ku Klux Klan, aided by the film, worked to harass African Americans to participate in the First World War effort.[28]

Now, this argument may need some context. From the early 1930s, but particularly from 1939 until the end of the Hitler-Stalin pact, the *Daily Worker* took an antiwar stance. Part of that project was an appeal to individuals such as blacks to see the European events not from a nationalist perspective but from one of class. This was not their fight since it was not that of any member of the working class; neither capitalists in the United States nor fascists in Germany were the blacks' friends. In early 1940, the *Daily Worker* and its supporters participated with blacks in picketing theaters reviving *The Birth of a Nation*.*[29]

Platt's act had a tradition in marxist aesthetic criticism: demonstrating the complicity of a film or literary text with capitalist goals was a well-established approach to art evaluation and the activation of political sensibilities. Furthermore, after 1915 *The Birth of a Nation* had been continually criticized for its racism by individuals not all of whom were particularly aligned with radical-Left politics. For instance, in 1938 in *Current History*, V. F. Calverton published an outstanding analysis of the historiographical problems of the film, pointing out "its inaccuracies, exaggerations, and historical indecencies and distortions."[30]

In February 1940, Platt continued his assault, printing a series of seven articles reviewing the representation of blacks in Hollywood and painstakingly developing the thesis that Hollywood, in cooperation with capitalist interests, "deliberately and carefully fostered" prejudice "to divide Negro and white and rule both." Citing the 1933 Payne Fund Studies and evidence of an increase in lynching in 1915, Platt implied that the film was directly responsible for changes in attitude and behavior.[31]

Whether because of a personal change in politics, a response to Platt's articles, or another cause, Seymour Stern took up in 1940 the defense of the film. Stern was to claim later that articles he wrote in 1940 "provoked a bitter reaction": "former friends and acquaintances ceased to be such." Writing for the socialist and, in his words, "anti-Stalinist" *New Leader*, Stern accused "Negro leaders and left-wing liberals" of attacking Griffith as being "anti-Negro." He went on to claim that after Platt's February *Daily Worker* articles, growing evidence indicated "a well-organized, underground boycott campaign against 'The Birth of a Nation,'" a "campaign of boycott and terrorism." "Several days [after Platt's articles], Communist Party agents and stooges from innocent-front organizations, who had gotten wind of the proposed revival [of *The Birth of a Nation*], visited the manager of the theatre and proceeded to terrorize him in much the same manner as the alleged clansmen in the picture terrorized Negroes."[32] The *New Leader*'s editorial note accompanying Stern's essay said that the article was

the first of a short series on Communist activity in the movie business, [which] shows how, in accordance with the new Stalinite [*sic*] line on the

Negroes, the caviar comrades are trying to suppress the showing of "The Birth of a Nation." . . . The next articles by Seymour Stern, who has spent more than a decade in Hollywood writing motion picture scenarios, will reveal the Communist ramifications in the Museum of Modern Art Film Library and in the documentary [filmmaking] field.*[33]

The Dies Committee was already investigating Hollywood for communists when this invective appeared.

What is happening becomes, in retrospect, ironic and sad. For Stern *and* Platt, along with Lewis Jacobs and Harry Alan Potamkin, had started the 1930s on a high and cooperative note. In 1930, these four individuals were cofounders and editors of *Experimental Cinema*, an early progressive film journal.*[34] However, several factors during the decade were to split these people and their associates into bitter factions.

Among the most significant of these factors were debates by leftists over the connections between literature and social or political policy, the appropriate roles of artists concerning approved party aesthetic policies, and the analysis of subject matter and narrational procedures. The vicissitudes of radical progressive thought in the 1930s about these concerns are extensive and complex. In only the most general terms, in the 1920s, marxists equated "good art with successful propaganda" but considered aesthetic experimentation permissible. Liberals such as Stark Young at the *New Republic* or Joseph Wood Krutch at the *Nation* dissented from that view, emphasizing internal structure and personal responses over content. This judgment reversed in the next decade. By the mid-1930s, splits among leftists developed over the artists' responsibilities to people, given the crisis of the depression. Could artists afford to detach themselves or their art from social communication? Richard Pells argues that Edmund Wilson's *Axel's Castle* (1931) participates in laying the groundwork for the need to communicate with people, developing the thesis that the symbolists and avant-gardists unconsciously absorbed the worst features of bourgeois individualism: intense subjectivity was inappropriate. Not all radicals agreed.[35]

Another factor, most important at the end of the decade and interpenetrating with aesthetic and cultural theory, was artists' increasing disenchantment with the Communist party as it changed policies during the 1930s. Daniel Aaron argues that the execution of Nicola Sacco and Bartolomeo Vanzetti in August 1927 mobilized many liberals into more radical politics. Furthermore, the depression deepened individuals' beliefs that capitalism was a bankrupt economic system. But after 1937, Stalinism began to seem as threatening as European fascism. The causes for this shift included the purges, dissatisfaction with party policies during the Spanish Civil War, and the blow of the Hitler-Stalin Pact on 23 August 1939, followed by Germany's invasion of Poland a week later. It should not be surprising that conservatives and even liberals attacked Bolshevik marxists at this point, but progressives such as socialists did as well. Max Nomad in the *New Leader* proceeded to redefine allies and enemies: "'The Socialist system of collective ownership is compatible with totalitarianism,'" he wrote in January 1941.[36]

Experimental Cinema started publication in 1930. Its initial and consistent stance in favor of Soviet cinema was, as George Amberg put it, "in 1930, . . . implicitly involved [in] a taking of sides, if not a political commitment. The position adopted and advocated by *Experimental Cinema* was unequivocally socialist."*[37] However, in 1934 a "bitter dispute" among the journal's staff and supporters developed. The communist Workers' International Relief commissioned Stern and the editors of *Experimental Cinema* to make a film dealing with exploitation of Mexican migrant workers in Imperial Valley, California. Eighteen thousand feet of film were exposed, which the Workers' International Relief claimed publicly in the *Daily Worker* comprised mostly arty shots of cantaloupes. Stern responded that *Experimental Cinema* wanted an "artistic achievement as well as a piece of agitative propaganda." Furthermore, in the same (and to-be-last) issue of *Experimental Cinema* with Stern's justification appeared a tribute to Potamkin, who had recently died. Samuel Brody, writing in the *Daily Worker*, criticized *Experimental Cinema* for printing the tribute, since *Experimental Cinema* had disagreed with Potamkin's aesthetics. Brody wrote that in the previous three years divergent roads had been taken: "Potamkin Leftwards, E. C. to the Right."[38]

In early 1935, *Experimental Cinema*'s major support, the Workers Film and Photo League, broke up, and members adopted variant positions regarding politics and aesthetics. Jacobs remained independent in the far Left. Platt joined the *Daily Worker* as a staff writer, as well as working for other communist cultural publications. Stern continued on as a filmmaker and writer. His articles reflect his taking the position that judgments about aesthetics and narrational procedures were separable from those about subject matter and representation. Later, Stern became a strong anti-Stalinist while defending Griffith and *The Birth of a Nation*.

Given the political and personal context, Stern's 1940 vituperative response to Platt's strongly worded attack—Platt's charge that *The Birth of a Nation* as reactionary and racist—set off an escalation of charges and countercharges that would continue for the next fifteen years and beyond as Stern took on more critics of Griffith. Somewhere along the line Sergei Eisenstein's name must have been invoked, for in January 1941, Eisenstein telegraphed the *Daily Worker* to deny that he had praised *The Birth of a Nation*. His aesthetic choice was clear: "The disgraceful propaganda of racial hatred toward colored people which permeates this film cannot be redeemed by purely cinematographic effects in this production." Eisenstein also refers to his forthcoming article about "the interrelation between Soviet Cinema and the 'old man' of American films," most likely meaning his "Dickens, Griffith, and the Film Today" (1944). There Eisenstein argues that narrational procedures are isomorphically related to ideological development.[39]

In 1946, Peter Noble published "A Note on an Idol" in *Sight and Sound*. Noble accused Griffith of being "a pioneer of prejudice," albeit he was also a pioneer of technique. Noble's reading of the film is extreme, exceeding any 1915 account that I found. He describes Silas Lynch as attempting to rape Elsie Stoneman, whereas initial spectators saw Lynch as violently forcing her to marry him. Additionally, Noble describes Gus as "frothy-mouthed" in his pursuit of Flora.[40] (Every 1915 review did assume though that Gus intended to rape Flora Cameron.)

In the following *Sight and Sound* issue, both Griffith and Stern reply. Griffith writes that "my attitude towards the Negroes has always been one of affection and brotherly feeling. I was partly raised by a lovable old Negress down in old Kentucky." He also claims that the film was historically accurate. Stern begins his response with what can only be considered Red-baiting, given the political climate at that time. He compares Noble's remarks to the pre–World War II "anti-Griffith libel issued periodically, and often in the identical phrases, from certain political publications in the U.S.A and the U.S.S.R." Stern then proceeds to argue and expand upon many of the themes that appeared in the 1915 defenses. *The Birth of a Nation* is historically accurate. In fact, Stern claims that it is based on Woodrow Wilson's *History of the American People*. He accuses Noble of basing his analysis on Jacobs's history of American film, a book filled with "errors, falsehoods and fanciful misinterpretations of American film in general and Griffith and his work in particular."[41]

The second theme is the representation of blacks. The villains in the movie are not "the uneducated and newly-freed Negroes but the *doctrines* of certain fanatical and vengeful Northern whites, who duped the Negroes with glittering promises of wealth and power."*[42] Moreover, the film shows good as well as bad African Americans: "In racial hatred, race is race, black is black, and there can be no exceptions."

Stern makes three additional observations. For one, he compares the South during the Reconstruction era to France and Norway during the Nazi occupation. Resorting to reading by allegory, Stern suggests that the South is rejecting the "totalitarianism" of northern radicals (e.g., Stoneman/Thadeus Stevens): "*The Birth of a Nation* exposes the ideology and tactics of a revolutionary movement; it dramatises the defeat of this movement by a counter-revolution, the leaders and protagonists of which are the people themselves." By paralleling northern carpetbagger politics to fascist totalitarianism and, eventually, to Stalinism, Stern makes *The Birth of a Nation* express liberal, democratic doctrines.

Additionally, Stern explains that it is communist propaganda to call Griffith a pioneer of prejudice:

> [Noble] is, of course, merely echoing in strangely familiar accents and phrases the astounding falsehoods and unbelievable nonsense on the subject which already have poured in volume from the presses of the N.Y. "Daily Worker," the "New Masses," the defunct "Friday" and "New Theatre," or from such specious and shockingly misleading politico-economic tracts as "The Rise of the American Film."

In this list, Stern ignores several decades of African-American protests. Finally, Stern counters the leftist claims that films have effects. He writes: "Surely Mr. Noble cannot but know that films do not start attitudes or trends in political or social relations; they merely *reflect* them."

The debates continued for several issues in *Sight and Sound*. In 1948 Noble published a monograph, *The Negro in Films*, only slightly modifying his stance. And in 1950, V. J. Jerome, considered a mainstream Communist, wrote *The Negro in Hollywood Films*—a sophisticated analysis of the ideology of racism in American films.[43]

Stern continued his defense of Griffith, admitting that the man's films had some faults but maintaining a spirited attack centered on communism and Stalinism as the source of Griffith's troubles. In 1949, as the U.S. Congress stepped up its repression of left-wing radicals and sent the Hollywood Ten to prison, Stern dates the "'official'" start of the marxist attack on Griffith as 1940, when "the would-be cultural dictators of the Left—the new generation of Marxist film critics and self-styled film 'historians'" tried to destroy Griffith, who "stands in challenging and diametric opposition to contemporary Marxist-Stalinist ideological values." He expands this theme in 1956, publishing "The Cold War against David Wark Griffith," where he asserts that Communists also manipulate film scholarship: "Since the Communist movement is as much an ideological and cultural conspiracy as it is an economic, military and political one, it is not surprising Communists the world over devote considerable time and energy to influencing, and controlling, film criticism and history." Stern's position mellows somewhat in the 1965 number of *Film Culture*, in which Jonas Mekas gives over the issue to Stern's wealth of material about *The Birth of a Nation*.[44] If the film was not one already appropriated by Communists as a cause célèbre, Stern's attacks gave it to them.

Readings of *The Birth of a Nation*'s reception have traditionally been structured by the axes of region (North versus South) and racial attitude (liberal versus racist). This reconsideration has extended the film's reception into history, refusing to assume that the conditions for reception are restricted to the context of the film's original exhibition. I believe that historicizing the reception of *The Birth of a Nation* transforms the text's polysemy, for the political foundation underlying some of the historical debates becomes more apparent. In the film's later reception, racial attitudes are not autonomous effects; they relate to the political agendas of the debaters, causing strange alliances in which a former progressive defends the film using much of the rhetoric and arguments of 1915 radical conservatives. Additionally, complex theoretical questions such as the relation of subject matter and narrational procedures or possible effects of films and the consequences of those effects for social policy (censorship versus free speech) are lost to name-calling and a hardening of lines among the combatants. Consequently, this "encrustation" of the history of *The Birth of a Nation*'s reception has a double implication. For while the conditions for interpreting the film now include those years of political antagonisms, the "crust" that surrounds that interpretation also prevents a clear perception of what was once, and is still, at stake in the evaluation of the movie.

For *The Birth of a Nation* is not a simple problem. Its racism is obvious; its significance in the development of narrational procedures is also apparent. Following codes (or schemata) developed from the aesthetics of the nineteenth century, if not earlier, film histories have separated subject matter and narrational procedures, "content" and "form"; viewers have too.*[45] However, what aesthetic, social, and political theories vie in promoting or refusing to accept this separation? For these aesthetics have been sites of contestation. Additionally, how does social policy connect to this question? What are the merits of free-speech-versus-censorship debates?

Currently, these difficulties still face film scholars. Racism appears in numerous films (for example, the *Indiana Jones* and *Star Wars* series). So do all sorts of abhorrent representations of gender, sexual preference, ethnicity, nationality, and class. But the plea for free speech over censorship, the ambiguities of claims of effect, and the shifting vicissitudes of interpretation in relation to historical political contexts make any final evaluation difficult. Consequently, in any historical instance of the reception of a film, particularly ones not so obvious as *The Birth of a Nation*, some moments of that sequence of determining meaning and significance to an individual may be progressive; others, regressive; some may be subversive; others, reactionary. Labeling any single interpretive response as one thing or the other may be very difficult.

That a splinter group of the Communist party would protest the 1978 Ku Klux Klan screening of *The Birth of a Nation* is due to a forty-year history of progressive radicals' using that film as a nodal point for their argument that connections exist between racism and class exploitation and that the representations of films matter to social spectators. The act of defending the film's showing, however, does not automatically associate the proponent with the racists of 1915 or the Red-baiters of 1946, but defenders ought at least to be aware of that part of the encrustation surrounding *The Birth of a Nation*. Thus, the conditions for the continued reception of *The Birth of a Nation* are now very complicated.

CHAPTER EIGHT

The Logic of Alternative Readings:
A Star Is Born

IN REVIEWING the literature on reader-response speculation, Terry Beers points out that a major responsibility for theorists is explaining different readings of a single text.[1] Beers notes that, on the one hand, in "Interpreting the *Variorum*," Stanley Fish postulates that variant readings are due to people's belonging to different interpretive communities, with some overlap of conventions between one community and the next. Such a proposition, however, leads to a proliferation ad infinitum of communities. On the other hand, in his affective stylistics approach, Fish employs a normative-reader solution. This suggestion also has its difficulties, for it implies that those who do not read in the manner Fish describes as normative could be understood to be stigmatized as less than adequate readers. Beers continues the survey, detailing Jonathan Culler's and Steven Mailloux's "middle ground": different communities have accepted notions of competence in reading, and these conventions both explain and constrain variations among readings. While Beers believes this approach to be the best thesis provided so far, he offers an alternative solution. Using a schemata theory of reading, much like David Bordwell's cognitive psychology approach described in chapter 3, Beers believes that people read from an orientation influenced by specific goals. "Idiosyncratic" readings, Beers argues, are due to goals different from the normal.[2]

Indeed, a major responsibility for any research on historical reading formations is to account for variety. Moreover, however, variety that seems consistent within a group of individuals is an even more compelling problem, since that variation/conformity must have been achieved through some social and cultural practices which elicited a similar construction of goals and self-identities for people who consider themselves part of that group. As I pointed out in Part One, Elizabeth Ellsworth cues right into one possible explanation of the dynamics among individuals, groups, and texts: "Social groups use cultural forms in the process of defining themselves."[3] Conversely, I would argue, groups may interpret texts similarly but variably from the "normative" if in that process of self-definition they also construct schemata or interpretive communities or conventions to read cultural forms in ways related to that self-definition. Ellsworth's research particularly focuses on organized group processes such as consciousness-raising groups and feminist collectives. Yet, obviously, less formal, ad hoc groups exist that might also function in the same way.

What this chapter attempts to study is alternative reading processes—or at least one historical instance of such an activity. Its focus will be on *methods to reconstruct that history* more than on major revelations about interpretations. Others have noticed that some gay men have had a special attachment to Judy Garland. My questions are, What particular historical conditions permitted such an association? What effects did those contexts have on interpretive procedures for Garland's films? How can a historical materialist approach to reception studies contribute to verifying previous claims about gays and Garland? And, How do the reading strategies of a repressed group such as gay men in the 1950s compare with dominant interpretive procedures? Thus, I shall be building on the work of Richard Dyer, Joe McElhaney, and other scholars of gay reading formations. But to raise such questions requires a number of caveats prior to the study. These caveats include discussion of the issues of appellations regarding types of readings and categories of individuals.

CAVEATS AND CLARIFICATIONS

As discussed in chapter 3, numerous difficulties exist in segmenting readings into a continuum from preferred through negotiated to resisting. For one thing, it is sometimes hard to figure out which is which, since criteria for categorizing are undefined and many readings are so disunified that portions of the readings may represent all of the possibilities. Additionally, discourses and interpretive strategies in a social formation are likely contradictory. Does that put a reading that follows the dominant views and normative procedures into a preferred category? Or is the reading, as a reflection of the contradictions, already negotiated?

These issues have been raised by others at different junctures in reading research. One of the early and influential books polemicizing the act of interpretation was Judith Fetterley's *The Resisting Reader*, published in 1978. Fetterley states her thesis succinctly:

> Though one of the most persistent of literary stereotypes is the castrating bitch, the cultural reality is not the emasculation of men by women but the immasculation of women by men. As readers and teachers and scholars, women are taught to think as men, to identify with a male point of view, and to accept as normal and legitimate a male system of values one of whose central principles is misogyny.[4]

Her suggested first step in combating this status quo is to become a "resisting reader," by which she implies a self-consciousness about gender representations in texts and gender issues in responses. Such a self-consciousness has become central to gender studies to the point that a major strategy in feminist scholarship is teaching methods by which to recognize sexual and gender images and biases in representations. As Mary Crawford and Roger Chaffin suggest, reinforcing Beers and Ellsworth, "The development of a uniquely female viewpoint has been a major part of the work of the women's movement. To have a 'raised consciousness' is to have schemata for a woman's viewpoint."[5]

Despite this happy view, Crawford and Chaffin are quick to point out that such schemata are unlikely to be totally deviant from that against which they resist: "The standard, male, viewpoint on an experience might be viewed as a very high-level schema or set of schemata. Because the male viewpoint is diffuse and pervasive, neither men nor women can readily step in and out of it as they attempt to apprehend their experiences." Furthermore, "to discard it entirely would require an alternative schema," but "alternative viewpoints, according to muted group theory, are less well articulated, or they may not exist."[6] Resisting readers may resist, but can they totally resist?

Crawford and Chaffin's review of the literature reveals that in schemata-theory research, gender and gender-role identification studies show evidence of variant but not completely different procedures. Other writers support that thesis, even arguing as Annette Kolodny does that some *theories* of reading are themselves gender biased. She particularly targets Harold Bloom's idea of the anxiety of influence, that writers misread because of oedipal romances with their predecessor-fathers, a theory Kolodny considers founded upon ignoring that women have been excluded from "the Great Tradition."[7]

Of course, it is also not clear that every aspect of reading a hegemonic text is divisible along gender lines. Is following the hermeneutic code and postulating hypotheses about the ending necessarily contrary to a female or feminine point of view?*[8] Nor is it clear yet what constitutes a hegemonic or normative reading. But most important is that a negotiated or resisting reading may not indicate any progressive act at all. Negotiated and resisting readings may merely be evidence of an oppression by the dominant system. Such readings may be signs of class (or gender or racial) struggle, but the terms for resistance have still been set by those in power, those who produce preferred readings.

Because of the complexity of categorizing readings, alternative readings are to be understood neither as less than competent nor as irrational interpretive practices. One of the points of this chapter is to explicate the logic—historically and textually—for alternative readings, particularly ones shared by numerous individuals. As I hope I shall make obvious, rules and conventional procedures not unlike those for preferred readings likely operate in many nondominant receptions of films.

For the sake of this chapter, then, what I am going to count as preferred or hegemonic are readings taken from the mainstream press. I shall consider as alternative those that do not match. I shall not, however, attempt to label these alternative readings as negotiated or resisting. I shall also not attempt to characterize those alternative readings as conservative or progressive, particularly in this case since I do not believe that I am in the position to judge the politics of gay cultural life. Here and there I will indicate what others have argued, but my interest is in thinking through how to come to terms with the conditions as they have been produced. Trying to provide some procedures by which to understand the historical antecedents and practices is my contribution to discussions.

If considering what readings are called needs some cautionary remarks, more important, so too does categorizing individuals. As I indicated in chapters 3 and 4, post-structuralist theorizing of the individual suggests that how people construct their imaginary self is significant in an interpretive act. What imaginary self counts, though, is not an a priori categorization by a researcher but what seems valid to the individual experiencing the process of the textual moments. This issue has been elegantly argued by Richard Dyer regarding his 1977 monograph on the representation of gays in cinema:

> Since *Gays and Film* came out, some discussions of homosexuality have cast into doubt the validity of producing such a book. Broadly, these discussions centre on the very category "homosexual" itself. Work by, for example, Foucault, [Mary] McIntosh, and [Jeffrey] Weeks argues persuasively that while homosexual activity is universal, the category of persons called "homosexuals" is of relatively recent date in this culture. In this perspective, work which addresses itself to this category seems to be accepting a purely historical division of sexuality into hard and fast categories which cut across the fluidity of human sexuality.
>
> However, because a category is historically and socially constructed, it is not any less real. (All social constructions limit humanity, but they are also the only means by which we can be human at all.) "Homosexual" is an historical category by which people really live.

Dyer continues, taking a polemical stand that because of the "invisibility" of homosexuals, "some form of recognisable representational form is a political necessity for gay people."[9]

Given this, of course (and Dyer warns about this in his statement), the opposite procedure should not occur. Even if one represents one's self as homosexual, that imaginary construct is not all that a person may consider him- or herself to be. Two other individuals caution against misrecognitions that such a social construction might produce while pointing out the contradictory problem of being homosexual in a heterosexual society. Gerald Hannon writes:

I define myself as gay. I know life is broader than that, I know sexuality isn't everything, I *know* I'll spend only a minute fraction of my life making love: I've heard all the arguments. And yes, I read novels, I go to movies, enjoy photography but, damn it, it's because I'm gay that movies only infuriate me now with their endless variations on the same drab heterosexual themes, because I'm gay that much of my life is spent struggling for what so many take for granted.[10]

Ken Popert warns, "If we assume that we can spot all the messages relevant to gay people in [*Cruising*] or any other movie or book or song, then we are assuming that we know all there is to know about gay people, about ourselves."[11]

Each of these individuals implicitly foregrounds the fallacy of self-definition. Yet particular historical conditions may force those definitions to the forefront of self-consciousness. Political strategies of promulgating that self-definition—such as those advocated by some feminists and gays—may, indeed, promote self-consciousness as a weapon against repressive representations and their social and political consequences.[*12] Despite the political advantages, however, and as Dyer notes, sexuality and the existence of individuals are not limited to historical categories of gender or sexual preference or anything else.[13]

As I have developed throughout this book, receptions are dependent upon specific historical configurations. To focus here on gays' reception of Judy Garland is to encounter a real moment in which defining one's self as homosexual counts much in the contextual interaction. Let me stress that I have tried not to force any categorizations on events; rather, the foundation for this discussion is the fact that some individuals counted themselves as gay and that gayness was pertinent to their experiences. The same method, I would argue, ought to be applied in any study of group alternative readings.

GAYS AND GARLAND

Judy Garland died on 22 June 1969; in the same month, police raided a New York City gay bar, provoking the Stonewall riots. For American culture, this conjuncture of events marks a major break in gay history. Within one year, gay liberation groups existed in more than three hundred U.S. cities. If the politicization for homosexual rights may be symbolically marked by the events around one gay bar, Garland's passing is also illustrative: her life had special meaning for the previous generation of American gays.

The thread of this heritage is still retained in contemporary gay rights activities. As the *Advocate* reported, the Radical Faeries, "who see gays and lesbians as a distinct and separate people, with our own culture, way of becoming, and spirituality," gathered in August 1989, to "commemorate the 20th anniversary of the Stonewall riots and Judy Garland's funeral, seminal events in Faerie mythology."[14] Among the Garland iconography were a pair of ruby slippers and "a coffin blaring Judy's greatest hits." The same summer was also the fiftieth anniversary of *The Wizard of Oz*, which occasioned a nostalgic visit by *Advocate* reporter Kent Bakken to Garland's hometown in Grand Rapids, Minnesota, where a Judy Garland festival is held yearly by the townspeople.[15]

Debated among gays are the politics of retaining an interest in what for some contemporary homosexuals symbolizes a period of their repression. Other gays argue that such reminders are important for political consciousness and also as gestures toward brothers and sisters living under different historical circumstances.*[16] However, regardless of the range of political views about this retention of Garland iconography, gay history recognizes that Garland has mattered to many homosexuals. The questions have been, rather, What has Garland meant? How have gays interpreted her and the films in which she appeared?

Several researchers provide information about the significance of the Garland cult. In his "Camp and the Gay Sensibility," Jack Babuscio concludes a discussion about camp and theatricality by commenting that it is the intensity of a character's performance which seems to interest gay spectators, particularly when the performer can be understood to be expressing both a character and a personal experience. Babuscio notes that Garland especially figures in this arena for gays: "Garland's popularity owes much to the fact that she is always, and most intensely, herself." Additionally, "many of us seem able to equate our own strongly-felt sense of oppression (past or present) with the suffering/loneliness/misfortunes of the star both on and off the screen."[17]

As Dyer notes, what counts in explaining the Garland case is the degree to which gay men could associate her situation with their own. The premise, then, for an instance of association*[18] is this:

> What seems to be happening in such cases is a coming together of two homologous structures—a star image . . . and a way of interpreting homosexual identity that is widely available in society in both dominant and subcultural discourses. . . .
>
> There is nothing arbitrary about the gay reading of Garland; it is a product of the way homosexuality is socially constructed, without and within the gay subculture itself. It does not tell us what gay men are inevitably and naturally drawn to from some in-built disposition granted by their sexuality, but it does tell us of the way that a social-sexual identity has been understood and felt in a certain period of time.[19]

Dyer's emphasis on a founding recognition of sufficient similarity between the constructed star image and the constructed gay image is a tenet to be foregrounded. (I cannot stress too strongly here the difference between an actual individual and an image of an individual. Here and below I shall be stressing not what Garland or gays are, but how they are constructed in discourse.) Once such a recognition is in place, material means of perpetuating and disseminating that recognition might account for its wider existence, but Dyer points out that if the socially constructed images are homologous (or near enough), the connection does not necessarily need to be conscious.

Two points of structural similarity between images of Garland and gays are suggested by Babuscio: theatricality and oppression. But Babuscio's analysis takes on something of an ahistorical tone. He writes as though gays have a universal rather than historically specific sensibility, while Dyer underscores the importance of historical circumstances. He and another scholar, Joe McElhaney, have attempted to understand the Garland phenomenon as peculiar to an era.[*20]

However, both researchers depend on limited sources of information about gay views of Garland during the 1950s and 1960s, when the terms of the homology were developed and, perhaps, were most pertinent. Both rely on retrospective recollections by gay men. McElhaney uses as evidence his personal recollections as well as those of other gay men. Dyer placed a letter requesting responses in gay publications and sought out published remarks. However, as Dyer notes about his procedure, much of what he received from the solicitation and publications has to be understood in the circumstances of the changed political scene after 1969, when some sense of gay pride or liberation may have altered views of what Garland meant prior to that time.[*21]

Thus, on the one hand, McElhaney's and Dyer's findings are recognizably distorted. On the other hand, because of the repression of gay culture prior to 1969, traces of traditional attitudes are extremely difficult to find. After 1969, publications addressed explicitly to homosexual audiences start appearing (although, as Dyer notes, some journals were implicitly so directed prior to that time). In fact, perhaps one of the most pertinent records of gay views would be their own histories, but few of those histories exist in permanent form. Oral histories taken now would also be tinged with the changing perspectives. This difficulty with evidence applies to other groups similarly marginalized in society—even for women whose everyday lives, as others have noted, were not valued as worthy of the permanency implied by print or oral recordings.

It is not the case, however, that all traces and records are gone. One important source of information is not in documentary form but in fiction. During the 1940s, as I shall discuss below, gay literature began appearing,

as a break in oppressive attitudes seemed possible. This momentary opening, however, was quickly closed off when Joseph McCarthy and other
conservatives sought out not only communists but homosexuals as threats
to national security. However, circa 1945 to 1950, a number of fictional
representations incorporating gay men in a variety of narratives were published. Additionally, some individuals openly argued that gay rights were
as important as civil rights for blacks.

Consequently, what Dyer and McElhaney propose about gay views of
Judy Garland can possibly be checked against what evidence of gay images
is available from the period when the Garland cult began. Additionally,
moreover, Garland's contemporaneous image is somewhat available
through published publicity and news about her. Thus, after reviewing
McElhaney's and Dyer's information from recollections of gays' views of
Garland, I will compare their observations with an analysis of circa-1950
images of gays by gays and Garland's public representations. I will also
compare their views to those of the dominant popular press.

Thus, what I am contributing is a verification method for comparing
historically specific data with recollections gathered in later years. Although obviously this procedure is valuable mostly for groups of individuals still living, important possibilities exist for opening research on some
marginalized types of readers and interpretations. Interviewing women,
lesbians, blacks, Asians, Hispanics, and so forth might prove illuminating
if other secondary evidence can support the interpretive views remem-
bered. This is obviously a very traditional historical procedure turned to
the use of reception studies. Moreover, through subsequent comparison of
that group's views with those of another group, such as the popular press,
additional features about the alternative reading can be foregrounded.

What are the conclusions about gays' views of Garland postulated by
McElhaney and Dyer from their evidence? Both McElhaney and Dyer
agree with Babuscio that theatricality and oppression are major structures
of comparison between gays and Garland, but these authors expand the
analysis, placing those observations within a historical context and cautioning that the interpretation was developed during a time in which gays
were officially and socially repressed. Thus, the themes of theatricality and
oppression are actually linked. According to Dyer, the public news of Garland's attempted suicide in 1950 sets off two chains of readings. One concerns the "break with Garland's uncomplicated and ordinary MGM
image"; the other is that she can now be considered to have "a special
relationship to suffering."[22] McElhaney agrees that Garland's image reverses from "the wholesome girl next door" to "a woman of instability,
dependent on drugs and alchohol, but also a victim—of Hollywood, of
M-G-M, of Louis B. Mayer, of her ex-husbands, of her mother." McElhaney continues: "It is not difficult to understand why gay men would

pick up on this. As Dyer points out, 'Her failures, her chaotic life, her problems with her appearance, her men, her career could also be used as an expression of what a mess gay men thought they were.'"[23] Thus Babuscio's remarks about identifying with Garland have a certain logic of analogy: if gay men of the 1950s believed their lives were "a mess" and they perceived similar features in Garland's career, the situation facilitated an association.

Dyer emphasizes that Garland's "ordinariness" is, as a result of the suicide attempt, turning out to be a surface hiding her not-ordinariness. Furthermore, her estrangement from norms can also imply—for a female—not being feminine (i.e., in Garland's case, not glamorous), and—for a male—not being appropriately masculine (i.e., gay). Dyer writes that gay men may represent themselves "as gender misfits . . . as physically deformed (if not bodily, at least biologically), and so on."[24] Thus, some gays accept the oppression constructed by dominant society with its attendant implications of inferiority.*[25]

Theatricality enters as a defense and a pose in response to this. Dyer's study of the material available to him suggests that closer to 1969, gay men viewed Garland as "representing gay men's neurosis and hysteria" but later this is transformed to "her representing gay men's resilience in the face of oppression."[26] Thus her comebacks are vital as confirmation of gays' specialness; i.e., the idea that gays are not inferior but, in fact, more authentic, emotional, sensitive, etc.*[27] Or, as Babuscio labels it, "intense." But such defeats turned into triumphs also invoke a performance metaphor of "the nerve and risk involved in living 'on the edge.'"[28] Hence, Garland is perceived as emotionally intense and authentic, a person who has lived through it all. Dyer quotes Kenneth Anger's description of Garland's death: "She was *hundreds* of years old, the oldest star ever, if you count emotional years, the toll they take, dramas galore for a dozen lifetimes. She was 'She,' who had stepped into the Flame once too often."[29]

The oppression/theatricality connection accounts for much in structured comparison between Garland and gay men. Garland was also not-ordinary in being "in-between" and androgynous. Both McElhaney and Dyer emphasize these attributes. McElhaney believes that since Garland was cast in her early film roles as an adolescent, as "in-between" child and adult, that that awkward state set up an image of her as "an outsider, of the necessity of repressing one's desires, and of the object of desire itself being remote and unapproachable." Once Garland moves into her adult film roles and her stage performances, particularly after 1950, that in-betweenness changes to an androgyny. Dyer phrases it as "a gender in-between."[30]

In his essay, McElhaney also discusses the trajectories of the films in which Garland starred. He argues that, not only do gays connect with general images, but the structuration of Garland's films helps feed into gay interpretive strategies. Here he notes that at least in Garland's early films, she often plays characters who moved from a "repressive small town" to an urban environment, although within a marginalized sector, often "show business." Such a pattern, McElhaney believes, replays the experiences of many gay men. Furthermore, McElhaney notes that the roles Garland plays permit her to desire male stars who often seem uninterested in her. In fact, if a gay is identifying with Garland, this permits a situation common to gay male life, passive acceptance of an impossible love. Often, though, in a film's resolution, Garland characters act on that desire, wooing and winning the man and producing a "miraculous and sudden turnabout."[31]

A final feature of the Garland/gay connection is the degree to which gay men read Garland's later work as camp. Dyer describes camp as a "characteristically gay way of handling the values, images and products of the dominant culture through irony, exaggeration, trivialization, theatricalisation, and an ambivalent making fun of and out of the serious and respectable."[32] Dyer stresses that Garland is considered to camp, not seen as an individual to *be* camped, although her mannerisms and persona are easy to imitate.[*23] Dyer stresses that this aspect to the perception of Garland seems to develop in the 1960s and may well have been due to Garland's own recognition of her growing popularity among gay men. That is, she may well have adopted the attitude in complicity with her audience. Subsequently, McElhaney argues, it becomes easy to read all of Garland's film performances as having either an intuitive camp sensibility or else an actual camp.

In fact, while Dyer's thesis explicitly proposes that what might initiate a gay reading of the sort that I am discussing here is that homologous structures existed between a star image and a fan's self-image, it is the case that one feature in the Garland cult is the transmission of speculation making Garland "one of us." In particular, McElhaney points out that gossip—true or false—circulates to link Garland with gay culture. "Among gay aficionados of Garland" are the following rumors: "Judy's father was gay; all of her husbands except Sid Luft were gay; Judy had lesbian affairs during the 40s; and most of the men who worked on her musicals were gay."[34] This discursive formation removes Garland from the world of straights and permits a different reading of her image, thus substantiating that sense of theatricality and role-playing.

This overdetermination of imagery sets up the potential for alternative readings to films in which Garland appears. Yet before moving to that problem, I would like to verify that what Dyer and McElhaney propose as gay men's readings might have some validity for the period of the 1950s. Perhaps ultimately this does not matter; perhaps if this is the Garland of the postliberation era—which is at any rate hardly a period of major changes in attitudes about homosexuality—then it does not matter whether this description is accurate for that earlier decade. But it does matter in that McElhaney and Dyer claim these readings to have something to do with pre-1969 gay heritage. In addition, my verification effort may be a way to confirm recollections and to understand the type of alternations such readings have from any apparently preferred reading. I shall look first at the public discussion around Garland and then at period discourse about gays.

THE CREATION OF THE GARLAND CULT

Mikhail Bakhtin mentions that in the second half of the eighteenth century, "local cults" appeared.[35] As he describes these, he indicates that in the case of a fictional tale which used actual historical places, people would visit the site, as though to associate themselves with the fictional characters they were so taken with. Thus, Goethe devotees ("The New Paris") stopped at Frankfurt's city wall, Rousseau fans (*La novelle Héloïse*) went to Lake Geneva, and Kamamzin cultists (*Poor Lisa*) enjoyed a pool outside of Moscow.

"Friends of Dorothy" visited Judy Garland. Just when gay men began to consider Garland as significant to them is not known. Dyer remarks that it begins after 1950—when Garland's recent suicide attempt was revealed—and that by 1961 the following was widely enough known that straight reporters in mainstream newspapers referred to gay audiences when describing Garland's performances.[36]

Biographies of Garland do indicate that the first revelation of something like a cult appeared in the fall of 1950, although different writers mark the moment by different events. Thomas J. Watson and Bill Chapman, great defenders and fans of Garland, consider Garland's arrival on the east coast, on 5 September 1950, as important: "Admirers in New York City staged what show business historians would cite as the first evidence of a 'Garland cult.'" Garland was met by fans yelling, "'Judy! Judy! We love you!'"[37] Anne Edwards dates the surfacing of the cult also in fall 1950 when Garland was introduced with some fanfare to Wayne Martin, who had for fourteen years been absorbed in Garland's career.[38]

Nothing, however, in these accounts indicates that either the mass of admirers or Martin was gay—or straight—and certainly Garland's appeal was not only to homosexuals. Cynically, one might take the view that both events were stage-managed to offset the bad publicity of the previous summer. However, Edwards does provide good evidence that Martin was a longtime fan, and it is the case that Garland's comebacks in the next few years and later had something of a reputation for an outpouring of fan behavior.

That said, it is difficult for me to believe that Garland was suddenly perceived after her suicide attempt as a figure for cult status. But instead of dating the transformation later, I would argue that prior to June 1950 her star image*[39] was already at odds with her film roles. This is important, I think, in providing sufficient groundwork for the "sudden" arrival of the cult after her attempt on her life.

Garland's career itself is less important here than the public representation of her. In such mainstream public press as I could find, it is apparent that Garland was consistently plagued with observations about her physical features, and that rumors about her instability and insecurity circulated much prior to her unfortunate suicide attempt in 1950. Watson and Chapman note that the reviews of Garland's first film, *Pigskin Parade* (1936), included the comment from the *New York Times*, "'She's cute, not too pretty, but a pleasingly fetching personality, who certainly knows how to sell a pop [tune].'"[40] Her notice in *Current Biography 1941* starts with a joke about Garland's first show as a thirty-month-old baby: "It is probable that the audience discovered neither the sex nor the latent talent. Those who saw and heard the performance of Judy Garland in *The Wizard of Oz* 15 years later, however, doubted neither her femininity nor her competence"; the notice later indicates that when Garland was offered a chance in the movies, "legend has it that Mrs. Gumm demurred because she didn't think Judy was 'pretty enough.'"[41]

Through the 1940s, Garland continues to be represented in ways that could later play into the image of inadequacy emphasized by McElhaney and Dyer (although, of course, other aspects of her persona are also part of the picture). In July 1941 when Garland's marriage to David Rose was reported, Sidney Skolsky, in "Tintypes," not only stresses Garland's youth (she was nineteen), but he mentions she is now slimmer, losing her "baby fat." Sheilah Graham remarks two years later, "Judy is still too thin, although a little heavier than while making 'For Me and My Gal,' when she dropped to a low of 96 pounds. She is overworking." While discussing Garland's secret for success as youthfulness and playfulness, Jerry Mason adds, "She is not [M-G-M's] greatest actress. She's no overwhelming beauty. Her figure is not the envy of 25 million wives. . . . Judy seems to symbolize the girls soldiers left back home. . . . Judy is probably the only star who has ever gone out on a camp tour and gained weight doing it." Garland's debut with an orchestra in the same year begins, "Judy Garland was never so petrified in her life," but by the end "the crowd roared, stamped, clapped, and whistled."[42]

Thus even before Garland and Rose divorce, a number of motifs are apparent: her physical appearance is consistently referred to as not conforming to some ideal type; she is, however, typical of American girls. Moreover, though, something is out of sync: overwork produces either too slim or too heavy a body. Or does this have something to do with stage fright?

Between this set of representations and those of the later 1940s, Garland's activities were beginning to show the symptoms of her use of barbiturates (from the late 1930s), her stress from work, and her sufferings in personal relations. Around 1943 her difficulties in showing up for shooting begin, increasing significantly after 1946. In July 1947, Garland checked into a sanitorium after a halfhearted try at committing suicide. Knowledge of the suicide attempt was suppressed, but Garland's retreat was publicly explained as due to a neurotic illness: "nervous exhaustion." In July 1948, Garland was suspended by M-G-M, and later that year her marriage to Vincente Minnelli was, for all purposes, over. Then from spring 1949 on, a series of suspensions and hospitalizations culminated when Garland cut her throat on 17 June 1950. The public press had the news within forty-eight hours.[43]

Hollywood uses publicity to stimulate a market for its films. A corps of reporters are set to gain from that need. Thus, in the late 1940s, public discussion and explanations of Garland's known behavior were extensive. In November 1947, Elaine St. Johns gave *Photoplay* readers "The Truth about Judy Garland's Health." St. Johns's subhead is: "When people say Judy is dying, it's time to treat rumors with an injection of facts."[44] St. Johns countered with all sorts of evidence that nothing was seriously wrong with Garland. Garland was only "overtired."[45]

Another explanation adduced was her personality. The following year, Maxine Arnold writes:

> You feel that Judy Garland, of the haunting brown eyes, sensitive face and the voice with that heart-catching quality, has never relaxed. And certain it is that the very emotional intensity that has contributed to her success as an actress has been a jinx in her personal quest for happiness.
>
> One day Judy is loaded with enthusiasm. The next, tight and tense, moody and distrait, she will go home weeping over some small incident; a scene she feels she could have done better, a scene she wasn't up to doing. . . .
>
> She has "opening day" jitters on every picture she makes. . . .
>
> She talks with the same intensity with which she acts, dances or sings.[46]

Thus, images of Garland as "intense" and insecure, terms that Babuscio, McElhaney, and Dyer will use later to describe her, are already evident in mainstream representations of the actress even prior to her 1950 collapse. When that breakdown does happen, old vocabulary is repeated: "ill at ease," "uncertain," unable to relax; new words are added: "hysterical" and "despondent." *Newsweek* reported the June 1950 story such that Louis B.

Mayer was presented as a substitute father who contributed to her problems, particularly that of her weight. Her use of drugs was overtly discussed.[47]

At this point, Garland's career shifts dramatically. M-G-M and she terminated her contract, and Garland begins the series of comebacks that become part of the lore of her appeal. By then, however, much of her image is set. In place were the representations of oppression (the ordinary/not ordinary contradiction and her physical deformity and victimization) and theatricality (Garland's intensity, hysteria, and emotional authenticity). The breakup with Minnelli also was available to reinforce an image of desire for finding her dream but her inability to succeed—"somewhere over the rainbow." Her stage shows in both London and New York in 1951 emphasized "comebacks" and the dream of romance and eventual success.*[48] Of the set of terms that Babuscio, McElhaney, and Dyer offer, only yet to appear are those related to "in-betweenness" or androgyny and camp. The former set appears at least as early as March 1952 in a review by Clifton Fadiman of Garland's performances at the Palace. Fadiman writes:

> Of *course* we wanted her to be wonderful, as if her triumphs could somehow help to wipe out our own sorrows and weaknesses. But there was more to it than that.
>
> Much more. As we listened to her voice . . . we forgot—and this is the acid test—who she was, and indeed who we were ourselves. As with all true clowns (for Judy Garland is as fine a clown as she is a singer) she seemed to be neither male nor female, young nor old, pretty nor plain. She had no "glamour," only magic.[49]

Fadiman would go on to call her an "elf."*[50]

If by 1950–1952, Garland's star image conforms to what is reported later as important to gay men, can the same be said about gay men? How did they think about or represent themselves during this time frame? These are much more difficult questions to answer, particularly since no reason exists to think that at any historical time there has existed a single "gay" image, especially as constructed by those who considered themselves as within that category.

In one of the few histories of U.S. gay culture, John D'Emilio points out, as Dyer and Jeffrey Weeks do, that the appearance of the notion of homosexuality as a label by which people can be considered may have come as recently as the nineteenth century.*[51] D'Emilio goes on to assert that as the label was employed during the 1920s to 1960s in the United States, "medical theories made homosexuality not a deed that one avoided but a condition that described who one was." Thus, common in those years was the proposition by experts, with all of their social authority, that some sort of essence existed to gayness. Among its characterizations were that gays were "less moral, less respectable, and less healthy than their fellows."[52] David F. Greenberg supports D'Emilio's presentation by detailing the social-scientific theories prevalent in the United States to explain gay behavior. These theories included postulations that homosexuality was innate, that gays were hereditary degenerations from normal individuals, or that (following Darwinian theory) they were throwbacks to more primitive people who were perhaps once bisexual or hermaphroditic. Havelock Ellis, the popular American psychologist of sexuality at the turn of the century, described homosexuality as an "inversion"; others, such as the German Karl Heinrich Ulrichs, thought gays might be a "third sex."

Greenberg stresses that such a medical and social-scientific discourse could justify state intervention and regulation of these supposed deviations from appropriate biological development. Thus the discourse of public experts took over, duplicating the position, while replacing the authority, of religious leaders. The economic and social determinants of the early 1800s for regulating sexuality in the name of patriarchy could continue.[53]

Such postulates of deviancy seem to be believed by representatives of one of the first American gay rights organizations. Dyer quotes the Mattachine Society's prospectus of 1950:

> We, the androgynes of the world, have formed this responsible corporate body to demonstrate by our efforts that our physiological and psychological handicaps need be no deterrent in integrating 10% of the world's population towards the constructive social progress of mankind.[54]

In the early 1950s, such a declaration marked an important moment in gay men's history, for after World War II, gay culture began coalescing in ways it had not before. D'Emilio argues that the war in some ways helped a coming-out for gays. Sheer mobility and concentration of males during their time in the armed forces created a recognition of how widespread and common homosexual activity was. D'Emilio characterizes the postwar era as a time of development of gay communities, of the appearance of gay bars and social groups in numerous urban areas. Gay literature was published. The Kinsey reports of 1948 and 1953 reinforced the notion that every sixth man was gay. The vocabulary of the Mattachine manifesto suggests as well that gays were linking their minority status with the general postwar civil rights movements of the blacks.*[55] Integration was called for.

The hopes of the early 1950s were, however, to be dashed when homosexuality was linked with communism as a threat to national security.[56] From the mid-1950s through the 1960s, an era of tense conflict witnessed homosexuality's becoming an arena of social attention. For instance, Vito

Russo notes that the first positive images of gays in mainstream films come in the early 1960s from Britain: *A Taste of Honey* (1961) and *Victim* (1961). *Advise and Consent*, in the United States, was released in 1962.[57]

Some documents do survive from the postwar era and the early fifties. An excellent piece of evidence is the published diary of an individual living in New York City in a gay community. Donald Vining's journal spans 1933 to 1967 and gives a remarkable sense of the day-to-day style and difficulties of a gay man of this time.[58] Another important document was published in 1951 by Donald Webster Cory (a pseudonym): *The Homosexual in America*, an insightful sociology of gay men's lives at the time. Cory lists a number of stereotypes and myths then prevalent among *both* gays and straights: (1) the "male homosexual is effeminate" (Cory attacks this stereotype as potentially inducing behavior that is actually held in low esteem by some gays); (2) "all homosexuals are alcoholics"; and (3) "the homosexual is a depressed, dejected person frequently on the brink of suicide." If those are versions of the gay of 1950, the consequences of those views and social realities have produced group traits. Cory continues, "If there is any characteristic of homosexual life that has been instrumental in the development of homogenous group traits, it is probably the pretense and the mask." This performance leads to lies. Additionally, "widespread instability . . . characterizes gay life. It is not only that many go from love to love, but seem to flounder hopelessly in a search for direction in education, in preparation for a career, in holding a job, in organizing a sound financial and social life." Cory also argues that because of the subjection to a hostile world and the belief that the self is inferior, "we create a new set of beliefs to demonstrate that our gay world is actually a superior one. For some reason or other that few of us stop to investigate, we come to believe that homosexuals are usually of superior artistic and intellectual abilities," hence, the search for those of like nature who are "brilliant."[59]

Terms familiar to the constructed gay image exist in Cory's description of gay culture and group norms in 1950. The ideas of inferiority or abnormality but superior sensitivity, of performance and masks, and of an otherness abound. Cory also lists books that he thinks could be interpreted to be stories about gays. Thus, another set of documents exists: period fiction perceived by a gay man to present gay characters. Of the list that Cory supplies, I read in depth nine novels published between 1948 and 1951 that seemed to me to represent a gay individual as a major character in the plot and in a way that would suggest the writer was intimate with gay culture. The nine were: *Quatrefoil* (James Barr, 1950), *Lucifer with a Book* (John Horne Burns, 1949), *Other Voices, Other Rooms* (Truman Capote, 1948), *The Gay Year* (Michael DeForrest, 1949), *Parents' Day* (Paul Goodman, 1951), *The Bitterweed Path* (Thomas Hal Phillips, 1949), *Twi-*

light Men (André Tellier, 1931; second printing, 1948), *Stranger in the Land* (Ward Thomas, 1949), and *The City and the Pillar* (Gore Vidal, 1948).*[60]

These books are valuable textual sources for deriving information about circulating representations of homosexuality. Introducing *Quatrefoil*, Samuel M. Steward describes gay fiction of the 1930s as having plots "with the protagonist always getting killed or committing suicide, thus showing the guards of public morals that Sin, especially homosexual Sin, always comes to a bad end."[61] *Quatrefoil*, he believes, is among the best of the new wave of fiction, and I would agree.

For the most part, *Quatrefoil* thwarts the stereotypes and myths that Cory indicates are dominant. Its plot seems more to invoke a Greek ideal of the relationship between an older and a younger man. At *Quatrefoil's* start, Ensign Phillip Froelich finds himself in deep melancholy, feeling ill at ease or at odds with himself. He is also about to be court-marshaled for general insubordination to his captain, whom he believes to be incompetent. Tim Danelaw, an aide to the admiral, subtly helps Froelich defend himself, as well as introducing Froelich to a cultivated social group. An attraction to Danelaw that Froelich attempts to deny culminates in a one-night affair. Although Froelich is to return home to a marriage of convenience and the leadership of his town, he gradually finds Danelaw educating him into a life of balance and harmony. After a brief visit to his family, during which time Danelaw is "intuitively" accepted by them, Froelich breaks off the engagement to his girlfriend, and he and Danelaw very quietly continue their love. Danelaw is killed in a plane crash, but Froelich, after contemplating suicide, conquers his thrust toward "self-destruction."

A deftly written romance, *Quatrefoil* still exhibits traditional symptoms of the dominant culture's view of homosexuality. Throughout, Danelaw and Froelich assume their activities are degenerate. What saves them, according to the novel's ethos, is that their adherence to one perfect affair prevents their further deterioration. Furthermore, a distaste for other gay men is expressed. One of Danelaw's lessons to Froelich is how to lead a solitary but satisfactory life: "a new kind of freedom." Thus, Froelich is counseled not to identify with a group even if he now recognizes his homosexuality.

Quatrefoil, thus, offers a view of gay life somewhat at odds with stereotypes of effeminacy, even if it falls into another tradition in gay culture. It does not break free of the notion that alternative sexual preferences are to be suppressed. In fact, it accepts the oppressive notion that sexuality between men is degenerate. In compensation *Quatrefoil* suggests that both Danelaw and Froelich are superior in other ways: natural leaders of men. But the homosexual aspect of the men's lives requires something of a performance, if not a theatricality.

Three of the other nine novels deal with schoolteachers in love with their students: *Lucifer with a Book, Parents' Day*, and *Stranger in the Land*. In the former two, the instructors are bisexual, with the protagonist in *Lucifer* eventually having an affair with one of the female teachers and leaving with her. Both *Lucifer with a Book* and *Parents' Day* provide rich, sympathetic, and unstereotypical images. The one exception is that ex-veteran Guy Hudson (in *Lucifer*) has a horribly distorted mouth as a result of war injuries (i.e., he is abnormal and ugly). Both books are also moderately satirical about the teaching profession in private schools, exhibiting more venom directed toward hypocrisy in others than concern about the protagonists' own plights as gays.

Stranger in the Land, however, fits the hypotheses of gay imaging much too well. Raymond Manton is being blackmailed by young Terry Devine, who is responding to Manton just for the money. Manton wishes he could leave the small town of Chatford and move to New York where he could be himself: "All the most vivid memories of his boyhood were milestones along the endless road of his humiliation."[62] But his mother needs his money, and he does not want her to discover he is a "degenerate." In the final chapter, Manton drowns Devine.

Such depressing conclusions and self-hatred permeate the other five novels. In *Other Voices, Other Rooms*, a young boy finds himself trapped with his family, including Cousin Randolph who is given to cross-dressing: "The man in the mirror was not Randolph, but whatever personality imagination desired him to resemble."*[63] In *The Bitterweed Path*, Darrell Barclay's desire for Malcolm Pitt and his son Roger culminates in an affair with Roger that ends. *Twilight Men*, written in 1931, but republished in 1948 and hence considered among the group, is perhaps the most typical of one vision of gay culture. A series of liaisons and jealousies occur because the two protagonists believe that monogamy is impossible for the "inverted." Armand, a writer, slips into drugs and lying. Eventually the novel ends when he kills his father and dies of an accidental overdose of morphine. In *The City and the Pillar* Bob and Jim, who were lovers, meet again years later. When Jim realizes Bob is not gay, Jim kills him, and the novel offers implications of his own suicide to come.

Finally, in *The Gay Year*, the novel opens with a narrator querying whether he could someday play the role of a madman. He cannot work or face the outside; he was teased as a child for looking like a girl: "'They' insulted and snubbed him years ago, even the features that might produce his abilities to be an actor or dance." As a child he was fat, so he lost weight. The novel then begins with a representation of gay life in New York in the late 1940s. The opening scenes are of Joe Harris meeting a blind date, Roger Stuart, and after a bit of delay and subterfuge, sleeping with him (between chapters). The next morning, Harris worries that he might become "camp" and denies he is gay to three homosexual men who live in his building. Numerous scenes depict characters such as Donald K. Jeffries (a divorced and lonely gay alcholic), who commits suicide; jealous Teddy Knight, who accuses Stuart of cruising while doing the same thing himself; Charles Evans, who counsels against thinking you love whom you sleep with; rich Reginald Hartley, who keeps Harris when Harris becomes cynical; Lois and Hi, who start a gay bar; and Katherine, who tries to convince Harris he is not an "invert." Harris nearly agrees with Katherine, but at the last minute, Stuart arrives to convince Harris otherwise. Of course, Stuart does not stay with Harris, so Harris begins singing in Lois and Hi's bar and is an immediate success: "a sad beauty"; "he sums up all the happiness and misery we all know in our lives, and throws it at you in a song." In the concluding chapters, Harris decides, "'I'm not really 'gay,' . . . I've never really been homo. I've only been lonely.'" He leaves the gay bar and goes into an uptown musical: "'I'm going to be all right. I know.'"⁶⁴

The variety of images in this set of novels suggests that, as now, a range of politics and fantasies propel fiction addressed to and written by gay men. This is immensely important in requiring that gay culture of the late 1940s and early 1950s not be solidified into a homogeneity that neither existed then nor exists now. Yet among these fictional representations are many indications that the images of the self constructed by gays then are similar to those images postulated by McElhaney and Dyer and justify an analogy to the discursive formation around the life of Garland. In many of the novels or parts of them are representations of gays that offer homologies to the image structure that was being constructed for Garland during the same period.

Consequently, some justification exists for assuming that the postulations about readings of Garland that McElhaney and Dyer are able to construct from their evidentiary sources have foundation in information from the period under consideration: the postwar, pre-Stonewall era. Reason exists to believe that some gay men (although likely not all of them) might view themselves in ways that could facilitate their equating Garland's ordeals with their own. The consequence of this is a structured logic to an alternative reading of her films.

GAY READINGS OF GARLAND FILMS

In Part One, I discussed how scholars of the reception of film have constructed text-activated theories of reading. Furthermore, I have argued that those theories actually only indicate socially or academically bound *norms* of reading, such as "competency" or "ideological complicity." Thus, when alternative readings for Garland films are considered, three readings are pertinent: competent or ideologically complicit readings ("preferred" readings), actual historical readings within dominant cultural realms, and alternative readings. The function of considering actual historical readings is to control the claims of what might be anticipated by hypotheses about preferred readings: that is, the context of the historical moment may produce a reading at odds with the preferred reading. But knowledge of that historical interaction is required to contextualize any alternative one.

To keep this in hand, I am going to use Garland's 1954 comeback film, *A Star Is Born*, as the reference film. *A Star Is Born* is useful since it was Garland's first film after her suicide attempt and successful stage act. Additionally, her fan contingency was already active. Finally, when checked against actual historical readings, the effects of Garland's post-1950 image should be apparent in the dominant readings. Thus, the variable of rereadings of earlier films by gays can be eliminated for this film: everyone knew Garland's troubles and her triumphs.

What would be the preferred reading? In chapters 3 and 4, I described how contemporary linguistics, cognitive psychology, and British cultural studies treat this problem in current film theory. In something of a reduction and combination of those views, I would suggest that four features could be pertinent. For one thing, a reader would presumably follow the hermeneutical puzzle, proposing hypotheses and revising them as the plot proceeded. Connected to this would be a search for coherency, tying all the events into a chronological story.

Additionally, readers would assume characters functioned for plot development. Readers might also either identify with characters or consider them objects of desire. Here gender issues would be pertinent, particularly for a Lacanian approach to a preferred reading. Furthermore, verisimilitude would be expected. Judgments about realism and credibility in the combination of events and character motivations would be made. Consideration of generic conventions should temper these evaluations. Finally, readers would interpret messages or propositions they assumed were made by the film, accepting those messages. Those messages might be presumed to come from some external source, likely the director or screenwriters.

In the contemporaneous response of the mainstream press to *A Star Is Born*, only some of these hypotheses about a preferred reading are met.[65] One important reason for this is that I am using mainstream press reviews which are governed by the conventions of their genre; that is, they are reviews rather than full-fledged interpretations. Additionally, in the case of the first feature of the preferred reading—viewers will attempt to solve the hermeneutic riddle—*A Star Is Born* is one of those cases for which this assumption is troublesome. *A Star Is Born* was a remake of a 1937 film, and its plot (which was not changed from the 1937 version) was generally known. Hence, reviews spent little, if any, time recapitulating plot, something reviews often do not do anyway.

The reviews do indicate, however, that the reviewers were quite interested in a different goal, perhaps because of the fact that *A Star Is Born* is something of a generic hybrid. It is a drama, but it is also a musical. Hence, most of the reviews evaluated the degree to which the writers were entertained. Although most of the reviewers wrote that the film was great, a few thought not. Much of the credit for the judgment depended on Garland's performance. Of the fifteen reviews examined, eight emphasized that the film was a comeback movie for Garland—and she was a success. Others did not foreground the extratextual situation so overtly, although similar goals were at stake in their discussions.

Only three reviews indicated that the film itself had features which might be considered autobiographical in nature. It is here that the recollections of gay readers detailed by McElhaney and Dyer seem to deviate from mainstream press readings. For in discussions of *A Star Is Born* by gay readers, one central feature seems to be equating the events in the film with Garland's life. Furthermore, some readings include an almost minute knowledge of the production circumstances for individual scenes. *A Star Is Born* was not without the usual Garland problems. Many of the reviews and adjacent stories emphasize that Garland delayed shooting, boosting costs to double what was expected. Her weight fluctuated. Gay connoisseurs of the film today have described to me the order in which scenes were taken, accounting for Garland's physical status in each shot.*66

Now, I doubt that most gay men in 1954 were likely so versed in the production history, but here is an instance in which the blanks Wolfgang Iser posits in texts are being created and filled in ways quite beyond what a text-activated theory would propose. *A Star Is Born* becomes as much a plot about Garland's suffering and difficulties, her performance in spite of it all, as it is about Esther Blodgett's rise to fame. In chapter 3, I discussed how Ellsworth's research indicated that the readers of *Personal Best* did not reject overt information provided by the text, although they might manipulate it in unexpected ways. Finding biographical analogies or comparing the scenes with a different story chronology (the story of the production of *A Star Is Born* instead of the textual plot) has a logic, particularly from the position of the star image's being found homologous to that of the reader. *A Star Is Born* for a gay reader is not about the making of a star but about the comeback of a performer who has been oppressed. Garland's abnormality, her weight problem, is of particular notice. For a gay alternative reading of the plot, then, the goal of the reading is not a game to solve the riddles of the text, nor is it to be entertained. It is, rather, to provide a hermeneutics of Garland's life.

So Blodgett/Garland is the character of focus for an alternative reading. She is, as well, the center of attention for most of the mainstream reviewers. Although two reviews argue that James Mason, playing Norman Maine, takes charge of the film, the others dwell on Garland. Little indication exists in the mainstream reviews, however, of treating Garland as a figure of identification or of sexual objectification. At least two reviews mention that she has something of a gamin quality. That feature becomes androgyny for the gay readings described by McElhaney and Dyer, perhaps explaining the rather distanced attitude toward Garland evinced by all readers. Mostly, Garland is considered to be a performer who keeps the film moving. The numbers attracting most comment are "Born in a Trunk" and her pantomimed number for Maine in their home.

The dominant-culture readers' interest in Garland's performance produces something of a conflict since approbation for that acting style and expansiveness had to be tempered by those readers' demand for verisimilitude in the plot. Several reviews remarked that happily the musical numbers were motivated as rehearsals or stage performances. Beyond these, opinions are mixed. A number of reviewers thought the film and Garland had "a ring of authority" or authenticity; others remarked that the stress on her showing off her ability to entertain through so many numbers reduced the credibility of the drama. Several reviewers wondered if the 1937 plot were not a bit creaky. Regarding Maine's altruistic suicide, a reviewer sneered: "One keeps wondering why he didn't simply join Alcoholics Anonymous."[67]

Gay alternative readings do not seem to value the criterion of verisimilitude as much as the popular press reviewers did. Perhaps this is due, if McElhaney and Dyer are correct, to a stronger emphasis on theatricality and a camp sensibility. That is, an intense, emotional performance that is perceived as such may rate higher. Dyer remarks that Garland's acting is particularly "intense" following Maine's death scene: it is a "knife edge between camp and hurt."[68] None of the mainstream press reviews even mention this scene. Five of the reviews do remark about the emotions elicited by the experience of watching the film, one mentioning its "eight-Kleenex ending."*[69]

What is significant here is not so much that emotionalism belongs to one reading or the other, but that there are differences in the sources of those emotions, the processes of identification or equation producing those experiences. If McElhaney and Dyer are accurate in claiming that some gays consider the roles played by Garland as having a relation to their own circumstances, then the degree to which they take her situation to be like their own can account for the intensity of tragedy in their experience of Maine's death. Contained within so many scenes of gay culture in the early 1950s were images of alcoholism, despondency, the sense of inferiority in the face of others' successes, and suicide. Blodgett/Garland's response to Maine's sacrifice might well have provoked instances of personal recognition of such difficulties. Dyer notes as well that Blodgett/Garland's "coming-back" after the suicide was an important part of the film's significance for him. In the face of adversity and suffering, the true performer went on with the show.

Such a message for an alternative reading might be quite similar to that constructed by a dominant-culture reading. Neither group is without its personal difficulties. Yet few of the press reviewers were explicit in what they took to be the significance of the film. Six of the fifteen reviews do suggest that one of the activities of *A Star Is Born* is satirizing Hollywood. But on the whole, they assume the point to be self-evident (if the film was about anything at all).

That Dyer as a gay reader thought a point was being made is itself significant. In a culture in which gay men have had few positive images of themselves and their lives presented on the screen, Dyer and Cohen argue that finding equivalent experiences from which to develop a politics of response to oppression is important.[70] One of the procedures gay men seem to have used is to find homologous image structures between themselves and others—of the same or different gender and sexual orientation—and to apply those individuals' experiences to their own circumstances. Without images of their own, this seems, unfortunately, a reading strategy much like that of any repressed group's struggle over the meaning of a sign.*[71] Here the scene chosen for special recognition is important in the overall thrust of a narrative, but elsewhere alternative readers find isolated moments that are of personal importance, and they stress those, counter to the dominant textual reading. (Such a reading procedure also occurred among lesbians' interpretations of *Personal Best*.)

This chapter has concluded by comparing three types of readings for a Garland film—preferred, dominant-culture, and alternative. In the case of *A Star Is Born*, I am hypothesizing that gay men find the external plot of Garland's life more important than the textual one, characters are judged by standards not of verisimilitude but of experiential similarity, theatricality and performance are more valued than any realism, and personal messages of significance to private lives matter. This type of alternative reading, however, may be peculiar to the Garland phenomenon—although I suspect that some of the strategies are quite common among not only gay men but other groups of alternative readers. The prospect of learning more about such activities is exciting.

It seems to me that alternative readings, when they can be useful for a progressive politics, need to be cultivated. The ones surrounding Garland may not in all (or any) ways contribute to an alteration in power structures. Yet they have their own logic within the culture in which they have developed and the context in which they existed. Alternative readings confront preferred or dominant reading patterns with the fact that those readings are hypothetical or specific to a group (not universal). Competency is not necessarily finding a solution to a riddle or judging the verisimilitude of a character; competency may be finding in a film the strength to continue the struggle for a humane life.

With the Compliments of the Auteur: Art Cinema and the Complexities of Its Reading Strategies

ONE POSSIBLE contribution of reception studies to film criticism and history is through offering an understanding of how individuals have analyzed groups of moving pictures such as those defined by genre or mode of film practice. Reception studies may provide new observations about developments in stylistic and narrational history, individual films, and stars; it ought also to help with other routine textual and historical activities. Coming to terms with how historical spectators and film viewers group films and then read them (or read, then group) is necessary in developing a materialist history of filmic interpretation.

A reception studies approach to grouping films is an alternative to organizing texts by formal means. While I will not speculate here on audiences' ideas about what does or does not belong in a particular category, I will explore one historically important interaction: how popular journalistic criticism of post–World War II foreign imports came to terms with a cinema it perceived as significantly different from the conventional Hollywood fare. The films in this group are generally clustered under the rubric "art cinema," and part of my project will be to determine how so many different kinds of film could be gathered into this species. In doing so, I will also consider the complexities of the reading strategies employed by a group of writers and describe the sequence of moves that led these critics to read the movies much as academic film critics have. Of particular importance will be two features of the films' historical context: one, the perceived differences of these films from the standard Hollywood fare (a perception that promoted an opposition of Hollywood versus foreign films); the other, the development within American business practices of differentiating consumer groups.

ART MOVIES AND AUTHORS

That the set of films referred to as art cinema might provoke an altered text-audience relation has interested the scholarly community already. Almost as soon as Hollywood began exhibiting some symptoms of taking on attributes associated with art movies, scholars began trying to articulate a series of oppositions delineating where deviation from the conventional movie occurred in order to chart a move toward "new Hollywood." Peter Wollen had already attempted such a list for particularly radical film practices, such as those employed by Godard in the late 1960s.[*1] So in 1976, drawing from observations made by Thomas Elsaesser and Robin Wood, Steve Neale sets out the terms for "'New Hollywood Cinema.'"[2] Neale provides three major variations between the old and the new: the "dramatic and spatio-temporal unity that founded classical mise-en-scene with its economy, density and 'subtlety' of signification" gives way to an overtly articulated mise-en-scène as zoom and telephoto lenses, slow-motion, and split-screen devices call attention to the narration of the action. Characters change too: "plot-linearity and its corollary, the goal-oriented hero" are "replaced by narrative fragmentation and troubled, introspective protagonists." As narration and narrative alter, so do conventions of presenting subject matter. Genres fall apart, but they are "replaced by a 'realism' compromised by traditional dramatic values and the exigencies of narrative conventions or a use of older generic conventions invested with an empty nostalgia or a knowing cynicism, or both."[3] The American art cinema is born.

Neale also summarizes and expands on possible causes for this metamorphosis. He points out that *Movie* and *Monogram* essays attribute the new cinema to a loosening up of censorship restrictions, a shift toward selling some films to subsets of the general audience, a concomitant exploitation of the director-as-auteur, and a "'breakdown of confidence in traditional American values.'"[4] Neale, however, also links those factors to the use that monopoly capitalism can make of the new cinema. While such a cinema might include spectacle and options enjoyed by groups that hold values counter to the conservatism catered to by mainstream cinema and American television, the techniques were also economically advantageous in terms of both providing profit to finance capitalism and offering less expensive procedures, appearing to supply a "realism" set into place by New Wave and ciné-vérité films.

Neale is moderately skeptical as to whether new Hollywood actually produces a progressive cinema. He argues that the effect on the spectator remains the same as with old Hollywood films. While the narration may be more apparent, this does not mean that the origin of narration is called into question. In fact, the narration can easily be referred to a human source, the director as "auteur," rather than materialist practices having some uneven relation to the mode of production and social formation. Narratives may "have an impression of open-endedness or ambiguity"[5] but only within the limits of the text and those of a speaking consciousness embodied as the giver-of-the-message. The message may be something about the difficulties of communication or the unsureness of representation, but in the age of modernism, that significance is still within the bounds of a unified speaking subject as both maker and receiver of the message. In other words, new Hollywood cinema is still a cinema within the hegemony of Western pre-structuralist epistemologies. Spectators use authorship to make the experience coherent.

Neale's discussion of new Hollywood films refers to technical devices borrowed from New Wave and ciné-vérité films. Certainly the larger tradition from which new Hollywood was harvesting ideas was art cinema in general. In 1979, David Bordwell provides another set of oppositions, contrasting this time Hollywood films and "art cinema." Bordwell argues that not only did art cinema exist within certain historical conditions and operate conventionally, but it produced "implicit viewing procedures."[6] For the conventions, Bordwell describes art cinema as having a looser narrative structure with gaps in the plot and resolution, motivated either as realism or as authorial expressivity. Character goals were ambiguous or weak, producing something of a rationale for the episodic plots.

Bordwell then lays out a diagram of reading strategies that differs from those for Hollywood cinema (for which he postulates that viewers tend to read for plot unity, verisimilitude to notions of everyday life, and generic appropriateness). When the spectator is confronted by non-Hollywood types of narrative form, "violations of classical conceptions of time and space are justified as the intrusion of an unpredictable and contingent daily reality or as the subjective reality of complex characters." The first reading strategy is to explain the formal variations as conforming to either an "objective" or a "subjective verisimilitude." Added to this is the second strategy of imputing the narration to an author or, in the case of film, its director (the strategy Neale has noted for new Hollywood). Assumed in the authorship strategy is that an "overriding intelligence [is] organizing the film for our comprehension." Thus, authorship is used to "unify the text."[7] A "competent viewer" of the "authorial code" looks for stylistic repetitions across series of films, for variations from the Hollywood cinema as marking out the author's commentary, and for a resolution to the movie that is not the solving of a plot (which is anyway often left unclear) but the elucidation of a significant message. Bordwell believes that the two reading strategies—verisimilitude and authorial expressivity—can be contradictory. Thus, the reader tries realism (either objective or subjective) first; failing that and confronted by some ambiguity, the reader turns to the latter, authorial commentary, to close off the text. Bordwell cites an example of such a critical reading from the scholarly community: Robin Wood's "Smart-Ass and Cutie Pie: Notes toward an Evaluation of Altman," one of the *Movie* essays informing Neale's discussion of new Hollywood.

Both Neale and Bordwell return to the subject of art cinema, adding valuable comments to their earlier observations. In 1981, Neale stresses that several types of art cinema have existed (e.g., the neorealist films of postwar Italy and the films of "subjective expressivity" such as Antonioni's).[8] These variations may be attributed in part to "high art and the cultural traditions specific to the country involved" in producing the cinema, but with the difference being marketed in capitalist manner: the "author as a 'brand name.'"[9] Bordwell also implies that art cinema might well be broken into at least two types. He writes that *Last Year at Marienbad* (1961) was very influential, adding or "pushing the art cinema toward extreme exploration of character subjectivity," the polar opposite of the objective realism art film of the 1950s.[10]

If Neale and Bordwell describe common reading strategies, it is the case that their remarks, when drawn from analysis of actual interpretations of art movies, take as their sources scholarly essays. Furthermore, those scholarly essays are written within the time frame in which auteurism is already a reading strategy. Bordwell argues in his *Making Meaning* that Bazin's cinema of authorship was promoted in France in the 1940s and disseminated in the mid-1950s in the United States through Andrew Sarris's writings.[11] By the start of the 1960s, New York film critics begin "to embrace auteurism," applying it not only to the films of foreigners but retrospectively to some American directors such as John Ford, Nicholas Ray, Douglas Sirk, and Samuel Fuller. In its most rigorous form, auteurism produced an "exegetical film criticism," seeking "'an inner consistency of theme, structure, and technique.'"[12] (Auteurism, of course, also has roots in American New Criticism.) Thus, for Bordwell, the auteurist strategy of reading informs how art movies are made meaningful by scholars.

While auteurism may now be a reading strategy commonly applied by academics to the group of films called art cinema, my question is, was that always the case? Or conversely, is authorship an older reading strategy that came to be applied to art movies when more traditional viewing procedures proved in some way deficient? Or, does another possibility exist?

I believe that it does. In the next sections, I shall suggest that tracing the context for the institutionalizing of art theaters in the United States indicates that authorship as a reading strategy was common prior to the introduction of auteurism by the scholarly community (although the strategy does perhaps owe something to that group of readers). Furthermore, films classified as art movies were first distinctive to a more general audience on the basis of their difference from Hollywood fare, but that difference is originally articulated, not only as being "realistic" in terms of some narrative or narrational features, but also as having subject matter considered "serious" or socially conscious. Consequently, a "message" was inferred, and that, logically, had to come from somewhere, that somewhere being the traditional pre-structuralist source: an "author."

Thus, while narrative and narrational conventions differ for art cinema, the stimulus for employing the traditional reading strategy of authorship is not those formal conventions per se, but what audiences took to be a potential communication relation between them and the film's producers. Furthermore, that relation was assumed to be somewhat interactive. Ironically, then, one of the early reactions to ambiguity in art films is for journalistic reviewers to argue that some films permit interpretative freedom for their viewers. The reading dynamics between art movies and their audiences suggest a complex history.

A CINEMA FOR "EGGHEADS"

In April 1962, Dwight Macdonald, certainly one of the more famous cultural commentators of the era, wrote:

> I have been viewing some of [Cinema 16's] current offerings and I think it is time to cast a cold eye on what is known as "the art film." (By "art film" I do *not* mean the work of such directors as Bergman and Resnais but rather films made outside the normal commercial set-up.) Its ideals are high and it is dedicated to truth—no escapism, no box office.[13]

"Mosk," a reviewer for *Variety*, also tries to distinguish this mode of film practice. While discussing *The Connection* (1961), Mosk declares that Americans can also make art movies: "If by art film is meant one dealing with an unusual theme in a non-conventional and frank manner, this pic fits this description aptly."[14]

Now, the sketch of what might count as an art film is quite different for each person, but what makes the definitions similar is their emphases on the treatment of a very particular kind of subject matter. Art movies are no-holds-barred, frank; they are serious. This view comes from both an intellectual and a correspondent for one of the most commercially oriented papers in the film business.

This designation also comes some fifteen years into the routine circulation of foreign films in the United States. Although imported movies had been shown in ethnic neighborhoods and in some very large urban areas from the 1920s, after World War II an art cinema circuit developed of sufficient size to support something of a national attention to, and familiarity with, films from Italy, France, and other European countries.

That Americans might be interested in movies other than those produced by its own film industry was publicized as the U.S. industry was experiencing its postwar drop in attendance. In February 1947, the *Motion Picture Herald* headlines that "Importers Seek Theatre Outlets: Mushrooming of New 'Art' Houses Is Foreseen to Give Playing Time."[15] The influential trade paper provides not only a term used from the 1920s for this informal chain of theaters, but it notes the potential profitability of Italian and French pictures such as *Open City* and *The Well-Digger's*

Daughter, both of which had already achieved runs of several months in New York City. The *Motion Picture Herald* speculated that some 125 to 150 foreign films would be imported during 1947. Concerning these films' marketing, the paper described what would now be called an "open small" strategy: inexpensive theaters with low overheads were rented so that they could stay open while reviews and "word of mouth" built interest in the films. At that point, descriptions of the audiences focused on a "French-culture-conscious 'intelligentsia'" as well as the thousands of GIs who had just returned from Europe. What the article also noted is that the phenomenon was wider than New York City. Two art theaters had opened in Boston, while Cleveland had one and Chicago, Washington (D.C.), Los Angeles, and San Francisco each sported at least three.

One other cause mentioned in the article for the appearance of these theaters is worth noting. After the war, the Hollywood majors continued to reduce the number of films they produced yearly as well as holding them over at first-run theaters to increase profit taking. Smaller theaters were being squeezed out of the Hollywood distribution system. Thus, imported films provided small theaters with an alternative product, enabling them to stay in business. In fact, the growth of art houses may have been due less to any new audience demand per se than to an opening of exhibition options arising from changes in the U.S. film industry's structure and conduct.*16

Just who was attracted to these movies would be a running theme in trade discussion of the exhibition scene. For example, later that year, a *New York Times* writer details the continued mushrooming of these theaters. By June 1947, at least ninety U.S. theaters were showing French films part- or full-time; New York City had twenty-five theaters. Who was coming? "Socially conscious" patrons, the groups who are tired of Hollywood fare and "crave the stronger realism of the better grade imported film," language students, and GIs. At that point, *Open City* had just completed its seventieth week at the World theater, making it the runner-up for all-time longevity at movie houses in New York. By early 1948, *Open City* had earned one million dollars, and distributors were indicating that less than 15 percent of the audience were attending because of national ties to the imported product.17

Not coincidentally, another aspect of the postwar American film industry's activities operated to reinforce the notion that patrons of these art houses were different in particular ways from the average moviegoer. Market analysis and audience segmentation were beginning to be applied assiduously to theatrical distribution of films. The use of firms such as Audience Research, Inc. (ARI), organized by George Gallup, and Leo Handel's Motion Picture Research Bureau started in the film industry in the early 1940s. In 1946, eleven studios hired ARI to preview audience response to proposed movies, and later in the decade, independent production companies discovered that having ARI statistics improved receptions at loan institutions.[18] Demographics provided by ARI and Handel's firm indicated to the majors that by 1950 young people were at the movies more than older individuals, that "persons in higher socio-economic brackets attend[ed] more frequently than those in lower levels,"[19] and the better educated people were, the more likely they were to see films. Furthermore, recent ARI statistics indicated a potential audience of ten to fourteen million people for the art houses. The film industry trade association offered to organize an advisory unit to facilitate foreigners desiring to distribute films in the United States.*[20]

This representation of audiences as no longer a "mass" but segmented opens the way to current marketing strategies in which consumer interest in specific brand names is developed, producing apparent monopolies and permitting increases in prices beyond levels at which they would remain in a purely competitive situation.[21] Thus, the film industry's activity occurs in connection with two wider, interrelated economic and social phenomena. At the basis of this are intensifying moves to expand capitalist markets as prewar imperialism is redefined into postwar trading circles. Hence, the Cold War heats up as international markets are staked out by the first and second world countries.[22]

To aid in the expansion both domestically and abroad, social scientific research in alliance with advertising agencies devotes more and more attention to defining audiences and analyzing their purchasing behaviors. By the mid-1940s, social science researchers such as W. Lloyd Warner and August B. Hollingshead had moved beyond grouping people by economic class to delineating "social classes" that seemed to have their own "class cultures." For Warner and Hollingshead, social classes had two objective variables—occupation and income—and two subjective variables—values and attitudes. These make up the "'style of life' of social classes."[23] By the late 1950s, businesspeople were being trained to think of consumers as more complex than "impersonal economic entities." "As behavior in the market place is increasingly elaborated, it also becomes increasingly symbolic. This . . . means that sellers of goods are engaged, whether willfully or not, in selling symbols, as well as practical merchandise."[24]

This business and social scientific representation of a differentiated clientele with cultures of tastes had overt public reinforcement. As the decade of the 1950s began, the notion of variant tastes distributed among categories of people is also a popular discursive trend. For example, the April 1949 *Life*, discussed in chapter 4, categorized people on the basis of intellectual tastes: "High-Brow, Low-Brow, Middle-Brow: These are three basic categories of a new U.S. social structure; and the high-brows have the whip hand." What will become the current "life-styles" image of diversity within the American social formation is beginning.*[25]

Thus after World War II, as the film industry saw its attendance decline, general developments in the economics of U.S. capitalism, its politics, and discursive strategies confirmed for consumers the need to consider products as indicating variable preferences and self-identities. For the industry, the availability of apparently scientific research procedures—procedures that might guarantee an ability to forecast the appeal of some movies to those most likely to want to see them—seemed a tremendous opportunity to some. With art houses doing a steady business, researchers investigated who was going to these films and why they went.

The answers indicated that earlier ad hoc representations were still accurate. In a study conducted between November 1951 and April 1952 in Champaign-Urbana, a team of researchers headed by Dallas W. Smythe surveyed the audience for one art house.[26] The fare for the 323-seat Illini included foreign films, reissues of "classics," "'offbeat' pictures with specialized appeal," and some subsequent-run Hollywood movies. Among its more revealing conclusions was a high correlation between education and art-theater attendance: 87 percent of the patrons had at least completed high school, while almost 25 percent had at least one year of college graduate work. (That figure should not seem surprising since the Illini was near the University of Illinois, but observers had already made a positive correlation between art houses and institutions of higher learning.)

If these were the people attending, why did they go and what did they like? Smythe et al. discovered that stars were not very important to these customers. Rather, acting and story mattered much more. Furthermore, art-house audiences seemed to like serious films. In fact, when queried about their reasons for liking foreign movies, their most frequent response was "realism," with "better acting" also important.*[27]

These statistics are in sharp contrast with data provided for the general population. Handel was reporting that 51 percent of the population liked improbable happenings in the movies, while only 26 percent disliked them. Furthermore, "socially significant pictures" were not a big draw. Out of eighteen "genres," these films ranked second to last, although "serious dramas" made a better showing.[28] This is important because, as I shall show below, one of the major threads in journalistic reviewing of art cinema was not only realism but social statement. Thus, while the "masses" were not especially attracted to "realism" or "message" pictures, art-house audiences were being typed as preferring those films.

Such an image continued during the 1950s. A 1959 study tested Smythe's analysis and generally reaffirmed as well as adding to it. Art-film audiences liked moving pictures that were "a realistic treatment of a social problem" and that were different from Hollywood. Not only were they better educated than the average American; they were more likely to have "more prestigious occupations." They were also more likely to attend concerts, operas, plays, and ballets, to listen to FM (classical music) stations, to prefer news magazines and the *New Yorker, Harper's, Atlantic,* and the *Reporter.* They were less likely to own a television. As the scholar summed it up, the art-house patron was "an egghead."[29]

Thus, while it is always wise to be somewhat suspicious of social science data about audiences, the best information available suggests that a better-educated section of the American population enjoyed films they perceived to be "realistic" and socially significant. The social scientific representation of the audience was also available, not only to the scholarly community, but also to the distributors of foreign films and the owners of art-cinema theaters, who might exploit it in their advertising. This social scientific information, however, does not prove causality: given the period's typing of these films as indicative of the fare a "highbrow" should enjoy, influences could be quite circular. Perhaps those who wished to be so categorized (as "highbrow") attended the films and became familiar with the films' textual features and "highbrow" methods for interpreting them.

If a pertinent fact in the constituency of who might be enjoying what in the art houses is the appeal to intellectuals, it is also the case that the journalistic circle often declared the foreign films to be as good as, if not "better" than, ones produced in Hollywood. In 1946, Bosley Crowther, the major reviewer for the *New York Times,* reported that among the ten "best pictures" for that year were five imports: *Open City, The Well-Digger's Daughter,* and three British films.[30] This evaluative tendency persisted through the following years until the *New York Times* relegated foreign films to their own category.

Also striking was that the reputation of American-produced films was poor in the international festival circuit. According to one observer, until 1951, the U.S. did not particularly try to compete in foreign-award competitions such as Cannes. That year it did, sending the Academy Award winner *All about Eve.* The film received scarcely any attention. Instead, the winners were European films: *Miracle in Milan* (Italy) and *Miss Julie* (Sweden).*[31]

Thus, by the early 1950s, art cinema was moderately well established in certain ways. Its profile included an appeal to audiences who enjoyed "realistic" and socially conscious cinema. Its films also had significance as being among the "best" according to both journalistic reviewers and festival judges. The audiences who watched these movies were better educated than the average American, and they were more likely to fit some general representation (or self-image) of being "highbrow." This is an important part of the context for reading these art films. How, then, might this audience be interpreting these films?

A FRANK AND SERIOUS CINEMA

When *Open City* premiered in New York City in spring 1946, reviewers were impressed by its narrational techniques. The film was, as others have noted, considered "documentary," but less for its plot than for its visual features. *Open City* did not, however, fool its reviewers: "'Open City,' may I quickly point out, is not a documentary. Yet it gives the illusion of being one." This is because the cinematography "approximates the flat reality of a newsreel." "'Open City' shocks you because of its excessively realistic look. Of all the super-naturalistic movies that have been made, this has an appearance of actuality that you used to get in old-time newsreels." It is "a film that has all the appearance and flavor of a straight documentary." Characters act and tell the story "with newsreel-like simplicity and telling realism."[32] While the narration had a sharply distinctive quality, some reviewers considered the narrative melodramatic—although one writer excused its contrivances as due to the subject matter of the war rather than the fancies of a scenarist.

The impact of the film was, however, equally due to what was perceived as its tone in relation to its content. *Open City* is a "bitter tale." It is not easy to watch. It has an "extreme morbidity." "All these details are presented in a most frank and uncompromising way which is likely to prove somewhat shaking to sheltered American audiences." Its "violence and plain sexiness steadily project a feeling of desperate and dangerous struggles which Hollywood seldom approaches." "It tells a brutally frank story."[33] Lessons were drawn: "Because of [the characters'] ability to die as they do, our faith in man's living is renewed." *Open City* provides its audiences "with a candid, overpowering realism and with a passionate sense of human fortitude."[34]

The film was frank; it was serious; it had a message. It was different from Hollywood. As John Simon expresses it some twenty-five years later, if Hollywood cinema is entertainment, art cinema is "saying something."[35] That the art film should rapidly attract the interpretive strategy of the director-as-origin is hardly surprising, for when movies are fun, who needs to know how the entertaining ones happened to come into existence.

Messages, on the other hand, imply senders. And for educated Americans, that means authorship. Although none of the eight reviews of *Open City* that I read discussed its director by name, Roberto Rossellini's next film provoked nascent authorship readings.[*36] A particularly overt one is that of Robert Hatch in the *New Republic*, which is subtitled: "Director's Picture." Hatch bubbles: "By itself, 'Open City' might have been a super-latively lucky accident; 'Open City' and 'Paisan' together are conclusive proof that Roberto Rossellini is among the greatest living practitioners of the motion picture." "['Paisan'] is preeminently a director's picture" al-though "it would be difficult, I think to find the Rossellini signature on the work he has sent the US thus far." This is because Rossellini has la-bored within "existing conventions."[37] Of the seven reviews surveyed, every one of them mentions Rossellini as the director and attributes to him the film's effects.[38]

The "Rossellini signature" may not yet be distinct enough to elicit a full-blown auteur reading such as those practiced by André Bazin, the *Cahiers du cinéma* critics, and Sarris in the 1950s, but Hatch matches Alex-andre Astruc's observation in the same year that cinema may now be capa-ble of expressing ideas written by its directors.

The notion of looking for a signature did not, however, necessarily, or even likely, come from French criticism. The director-as-author was a po-tential discourse within American intellectual circles from at least the 1920s, and recall that Hatch is writing for a highbrow magazine, the *New Republic*. From the time of the early distribution of foreign movies in the 1920s as art cinema, such an interpretive strategy was promoted through journalistic reviews, as well as via programming practices. As Michael Budd has argued, during the 1920s a short-lived art cinema circuit existed in the U.S. in part because of promotions by the cultural elite.[39] A signifi-cant strategy of programming was by the director's name. Furthermore, groups that organized the theatrical showing of art films might implicitly suggest that audiences investigate these films for authorial styles. In 1930, Howard Thompson Lewis describes one association's procedure: "The Guild was the first to focus particular attention on the abilities of an indi-vidual director by originating programs of one week's duration given over to the showing of one director's work."[40]

Thus, from at least as early as the 1920s, and I would argue throughout the era of the existence of films, a common interpretive strategy among the cultural elite and "better-educated" audiences was attributing the origin of filmic meaning to the director. It was not routinely practiced, however, for films of mere entertainment. The authorship procedure seems to have been reserved for those films considered to be serious, and, hence, art. Conse-quently, when *Open City* and *Paisan* are taken as frank (i.e., not Holly-wood fluff), the art/message/author association is activated. And Hatch and the other reviewers proceed to apply very standard literary and dramatic conventions to "reading" the art films for their social com-mentary.

Several institutionalized factors reinforced this. First of all, a survey of the *New York Times* between 1941 and 1949 turns up very few articles discussing directors. For foreigners, Rossellini immediately stands out as receiving unusual consideration. In fact, a 1949 report, "The Personal History of Roberto Rossellini," even calls attention to this.*[41] Articles about these new foreign filmmakers begin to appear more frequently in the early 1950s, but equivalent essays do not often exist for Hollywood directors. One stab at discussing American filmmakers does occur in 1952. Gertrude Samuels writes about "The Director—Hollywood's Leading Man," interviewing John Ford, Fred Zinnemann, Michael Curtiz, and Henry Koster. Furthermore, as discussed in chapter 4, Hitchcock was promoted as a something of an author. However, generally through the 1950s, directors accorded such an honor were almost uniformly those now associated with art cinema.*[42]

Another institutional factor is the development of film societies and increased attention by cultural leaders to promoting a director's cinema. Cinema 16, an important New York-based film society that showed films in sixteen millimeter, was founded in 1947 by Amos Vogel. By 1956, its membership was at six thousand. In 1949, a *New York Times* writer described the ciné-club tradition of France, ending his essay with the query, would not such a practice be a "tremendous cultural force in the United States as well?" Within six months, the *New York Times* reported that the "Film Society Movement Catches On": two hundred societies showing films in nontheatrical gauge existed, with over one hundred thousand members.[43]

The Museum of Modern Art and the San Francisco Museum of Art also promoted an art cinema. Perhaps striking here is that like the *New York Times*, these institutions explored not only foreign films and the new avant-garde of the United States but also Hollywood for signs of authorship. (A possible influence for this is the economic advantage of transferring to Hollywood fare the features that led to foreign films' successes among the intelligensia.) In 1954, the Art in Cinema program at the San Francisco Museum of Art hosted a fourteen-film series in which active directors discussed the "arts of good filmmaking." Furthermore, the program was structured around great filmmakers and genres from Hollywood. Opening the series was Rouben Mamoulian on D. W. Griffith. He was followed by Mitchell Leisen discussing Cecil B. DeMille and spectacles, Kenneth Macgowan on John Ford and westerns, Fred Zinnemann on realism, and Vincente Minnelli on musicals.

If authorship was an early and significant reading strategy, it is not until *Hiroshima, mon amour* and *Breathless* that journalistic reviewers practice a full-fledged auteurism in which narrational style is linked to subject matter and attempts are made to unify the film under some broad generalization.

This does not mean, however, that earlier reviewers did not observe narrational practices. It is just that until those films are exhibited, reviewers tended to treat technique as separate from subject matter. With those films, style begins to be explained in ways that the earlier films' techniques apparently did not require: reviewers begin to try to correlate style and subject matter. Through the 1950s, however, reviewers seek messages from directors in films they continue to consider as serious, frank, and, consequently, worthy of interpretation.

"GODARD HAS SENT HIM TO HELL IN STYLE"

In moving toward an "explication de auteur," popular press reviewers also expressed numerous approaches to the narrative, narration, and subject matter that would constitute what Neale, Bordwell, and others have described as art cinema. Generally, they end up conforming to what Bordwell argues is the art cinema interpretive strategy for accounting for ambiguity in a movie. However, reviewers do not jump to that solution but work toward it, abetted, I believe, by several films for which editing practices solicited associations with modern art. Then reviewers began assuming (as they were already accustomed to doing for contemporary paintings) that technique *was* part of the subject matter. Earlier reviews do not operate on this assumption.

To study the historical development of these reading procedures, I chose thirty films distributed in the United States from 1946 through 1974. They included all films listed by Bordwell in his essays, plus several others.[*44] I also selected eight sources for reviews: a major U.S. newspaper (the *New York Times*), a major trade paper (*Variety*), three mass-media publications (*Life, Newsweek,* and *Time*), and three highbrow periodicals (the *New Republic,* the *New Yorker,* and *Saturday Review*).[*45] How, then, did these reviewers move to an auteurist approach to narration?

Failing to conform in some ways to classical systems of editing time and space can be taken as a type of objective realism, and what counted as realistic in the first year of the postwar art cinema was related to such narrational techniques. As I mentioned earlier, in the case of *Open City* its acting, locations, and shooting style provoked the assertions of its "documentary tone." Yet its plot was described as melodramatic, not the fragmented and goal-less narrative of later art films.

However, with *Shoeshine* (reviewed in fall 1947), what counted as "realism" changed meaning. Instead of implying a documentary expression, realism was related to presentation of subject matter: an emotional or experiential truth, often of a social or personal nature, had been stated by the film. In the words of the *New York Times* reviewer, it has "such uncompromising realism that the roughness of its composition is overshadowed by its driving, emotional force. . . . 'Shoe-Shine' is not an entertainment; rather, it is a brilliantly executed social document."[46] *Bicycle Thief* receives the same treatment: DeSica "has laid hold upon and sharply imaged in simple and realistic terms a major—indeed, a fundamental and universal—dramatic theme. . . . [He is] holding a mirror up to millions of civilized men."[47] Realism in these and other art films rapidly shifts from some technical process of narration to dramatic truth and social acuity—the subject and tonal features apparently particularly compelling to a highbrow audience.

Part of this ostensible realism obviously was the introduction of topics previously not considered directly by Hollywood, in part because of its production code. Thus, violence and sexuality receive particular attention in reviews. *Bitter Rice* reaches something of a climax: Crowther found it presenting "slices of life in the raw" but "excessive" in showing "elemental passions" and "carnal hunger." *Newsweek* commented that the film was "social significance with a liberal dose of sex."[48]

Not until *La Strada* is shown in the summer of 1956 is a film called realistic because its narrative is fragmented and characters are only slightly motivated. H. A. Weiler links *La Strada* to other Italian "neo-realist" films. *La Strada* is a "parable": "Like life itself, it is seemingly aimless, disjointed on occasion and full of truth and poetry." Yet the other current notions of realism also count. Another reviewer explains, "It is a 'neorealistic' work, meaning, among other things, that it makes an enormous effort to tell the truth in an original way." (That is, it is different from Hollywood.) Arthur Knight, writing for *Saturday Review*, declares that *La Strada* is "neo-realism on a new plane," for it is a "mixture of realism and poetry." *Time* describes it as "a blend of myth and surrealism."[49]

La Strada seems to have struck its reviewers, as Weiler remarked, as a parable. James Reichley for the *New Republic* provides the first extended thematic interpretation among the reviews sampled.

> On one level the theme is the eternal one of the conflict between body (the strong-man), mind (the clown), and spirit (the girl); but on another and perhaps more pertinent level the strong-man may represent the brutish forces that have been unleashed in all the Western world by the success of democracy; the girl represents the simple verity in the hearts of ordinary people assumed by democratic sentiment; and the clown the intellectuals who have risen on the tide of democracy, yet owe an allegiance to the culture of a class-structured past.[50]

Thus the episodic narrative structure of *La Strada* plus the notion of authorial expressivity produces an allegorical reading that might account for many of the sense-data of the film. Possible ambiguities of meaning are closed off, not as objective or subjective realism, but as a riddle from the author for the viewer to solve.

What is somewhat conspicuous about these reviews is how seldom they do consider ambiguities to exist. (No one seems perturbed by Patricia's actions in *Breathless*, for instance.) And when they do confront ambiguities, the explanations they attempt are striking. At least through this period, journalistic reviewers seldom attribute ambiguity to objective or subjective realism. Or to authorial expressivity about reality. An early art film that might provoke some difficulties in regard to ambiguity is *Rashomon*. Described by Crowther as a "slice of life," it was seen by one reviewer as being about "moral ambiguities," but that reviewer then also argued interpretive freedom: "It is up to the customer to decide whether the death of the samurai is suicide or murder and by whom."[51] Thus, while this vagueness might be taken as a statement regarding authorial expressivity, also implied is something of a notion of free-floating messages and variability in significances.*[52]

A more difficult film in terms of ambiguity was *Diary of a Country Priest*. There the character of the priest seemed unmotivated, perplexing many of the writers. Again, however, the problem was not attributed to authorial expression about objective or subjective reality. Instead, two propositions were made relating to production causes: George Bernano's story was about the "abstract regions of the soul" so perhaps the script was obtuse. Or maybe "Bresson is not too successful in explaining his motivations." Alternative hypotheses found the failure of clarity in plot linkages to be the reviewer's problem. "The movie does demand some willingness from the viewer to add his own interpretative abilities to what is shown." But perhaps the reviewer just does not sufficiently know theology.[53]

This willingness on the part of the reviewers to assume that films could have multiple interpretations depending on the spectator somewhat contradicts the idea that an author is sending a message, such as that life is ambiguous. More cynical was Stanley Kaufmann's assertion that *The Seventh Seal* was "pretentious . . . [it] was, to me, symbolically opaque and allegorically illogical; the net effect was something like those *New Yorker* stories whose chief purpose seems to be to make you feel cretinous if you find them obscure."[54]

By the late 1950s, however, narrational style that might seem strange is increasingly explained as subjective realism. In the early 1950s, reviewers were accustomed to describing stylistic activities. *Day of Wrath* is praised for its visual images, which reviewers linked to fine art traditions of European classics. Acting and camerawork in *Rashomon* are due to cultural differences. *Diary of a Country Priest* receives numerous compliments on its poetic tempo. *The Seventh Seal* is an allegory.

However, in summer 1959, *Wild Strawberries* is the first film to provoke enough of a crisis to push the reviewers beyond criteria of pure "style"; this film's narrational tactics demanded an explanation related to some thematic or narrative point. Reviewers had no trouble, though, finding a solution. *Wild Strawberries* presents some kind of subjective realism. Crowther thinks it is a "surrealist exercise," exploring a person's "feelings and the psychology of an aging man." "Mosk" for *Variety* offers lots of solutions: "Nightmares, dreams and reminiscences are expertly blended as space and time are broken to work on the various levels of the man's thoughts." The *Time* reviewer also connects the narrational strategy to subject matter. The film is "a series of dreams and daydreams that reveal to [the protagonist] the meaning and unmeaning of his existence."[55]

A similar naturalization process (such as that which Jonathan Culler predicts and is described in chapter 2) works for *Hiroshima, mon amour*. The fragmented, elliptical style is actually fairly calmly received but leads to all sorts of interpretive solutions. One is, again, subjective realism. The narration is like a dream, or it is in a "Proustian style" of personal memories of one of the characters. More often, though, *Hiroshima, mon amour* is described as a poem and interpreted thus. The *Time* reviewer remarks that the crosscut opening suggests the couple are making love in a mass grave and continues from there in something of an explication de texte. But every writer thinks that the film is cinematic and its narration matches its subject matter.[56]

For these reviewers, the solution to problems of stylistic quirks, narrative ambiguity, and nonconventional subject matter ends up the classic auteurist reading strategy that Bordwell predicts. The director's every portion of the film expresses messages. But to achieve that solution, reviewers have to find some parallels between form and content. Obviously, here, the textual features are perceptually different to a viewer trained in the codes or schemata of Hollywood films. However, the texts themselves are not the sole determinants of this need to interlace sense-data into a coherent pattern. Contexts also matter: the films' being represented as "art"; highbrow protocols of reading serious material, such as those being taught in academic institutions (e.g., American New Criticism); and social and discursive assumptions that the films had something coherent to say.

Breathless becomes a good summary case, in part because of the unfamiliar narrational techniques of Godard's jump cuts: the reviewers seem to feel compelled to explain this editing practice. Crowther writes, "It goes at its unattractive subject in an eccentric photographic style that sharply conveys the nervous tempo and the emotional erraticalness of the story it tells." "Mosk" specifically names the editing tactic a "jump cut" and explains, "But all this seems acceptable for this unorthodox film moves quickly and ruthlessly." Kauffmann concludes, "Form and subject are perfectly matched in this work."[57]

This solution is most certainly within the boundaries of typical literary and dramatic interpretation practiced by "better-educated" Americans in the 1950s. But *Time*'s reviewer takes one further step. Godard's practice is modern art. Titling the review "Cubistic Crime," the *Time* writer not only finds ways to link the narrational activity with subject matter but argues that Godard has achieved a truly contemporary realism.

> More daringly cubistic is the manner in which Godard has assembled his footage. Every minute or so, sometimes every few seconds, he has chopped a few feet out of the film, patched it together again without transition. The story can still be followed, but at each cut the film jerks ahead with a syncopated impatience that aptly suggests and stresses the compulsive pace of the hero's doomward drive. More subtly, the trick also distorts, rearranges, relativizes time—much as Picasso manipulated space in *Les Demoiselles d'Avignon*. All meaningful continuity is bewildered; the hero lives, like the animal he is, from second to second, kill to kill. A nasty brute. Godard has sent him to hell in style.[58]

The same sort of reading practice occurs for *Last Year at Marienbad* a year later. It is a dream, it is Pirandello, it is Einsteinian, it is twelve-tone music, it is *Finnegans Wake*. When in doubt, call it modernism, a mirror of the times. Such a move also reaffirms films as high art, reinforcing the "highbrow" association. This reading strategy continues through the decade of the 1960s. Michelangelo Antonioni explains to *Newsweek* that *L'Avventura*'s pace is "'the internal rhythm of the times.'" *Newsweek* thinks he is the "first man from the movies to get there." The film is also compared to a Chirico painting and an avant-garde novel.[59]

Thus, while the early narrational practices of camerawork by the Italian imports of the early 1950s failed to confound the reviewers (they praised the visual styles as documentary realism or poetic pictorialism), editing provoked enough notice to require its being explained as more than quirkiness. Either subjective realism or modernism becomes the justification. Then all alternative practices are subject to such treatment. Yet all solutions are still within the authorship ideology. An originating source (the director) expresses a message in the dialect of the times. Spectators who enjoy socially conscious discussions may opt to visit the art cinema, interpreting those messages and unifying subject matter and narrational techniques. Perhaps the audience can even find patterns among a director's films. Now, the art cinema comes with the compliments of the auteur.

Thus, the movement toward what has been described by scholars as the art cinema reading strategy has certain contextual logics. While the films did provoke a need to alter procedures applied to Hollywood films, the films—by themselves—scarcely tell the whole story. When the early art films deviated in subject matter as well as in narrative and narrational procedures, and when that deviation suggested the possibility that serious issues informed the film, a very traditional solution was used to interpret the text: the messages came from authors. Later, as divergence came to be more profound, academic rules for making the text coherent may have been particularly available, for the audience of the art cinema was "better educated." Furthermore, lots of explanations for odd narration were public discourse: documentary or subjective realism, pictorialism or modernism. All of these reading strategies permitted a public differentiation of the art cinema and its audience, maintaining a viable product for a specific audience to view. Thus, historical context helped journalistic reviewers and audiences keep the movies within the bounds of the interpretable and the consumable.

CHAPTER TEN

Chameleon in the Film,
Chameleons in the Audience;
Or, Where Is Parody? The Case of *Zelig*

To the Marxists [Zelig] is one thing, to the Catholic Church another. To Professor John Morton
Blum, author of "Interpreting Zelig," he reflects
the Jewish-American experience in that he wants
to "assimilate like crazy."
(Rob Edelman, 1984)

THE VARIETY of significances attributed to the titular character Zelig in the 1983 film provides a fitting conclusion for a project concerned with the historical interpretation of texts.[1] For Zelig and *Zelig* change depending upon their context: when Zelig encounters gangsters he adopts their bravado; when he hears black musicians he plays jazz with them; when surrounded by fat people he gains two hundred pounds. Zelig, the "human chameleon," metamorphoses from Republican to Democrat to Fascist; from African American to Chinese to Greek to Indian to Jew to German; from household help to baseball player to psychiatrist to actor to aviator. As one of those individuals interviewed in the fictional documentary about Zelig's life explained, "French intellectuals regard him as the symbol of everything." But John Morton Blum also notes that "no two intellectuals . . . agreed what he meant."

Indeed, the reviews of *Zelig* also evince that the film's significance[*2] changes as rapidly as Zelig did. In a survey of thirty-two reviews in mostly U.S. journals and newspapers, twelve writers thought that *Zelig* was commenting on the status of celebrities. Close to that theme was the notion, held by three reviewers, that the film was about "capricious social opinion." Three other reviewers indicated that insanity or psychosis was the subject matter, but other possibilities included "insignificance" (one) and proof of existence (one). Some overlap with the latter ideas exists among the nine reviewers who considered conformism to be the point of it all, although two thought "being oneself" or "self-identity" was closest to *Zelig's* core. Whatever above themes might be privileged, they also reflected on "the modern man" (four reviewers), or "Everyman" (three), or "the non-hero" (one). Of course, Zelig had identity problems, so that for one reader *Zelig* replayed the Lacanian mirror stage story. Being liked (one), being a success (one), being redeemed through love (two), being or not being Jewish (three), and being Woody Allen the auteur-celebrity (nine) also were rival theses.*[3]

Such a range of opinions is quite understandable from the viewpoint of the historical materialist study of reception. In this case, of course, the fact that most reviewers also thought that *Zelig* was a parody or satire also adds richness to the example. More than two-thirds of the reviewers (twenty-three) noted that *Zelig* was having some kind of fun with the genre of the documentary. Second on the list was that *Zelig* was parodying the recently released *Reds* (twenty). Other competitors for what constituted the objects of satire or intertextual reference included *Citizen Kane* (eight), the Elephant Man (four), Melville's confidence man (two), the real-life Jew Stephen Jacob Weinberg (one), and the interviewees—Susan Sontag, Irving Howe, Saul Bellow, and Bruno Bettelheim (two). Parody of rampant commercialism (one), life in the 1920s (three), and psychoanalysis (two) were also proposed. And one critic even thought that *Zelig* was satirizing attempts at interpretation.[4] Indeed, *Zelig* does present a choice example for studying a very specific but common interpretive problem—the determination of voice and tone, the explication of parody.

Parody is particularly an interpretive problem for two reasons. First of all, internal evidence in a text could never be sufficient to settle critical disagreements about the meaning of the text or to what it refers since part of the process of parody is *extra*textual referencing. Parodies imply an intent (from the source of the text), and they require another text as a referent. As David Bennett notes, "There is nothing intrinsic to the text that predetermines a parodic reading. . . . the parodic can be seen as contextually, not intrinsically, defined— . . . parody is the effect of a particular, intertextual strategy of reading." [5] Thus, considering context is a normal referential act by a reader who believes parody to be occurring.

A theory of parody benefits from post-structuralist hypotheses about language. For a sign in the text to be readable as parodic requires that it have two simultaneous signifieds: its meaning within the text and its intertextual signification, derived from the reader's recognition that another referent is imbricated in the communicative process.

While several writers of post-structuralism have broached the issue of intertextuality (especially Julia Kristeva), one of the more important scholars of the phenomenon of parody is Mikhail Bakhtin, whose work has recently entered European and American scholarly communities, hailed by individuals such as Tzvetan Todorov as potentially providing an entirely new theory of communication. For Todorov, Bakhtin is something of a savior since Bakhtin's translinguistics might provide an alternative to the discredited structuralism of Saussure and applications of that linguistics to the criticism of texts. Bakhtin and his compatriot, V. N. Vološinov, also furnish the communication theory base for the British cultural studies approach discussed in Part One. Rejecting structuralism, the British cultural studies scholars believe that Bakhtin and Vološinov offer a cultural and social theory which explains the *possibility* for variations in readings.

The extent to which the theories of Bakhtin might be of use in post-structuralist research about the *production* of texts is an important question. In fact, in the case of *Zelig*, Robert Stam suggests that "the categories of Mikhail Bakhtin" are particularly useful in "attempts to disengage the film's generic intertext and explore the strata of its allegorical palimpsest: film as chameleon, the artist as chameleon, the Jewish experience as chameleon, the self as chameleon."[6]

However, another question is whether Bakhtin's translinguistics as is currently constituted by the scholarly community can account for the *reception* of texts, especially the "double-voiced," parodic texts for which his theory seems especially suited. It is the reception side of Bakhtinian theory that I wish to ponder in this chapter. Yet even if I conclude that Bakhtin's translinguistic model is flawed, I believe that the historical materialist approach to reception presented within this book can provide an explanation *using Bakhtin's model* for why that model has difficulties accounting for variation among interpretations of significance and intertextuality. A closer examination of the critical response to *Zelig* can provide some data useful toward that understanding. In the long run, then, I also believe that Bakhtin's translinguistics might be revised so as to be useful in reception studies, a proposition I hinted at in Part One in discussing the values of the three dominant approaches in film studies for analyzing interpretative acts.

BAKHTIN'S TRANSLINGUISTIC THEORY OF COMMUNICATION

It is not my purpose here to enter the fray over some of the problems of Bakhtin scholarship.*[7] What I shall try to provide is something of the received opinion regarding Bakhtin's theory of communication. Ultimately, I agree with Allon White that translinguistics provides several criticisms of structuralism, linking Bakhtinian language theory to post-structuralist models of communication. These differences include the belief that texts are not autonomous, closed structures and that meaning is determined from contextual conditions.[8] The latter point, however, removes Bakhtin from the camp of the deconstructionists, a factor that will wreak havoc with use of his translinguistics—as currently constructed—for reception studies.

In synopses of Bakhtin's work, a distinction is made between *linguistics* as the study of language and *translinguistics* as the study of discourse, or the process of individual exchanges. Bakhtin is interested in the latter; that is, the study of communication is his object of research. Unlike Saussure, whose domain is language and whose minimal unit is the sign, Bakhtin considers his fundamental unit to be the "utterance."[9] According to Todorov's version of Bakhtin, an utterance has two facets: its linguistic matter and the context of its enunciation, which is "'a necessary constitutive element of [an utterance's] semantic structure.'" This enunciative context is further broken into three subfacets: "The spatial *horizon common* to the interlocutors"; "*knowledge and understanding of the situation,* also *common* to both"; and "their *common evaluation* of the situation," including the object of discussion.[10]

Consequently, Todorov sees Bakhtin's model of communication as contrasting with that of the Saussurean-lineaged Roman Jakobson. Jakobson broadens the standard Speaker-Message-Receiver diagram to incorporate context, contact, and code, where contact is the "physical channel and psychological connection between the addresser and the addressee" and the code is a partially or fully shared language system.[11] Thus Jakobson diagrams an act of verbal communication:

Jakobson's Model of Communication

	Context	
Addresser	Message	Addressee
	Contact	
	Code	

Alternately, Todorov[12] presents Bakhtin's model as:

Bakhtin's Model of Communication

	Object	
Speaker	Utterance	Listener
	Intertext	
	Language	

This substitute model may at first glance seem merely a change of terminology. However, part and parcel of the Bakhtinian theory are the visions of the constructed and social Self and the dialogical process of communication.

From Vološinov's *Marxism and the Philosophy of Language,* which Bakhtinian scholars believe constitutes part of Bakhtin's writings and beliefs, comes the theory that the individual's acquisition of language is socially based. Furthermore, if given a post-structuralist twist, since the "Self" is itself a representation and thus a sign, the traditional split between Self and society is a false opposition. Rather, the notion of the Self (and the constitution of an individual into a Self) derives thoroughly from the social base through the individual's entrance into representation via society's pregiven language. As this is often put, the individual and the individual's language are, through and through, social, always already incorporating the Other.

This disruption of traditional boundaries (Self/Other) appears again in the representation of the dialogical. For Bakhtin, in any instance of communication, the speaker is already constituting the listener as an Other prepared to respond to the speaker's discussion. The same applies to the listener. In an extended criticism written in 1952 of the Saussurean model, Bakhtin stresses that the listener is not passively taking in a speaker's words but is "inherently responsive": "he either agrees or disagrees with it (completely or partially), augments it, applies it, prepares for its execution, and so on." But a speaker assumes this.

> He does not expect passive understanding that, so to speak, only duplicates his own idea in someone else's mind. Rather, he expects response, agreement, sympathy, objection, execution, and so forth. . . . Moreover, any speaker is himself a respondent to a greater or lesser degree. He is not, after all, the first speaker, the one who disturbs the external silence of the universe. And he presupposes not only the existence of the language system he is using, but also the existence of preceding utterances—his and others'—with which his given utterance enters into one kind of relation or another (builds on them, polemicizes with them or simply presumes that they are already known to the listener). Any utterance is a link in a very complexly organized chain of other utterances.[13]

Consequently, within the speaker's message is the anticipated dialogue*[14] with the Other's speech. Communicative exchanges are not bounded messages; every utterance already includes the response of the receiver. As Michael Holquist explains:

> "Utterance" is Bakhtin's overall term for a *duality* of roles that previously has been obscured by the assumption that speaking and listening were mutually opposed, unitary activities: a person *did either* one or the other. In fact, of course, we do both simultaneously. Discourse is an action. It is an activity more complicated than that of machines which must, due to mechanical limitations, transmit and receive *sequentially*.[15]

Furthermore, no utterance is an "individualistic subjectivism"[16] since the speaker and speaking are already social. As Charles I. Schuster writes,

"Language is not just a bridge between 'I' and 'Thou,' it is 'I' and 'Thou.'"[17] This is the way that "[Bakhtin] demolishes the notion of the atomic self, authentic in its privacy only, clearly separable from other selves and identified as free to the degree that it has purged itself of 'external influences.' For him . . . what I call my 'self' is essentially social."[18]

Because of the already-answering nature of speakers' utterances, utterances are not bounded but always intertextual—they refer to and thus image the words of the Other; they "report" the speech of the Other. The intertext is the projected dialogue of the listener that features in the construction of the utterance, just as do the object and the available social language. Immanent, then, within the character of utterances is the feature of polyphony. For Bakhtin, polyphony describes the multi-voiced expression of every communicative process.[19]

Let us return to Todorov's diagram of the communicative exchange as utterance. It is now more apparent why the new model, while similar to its predecessor, is not merely a substitution of vocabulary. Todorov indicates that the terms "object" in Bakhtin's model and "context" in Jakobson's might both be translated as "referent." However, the rest of the diagram is different. In place of Jakobson's "contact" is Bakhtin's "intertext," a notion that does not figure in Jakobson's model because Jakobson assumes an autonomous speaker encoding and then a listener decoding. As indicated above, intertextuality is, like the object, part of the contextual situation in play for any utterance. Intertextuality produces polyphony—the multi-voicedness of any utterance. (If the intertext is of another language,*[20] say the language of a repressed minority, then heteroglossia—many-languagedness—is also occurring.)

Additionally, Todorov stresses that his whole schema needs to be used with care, for the term "language" should not be considered at the same plane as the other terms since the model "cannot account for the fundamental difference between discourse and language." Language is the starting place for utterances that make up discourse; it is not the means by which utterances are understood and made meaningful (as codes may be said to function in language). Rather, the entire communicative *relation* or its *context* is what constitutes the production of meaning. As Bakhtin writes, "The authentic environment of an utterance, the environment in which it lives and takes shape, is dialogized heteroglossia, anonymous and social as language, but simultaneously concrete, filled with specific content and accented as an individual utterance."[21] Thus, Schuster also contrasts Bakhtin's model against the similar Aristotelian paradigm of speaker-subject-listener in which, Schuster notes, Aristotelian critics are interested in the *denotative* meaning of statement. Bakhtin's intertextual model is after the *connotative* implications of the discourse for that historical space and time. Ken Hirschkop underlines the theory's significance: "The dependence of textual meaning on social situation is by now an accepted Bakhtinian axiom."[22]

Such a theory of communication might seem eminently amenable to the reception studies method proposed in this book. In fact, it might be, were it not for an assumption made by Bakhtin and many of his disciples. This assumption repeats that of the text-oriented critics: that the object and projected intertext, and thus the context, are the same for both the speaker and the listener. While the problem of contextual referencing exists for any utterance, it is most apparent in overt instances of "double-voiced" speech, in the cases of explicitly reported speech, stylization, *skaz*,*[23] and parody. To see this at work requires considering Bakhtin's theory of communication in relation to voice.

PARODY: A FEW DIS-CONTENTS

Bakhtin believed that "to a greater or lesser extent, every novel is a dialogized system made up of *images* of 'languages,' styles and consciousnesses that are concrete and inseparable from language."*[24] Moreover, he especially concerned himself with a special type of dialogization: instances in which a discourse referred simultaneously to the object of discussion as well as to a second object, an imaged intertext. He wrote: "A single trait is common to [stylization, parody, *skaz*, and dialogue] despite their essential differences: in all of them the word has a double-directednesss—it is directed both toward the object of speech, like an ordinary word, and toward *another word*, toward *another person's speech*."[25] So that, for instance, for *Zelig* to parody *Reds*, the filmic interviews with Sontag, Howe, Bellow, and Bettelheim must contextually reference the object of discussion, Zelig. Additionally, though, those interviews must be directed toward and incorporate a second object, the imaged speech of the filmmakers who produced *Reds*. Bakhtin will call such an event an "intentional hybrid."[26] Finally, however, for parody to occur, the utterance must also suggest a particular attitude or tone about the relation between the object of reference and the imaged speech, an attitude or tone judged parodic. In other examples of double-voicedness, the relationship implied takes a different tone, perhaps merely that of neutrality in the case of reported speech.

Such an intentional hybrid, thus, is not without its distortions. As I noted above, the parodying utterance produces an *image* of the parodied language. Consequently, transformations and metamorphoses occur. Bakhtin acknowledges this: "It is the nature of every parody to transpose the values of the parodied style, to highlight certain elements while leaving others in the shade: parody is always biased in some direction, and this bias is dictated by the distinctive features of the parodying language, its accentual system, its structure. . . . Thus, every parody is an intentional dialogized hybrid."[27] Such a proposition inflects on the thesis of Vološinov's to which I have referred often: that a region for class struggle is the accent of signs.

All of this, it seems to me, is viable for arguments about the production of utterances and, in particular, parodies. However, some twisting is necessary for the model to function as a theory of reception. In an attempt to apply Bakhtin's commentary to parody, Linda Hutcheon points out that Bakhtin's discussion is structural rather than pragmatic. For a listener to participate, the listener has to have at least a notion of the speaker's intent.[28]

Thus, Bakhtin seems to assume, as do so many other structuralists, harmony in understanding between speaker and listener. This works only if you assume that language is monoglossic—an assumption that Bakhtin himself denies. Furthermore, in Bakhtin's model, a listener would have to share with the speaker something of an isomorphic judgment of (1) the object of the utterance's reference, (2) the image of speech being parodied, (3) the tone or attitude toward the relation between (1) and (2), and (4) the intertext. In fact, such a notion of the homogeneity of context is implied in Todorov's description of the act of utterance. Recall that Todorov uses the phrases "spatial *horizon common* to the interlocutors," "*knowledge and understanding of the situation*, also *common* to both," and "their *common evaluation* of the situation."[29] As I have been at pains to construct throughout this book, such a representation of the speaking event, while possible, is not probable, given the heterogeneity of social and historical contexts. Even Bakhtin seems finally to limit the understanding of utterances to very specific moments.

> The linguistic significance of a given utterance [for a listener] is understood against the background of language, while its actual meaning is understood against the background of other concrete utterances on the same theme, a background made up of contradictory opinions, points of view and value judgments—that is, precisely that background that, as we see, complicates the path of any word toward its object. Only now this contradictory environment of alien words is present to the speaker not in the object, but rather in the consciousness of the listener, as his apperceptive background, pregnant with responses and objections. . . . Understanding comes to fruition only in the response. Understanding and response are dialectically merged and mutually condition each other; one is impossible without the other.*[30]

Now, a deconstructionist would argue that at no time is such a dialectical *merging* possible. This is so for two reasons related to the notion of the boundaries of context. First of all, if Bakhtin does theorize the Self as constituted in language as a sign, and if language is polyvocal and heteroglossic, then so is the Self. The Self in reporting its identity is never in identity with the Self that is reported: "When I say that I performed such and such a deed at such and such a time, it is no longer the same 'I' who speaks as the one who performed the deed."[31] Thus, even if the speaker is constituting an utterance through the dialogized intertext of the listener, the listener, in turn, is confronted with being in a chaining discourse: the listener's understanding of the utterance requires a permutation based on the speaker's merging activity. Speaking is a process and transformation, not a structure.

This relates to the second difficulty with the bounds of context. Given the "double-voiced" feature of language, given variable accents and heteroglossia, and given the process (rather than structure) of utterances, it would be extremely difficult to determine with certainty the intention of an utterance in relation to objects of reference and intertextuality. Even in a face-to-face exchange, the listener could never verify the speaker's intent since the speaker's Self would be consistently not the Self previously speaking.

The upshot of this is that every listener is ultimately not truly a "listener" but another speaker, a producer of meaning. The listener may attempt to consider what the speaker's object(s) and intertext(s) are, but the context has changed. No assured exchange occurs. This problem of context slips into Bakhtin's analysis even though he seems to wish to focus on explication of texts and utterances as though they could be frozen for analysis (he produces a text-oriented criticism). Bakhtin points out: "There is neither a first nor a last word and there are no limits on the dialogic context (it extends into the boundless past and boundless future). Even *past* meanings, that is, those born in the dialogue of past centuries, can never be stable (finalized, ended once and for all)—they will always change (be renewed) in the process of subsequent, future development of the dialogue."[32] In fact, parody is particularly susceptible to deterioration of context: it "may under certain circumstances be easily and quickly lost to perception, or be significantly weakened."[33]

Despite the problem of context and his own theory of the constitution of the Self as social and dialogical, Bakhtin's model of communication is still perhaps of value to the consideration of what happens in the reception of parody (or single-directed discourse). For the model does mime several features of reception not obvious in the Jakobson model. How this might work can be outlined in the *Zelig* affair.

THE CASE OF ZELIG

If the reviewers of *Zelig* are considered not as listeners but new speakers in dialogical exchange with *Zelig*, many of the inconsistencies and yet similarities among the reviews can be explained. For each review-as-utterance, the reviewer posits *Zelig* as one object of reference; a second object, the imaged speech of an Other to which *Zelig* refers; a tone to the relation (such as parodic); and, as a fourth variable, the intertext of the reviewer's own listeners. Even if I granted that *Zelig* had an immanent meaning (which I have been arguing against throughout this text), the other three variables are sufficient to account for variations among the critical interpretations of the film's significance. Each writer images the speech with which *Zelig* is in dialogue: this is often and casually termed the *subtext*, a rather apt metaphor in the instance of this model. For it is, indeed, a text within the context of the reviewer's utterance but lying outside the boundaries of the object and the utterance. Thus, for agreement among critics to occur, all critics would have to construct the same subtext, having the same features in the subtext's image of speech which *Zelig* will mimic by accentuation. Additionally, for parody, all critics would have to agree to the attitude expressed in the voice of the reported speech.

But even more than that, each reviewer would have to construct the same intertextual dialogue with his or her listeners. Recall that Bakhtin's model understands utterances as dialogical. Incorporated within the speaker's utterance is the speaker's presupposition of the Other to which the utterance is already in response, hence an utterance's polyphonic and heteroglossic nature.*[34] Thus, speakers become chameleons: they take on the coloration of those whom they address in their attempts to respond to the listeners even as they speak—without, however, losing their own identity.

Even if critics all agreed on the variables of the subtext and voice, however, no speaker's intertext can be the same as any other speaker's intertext since each speaker exists within a different context as an uniquely socialized member of a language community. What maintains the possibilities for communication, I believe, are the material constraints on the set of heteroglossias functioning within any historical social formation. This I have stressed throughout the book.

If this thesis has validity, then some evidence of it should be discernible in the reviews. I believe that it is. This time, I surveyed thirty-two reviews mostly in U.S. journals and newspapers. Although I entered the case of *Zelig* having in mind its possible use for considering Bakhtin's commentary on the dialogic and parody, wanting an example from the decade of the 1980s, and knowing that at least Robert Stam had considered the film in relation to Bakhtin's theories of polyphony, I more or less went into the reviews "blind." That is, I did not preselect the case because I knew the reviews would confirm my thesis.

What I found are several remarkable correlations between critics' subtexts and intertexts. Let me give two connected examples of this. One instance involves those critics who claimed that *Zelig* deals with being or not being Jewish. Three writers mention this: Richard Combs writing for *Monthly Film Bulletin* and Samuel Dresner and Aryeh L. Gotlieb for *Midstream*. On the one hand, Combs remarks in passing that the film is "almost a dissertation on the Jewish joke" which Combs connects to "assimilation anxiety"; he also suggests parodies or allusions to *Reds, Elephant Man*, and *Citizen Kane*, listing as many films or other books as possible subtexts as do Pauline Kael and Stanley Kauffmann of the cultural incrowd periodicals, the *New Yorker* and the *New Republic*. Most of all, though, Combs focuses on Zelig as a "perfect expression of [Woody Allen's] non-hero," a character Combs believes runs through the films directed by Allen. Thus, while Combs mentions Jewishness as a possible subtext, he does not consider it as centrally establishing a significance he finds more general to Allen's oeuvre. As a writer for *Monthly Film Bulletin*, a periodical for movie aficionados, Combs argues that "this is the non-film Allen has always been working towards." (Obviously, Combs is continuing the authorship themes that I have suggested permeate twentieth-century American film criticism.)

Dresner and Gotlieb, on the other hand, do not take the "Jewish joke" so lightly, writing as they do for a "Zionist publication." Instead, their intertext assumes dialogue with a very specific ethnic and national listener, the American Jew, at a time when the issues of Jewish heritage and Israeli-U.S. politics are of signal importance to readers of such a magazine. Dresner and Gotlieb seem as well to be in dialogue with each other, publishing their pieces sequentially in the same issue of *Midstream*. Dresner draws evidence from *Zelig* to show that "Allen is examining Jewish conformism, albeit of American Jews." (Note that the conformism is not just any conformism, a general theme of significance to eight other writers but specified as "Jewish" only in Dresner's case.) Dresner continues: Zelig's transformations refer to "all the adjustments of noses, accents, names, and creeds that Jews have undergone so that they can be accepted into the club, the church, the business, the family." The final cure for the assimilation desire is intermarriage and the dissolution of the Jew. Gotlieb "counters": Zelig does not disappear; "Zelig at the core survives." This is because "wherever he is, the Jew takes on the color of his environment, but he does not disappear into the background. He doesn't even blend. He stands in the foreground as a major contributor—no one forgets that he is a

Jew." Rather than assimiliation, Gotlieb believes acculturation to be the message.

This is what two Jewish writers conclude. By contrast, the specifically Christian magazines reviewing *Zelig* do not raise "being or not being Jewish" as a point of the film. Three overtly religious journalists covered *Zelig*: Richard A. Blake of *America* (Catholic), Harry Cheney of *Christianity Today* ("evangelical"), and J. M. Wall of *Christian Century*. Wall's review is brief, although it notes "scenes that parody the rise and fall of the heroes of the '20s and '30s." Blake and Cheney provide more extended exegeses. Blake perceives *Zelig* as "a statement on the plight of modern man": "Modern man can be so dominated by his environment that he loses his personality. Love . . . liberates the true self. Psychosis lies at the root of genius; perfect adjustment destroys creativity. Woody Allen, the modern Everyman, fears annihilation." Blake also believes that *Zelig* critiques interpretation: "[The interviewees] deflate through parody the pomposity that so often accompanies a quest for recondite meanings in Woody Allen's works and in their own." Although Blake notes that Zelig is the son of Jewish parents, "since Leonard has no personality, his Jewishness does not stick," and Blake moves on to his more important observations.

Cheney finds significances in *Zelig* not observed by anyone else. He reads the film as an allegory: the "ironic confession of the neurosis-riddled Everyman." This Everyman "discovers how difficult it is to co-exist peaceably with anyone—including himself and God—yet earnestly desires such an arrangement all the same. . . . Desperate to join any club, Leonard pays the exorbitant membership fee with his own soul." Zelig is not made to perish in hell, however. "The 'chameleon man's' greatest feat is his final transformation into a loving human being: a liberated Lazarus freed from the burial cloths of fashionable conformity and public opinion. The most satisfying resurrection is Woody Allen's visual paraphrase of Saint Paul's admonishment that we 'be not conformed. . . .'"

Thus, for Jews in America, *Zelig* teaches a message about the Jew in America; for Christians, *Zelig* fulfills New Testament parables about love transforming the self into an independent being freed from social pressures for conformity. It is a long-standing thesis in rhetorical studies that speakers consider their audiences when preparing addresses. Bakhtin's model suggests that not only are those audiences considered but the speaker assumes and speaks, dialogically, those audiences' voices in speaking her or his own. As I argued in Part One, how individuals construct or imagine themselves—the specific gender, ethnic, racial, national, or, here, religious identities by which they establish their Selves—becomes part of the constituent terms in a relation of a text's reception. Bakhtin's model of communication may be transformed into a sophisticated proposition about how that constitution occurs within a contextual chain of utterances when, as a theory of reception, the model places the listener into the position of being a new speaker. Such a historical and contextual approach differs from preconstituting the listener's identity, a practice, as I noted, of the British cultural studies scholars.

Other examples of the selective visions of subtexts and intertexts exist for *Zelig*. For instance, the eight writers who mention *Citizen Kane* as a possible intertextual reference are all writing for journals or newspapers with an audience presumably well educated in film history. These are: the *New York Times, Monthly Film Review*, the *New Yorker, Newsweek, Films and Filming, Sight and Sound, Village Voice, Film Journal*, and *Cinefantastique*.*[35] The two individuals who reference Melville's confidence man are writers with a cultural elite audience, Kael (the *New Yorker*) and Kauffmann (the *New Republic*).

Variations occur. Although three writers generalize that *Zelig* speaks about "Everyman," what *Zelig* says for every person differs. Cheney thinks it is everyone's battle against "conformity"; John Coleman of the *New Statesman* describes everyone's problem as "insecurity"; and Colin L. Westerbeck, Jr., for *Commonweal*, posits the subtext, everyone's, as the "emptiness" of fame. In fact, these differences raise the second example for which the model must also account. Only a few of the thirty-two writers attempt an overarching, unifying theme for the film's significance. In chapter 4, I noted Jonathan Culler's argument that four protocols for unifying a text often operate: (1) noting that the particulars of an individual apply to a class; (2) exploiting shifts in meaning, arguing that what comes second is what is true; (3) using local materials to argue parallel, connotative, or ironic semantics; and (4) counting closings more than anything else. Of all of the reviewers, Cheney most adheres to the position of Culler's competent reader. Most people, like Blake, string observations together with little attempt to unify their interpretation. Likely this is due mostly to the convention that reviews (and general audience responses) do not require such a rigorous interpretative approach. Consequently, numerous writers mention several propositions that might be taken as statements about *Zelig*'s significance without attempting to be sure a consistent logic underpins every observation. Such a manifestation, however, is easily explained: the critics determined multiple subtexts that seemed relevant. Given the variety of possibilities available to an early-1980s viewer of film, the historical discursive determinants are specific, although numerous. In an extended example, then, each individual's context, self-identity, and imagined audience would also need to be connected to issues in the social formation (such as themes of identity and fame in a postmodernist era).

What does seem to happen, at least among the thirty-two writers surveyed, is that subtexts begin to overlap one another: writers combine similar subtexts into what appear to be original views of the film (and they are). For instance, David Denby (*New York*) couples the chameleon motif with the subtext of Woody Allen's career to produce this utterance: "We're more likely to say that a story about a man who becomes whomever he's with is a kind of drastic metaphor for the actor and the comedian." Richard Grenier (*Commentary*), who spends almost one-half of his essay describing the remarkable feats of "the greatest imposter," Stephen Jacob Weinberg, associates the period in which the events are set (the 1920s) with the conformist theme thus: "But the notion of the 20's as a *conformist* period is also somewhat staggering." I would not venture to say that a limited set of fundamental subtexts determines the range of a finite number of possible permutations; however, I would stress that within a historical context, a film with the material of *Zelig* and readers with specific arrays of discourses and interpretive strategies are likely to produce determinant clusters of subtexts. Each critic, depending on his or her socialization, constructed Self, and the historical context for the utterance, will produce a specific, but understandable, variation on *Zelig*'s significance.

Stam and Ella Shohat believe *Zelig* exemplary of "what Bakhtin would call 'the interpersonal definition and fabrication of the world's meaning.'" In this I would agree, provided that it is clear that critics do not remain within the world of *Zelig*. Stam and Shohat point out that although everyone interviewed in *Zelig* interpreted Zelig differently, all the interviewees saw themselves in him: Howe "interprets Zelig as a quintessential exemplum of the transformations involved in assimilation"; Sontag, as "a rebel and maverick"; Bellow, as ambiguous and conformist.[36] Stam and Shohat thus notice that not only is Zelig a human chameleon but he produces in his viewers a similar dialogical rewriting. Stam and Shohat remain, however, within the field of textual criticism rather than taking their observation one step further: that each reviewer also becomes a chameleon in interpreting *Zelig*.*[37]

   If Bakhtin's theory is of use as a model of communication, then receiving a text such as *Zelig* results in a dialogical production of an utterance about the film's significance. This dialogical utterance derives from the audience's perception of the film's context, subtext, and intertext. The audience quotes this dialogical utterance when it interprets the film. As Zelig took on features of his contextual surroundings while still remaining Leonard Zelig, so are audiences both changed and unchanged. Such an observation also suggests that while the dialogic may be "in" the text, the text's *significance* derives from the contextual determination of the reader's interpretation as a process of reception.

Epilogue

INTERPRETING FILMS, interpreting television shows, interpreting events in our daily lives—over these activities we believe we have great mastery. And we do. But as I have struggled to argue, the contextual discourses derived from our social formation are critical in the reading strategies available to individuals. Consumers may make producers producers, as Marx points out, but the historical conditions involving such a constitution of that relation cannot be ignored. Furthermore, inequities that unfortunately still exist in all social formations produce not merely diversity but conflict among interpreters. Discourses are not neutral but connected in complex and often uneven relations to those social arrangements. Class, gender, race, ethnicity, national origin, sexual preference—these are but a few of the categories by which specific social formations have arranged people into subject positions, defined hierarchies of authority and privilege, and devaluated or even attempted to eliminate diversity.

Some of the manifestations of those inequities show up in interpretive activities and, in particular, in contested signs where meaning is not uniform among readers. The significance of a struggle over semantics, however, seldom manifests itself in a direct way. In fact, I would argue that contested signs can occasionally be diversions from more profound difficulties. A strategy of the dominant class has been diverting attention from real issues to ones of lesser import, displacing energies to phony battles. In chapter 1, I recounted Robert Darnton's suggestion that for the French the displacement whereby the furor over *Danton*'s interpretation led to concerns about their educational system masked a deeper anxiety about France's economic difficulties and political leadership.

Something of a similar event has occurred recently in the United States with conservative calls for reasserting agreement on, and reestablishing curricular attention to, older canons of great books. Such cries divert attention from, most directly, inadequate minority student recruitment, increasing costs of higher education (effective for lower- and, now, middle-class repression), stagnant faculty salaries, and intensified military-industrial state involvement in financing universities. Among the many political and social implications, the suggestion of a "supraclass" set of books indicates the desire to reinforce the continuing function of educational institutions to reproduce the dominant class's ideology—an ideology that is failing in relation to increasing economic difficulties and rising numbers of non-Anglo-Saxon Americans. Hegemony is in crisis.

Thus, this discussion of interpretation, for me at least, has wider implications than a mere struggle over critical approaches to autonomous literary or cinematic texts. I have tried to theorize a reception studies that has the following features: objects are not containers with immanent meaning but are constituted in historical context and sometimes conflict; signs are not fixed but may be contested; variations among interpretations are not random but have connections—usually uneven—to available discourses and interpretive strategies and to the real conditions of existence in a specific social formation; and interpretations are not predestined by social scientific categories of people but are related to individuals' constructed self-identities and the relation of those identities to apparent textual address determined by available interpretive strategies and discourses about the Self.

This endeavor has by no means covered the grounds that would be necessary to an eventual understanding of the process of interpretation in any specific social formation, much less all those available at any one historical moment or through history. This study has not dealt directly with nontutored readings; it has unfortunately in many cases focused solely on popular press reviews. Only indirectly has this study asserted claims about people who have traditionally had no access to public and printed records of communication. Such an unspoken mass deserves as much attention as does the popular press—if not more. How to do this for historical readers in a responsible scholarly way, however, is a very real problem.

Nor are these audiences one thing. In any process of reading, any number of possible self-identities may come into play simultaneously or successively. For a historical account of interpretation, seeking coherent readings is fallacious. So is assuming that all readers of the researcher's category will operate similarly. That fallacy returns reception studies to a text-activated, ideal-reader theory. The real diversity of interpretations and self-identities, moreover, requires analysis, for the diversity is not random but structured in relation to available discourses and self-identities, interpretive strategies, and historical conditions. Here, too, the choices of possible self-identitites are being determined. Marxism has traditionally emphasized class as the most pertinent aspect of self-identity, but it seems harder and harder to maintain this self-identity as one that individuals use often for interpreting. The preferred choices of self-identity (occupation, life-style, race, ethnicity, gender, sexual preferences, nationality, and so on) may or may not be progressive or capable of being mobilized for progressive activities. Political and historical analyses need to consider this question as well.

This book is not a reception history. Although I might be tempted to make some linkages among the case studies, asserting trajectories of critical procedures among some readers, such as mass media writers, those claims would have to be so tentative as to be almost worthless. For instance, from the start "authorship" seems a strategy for unifying film texts either internally or across several films. Although Michel Foucault argues that this is a historical reading strategy of several centuries' duration, more specific case studies of readers are necessary before assertions of continuities and discontinuities in procedure can be determined. Then, too, "authorship" 's particular configuration in relation to the collective production of texts needs to be sorted out for mass media such as the dime fiction of the late 1800s as well as twentieth-century film and television. "Reflexivity" is another such reading strategy. Its appearance in film studies must relate to modernism, and much more can be done in sorting that out through the multiple avant-gardes that appear beginning in the mid-nineteenth century. The "form/content" split is another strategy that must connect with wider sociologies and semantics of art. Shifting histories of the construction and employment of various self-identities are more significant strands that ought to be followed in the effort to understand what has occurred.

For a materialist history of reception, the isolated cases I have presented will need to be put together with other studies. Reception studies is not textual interpretation but a historical explanation of the activities of interpretation. The significance of the specific cases presented here in relation to historical change requires understanding of the rate, direction, and probable outcome of the changes that have taken place and are taking place as a result of conflicts of forces. Thus, judgment calls about the political effectivity of specific interpretations remain tenuous until wider knowledge, cross-culturally and temporally, is available. Ultimately, though, I hope that reception studies can have use-value for progressive political change.

Notes

Chapter One
The Use-Value of Reception Studies

1. Karl Marx, *Introduction to The Critique of Political Economy* (1857; published 1903), quoted in Manfred Naumann, "Literary Production and Reception" (1973), trans. Peter Heath, *New Literary History* 8 (Autumn 1976): 108.

2. Roland Barthes, "The Death of the Author" (1968), in *Image, Music, Text*, trans. Stephen Heath (New York: Hill and Wang, 1977), p. 143; John Paul Russo, "I. A. Richards in Retrospect," *Critical Inquiry* 8, no. 4 (Summer 1982): 743–60; I. A. Richards, *Practical Criticism: A Study of Literary Judgment* (New York: Harcourt, Brace & World, 1929).

3. An asterisk preceding a footnote number indicates that the note is substantive, not purely bibliographical.

Here and elsewhere in this opening I shall use words, such as *meaning*, as though their definitions were obvious. Later I shall take up certain problems associated with these words.

4. Arthur Danto, "The Artworld," *Journal of Philosophy* 61 (1968): 581.

5. Directed by Andrzej Wajda, released in France in 1983.

6. Robert Darnton, "Danton and Double-Entendre," *New York Review of Books*, 16 February 1984, 19–24.

7. Ibid., p. 19.

8. Ibid.

9. Ibid., p. 23.

10. Ibid., p. 20.

11. Ibid.

12. Darnton also places the controversies within significant upheavals in French historiography, suggesting that the replacement of political histories by social histories (of the *Annales* school) also muddied the lines of dispute.

13. V. N. Vološinov, *Marxism and the Philosophy of Language* (1929), trans. Ladislav Matejka and I. R. Titunik (New York: Seminar Press, 1973).

14. Ferdinand de Saussure, *Course in General Linguistics* (1915), trans. Wade Baskin (New York: McGraw-Hill Book Company, 1966), pp. 15–17.

15. Vološinov, *Marxism*, p. 21 (italics in original).

16. Ibid., p. 23 (italics in original).

17. Darnton, "Danton," p. 19.

18. I am using the term "paradigmatic structure" and the notion of a transformation with all its implications in the sense explicated in Thomas S. Kuhn, *The Structure of Scientific Revolutions*, 2d ed. (Chicago: University of Chicago Press, 1970).

19. Jonathan Culler, *The Pursuit of Signs: Semiotics, Literature, Deconstruction* (Ithaca: Cornell University Press, 1981), p. 13. Culler is specifically referring to the *rezeptionsästhetik* of Hans Robert Jauss.

20. Culler, *The Pursuit of Signs*, p. 5.

21. Jane P. Tompkins, "The Reader in History: The Changing Shape of Literary Response," in *Reader-Response Criticism: From Formalism to Post-Structuralism*, ed. Jane P. Tompkins (Baltimore: The Johns Hopkins University Press, 1980), pp. 201–32. Also see Victoria Kahn, "The Figure of the Reader in Petrarch's *Secretum*," *PMLA* 100, no. 2 (March 1985): 154–66.

22. See philosophy of history debates such as those described in William H. Dray, *Philosophy of History* (Englewood Cliffs, N.J.: Prentice-Hall, 1964); R. F. Atkinson, *Knowledge and Explanation in History: An Introduction to the Philosophy of History* (Ithaca: Cornell University Press, 1978).

23. Etienne Balibar and Pierre Macherey, "Sur la littérature comme forme idéologique: Quelques hypothèses Marxistes," *Littérature* 13 (1974): 30, quoted in Pierre Kuentz, "A Reading of Ideology or an Ideology of Reading?" trans. Wayne Gymon, *Sub-stance* 15 (1976): 82–93 (italics in original).

24. An excellent survey of the difficulties of working from either an "apparatus" or an "individual" approach is Barbara Klinger's "In Retrospect: Film Studies Today," *Yale Journal of Criticism* 2, no. 1 (1988): 129–51.

25. Martin Allor, "Relocating the Site of the Audience," *Critical Studies in Mass Communication* 5 (1988): 219. Be sure to see the critical response to Allor's essay in the same issue. Also see Richard Johnson, "Culture and the Historians," in *Working-Class Culture*, ed. John Clarke, Chas. Critcher, and Richard Johnson (London: Hutchinson, 1979), pp. 41–71.

26. Terry Eagleton, *Criticism and Ideology: A Study in Marxist Literary Theory* (1976) (London: Verso, 1978), p. 73.

27. Judith Fetterley, *The Resisting Reader: A Feminist Approach to American Fiction* (Bloomington: Indiana University Press, 1978).

28. Marc Silberman, Review of "Holub's *Reception Theory*," *New German Critique* 33 (Fall 1984): 250.

29. See *Critical Inquiry* 10, no. 1 (September 1983) (special issue on canons); valuable comments are also in Peter Uwe Hohendahl, "Introduction to Reception Aesthetics," trans. Marc Silberman, *New German Critique* 10 (Winter 1977): 47; Peter U. Hohendahl, "Prolegomena to a History of Literary Criticism," trans. Jeannine Blackwell, *New German Critique* 11 (Spring 1977): 159; Janet Staiger, "The Politics of Film Canons," *Cinema Journal* 24, no. 3 (Spring 1985): 4–23; Jane P. Tompkins, "Sentimental Power: *Uncle Tom's Cabin* and the Politics of Literary History" (1978), rpt. in *The New Feminist Criticism: Essays on Women, Literature and Theory*, ed. Elaine Showalter (New York: Pantheon Books, 1985), pp. 81–84.

30. Barbara Herrnstein Smith, "Contingencies of Value," *Critical Inquiry* 10, no. 1 (September 1983): 18.

31. Ibid.

32. Gerald Graff, "The Genesis of Secrecy: On the Interpretation of Narrative by Frank Kermode," *New Republic*, 9 June 1979, 27.

33. Walter Benjamin, "Theses on the Philosophy of History," in *Illuminations*, ed. Hannah Arendt, trans. Harry Zohn (New York: Schocken Books, 1969), p. 256.

Chapter Two
Reception Studies in Other Disciplines

1. For a good survey of some of the consistencies and divergencies in approaches in new sociocultural histories, see Roger Chartier, "Intellectual History or Sociocultural History? The French Trajectories," trans. Jane P. Kaplan, in *Modern European Intellectual History: Reappraisals and New Perspectives*, ed. Dominick LaCapra and Steven L. Kaplan (Ithaca: Cornell University Press, 1982), pp. 13–46.

2. Robert Darnton, *The Great Cat Massacre and Other Episodes in French Cultural History* (New York: Vintage Books, 1984), pp. 215–56.

3. Peter Bürger, "The Institution of 'Art' as a Category in the Sociology of Literature," *Cultural Critique* 2 (Winter 1985–1986): 6.

4. For example, Clifford Geertz, *The Interpretation of Cultures* (New York: Basic Books, 1973), p. 46: "Undirected by culture patterns—organized systems of significant symbols—man's behavior would be virtually ungovernable, a mere chaos of pointless acts and exploding emotions, his experience virtually shapeless."

5. Cognitive science provides the basis of at least one major theory of spectator activity in film studies. I shall cover this research in more depth in chapter 3.

6. On use of Schleiermacher and the Hermeneutic Circle for contemporary research, see "*The Hermeneutics*: Outline of the 1819 Lectures" (1974), trans. Jan Wojcik and Roland Haas, *New Literary History* 10, no. 1 (Autumn 1978): 1–16, and the entire special issue; David Tracy, "Creativity in the Interpretation of Religion: The Question of Radical Pluralism," *New Literary History* 15, no. 2 (Winter 1984): 289–309. On Gadamer's work see Janet Wolff, "The Interpretation of Literature in Society: The Hermeneutic Approach" in *The Sociology of Literature: Theoretical Approaches*, ed. Jane Routh and Janet Wolff (Keele, England: University of Keele Press, 1977), pp. 18–31; Robert C. Holub, *Reception Theory: A Critical Introduction* (New York: Methuen, 1984), pp. 3–52. Holub also links in the Russian formalists and Prague structuralists.

7. Robert Weimann, "'Reception Aesthetics' and the Crisis of Literary History," trans. Charles Spencer, *Clio* 5, no. 1 (1975): 3. Marxists who prefer alternative influences to that of Iser and Jauss may choose to appeal to those debates.

8. Discussing the research of Terence Cave and Cathleen Bauschatz, Victoria Kahn delineates their view that prior to the 1500s, rhetorics assumed the reader to be a "passive recepient." However, quattrocentro humanists believed in the possibility of educating readers, which would imply some kind of change in knowledge or ideas. Cave argues that it is as a result of these pedagogical theses that the reader (as a character) starts appearing in texts. Kahn counters, however, that Petrarch considered reading as dangerous, provoking earlier addresses within the text to (implied) readers. Naomi Schor also considers this, by proposing that most modern fiction provides a character who interprets events. She claims, furthermore, that it is difficult for an actual reader to avoid identifying with this "interpretant." To flesh out her thesis, she considers the interpretant-characters in works by James, Proust, and Kafka, using two criteria: "quantity" (how significant to the text the interpretant is) and "quality" (the degree(s) of success for the interpretant

in interpreting). Kahn, "The Figure of the Reader in Petrarch's *Secretum*," 154; Naomi Schor, "Fiction as Interpretation/Interpretation as Fiction," in *The Reader in the Text: Essays on Audience and Interpretation*, ed. Susan Suleiman and Inge Crosman (Princeton: Princeton University Press, 1980), pp. 165–82.

9. Susan R. Suleiman, quoting Geoffrey Hartman, gives a succinct description of "negative hermeneutics": it criticizes, often by parody or play, "'master theories that claim to have overcome the past, the dead, the false.'" Negative hermeneutics accomplishes this "by focusing on those aspects of a text that reveal the vulnerability of any absolute statement about its meaning, and by making of the impossibility of a single interpretation the primary subject of criticism." "Introduction: Varieties of Audience-Oriented Criticism," in *The Reader in the Text*, ed. Suleiman and Crosman, pp. 38–39.

10. In chapter 3 I will discuss David Bordwell's reservations about using the term *reading* in reference to the process of viewing moving images.

11. Gerald Prince, "Notes on the Text as Reader," in *The Reader in the Text*, ed. Suleiman and Crosman, p. 225.

12. Prince is using those terms as developed by Roland Barthes in *S/Z* (1970), trans. Richard Miller (New York: Hill and Wang, 1974). See below.

13. Prince, "Notes on the Text," p. 229.

14. George L. Dillon, *Language Processing and the Reading of Literature: Toward a Model of Comprehension* (Bloomington: Indiana University Press, 1978), p. xvii (italics in original). As indicated, Dillon is presenting a psycholinguistic explanation of reading. In Harry Singer and Robert B. Ruddell's anthology, the authors offer four models of reading: psycholinguistic, information processing (theories that readers go from print to abstract entities but not by way of speech), developmental ("as an individual learns to read, he sequentially develops a mental structure that is complexly interwoven and functionally organized in at least three hierarchical levels" [pp. 619–20]), and affective (drawing on personality psychology, social psychology or psychiatry). *Theoretical Models and Processes of Reading* (Newark, Del.: International Reading Association, 1976), pp. 450–676. Most reception theory literature assumes ability to read, but claims about universality or about the relations between perception and interpretation seem to me to require investigation of these fundamental questions. For instance, the first three models offer variant notions of how language is learned and whether or not it is necessary for thinking. When discussing David Bordwell's application of cognitive science to film philosophy in chapter 3, I will return to this.

15. Dillon, *Language Processing*, p. xx.

16. Much the same position about interpretation's determining comprehension is taken by Alan Garnham in *Psycholinguistics: Central Topics* (London: Methuen, 1985), pp. 147–82. He writes, "Knowledge about the world is important in text comprehension. For example, it is often required to establish cohesive links between sentences" (p. 156). An analytical philosophy approach (James F. Ross, "On the Concepts of Reading," *The Philosophical Forum* 6, no. 1 [Fall 1974]: 93–141) concludes the same thing and even extends it: "perception occurs only when the subject forms an epistemic attitude which is the result of his interpretation, via some cognitive unit or other, of a sensory stimulus" (p. 103). "There may be no such thing as the simple apprehension of linguistic meaning with no *other* product;

... perhaps, there must always be an output (not necessarily bahaviorally manifest) of behaviorially discriminable epistemic, imaginative, associative or emotive states" (p. 94, italics in original).

17. Steven Mailloux, "Reader-Response Criticism?" *Genre* 10 (Fall 1977): 418. Also see Schor, "Fiction as Interpretation," p. 167.

18. Robert Crosman, "Do Readers Make Meaning?" in *The Reader in the Text*, ed. Suleiman and Crosman, p. 155.

19. Michael Baxandall, *Patterns of Intention: On the Historical Explanation of Pictures* (New Haven: Yale University Press, 1985), p. 11. Baxandall is also defining interpretation as the process of inferring an author's constructive intention.

20. Finally, I could take a post-structuralist stance about this: within the definition of interpretation is what it (only apparently) is not.

21. Steven Mailloux, *Interpretative Conventions: The Reader in the Study of American Fiction* (Ithaca: Cornell University Press, 1982), pp. 177–78.

22. Ibid., p. 178 (interpolation mine).

23. M. H. Abrams, "The Deconstructive Angel," *Critical Inquiry* 3 (1977): 426, quoted in Mailloux, *Interpretative Conventions*, p. 142.

24. Mailloux, "Reader-Response Criticism?" p. 414.

25. Culler, *The Pursuit of Signs*, p. 5 (italics in original). A classic expression of this is in René Wellek and Austin Warren, *Theory of Literature*, rev. ed. (New York: Harcourt Brace and World, 1970).

26. W. K. Wimsatt, Jr. and M. C. Beardsley, "The Intentional Fallacy," *Sewanee Review* 54 (1946): 468.

27. W. K. Wimsatt, Jr., "Genesis: A Fallacy Revisited," in *The Disciplines of Criticism: Essays in Literary Theory, Interpretation, and History*, ed. Peter Demetz, Thomas Greene, and Lowry Nelson, Jr. (New Haven: Yale University Press, 1968), p. 222.

28. However, also see Wimsatt and Beardsley's theses in "The Affective Fallacy," *Sewanee Review* 57 (1949): 31–55. The authors describe the affective fallacy as "a confusion between the poem and its *results* (what it *is* and what it *does*)" (p. 31, italics in original). This mistake, they claim, ends in "impressionism and relativism." Attaching emotions to objects is distinct from saying that objects have those emotions *in* them.

29. Dagmar Barnouw, "Review of *The Act of Reading* and *The Implied Reader* by Wolfgang Iser," *Modern Language Notes* 94 (December 1979): 1209. Barnouw is explicating Iser, but Iser is also quoted as referring to Frege and Ricoeur on Frege: "'There are two distinct stages of comprehension: the state of "meaning" ... and the stage of "significance," which represent the active taking over of the meaning by the reader'" (p. 1209).

30. Crosman, "Do Readers Make Meaning?" pp. 149–51; E. D. Hirsch discussed in Crosman; Wolff, "The Interpretation of Literature in Society," p. 30n; Culler, *The Pursuit of Signs*, pp. 50–51.

31. Crosman, "Do Readers Make Meaning?" p. 151.

32. Postulations of these readers, or pertinent comments about them, are in (by alphabetical order): Barnouw, "Review of *The Act of Reading*," p. 1211; Robert Crosman, "Some Doubts about 'The Reader of *Paradise Lost*,'" *College English* 37

(December 1975): 372–82; Jonathan Culler, *On Deconstruction: Theory and Criticism after Structuralism* (Ithaca: Cornell University Press, 1982), pp. 134–41; Robert DeMaria, Jr., "The Ideal Reader: A Critical Fiction," *PMLA* 93 (May 1978): 463–74; Fetterley, *The Resisting Reader*; Walker Gibson, "Authors, Speakers, Readers, and Mock Readers" (1950), 265–69, rpt. in *Reader-Response Criticism*, ed. Tompkins, pp. 1–6; James R. Kincaid, "Coherent Readers, Incoherent Texts," *Critical Inquiry* 3 (Summer 1977): 781–802; Victor Lange, "The Reader in the Strategy of Fiction," in *Expression, Communication and Experience in Literature and Language*, ed. Ronald G. Popperwell (London: The Modern Humanities Research Association, 1973), pp. 88–89; Mailloux, "Reader-Response Criticism?"; Gerald Prince, "Introduction to the Study of the Narratee" (1973), rpt. in *Reader-Response Criticism*, ed. Tompkins, pp. 7–75; Peter Rabinowitz, "Truth in Fiction: A Reexamination of Audiences," *Critical Inquiry* 4 (Autumn 1977): 122–41; William Ray, "Recognizing Recognition: The Intra-Textual and Extra-Textual Critical Persona," *Diacritics* 7, no. 4 (Winter 1977): 20–33; John Rutherford, "Structuralism," in *Sociology of Literature*, ed. Routh and Wolff, pp. 48–50. A bitter but perceptive criticism of reception theory, describing assumptions for ideal, implied, and empirical readers is in Didier Coste, "Three Concepts of the Reader and Their Contribution to a Theory of the Literary Text," *Orbis Litterarum* 34, no. 4 (1979): 271–86. Coste asserts that these three concepts are all "a displacement which works to extend the privileges of literariness and authorship" (p. 271).

33. DeMaria, "The Ideal Reader," p. 464.

34. A twentieth-century version of this may be Michael Riffaterre's "supper-reader" who is emptied of "idiosyncrasy-oriented responses (positive or negative according to the reader's culture, era, esthetics, personality) and goal-oriented responses (those of the reader with non-literary intent, who may be using the poem as a historical document, for purposes of linguistic analysis, etc.)." "Describing Poetic Structures: Two Approaches to Baudelaire's 'Les Chats'" (1966), rpt. in *Reader-Response Criticism*, ed. Tompkins, p. 37.

35. DeMaria, "The Ideal Reader," pp. 464, 465.

36. Ibid., p. 468.

37. For example, Crosman locates the ideal reader for Wayne Booth: "It is only as I read that I become the self whose beliefs must coincide with the author's. . . . the most successful reading is one in which the created selves, author and reader, can find complete agreement." Booth in *The Rhetoric of Fiction* (Chicago: University of Chicago Press, 1961), p. 138, cited in "Some Doubts," p. 372n.

38. Steven Rendall argues that the use of the "critical we" in describing audiences (as in "we read the text . . .") is "a *prescriptive* rather than *descriptive* enterprise" ("The Critical *We*," *Orbis Litterarum* 35, no. 2 [1980]: 97; italics in original). The "we" is an attempt to get the reader to enter the interpretative community of the critic.

39. Patrocinio P. Schweickart, "Reading Ourselves: Toward a Feminist Theory of Reading," in *Gender and Reading: Essays on Readers, Texts, and Contexts* (Baltimore: The Johns Hopkins University Press, 1986), p. 31.

40. See, for instance, Smith, "Contingencies of Value," pp. 1–35.

41. In one sense I will do this by arguing for study of historical spectators.

42. Judith Newton defines scholars practicing new historicism as assuming that "there is no transhistorical or universal human essence and that human subjectivity is constructed by cultural codes which position and limit all of us in various and divided ways. They assume that there is no 'objectivity,' that we experience the 'world' in language, and that all our representations of the world, our readings of texts and of the past, are informed by our own historical position, by the values and politics that are rooted in them. They assume, finally, that representation 'makes things happen' by 'shaping human consciousness' and that, as forces acting in history, various forms of representation ought to be read in relation to each other and in relation to non-discursive 'texts' like 'events.' . . . There is the notion that 'history' is best told as a story of power relations and struggle, a story that is contradictory, heterogeneous, fragmented. There is the (more debated) notion that hegemonic power is part but not all of the story, that 'history' is a tale of many voices and forms of power, of power exercised by the weak and the marginal as well as by the dominant and strong. Even the technique of 'cross-cultural montage,' or the juxtaposition of literary, non-literary, and social texts is not unknown." "History as Usual? Feminism and the 'New Historicism,'" *Cultural Critique* 9 (Spring 1988): 88–89.

43. Barnouw, "Review of *The Act of Reading*," p. 1211.

44. Kincaid, "Coherent Readers," pp. 781–82. The debates referred to appear in Wayne C. Booth, "M. H. Abrams: Historian as Critic, Critic as Pluralist," *Critical Inquiry* 2 (1976): 441; M. H. Abrams, "Rationality and Imagination in Cultural History: A Reply to Wayne Booth," *Critical Inquiry* 2 (1976): 457; Wayne C. Booth, "'Preserving the Exemplar': or, How Not to Dig Our Own Graves," *Critical Inquiry* 3 (Spring 1977): 407–23;

45. Kincaid, "Coherent Readers," p. 782 (italics in original).

46. Ibid., p. 783.

47. Rutherford, "Structuralism," p. 50.

48. Kincaid, "Coherent Readers," p. 785n, is discussing Ralph Rader, "The Concept of Genre and Eighteenth-Century Studies," in *New Approaches to Eighteenth-Century Literature: Selected Papers from the English Institute*, ed. Phillip Harth (New York: Columbia University Press, 1974), pp. 79–115.

49. Kincaid, "Coherent Readers," p. 786.

50. Gibson, "Authors, Speakers," pp. 1–2.

51. Culler, *On Deconstruction*, p. 55.

52. Barnouw, "Review of *The Act of Reading*," p. 1211.

53. Jonathan Culler, *Structuralist Poetics: Structuralism, Linguistics, and the Study of Literature* (Ithaca: Cornell University Press, 1975), pp. 120–21.

54. Ibid., p. 121.

55. Culler, *On Deconstruction*, p. 178.

56. Smith, "Contingencies of Value, p. 18.

57. Michael Riffaterre, "The Referential Fallacy," *Columbia Review* 57, no. 2 (Winter 1978): 22.

58. Ibid.

59. Russo, "I. A. Richards in Retrospect, p. 751.

60. Hohendahl, "Introduction to Reception Aesthetics," p. 31.

61. Ibid., p. 32.

62. Eagleton, *Criticism and Ideology*, p. 73.

63. Culler, *The Pursuit of Signs*, pp. 51, 47–48.

64. The epigraphs to this section are drawn from Barthes, *S/Z*, p. 16; C. Barry Chabot, "Three Studies of Reading," *College English* 37 (December 1975): 425–26; and David Coward, "The Sociology of Literary Response," in *The Sociology of Literature*, ed. Routh and Wolff, p. 8.

65. Steven Mailloux provides another organization, dividing the writers into groups called "subjectivism," "phenomenology," and "structuralism." My grouping is somewhat based on his. See his "Reader-Response Criticism?" p. 415. For "stories of reading," Culler (*On Deconstruction*, pp. 69–83) suggests three questions similar to mine: Who is in control, the reader or the text? What is "in" the text? What is the ending of the story of reading? He notes that "adventures of reading generally turn out well" (p. 78). Jane P. Tompkins has five comparative questions: What are the kinds of readers various texts seem to imply? What is the role actual readers play in determining literary meaning? What is the relation of reading conventions to textual interpretation? What is the status of the reader's self? What is the status of the literary text? "An Introduction to Reader-Response Criticism," p. ix.

66. Umberto Eco, *The Role of the Reader: Explorations in the Semiotics of Texts* (Bloomington: Indiana University Press, 1979), pp. 13–43. In this broad preview of his model of reading, Eco floats between describing interpretive activities and describing structures that promote interpretive activities. In my summary, I have tried to convert his nine parts to structure nomenclature since I believe he considers textual features as the cause for the actions of his "Model Reader": "the Model Reader is a textually established set of felicity conditions . . . to be met in order to have a macro-speed act (such as a text is) fully actualized" (p. 11). Eco does not deny the existence of sociopsychological readers who could read any "closed" text "aberrantly" (p. 11), but often one result of positing an ideal reader such as the Model Reader is producing a text-activated model of reading.

67. Riffaterre, "Describing Poetic Structures," pp. 27–28.

68. Mailloux, *Interpretative Conventions*, p. 67.

69. Mailloux, "Reader-Response Criticism?" p. 428.

70. Culler, *Structuralist Poetics*, p. 115. Also see Mailloux, *Interpretative Conventions*, pp. 126–27. There he proposes three types of conventions: traditional conventions of precedent, regulative conventions of agreement or stipulation, and constitutive conventions of meaning. In *Making Meaning*, David Bordwell uses cognitive psychology models rather than Culler's linguistic ones to argue that film criticism of a more academic nature uses semantic fields and routine procedures of mapping to build up meanings. An extremely valuable exploration, *Making Meaning* amplifies on (or offers another account of) how rigorous attempts to unify interpretations operate in the U.S. academic community. David Bordwell, *Making Meaning: Inference and Rhetoric in the Interpretation of Cinema* (Cambridge: Harvard University Press, 1989).

71. Stanley Fish, "Interpreting the *Variorum*" (1976), rpt. in *Reader-Response Criticism*, ed. Tompkins, pp. 164–84; Stanley E. Fish, "Interpreting 'Interpreting the *Variorum*'" (1976), rpt. in *Is There a Text in This Class?* (Cambridge: Harvard

University Press, 1980), pp. 174–80. Also see Mailloux, "Reader-Response Criticism?" 414–15, and James Phelan, "Data, Danda, and Disagreement," *Diacritics* 13, no. 2 (Summer 1983): 39–50.

72. Suleiman, "Introduction," p. 15. Also see Susan Rubin Suleiman, "Redundancy and the 'Readable' Text," *Poetics Today* 1, no. 3 (Spring 1980): 119–42.

73. Christine Brooke-Rose, "The Readerhood of Man," in *The Reader in the Text*, ed. Suleiman and Crosman, pp. 120–48.

74. Ibid., p. 144.

75. Susan R. Suleiman, *Authoritarian Fictions: The Ideological Novel as a Literary Genre* (New York: Columbia University Press, 1983), p. 43.

76. Suleiman, "Redundancy," pp. 136–39.

77. Terry Heller, *The Delights of Terror: An Aesthetics of the Tale of Terror* (Urbana: University of Illinois Press, 1987), p. 10.

78. I should stress that this is as practiced. Nothing in the work inherently presupposes such an ahistorical, unspecific view of the reader. Thus, I do not believe I am violating the models' findings or the integrity of my research by drawing these conclusions from their work.

79. Stanley Fish, "Literature in the Reader: Affective Stylistics" (1970), rpt. in *Reader-Response Criticism*, ed. Tompkins, p. 78. Fish is criticizing a Chomskian psycholinguistic approach that would seek meaning in deep structures rather than surface expression. He also disagrees with Riffaterre, counting only perceptual disautomatizations as aesthetic data (see below).

80. Summarized nicely by Richard Sherwood in "Victor Shklovsky and the Development of Early Formalist Theory on Prose Literature," *Twentieth Century Studies* 7/8 (December 1972): 36–37. Meir Sternberg suggests a number of ways to compare retardatory structures; Meir Sternberg, *Expositional Modes and Temporal Ordering in Fiction* (Baltimore: The Johns Hopkins University Press, 1978), pp. 159–62.

81. Jan Mukařovský, "Detail as the Basic Semantic Unit in Folk Art" (1942), in *The Word and Verbal Art*, trans. John Burbank and Peter Steiner (New Haven: Yale University Press, 1977), pp. 198–99.

82. Ibid., p. 199.

83. Gerard Genette, *Narrative Discourse: An Essay in Method* (1972), trans. Jane E. Lewin (Ithaca: Cornell University Press, 1980).

84. Sternberg, *Expositional Modes*, p. 50. Sternberg stresses that his idea of a gap is not that of Iser or Ingarden (p. 50n).

85. Fish, "Interpreting the *Valorium*," p. 474, cited in Mailloux, "Reader-Response Criticism?" p. 427; this is a good instance of a description of sequential interpretations.

86. See, for instance, Howard Anderson, "*Tristram Shandy* and the Reader's Imagination," *PMLA* 86 (October 1971): 966–67. Mailloux stresses that sequential approaches to response may still produce a "final holistic interpretation" (*Interpretative Conventions*, pp. 66–73). Also see Karlheinz Stierle, "The Reading of Fictional Texts," trans. Inge Crosman and Thekla Zachrau, in *The Reader in the Text*, ed. Suleiman and Crosman, pp. 83–105. Michel Beaujour proposes an ideological analysis of texts based on the (implied) relation between text and reader; while literature might be an exchange between two mature "individuals" (one

being the text), texts imply all sorts of dialogues: father-to-child, woman-to-man, etc. See "Exemplary Pornography: Barres, Loyola and the Novel," in *The Reader in the Text*, ed. Suleiman and Crosman, pp. 325–49.

87. Wolfgang Iser, *The Implied Reader: Patterns of Communication in Prose Fiction from Bunyan to Beckett* (Baltimore: The Johns Hopkins University Press, 1974), p. 282.

88. Barnouw, "Review of *The Act of Reading*," p. 1208; also see Culler, *On Deconstruction*, pp. 75–76; Mailloux, "Reader-Response Criticism?" pp. 423–24; Suleiman, "Introduction," pp. 23–24.

89. Iser, *The Implied Reader*, p. xiii.

90. Norman N. Holland, "Recovering 'The Purloined Letter': Reading as a Personal Transaction," in *The Reader in the Text*, ed. Suleiman and Crosman, pp. 350–70. Also see Norman N. Holland, "Stanley Fish, Stanley Fish," *Genre* 10 (Fall 1977): 433–41; Norman N. Holland, "UNITY IDENTITY TEXT SELF" (1975), rpt. in *Reader-Response Criticism*, ed. Tompkins, pp. 118–33; Mailloux, "Reader-Response Criticism?" pp. 416–18.

91. Holland, "Recovering 'The Purloined Letter,'" p. 363.

92. Mailloux, "Reader-Response Criticism?" p. 418.

93. Ibid., pp. 421–23; David Bleich, *Subjective Criticism* (Baltimore: The Johns Hopkins University Press, 1978).

94. Culler, *The Pursuit of Signs*, p. 63.

95. Also consider here Stanley Fish's theory of interpretive communities.

96. Culler, *The Pursuit of Signs*, pp. 68–78.

97. Walter Benn Michaels, "The Interpreter's Self: Peirce on the Cartesian 'Subject'" (1977), rpt. in *Reader-Response Criticism*, ed. Tompkins, p. 194.

98. Michaels, "The Interpreter's Self," p. 199.

99. Stanley E. Fish, "Normal Circumstances, Literal Language, Direct Speech Acts, the Ordinary, the Everyday, the Obvious, What Goes without Saying, and Other Special Cases," *Critical Inquiry* 4 (Summer 1978): 632.

100. Barthes, *S/Z*, p. 9 (italics in original).

101. Tony Bennett, "Text and Social Process: The Case of James Bond," *Screen Education* 41 (Winter/Spring 1982): 6.

102. Hans Robert Jauss, *Toward an Aesthetic of Reception*, trans. Timothy Bahti (Minneapolis: University of Minnesota Press, 1982). As he writes, "A literary work is not an object that stands by itself and that offers the same view to each reader in each period. It is not a monument that monologically reveals its timeless essence. It is much more like an orchestration that strikes ever new resonances among its readers and that frees the text from the material of the words and brings it to a contemporary existence" (p. 21).

103. Bennett, "Text and Social Process," p. 3, citing Pierre Macherey, *Red Letters* 5 (Summer 1977): 7 (italics in original).

104. See Culler, *The Pursuit of Signs*, pp. 54–58; Henry J. Schmidt, "'Text-Adequate Concretizations' and Real Readers: Reception Theory and Its Applications," *New German Critique* 17 (Spring 1979): 158–69; Suleiman, "Introduction," p. 37.

105. Jacques Leenhardt, "Toward a Sociology of Reading," trans. Brigitte Navelet and Susan R. Suleiman, in *The Reader in the Text*, ed. Suleiman and

Crosman, pp. 205–24. For numerous reasons, scholars pursuing context-activated theories of reception often approach evidential needs by doing empirical work. Empirical research should not be confused with empiricist or positivist epistemologies. Dialectical or historical materialists assume that theoretical propositions or abstractions direct their empirical research; they do not, however, assume that sense data are obvious or the observer objective in relation to those data.

106. Janice Radway, *Reading the Romance: Women, Patriarchy, and Popular Literature* (Chapel Hill: University of North Carolina Press, 1984), pp. 48, 208.

107. Naumann, "Literary Production and Reception," pp. 117, 119.

108. Bennett, "Text and Social Process," p. 5.

109. Ibid., pp. 5–6 (italics in original).

110. Ibid., p. 8.

111. In this view, the reading act·is considered contradictory. The text is material sense-data; it is not itself contradictory.

Chapter Three
Reception Studies in Film and Television

1. I will not particularly address the issues of avant-garde film or video viewing in this book. However, I believe you could apply with little difficulty to avant-garde texts the principles developed here for studying historical spectators. The determinants of conventional reading procedures and historical discourses about avant-garde art practices would obviously be influential contextual factors. The same applies to the documentary mode.

2. Annette Kuhn, "Women's Genres," *Screen* 25, no. 1 (January–February 1984): 18–28.

3. Patrice Petro, "Television Criticism, Television History: Realism, Modernism, and Reception" (Paper delivered at the Society for Cinema Studies Conference, Madison, Wisconsin, 26–31 March 1984). Also see her "Mass Culture and the Feminine: The 'Place' of Television in Film Studies," *Cinema Journal* 25, no. 3 (Spring 1986): 5–21.

4. J. Dudley Andrew, *The Major Film Theories: An Introduction* (New York: Oxford University Press, 1976). Andrew's questions derive from Aristotle and are informed by Siegfried Kracauer.

5. For instance, in his lectures, David Bordwell treats classical film philosophies from another question or set of questions. He asks, What are the propositions' ontological, epistemological, and aesthetic assumptions? As he moves through the philosophies in his lectures, he tends to equate the ontological and epistemological issues with the question of whether the theories are idealist or materialist. Thus, idealist theories have been written by Arnheim and Bazin, while materialist ones come from Eisenstein and Vertov. As you can note, this produces groupings different from the ones proposed by Andrew, but the differences are not due to major changes in the reading of the philosophies so much as to a change in the initial question. It is the question that causes the difference in the splitting and subsequent categorizing of the philosophies.

I do not mean to imply that I think any one of these questions is inappropriate, invalid, or irrelevant. In fact, the advantage of having both Andrew's and

Bordwell's set of queries is that each brings out certain relationships among the philosophical discourses, as well as providing means to contrast them. Optional categorizing is part of what academia considers the point of analysis—providing new information, which may require rearranging the same set of data through such new starting questions. David Bordwell, "Lectures in Film Theory," University of Wisconsin-Madison, Madison, Wisconsin, Spring 1978. In this, I have followed him but have revised the questions to ones of ontology, epistemology, and effectivity, with the last term stressing propositions of causality. John Fiske also defines effectivity as a "socio-ideological term" against "effect," "an individual-behavioristic one," and this is a good distinction. *Television Culture* (London: Methuen, 1987), p. 20.

6. For Bordwell's readings classical film philosophies offer a text-activated approach to the spectator. For an idealist philosophy of cinema, the spectator has certain a priori structures that organize the sense data (as in Arnheim). While individual films may differ, the a priori structures remain static and available, determining the spectator's ability to respond to the textual features of the specific film. Bazin's writings also end up with a text-activated theory. While some films (e.g., those of Renoir, Wyler, and Welles) may bring the spectator into a perceptual situation closer to that of the individual's relationship with reality, it is due to the film's formal and stylistic organization, not to any spectatorial intention or activity. When Bordwell reads the materialist philosophies of Eisenstein and Vertov, again, he discovers that the organization of the film's materials determines effects.

7. Sergei M. Eisenstein, *S. M. Eisenstein: Selected Works*, vol. 1: *Writings, 1922–34*, ed. and trans. Richard Taylor (London: BFI Publishing; Bloomington: Indiana University Press, 1988), p. 183. Principal influences on my interpretation of Eisenstein for this period of his writing include Andrew, *Major Film Theories*; Bordwell, "Lectures"; Peter Wollen, *Signs and Meaning in the Cinema*, rev. ed. (Bloomington: Indiana University Press, 1972), pp. 19–73; David Bordwell, "Eisenstein's Epistemological Shift," *Screen* 15, no. 4 (Winter 1974–1975): 32–46; Philip Rosen, "Formalism, Reception and Eisenstein's Theoretical Development" (Unpublished paper, March 1980); Ken Slavin, "Generative Semiotics" (Paper delivered at the Society for Cinema Studies Conference, Madison, Wisconsin, 26–31 March 1984).

8. Slavin, "Generative Semiotics." A mentalist (i.e., Pavlov) in the Soviet Union in the 1920s believed that the mind was capable of mediating perceptions. The epistemological position is still, however, materialist.

9. Eisenstein, *Selected Works*, p. 47.

10. Ibid., p. 62 (italics in original).

11. Ibid., pp. 41–42.

12. Interestingly, while undergraduates are introduced to Eisenstein's early work (and not his later), scholarly debates have been most intense on the post-1930 period of Eisenstein's writing. My position in the debates rejects prior dismissals of Vygotsky as important because I believe that interpretations of Vygotsky's writings have been inadequate. I will not rehearse here my argumentation, but a valuable summary of the theory is in James V. Wertsch, *Vygotsky and the Social Formation of the Mind* (Cambridge: Harvard University Press, 1985).

13. Eisenstein, *Selected Works*, p. 236.

14. The distinction between meaning and sense appears in both Vygotsky and Eisenstein. It has a different connotation, however, from the distinction between meaning and significance described in chapter 2. For Vygotsky and Eisenstein "sense" has "sensuality," the private, psychological, affective feelings aroused by the sign.

15. Sergei M. Eisenstein, *The Film Sense*, ed. and trans. Jay Leyda (New York: Harcourt, Brace & World, 1942), p. 18 (italics in original).

16. Ibid., pp. 16–17 (italics in original).

17. Ibid., p. 14.

18. Ibid., p. 172 (italics in original).

19. Sergei Eisenstein, *Film Form: Essays in Film Theory*, ed. and trans. Jay Leyda (New York: Harcourt, Brace & World, 1949), p. 151 (italics in original).

20. Hugo Münsterberg, *The Photoplay: A Psychological Study* (1916; rpt. as *The Film: A Psychological Study*, New York: Dover Publications, 1970), p. 17.

21. Ibid., pp. 19, 23, 29, 30 (italics in original).

22. Ibid., p. 31.

23. Ibid., pp. 31, 46 (italics in original).

24. Ibid., pp. 95, 96.

25. See a recent extension: Barbara Rogoff, *Apprenticeship in Thinking: Cognitive Development in Social Context* (New York: Oxford University Press, 1990).

26. Elizabeth Ellsworth, "Illicit Pleasures: Feminist Spectators and *Personal Best*," *Wide Angle* 8, no. 2 (1986): 45–56.

27. Ellsworth quotes the film pressbook's representation of the narrative: "'[Tory (Patrice Donnelly) and Chris (Mariel Hemingway)] met as strangers at the 1976 Olympic trials. They became friends, lovers, and ultimately competitors facing each other in the pentathlon at the Olympic trials in 1980'" (ibid., p. 50).

28. Ibid., p. 46.

29. Ibid., pp. 53, 54.

30. Ibid., p. 55.

31. Another recent advance in this area is the work of Barbara Klinger. See her "Digressions at the Cinema: Reception and Mass Culture," *Cinema Journal* 28, no. 4 (Summer 1989): 3–19, and "Much Ado about Excess: Genre, Mise-en-Scene, and the Woman in *Written on the Wind*," *Wide Angle* 11, no. 4 (1989): 4–22. These essays derive from her "Cinema and Social Process: A Contextual Theory of the Cinema and Its Spectators" (Ph.D. diss., University of Iowa, 1986). There she analyzes three reading formations for *Written on the Wind*: the academic, the industrial, and the mass cultural. See also Jacqueline Bobo, "*The Color Purple*: Black Women's Responses," *Jump Cut* 33 (1988), 43–51, although this article is theoretically less well-formulated.

32. This genealogy could be contested, but it is a common representation of direct influences on the individuals who were associated with one another during the 1980s at the Centre and functions at least to provide a few guideposts for those unfamiliar with the scholarship.

33. What follows is underdeveloped for the sake of concentration on the problem at hand. I assume reader familiarity with this model, but I also find helpful, particularly for the Lacanian addition, Rosalind Coward and John Ellis, *Language*

and Materialism: Developments in Semiology and the Theory of the Subject (London: Routledge & Kegan Paul, 1977). Most individuals working in the contemporary linguistic model also adopt structuralist marxist tenets. That, however, is not necessary to the linguistic aspect of the model, and I shall discuss the situation regarding structuralist marxism below in my coverage of British cultural studies.

34. I shall discuss the problem of commercial broadcast television below.

35. Christian Metz, *Film Language* (1968, orig. pub. 1971), trans. Michael Taylor (New York: Oxford University Press, 1974); Christian Metz, *Language and Cinema* (1971), trans. Donna Jean Umiker-Sebeok (The Hague: Mouton, 1974).

36. My phrasing may seem odd. I would argue that Metz's phenomenology underpins his linguistic theory, leading to the implication that perception and innate mental structures (the human mind has a diachronistic structure [*Film Language*, p. 47]) allow individuals to understand narratives. The grande syntagmatique is not an explanation of how people understand narratives but an after-the-fact categorization of film segments into temporal and spatial categories. See below.

37. Metz, *Film Language*, p. 62n.

38. Ibid., p. 27 (italics in original).

39. This idea also derives from structuralist marxism, which I will take up in the section on British cultural studies.

40. Ross, "On the Concepts of Reading," p. 95.

41. George M. Wilson, *Narration in Light: Studies in Cinematic Point of View* (Baltimore: The Johns Hopkins University Press, 1986), p. 191.

42. Robert Stam makes suggestions along this line in his support of Bakhtin's and Vološinov's contributions to cultural theory. See Robert Stam, "Film and Language: From Metz to Bakhtin," R. Barton Palmer, "Bakhtinian Translinguistics and Film Criticism: The Dialogical Image?" and Robert Stam, "Bakhtinian Translinguistics: A Postscriptum," in *The Cinematic Text: Methods and Approaches*, ed. R. Barton Palmer (New York: AMS Press, 1989), pp. 277–351.

43. Pierre Maranda, "The Dialectic of Metaphor: An Anthropological Essay on Hermeneutics," in *The Reader in the Text*, ed. Suleiman and Crosman, p. 185.

44. Ross, "On the Concepts of Reading," p. 95.

45. Rick Altman, "Television Sound" (1985) and Nick Browne, "The Political Economy of the Television (Super) Text" (1984), rpt. in *Television: The Critical View*, ed. Horace Newcomb, 4th ed. (New York: Oxford University Press, 1987), pp. 566–84, 585–99 respectively; Fiske, *Television Culture*. Some interesting contradictions exist among the writers on television specificity. What I indicate in the text should be understood as an uncritical synopsis of received opinion. Additionally, this general description is held by both contemporary linguistic theory and British cultural studies since the latter agrees with many tenets of the former.

46. Janet Bergstrom and Mary Ann Doane, "The Female Spectator: Contexts and Directions," *Camera obscura* 20–21 (May–September 1989): 13.

47. Singer and Ruddell, ed. *Theoretical Models and Processes of Reading*, pp. 450–676.

48. William Frawley, "Lectures in Psycholinguistics," Newark, Delaware, University of Delaware, Spring 1983. Two recent surveys are Garnham, *Psycholinguis-*

tics, and Danny D. Steinberg, *Psycholinguistics: Language, Mind and World* (London: Longman, 1982).

49. As I indicated above, the word-versus-thought debate seems a toss-up to me. Current neurological and language brain research concludes several things about this question, as well as about the issue of affect. A handy synopsis is Israel Rosenfield, "A Hero of the Brain," *New York Review of Books*, 21 November 1985, 49–55. Rosenfield gleans from the literature the following observations, which seem to me to have some interest for the issues at hand. (1) Psychological capacities such as "recognition of objects . . . were composites of independent brain operations" (not a function of the entire brain). "A man could see an object without recognizing it." (2) Speech "'has as a prerequisite the ability to form cross-modal associations.'" That is, information such as the spoken word "dog" can connect with the visual image of a dog. (3) It appears doubtful that writing evolved out of pictorial representation. Both notational systems and drawing developed at the same time. (4) A picture understood as a picture is deciphered by the visual system; "a picture used in writing is ultimately deciphered by the language centers." Apparently the brain makes distinctions depending on what it believes is the type of information desired. A related point: sign language is processed in language centers. (I wonder what happens in the case of moving images.) (5) Reading and writing, like oral language, require different and to some extent independent mechanisms. However, two recent books by Ronald A. Finke and Mark Rollins make powerful arguments for the pictorialist view; see the review by J. Michael Tarr, "The Mind's Eye," *Science* 249 (10 August 1990): 685.

50. David Bordwell, *Narration in the Fiction Film* (Madison: University of Wisconsin Press, 1985). As I shall describe below, Bordwell offers a constructivist cognitive psychology theory. Bordwell's model might inappropriately be combined with the work of two other individuals who do not agree with contemporary linguistic theory. These people are Noël Carroll and Edward Branigan. Carroll takes an analytical philosophy approach: while he agrees with Bordwell that the medium of the movies differs from language ("The Power of Movies," *Daedalus* 114, no. 4 [Fall 1985]: 79–103], he describes reading in terms of propositional logic. For instance, "The spectator is not free to make any inference he or she chooses for a given shot interpolation. Rather the induction must be constrained in terms of what is plausible to infer in virtue of the rest of the film and in terms of the cultural context of the film" ("Toward a Theory of Film Editing," *Millennium Film Journal* 3 [1978]: 93).

Branigan prefers a linguistic model indebted to the work of Noam Chomsky. This puts Branigan someplace between contemporary linguistic philosophy in film (with its Saussurean heritage) and a cognitive psychology position. Branigan writes: "It is my belief that a film spectator, through exposure to a small number of films, knows how to understand a potentially infinite number of new films. The spectator is able to recognize immediately repetitions and variations among films, even though the films are entirely new, and outwardly quite distinct. . . . I believe that this ability to understand—however it is acquired—is evidence of the prior knowledge, or competence, of a spectator. The goal, then, is to explain the 'reading act' in terms of the generally unconscious methods employed in decoding texts. Not that whether or not pictures themselves are held to be symbolic in nature, the claim here is merely that a narrative arrangement of pictures is symbolic and so permits certain linguistic analogies." *Point of View in the Cinema: A Theory of Narration and Subjectivity in Classical Film* (Berlin: Mouton Publishers, 1984), pp. 17–18.

51. Bordwell, *Narration in the Fiction Film*, p. 30.

52. Ibid., p. 31.

53. This example is derived from Katherine Nelson, "Social Cognition in a Script Framework," in *Social Cognitive Development*, ed. J. H. Flavell and L. Ross (Cambridge: Cambridge University Press, 1981), pp. 101–3.

54. Bordwell, *Narration in the Fiction Film*, p. 31.

55. Ibid.

56. Jan Mukařovský does appeal to a linguistic model to explain how meanings are developed in a text. See "On Poetic Language" (1940) in *The Word and Verbal Art*, pp. 50–53.

57. Bordwell, *Narration in the Fiction Film*, p. 30.

58. Ibid., pp. 149–50.

59. Ibid., pp. 213, 212, 242, 245, 287.

60. Ibid., p. 30.

61. As early as 1947, Jerome S. Bruner and Cecile C. Goodman argued that behavioral determinants such as "personality dynamics," "quasi-tempermental characteristics like introversion and extraversion," "social needs, and attitudes" affected basic perception; "Value and Need as Organizing Factors in Perception," *Journal of Abnormal and Social Psychology* 42, no. 1 (January 1947): 33. A nice summary of current psychochemical research on the mind is Israel Rosenfield, "The New Brain," *New York Review of Books*, 14 March 1985, 34–38.

62. Bordwell, *Narration in the Fiction Film*, p. 32.

63. Ibid.

64. Ulric Neisser, *Cognitive Psychology* (New York: Appleton-Century-Crofts, 1967), pp. 290, 296–99; Nelson, "Social Cognition," p. 105; Ragnar Rommetveit, "Language Acquisition as Increasing Linguistic Structuring of Experience and Symbolic Behavior Control," in *Culture, Communication, and Cognition: Vygotskian Perspectives*, ed. James V. Wertsch (Cambridge: Cambridge University Press, 1985), pp. 193–94; Michael Cole, "The Zone of Proximal Development: Where Culture and Cognition Create Each Other," in *Culture, Communication, and Cognition*, ed. Wertsch, p. 154. For a recent, succinct survey of the literature in relation to an application to feminist literary theory, also see Mary Crawford and Roger Chaffin, "The Reader's Construction of Meaning: Cognitive Research on Gender and Comprehension," in *Gender and Reading: Essays on Readers, Texts, and Contexts*, ed. Elizabeth A. Flynn and Patrocinio P. Schweickart (Baltimore: The Johns Hopkins University Press, 1986), pp. 3–30.

65. Bordwell, *Narration in the Fiction Film*, p. 149 (italics in original). Note that Bordwell says "innate mental *capabilities*" (italics mine). He does not say innate forms or categories. What he is probably suggesting is that the biochemistry of the human body has particular preset dispositions, but this comment should not be taken to imply either idealist or copy-theory epistemologies.

66. James W. Carey, "A Cultural Approach to Communication," *Communications* 2 (1975): 6; Horace M. Newcomb and Paul M. Hirsch, "Television as a Cultural Forum: Implications for Research," *Quarterly Review of Film Studies* 8,

no. 3 (Summer 1983): 47. Dudley Andrew also suggests this "social ritual" approach in "Film and Society: Public Rituals and Private Space," *East-West Film Journal* 1, no. 1 (December 1986): 7–22.

67. Vološinov, *Marxism and the Philosophy of Language*, p. 23.

68. Descriptions of the genesis of this position with critiques of prior approaches include the following (arranged in chronological order): Johnson, "Culture and the Historians," pp. 41–71; Richard Johnson, "Three Problematics: Elements of a Theory of Working-Class Culture," in *Working-Class Culture*, ed. Clarke, et al., pp. 201–37; David Morley, *The "Nationwide" Audience: Structure and Decoding* (London: British Film Institute, 1980), pp. 1–21; Stuart Hall, "Cultural Studies and the Centre: Some Problematics and Problems," in *Culture, Media, Language: Working Papers in Cultural Studies, 1972–79*, ed. Stuart Hall, Dorothy Hobson, Andrew Lowe, and Paul Willis (London: Hutchinson, 1980), pp. 15–47; Stuart Hall, "The Rediscovery of 'Ideology': Return of the Repressed in Media Studies," in *Culture, Society and the Media*, ed. Michael Gurevitch, Tony Bennett, James Curran, and Janet Woollacott (London: Methuen, 1982), pp. 56–90; Tamar Liebes, "On the Convergence of Theories of Mass Communication and Literature Regarding the Role of the 'Reader'" (Paper delivered at the Conference on Culture and Communication, Philadelphia, Pennsylvania, October 1986). Nonhistorical expressions of the positions and assumptions held are the following (arranged in chronological order): Iain Chambers, John Clarke, Ian Connell, Lidia Curti, Stuart Hall, and Tony Jefferson, "Marxism and Culture," *Screen* 18, no. 4 (Winter 1977/78): 109–19; Dick Hebdige, *Subculture: The Meaning of Style* (London: Methuen, 1979), pp. 3–19; Stuart Hall, "Encoding/Decoding," in *Culture, Media, Language*, ed. Hall et al., pp. 128–39; Stuart Hall, "Recent Developments in Theories of Language and Ideology: A Critical Note," in *Culture, Media, Language*, ed. Hall et al., pp. 157–62; Dave Morley, "Texts, Readers, Subjects," in *Culture, Media, Language*, ed. Hall et al., pp. 163–73; Stuart Hall, "Cultural Studies: Two Paradigms," *Media, Culture and Society* 2 (1980): 57–72; James Curran, Michael Gurevitch, and Janet Wollacott, "The Study of Media: Theoretical Approaches," in *Culture, Society and the Media*, ed. Gurevitch et al., pp. 11–28; Terry Lovell, "Marxism and Cultural Studies," *Film Reader* 5 (1982): 184–91; Samuel L. Becker, "Marxist Approaches to Media Studies: The British Experience," *Critical Studies in Mass Communication* 1 (1984): 66–80; (a dissenting view) Nicholas Garnham, "Contribution to a Political Economy of Mass-communication," in *Media, Culture and Society*, ed. Richard Collins, James Curran, Nicholas Garnham, Paddy Scannell, Philip Schlesinger, and Colin Sparks (London: Sage Publications, 1986), pp. 9–32; John Fiske, "British Cultural Studies and Television," in *Channels of Discourse*, ed. Robert C. Allen (Chapel Hill: University of North Carolina Press, 1987), pp. 254–89.

69. Louis Althusser, "Ideology and Ideological State Apparatuses (Notes towards an Investigation)" (1970), in *Lenin and Philosophy and Other Essays*, trans. Ben Brewster (New York: Monthly Review Press, 1971), pp. 127–86.

70. I hope that this particular rewriting by me (but based on many other scholars' observations) of Althusser's Ideological State Apparatuses essay eliminates some of the valid criticisms by him and others of his original statements (specifically its "scientificism" and "idealism").

71. Althusser, "Ideology," p. 162.

72. See particularly Hall, "Cultural Studies," and Morley, "Texts, Readers, Subjects."

73. Charlotte Perkins Gilman Stetson, *Women and Economics: A Study of the Economic Relation between Men and Women as a Factor in Social Evolution* (1898; rpt. New York: Source Book Press, 1970).

74. Conversations with Richard Johnson, Austin, Texas, 20–22 September 1990.

75. Morley, *The "Nationwide" Audience*, pp. 9, 10.

76. Ibid., p. 15.

77. Ibid., pp. 14–15.

78. Charlotte Brunsdon and David Morley, *Everyday Television: "Nationwide,"* (London: British Film Institute, 1978), p. v.

79. Morley, *The "Nationwide" Audience*, pp. 20, 21.

80. Hall, "Encoding/Decoding," pp. 136–38. What this looks like will be examined with specific examples in chapter 4.

81. Morley, "Texts, Readers, Subjects," p. 172.

82. Despite Morley's and others' remarks about the three frameworks' simplicity, individuals continue to use the tripartite system. See, for instance, Ien Ang, *Watching Dallas: Soap Opera and the Melodramatic Imagination* (1982), trans. Della Couling (London: Methuen, 1985); Fiske, "British Cultural Studies and Television"; Fiske, *Television Culture*; Tony Bennett and Janet Woollacott, *Bond and Beyond: The Political Career of a Popular Hero* (London: Methuen, 1987); Linda Steiner, "Oppositional Decoding as an Act of Resistance," *Critical Studies in Mass Communication* 5, no. 1 (March 1988): 1–15.

83. Johnson, "Culture and the Historians," p. 62.

84. David Morley, *Family Television* (London: Comedia, 1986).

85. Tamar Liebes and Elihu Katz, "On the Critical Ability of Television Viewers" (Paper delivered at the World Congress of Sociology, New Delhi, India, August 1986); Liebes, "On the Convergence of Theories." Also see Sonia M. Livingston, "Interpreting a Television Narrative: How Different Viewers See a Story," *Journal of Communication* 40, no. 1 (Winter 1990): 72–85.

86. Fiske, for instance, lists seven subjectivity positions (from J. Hartley): "'self, gender, age-group, family, class, nation, ethnicity'" (*Television Culture*, p. 50). Surprisingly, sexual preference is missing, something Fiske does not mention. I shall discuss this below.

87. Morley, *Family Television*, p. 10.

88. Richard Maltby, "'Baby Face' or How Joe Breen Made Barbara Stanwyck Atone for Causing the Wall Street Crash," *Screen* 27, no. 2 (March–April 1986): 22.

89. Ang, *Watching Dallas*, pp. 20 and 47. Likewise, Morley and Hall disagree with positivist social science's "uses and gratifications" psychology and imply that social explanations are the place to look. See Hall, "Introduction" to Morley, *Family Television*, p. 9.

90. Fiske, *Television Culture*, p. 225.

91. The publication date of *Television Culture*. Another version of this occurs in his later *Understanding Popular Culture* (Boston: Unwin Hyman, 1989), pp. 49–68.

92. Roland Barthes, *The Pleasure of the Text* (1973), trans. Richard Miller (New York: Hill and Wang, 1975), pp. 9–10, 14.

Chapter Four
Toward a Historical Materialist Approach

1. Jean Douchet, "Hitch and His Public" (1960), trans. Verena Conley, rpt. in *A Hitchcock Reader*, ed. Marshall Deutelbaum and Leland Pogue (Ames: Iowa State University Press, 1986), p. 10.

2. Norman E. Spear, "Retrieval of Memories: A Psychobiological Approach," in *Handbook of Learning and Cognitive Processes*, vol. 4: *Attention and Memory*, ed. W. K. Estes (Hillsdale, N.J.: Lawrence Erlbaum Associates, 1976), pp. 17–90.

3. Benjamin, "Theses on the Philosophy of History," p. 256.

4. Bordwell, *Narration in the Fiction Film*, pp. 29–47.

5. Other reviews and articles exist. For this study I have not done an exhaustive search for responses. However, the point of the exercise does not require this. The reviews and critical essays that I am using are the following: Jesse Zunzer, "Hitchcock's Scariest in Years Comes to Town," *Cue*, 7 August 1954, 15; John McCarten, "Hitchcock Confined Again," *New Yorker* 30, no. 25 (7 August 1954): 50–51; Bosley Crowther, *New York Times*, 5 August 1954, 18; Douchet, "Hitch and His Public" (1960); François Truffaut, *Hitchcock* (1966; rpt. New York: Simon and Schuster, 1967), pp. 159–66; Alfred Hitchcock, "Rear Window," *Take One* 2, no. 2 (1968/69): 18–20; Robin Wood, *Hitchcock's Films* (1969; rpt., New York: Paperback Library, 1970), pp. 65–76; Alfred Appel, Jr., "The Eyehole of Knowledge: Voyeuristic Games in Film and Literature," *Film Comment* 9, no. 3 (1973): 20–26; Laura Mulvey, "Visual Pleasure and Narrative Cinema," *Screen* 16, no. 3 (Autumn 1975): 6–18; Philip Strick, "Rear Window," *Films and Filming* 350 (November 1983): 38–39; Robin Wood, "Fear of Spying," *American Film* 9, no. 2 (November 1983): 28–35; and Robert Stam and Roberta Pearson, "Hitchcock's *Rear Window*: Reflexivity and the Critique of Voyeurism," *enclitic* 7, no. 1 (Spring 1983): 136–45. As I shall indicate below, Douchet also introduces the reflexivity motif: a reading connected to this line is R. Barton Palmer, "The Metafictional Hitchcock: The Experience of Viewing and the Viewing of Experience in *Rear Window* and *Psycho*," *Cinema Journal* 25, no. 2 (Winter 1986): 4–19. Again, this is by no means an exhaustive search of the reception and interpretations of *Rear Window*.

6. Stam and Pearson, "Hitchcock's *Rear Window*," pp. 136 and 142.

7. Culler, *On Deconstruction*, pp. 215 and 236.

8. McCarten, "Hitchcock Confined Again," pp. 50–51.

9. Zunser, "Hitchcock's Scariest," p. 15.

10. Douchet, "Hitch and His Public," pp. 7–8.

11. Truffaut, *Hitchcock*, pp. 160, 159.

12. Wood, *Hitchcock's Films*, pp. 66–67, 70. Wood's 1969 thesis sounds very much like Norman Holland's and David Bleich's mid-1970s theories. Obviously developments in psychoanalytical theory are affecting all of these individuals.

13. Ibid., p. 74.

14. Appel, *Film Comment*, p. 23 (italics in original).

15. Wood, "Fear of Spying," pp. 31, 32.

16. Stam and Pearson, "Hitchcock's *Rear Window*," pp. 136, 142, 143.

17. Ibid., p. 144.

18. Ibid., pp. 143, 145.

19. Bordwell, *Narration in the Fiction Film*, pp. 41, 42.

20. Ibid., pp. 40, 42, 40, 43.

21. A recent analysis of *Rear Window* provides a sophisticated ideological analysis of the film in relation to gender issues—if not class. See Tania Modleski, *The Women Who Knew Too Much: Hitchcock and Feminist Theory* (New York: Methuen, 1988), pp. 73–85.

22. Leo A. Handel, *Hollywood Looks at Its Audience: A Report of Film Audience Research* (Urbana: University of Illinois Press, 1950), p. 124. Specifically, in a story preference survey in which individuals chose which genre they liked most and least, women ranked love stories and romances first (18 percent) with musical comedies second (14.7 percent). Mystery and horror pictures were tied with gangster and G-men pictures for next-to-least favorite (12.7 percent each); least was westerns (14.4 percent). For men, mystery and horror stories ended up about in the middle of the rankings (6.8 percent liked; 5.6 percent disliked). Top-ranked in the "like" category for men were war pictures (15 percent), adventure and action pictures (11.8 percent), and musical comedies (10.0 percent). Most disliked for men were love stories and romances (11.4 percent), then child star pictures (9.1 percent).

Handel also reports genre preferences by class (p. 126). For *Rear Window*, results by class are less obvious than are those by gender. However, Handel's figures indicate that the high class generally disliked mystery and horror pictures (like—2.7 percent; dislike—11.5 percent) although upper-middle (4.6; 9.8), lower-middle (6.7; 7.9), and low classes (7.5; 9.1) accepted them. The figures for love stories and romances are as follows: high (9.3; 5.3); upper-middle (11.6; 6.1); lower-middle (11.6; 7.9); and low (13.1; 8.4). Love stories and romances were the lower class's most-liked genre, but this genre also came in fourth in the "least-liked" category. (The number of possible genre choices was eighteen.)

23. Since British cultural studies rejects psychoanalytical theses, I am not complicating the question of identification here. Instead I am assuming a rather simple "commonsense" notion of identification. In a psychoanalytical study informed by feminism, this would be quite unacceptable, and the issue, in particular, of women's identification with male or female characters would be much more complicated. Additionally, I am aware of, but bracketing off, sexual preference (e.g., hetero-, bi-, and homosexuality).

24. Robert E. Kapsis, "Hollywood Filmmaking and Reputation Building: Hitchcock's 'The Birds,'" *Journal of Popular Film and Television* 15, no. 1 (Spring 1987): 6.

25. Crowther, review, p.18.

26. Zunser, "Hitchcock's Scariest," p. 15.

27. McCarten, "Hitchcock Confined Again," pp. 50–51.

28. This can probably be explained since that opposition is a common motif in detective stories.

29. "High-Brow, Low-Brow, Middle-Brow," *Life*, 11 April 1949, 99–101.

30. McCarten's class is unknown and would need exploration if I were doing a more extensive analysis. His class background and current occupation as a writer may be in opposition to the period's dominant educational position on these issues and his assumed audience's class, thus significantly complicating his response. Additionally, long-standing concerns about mass culture by the intellectual elite need to be considered. Here the spread of theses by people such as Paul Lazersfeld and Harold Lasswell or Theodor Adorno may be affecting McCarten's views. More specifically, Richard H. Pells describes the 1950s intellectual scene and its contradictory views of mass media and culture in *The Liberal Mind in a Conservative Age: American Intellectuals in the 1940s and 1950s* (New York: Harper & Row, 1985), pp. 216–32.

31. Terry Eagleton, *Literary Theory: An Introduction* (Minneapolis: University of Minnesota Press, 1983), p. 107.

32. Nina Baym also points out in regard to the canon in American literature that theories of creativity privileging father-son conflicts exclude female writers. "Melodramas of Beset Manhood: How Theories of American Fiction Exclude Women Authors," in *The New Feminist Criticism*, ed. Showalter, pp. 63–80.

Chapter Five
Rethinking "Primitive" Cinema

This chapter is a revision of a paper first presented at the Society for Cinema Studies Conference, New Orleans, Louisiana, 3–6 April 1986.

1. A discussion of the various versions of this history appears in my "Class, Ethnicity, and Gender: Explaining the Development of Early American Film Narrative," *Iris* 11 (Summer 1990): 13–25. Examples of the position with which I am disagreeing include: Noël Burch, "Porter, or Ambivalence," *Screen* 19, no. 4 (Winter 1978/79): 91–105; Noël Burch, "Film's Institutional Mode of Representation and the Soviet Response," *October* 11 (Winter 1979): 77–96; André Gaudreault, "Temporality and Narrativity in Early Cinema, 1895–1908," in *Film before Griffith*, ed. John L. Fell (Berkeley: University of California Press, 1983), pp. 311–29; Tom Gunning, "Non-Continuity, Continuity, Discontinuity: A Theory of Genres in Early Film," *Iris* 2, no. 1 (1984): 101–12.

2. I would stress that this description applies to the United States and not to other national cinemas. Some of the problems in the broad description of early film and its relation to various classes stem from the practice of extending conditions in one country (such as England) to another (the United States).

3. See the various articles in *Film before Griffith*, ed. Fell, pp. 101–222; Robert C. Allen, "Film History: The Narrow Discourse," in *1977 Film Studies Annual*, ed. Ben Lawton and Janet Staiger (Pleasantville, N.Y.: Redgrave Publishing Company, 1977), pp. 9–17; Robert C. Allen, *Vaudeville and Film, 1895–1915: A Study in Media Interaction* (New York: Arno Press, 1980); Charles Musser, "The Eden Musee in 1898: The Exhibitor as Creator," *Film and History* 11, no. 4 (December 1981): 73–83, 96; Eileen Bowser, "Preparation for Brighton—the American Contribution," in *Cinema 1900–1906: An Analytical Study*, ed. Roger Holman (Brussels, Belgium: FIAF, 1982), pp. 3–29; Charles Musser, *Before the Nickelodeon* (film) (USA, Films for Thought, 1983); Charles Musser, "Archeology of the Cin-

ema: 8," *Framework* 22/23 (1983): 4–11; Charles Musser, "Another Look at the 'Chaser Theory,'" *Studies in Visual Communication* 10, no. 4 (Fall 1984): 24–44, and replies by Allen and Musser, pp. 45–50; Charles Musser, "The Travel Genre in 1903–04: Moving Toward Fictional Narrative," *Iris* 2, no. 1 (1984): 47–59; Charles John Musser, "Before the Nickeodeon: Edwin S. Porter and the Edison Company" (Ph.D. diss., New York University, 1986).

4. Besides sources listed above, see Janet Staiger, "The Central Producer System: Centralized Management after 1914," in *The Classical Hollywood Cinema: Film Style and Mode of Production*, by David Bordwell, Janet Staiger, and Kristin Thompson (London: Routledge & Kegan Paul, 1985), pp. 128–29.

5. Aspects of these can be reconstructed in part through other primary evidence, however, and Musser and others have been attempting to do this.

6. Musser, "Archeology," 5.

7. *Uncle Toms [sic] Cabin or Slavery Days* (Edison Company, copyright 30 July 1903, directed by Edwin S. Porter), synopsis produced from a Library of Congress print. The accompanying dramatic version is a compilation of the 1852 drama by George L. Aiken. An edition of the play was done by A. E. Thomas in 1934 and reprinted in Montrose J. Moses, ed. *Representative Plays by American Dramatists: From 1765 to the Present Day* (1925; rpt. New York: Benjamin Blom, 1964), pp. 605–93; A. E. Thomas, ed., *Uncle Tom's Cabin* (New York: D. Appleton-Century, 1934). This compilation, although in part from a text later than the period under discussion, most likely represents the status of the typical dramatic version around 1903. For background on the textual variants, see Montrose, *Representative Plays*, pp. 605–13; Thomas, *Uncle Tom's Cabin*, p. v–vii; Thomas F. Gassett, *Uncle Tom's Cabin and American Culture* (Dallas: Southern Methodist University Press, 1985), pp. 262–63; and discussion below.

8. Information about *Uncle Tom's Cabin* comes from Harry Birdoff, *The World's Greatest Hit: Uncle Tom's Cabin* (New York: S. F. Vanni, 1947), Montrose, *Representative Plays*, pp. 605–13; Gassett, *Uncle Tom's Cabin*; Frank Luther Mott, *Golden Multitudes: The Story of Bestsellers in the United States* (New York: Macmillan Company, 1947), pp. 7, 76–79. Jane Tompkins provides a cultural analysis of the novel and play for mid-nineteenth-century audiences; *Sensational Designs: The Cultural Work of American Fiction, 1790–1860* (New York: Oxford University Press, 1985), pp. 122–46. Some of the traces of this most likely lingered in various mediations by the turn of the century, but I will not attempt to consider the significance of the text for a 1903 audience.

9. Gassett, *Uncle Tom's Cabin*, pp. 269–71.

10. Quoted in Birdoff, *The World's Greatest Hit*, p. 299.

11. Ibid., pp. 317–18.

12. Gassett, *Uncle Tom's Cabin*, p. 382.

13. Besides the above sources, information on other tie-ins to *Uncle Tom's Cabin* comes from Mott, *Golden Multitudes*, pp. 117–22.

14. Birdoff, *The World's Greatest Hit*, pp. 358–59; Gassett, *Uncle Tom's Cabin*, p. 358.

15. Birdoff, *The World's Greatest Hit*, p. 371.

16. Musser transcribes the Edison catalog description of the film in his "Before the Nickelodeon" dissertation, pp. 286–91. Musser points out that the exposition

is very detailed and could have been used by an exhibitor to provide oral commentary during the screening. This might very well have been the case for "first-run" exhibition of the film, but period descriptions do not suggest that lecturers were common in the nickelodeons where *Uncle Tom's Cabin* continued to play; such a practice was not feasible for the low-profit-margin houses.

17. Also see Nicholas Vardac, *Stage to Screen: Theatrical Origins of Early Film: David Garrick to D. W. Griffith* (1949; rpt. New York: Da Capo Press, n.d.), illustrations 61–64.

18. Frank Trommler, "Working-Class Culture and Mass Culture before World War I," *New German Critique* 29 (Spring/Summer 1983): 60, 69.

19. Quoted in Musser, "Archeology," p. 5.

20. Ibid., p. 6.

21. M. M. Bakhtin, "From the Prehistory of Novelistic Discourse" (1975), in *The Dialogic Imagination: Four Essays*, trans. Caryl Emerson and Michael Holquist (Austin: University of Texas Press, 1981), pp. 45–46.

22. Frank C. Perkins chronicled the making of the film in "Photographing the New York Subway," *Scientific American* 93, no. 1 (1 July 1905): 12. His description, however, only states that the subway's details "were photographed with remarkable distinctness."

23. Some sense of the variety for New York City immigrants can be gleaned from Mary Heaton Vorse, "Some Picture Show Audiences," *Colliers*, 24 June 1911, 441–47.

Chapter Six
"The Handmaiden of Villainy"

This chapter is a revision of a paper first presented at the Ohio University Film Conference, Athens, Ohio, 24–27 October 1984, and subsequently published in *Wide Angle* 8, no. 1 (1986): 19–27.

1. The reviews, interviews, articles, and letters to the editor used for this study (and arranged by dates) are: "Foolish Wives," *New York Times*, 12 January 1922, 15; Harriette Underhill, "On the Screen," *New York Herald Tribune*, 12 January 1922, 8; "'Foolish Wives' at the Central," *New York Call*, 14 January 1922, 4; "Foolish Wives," *Variety*, 20 January 1922, 35; A. J., "A Million! A Million!" *Moving Picture World* 54, no. 3 (21 January 1922): 267; Fritz Tidden, "Foolish Wives," *Moving Picture World* 54, no. 3 (21 January 1922): 316; Harriette Underhill, "Von Stroheim's 'Foolish Wives' Not So Foolish," *New York Herald Tribune*, 22 January 1922, sect. 4, p. 4; Arthur James, "The Heavy Rental Prices Involved," *Moving Picture World* 54, no. 11 (11 February 1922): 599; "Foolish Wives," *Photoplay* 21, no. 4 (March 1922): 70; "'Cave Man Stuff' Still Goes, Says Director Von Stroheim" (unknown newspaper), ca. 5 March 1922, clipping file, "Foolish Wives," New York Public Library-Lincoln Center; Frederick James Smith, "Foolish Wives," *Motion Picture Classic* 9, no. 2 (April 1922): 48–49, 87; F.J.S., "Double Exposures," *Motion Picture Classic* 9, no. 2 (April 1922): 50; Dick Dorgan, "Solving the Million Dollar Mystery: A Slang Review," *Photoplay* 21, no. 6 (May 1922): 76, 100; Robert E. Sherwood, "Alas, Poor Hamlet: As Some Producers Would Do It," *Photoplay* 21, no. 6 (May 1922): 107; D.E.G., (letter to editor),

Photoplay 22, no. 2 (July 1922): 115; Frederick James Smith, "The Film Year in Review," *Photoplay* 22, no. 3 (August 1922): 57; Willis Goldbeck, "Von Stroheim, Man and Superman," *Motion Picture Classic* 10, no. 1 (September 1922): 18–19, 82–83; "A Yank Abroad" (letter to editor), *Photoplay* 22, no. 4 (September 1922): 113; Mildred R. Hut (letter to editor), *Photoplay* 22, no. 5 (October 1922): 117.

2. Richard Koszarski, *The Man You Loved to Hate: Erich von Stroheim and Hollywood* (Oxford: Oxford University Press, 1983): p. 88. That gross, however, did not even cover the film's unusually high negative costs.

3. Vološinov, *Marxism and the Philosophy of Language*, p. 23.

4. To what degree this semantic field and trajectory of desires are recent (post–World War I), how long they last, and whether they are isomorphic cannot be answered in a single case study. A wider study might, however, be quite suggestive. Yet as I shall indicate below, some comparisons seem to exist in the instance of Valentino, a popular star at the time of the *Foolish Wives* episode.

5. Suleiman, "Introduction," pp. 35–37.

6. John Higham shows that this view develops in the late 1800s due to economic difficulties. See his *Strangers in the Land: Patterns of American Nativism, 1860–1925* (New Brunswick, N.J.: Rutgers University Press, 1955).

7. Burl Noggle, *Into the Twenties* (Urbana: University of Illinois Press, 1974), pp. 84–121; Geoffrey Perrett, *America in the Twenties* (New York: Simon and Schuster, 1982), pp. 29–116; Frederick Lewis Allen, *Only Yesterday* (1931; New York: Harper and Row, 1964), pp. 38–62; William E. Leuchtenberg, *The Perils of Prosperity, 1914–32* (Chicago: University of Chicago Press, 1958), pp. 66–83; Sinclair Lewis, *Babbitt* (New York: Harcourt, Brace & World, 1922).

8. Noggle, *Into the Twenties*, p. 118.

9. "Capitalism and War," *New York Call*, 8 January 1922, 9. Also see H. A. Miller, "Problems of Nationality," *New York Call*, 17 January 1922, 8.

10. Raymond Williams defines *overdetermination* as the "recognition of multiple forces . . . and of these forces as structured." See *Marxism and Literature* (London: Oxford University Press, 1977), pp. 88–89.

11. It should be emphasized here especially that I am discussing what happened in this instance. These are not rules of reception and, in fact, given the abnormally negative reaction to this film, may be quite atypical.

12. Not von Stroheim's term, but implied in his discussion.

13. See Goldbeck, "Von Stroheim, Man and Superman," p. 82. In the same interview, von Stroheim claims that "Freud's 'Interpretation of Dreams' is the most widely circulated book in this country."

14. As noted in chapter 2, some reception theorists distinguish between "meaning" as an intrinsic property of the text and "sense" or "significance" as what a reader considers the text to suggest in terms of facts and ideas outside of that text. See Barnouw, "Review of *The Act of Reading*," p. 1209. Although I would disagree with the notion that any meaning is "immanent" in the text, I find useful the distinction between a reader's concept of what he or she assumes to be the intent of the text and what he or she considers to be that text's value.

15. I have just implied a psychoanalytical explanation for these metaphors—one that I believe is valid. However, George Lakoff and Mark Johnson suggest

that language is consistently underpinned by metaphorical organizations. One of these is the normalcy of the general metaphor "ideas are food," with attributes of taste and smell (p. 46). See their exciting *Metaphors We Live By* (Chicago: University of Chicago Press, 1980).

16. Assuming that no one is using a nom de plume and that obvious gender-specific nominations have occurred.

17. H. H. Van Loan, "H. H. Van Loan's Own Corner," *Photodramatist* 4, no. 8 (January 1923): 33.

18. A magazine of the period, published by the owners of Vitagraph.

19. Miriam Hansen, "Pleasure, Ambivalence, Identification: Valentino and Female Spectatorship," *Cinema Journal* 25, no. 4 (Summer 1986): 10. Hansen's essay was published between the original publication of my essay and this revision.

20. Dick Dorgan, "A Song of Hate," *Photoplay* 22, no. 2 (July 1922): 26.

21. Hansen, "Pleasure, Ambivalence, Identification," p. 6.

22. Fish, "Interpreting the *Variorum*," pp. 164–84; Jonathan Culler, "Prolegomena to a Theory of Reading," in *The Reader in the Text*, ed. Suleiman and Crosman, pp. 46–66; Tompkins, "The Reader in History," pp. 201–32; Timothy J. Clark, "Preliminaries to a Possible Treatment of 'Olympia' in 1865," *Screen* 21, no. 1 (Spring 1980): 18–41. Peter Wollen takes issue with Clark's interpretation of the critics' responses; see his "Manet: Modernism and Avant Garde," *Screen* 21, no. 2 (Summer 1980): 15–25.

23. According to these writers, but not essentially.

24. Willard Huntington Wright, "A Motion Picture Dictionary," *Photoplay* 22, no. 2 (July 1922): 82 (italics in original).

25. Albeit from the recent war enemy nation of Germany.

Chapter Seven
The Birth of a Nation

This is a revision of a paper first presented at the Society for Cinema Studies Conference, Iowa City, Iowa, 12–16 April 1989.

1. Gladwin Hill, "Polyglot City Is in Shock after a Melee," *New York Times*, 3 August 1978, A-14.

2. Joel Williamson, *The Crucible of Race: Black-White Relations in the American South since Emancipation* (New York: Oxford University Press, 1984).

3. Thomas Cripps, *Slow Fade to Black: The Negro in American Film, 1900–1942* (London: Oxford University Press, 1977), pp. 41–43; Thomas R. Cripps, "The Reaction of the Negro to the Motion Picture 'Birth of a Nation'" (1963), rpt. in *Focus on "The Birth of a Nation,"* ed. Fred Silva (Englewood Cliffs, N.J.: Prentice Hall, 1971), p. 111 (hereafter *Focus*). Thomas F. Gassett describes how Wilson contributed to reasserting segregation; *Race: The History of an Idea in America* (Dallas: Southern Methodist University Press, 1963), p. 279.

4. James M. McPherson, "The Antislavery Legacy: From Reconstruction to the NAACP," in *Towards a New Past: Dissenting Essays in American History*, ed. J. Barton Bernstein (New York: Random House, 1967), pp. 126–57; Williamson, *The Crucible of Race*, pp. 70–78. Williamson's thesis for the deepening of antagonisms between whites and blacks extends C. Vann Woodward's economic

and political determinations proposed in Woodward's *The Strange Career of Jim Crow* (1955) to include psychological and cultural factors. The deteriorating situation of the blacks was not isolated; racism extended to Jews and Asians as well, with segregation and discrimination particularly overt. The Anti-Defamation League of B'nai B'rith formed in 1913. See Oscar Handlin, ed., *Immigration as a Factor in American History* (Englewood Cliffs, N.J.: Prentice Hall, 1959), pp. 171–82. Also see Higham, *Strangers in the Land*.

5. Cripps, *Slow Fade*, pp. 52–64; "NAACP v. 'The Birth of a Nation': The Story of a 50-Year Fight," *Crisis* 72, no. 2 (February 1965): 96.

6. Williamson, *The Crucible of Race*, pp. 140–95.

7. Ibid., pp. 4–6. All of Williamson's "mentalities" are categorized from the position's view of the evolutionary potential of people of color, most likely a sensible system given the impact of social Darwinism on discourses of the period. Gassett, *Uncle Tom's Cabin and American Culture*, p. 346.

8. Quoted in Benjamin R. Tillman, *Congressional Record*, 59th Cong., 2d Sess. (21 January 1907): pp. 1140–44, rpt. in *Civil Rights and the American Negro: A Documentary History*, ed. Albert P. Blaustein and Robert L. Zangrando (New York: Washington Square Press, 1968), p. 319.

9. Grant worked at the American Museum of Natural History. His popular book counted as threatening Eastern and Southern Europeans as well as other groups of people. Handlin, *Immigration*, pp. 183–85. Also see material on this in my chapter 6.

10. Williamson, *The Crucible of Race*, pp. 140–48, 173–75; Gassett, *Uncle Tom's Cabin and American Culture*, p. 346; Cripps, *Slow Fade*, pp. 52–64.

11. "The Clansman," *Crisis* 10, no. 1 (May 1915): 33; "Fighting Race Calumny," *Crisis* 10, no. 1 (May 1915): 40–42, 87–88, rpt. in *Focus*, pp. 66–73. Later historical surveys of the events during this period include: "NAACP v. 'The Birth of a Nation,'" p. 96; Cripps, "Reaction," pp. 112–18; Goodwin Berquist and James Greenwood, "Protest against Racism: 'The Birth of a Nation' in Ohio," *Journal of the University Film Association* 26, no. 3 (1974): 39–44; Cripps, *Slow Fade*, pp. 52–64; Nickieann Fleener-Marzec, *D. W. Griffith's "The Birth of a Nation": Controversy, Suppression, and the First Amendment as It Applies to Filmic Expression, 1915–1973* (New York: Arno Press, 1980), p. 392–424; Richard Schickel, *D. W. Griffith: An American Life* (New York: Simon and Schuster, 1984), pp. 212–302.

12. In New York, the person who threw two eggs during the scene of "Little Sister" jumping off the cliff was a white, Howard Schaeffle. "Egg Negro Scenes in Liberty Film Play," *New York Times*, 15 April 1915, n.p.

13. For details on the alterations, besides the historical surveys (above), see "Films and Births and Censorship," *Survey*, 3 April 1915, 4–5; Seymour Stern, "The Birth of a Nation," *Cinemages*, special issue no. 1 (1955): 9. As Stern describes, among Griffith's deletions were some of the shots of blacks running through the streets of Piedmont, "flashes of screaming white girls being whisked by Negro rapists into doorways in back-alleys of the town," an epilogue "featuring, first Lincoln's forgotten letter to Staunton [*sic*], wherein Lincoln affirms that he does *not* believe in the equality of the black race with the white, and, finally,

full-scale images of the deportation of masses of Negroes from New York harbor to the (filmed) jungles of Liberia as a 'peaceable solution' for American and the Negroes." *Survey* (in 1915) describes an important insertion required by the National Board of Censorship in late March: "These [changes] are said to have been chiefly a substantial reduction in the details of the chase of the white girl by the renegade Negro, which in the original is said to have been the most dreadful portrayal of rape ever offered for public view; the insertion of various soothing captions, such as 'I won't hurt you, little Missy'; the entire excision of a lynching; and a toning down of the scene in which the mulatto all but marries a white girl by force" ("Films and Births and Censorship," p. 4). "'Wid'" in "Films and Film Folk" (ca. 13 July 1915), *D. W. Griffith Papers, 1897–1954* (Frederick, Md.: University Publications of America, microfilm) describes the Hampton Institute epilogue as a "shock," coming after *The Birth of a Nation*. Details on its production are in Nickie Fleener, "Answering Film with Film: The Hampton Epilogue, a Positive Alternative to the Negative Stereotypes Presented in *The Birth of a Nation*," *Journal of Popular Film and Television* 7, no. 4 (1980): 400–425.

14. Fleener-Marzec, *D. W. Griffith's "The Birth of a Nation,"* p. 483.

15. "NAACP v. 'The Birth of a Nation,'" p. 97; "Negroes Oppose Film," *New York Times*, 7 May 1921.

16. "Movies Turn Deaf Ear to Colored Plea," *Christian Century* 47, no. 2 (24 September 1930): 1140–41.

17. Ruth C. Peterson and L. L. Thurstone, *Motion Pictures and the Social Attitudes of Children* (New York: Macmillan, 1933), p. 38.

18. Although Cripps, Berquist and Greenwood, Fleener-Marzec, and Schickel provide accounts of the reception of *The Birth of a Nation*, three other studies deserve special note. In 1961, Charles L. Hutchins surveyed much of the critical discussion to date in his master's thesis, "A Critical Evaluation of the Controversies Engendered by D. W. Griffith's *The Birth of a Nation*" (Master's thesis, University of Iowa). Hutchins's purpose was to outline and evaluate "major controversial issues which have grown up around *The Birth of a Nation*" (p. 3). Two stand out for him: Griffith's "treatment of the Negro" and the historical documentation regarding the "treatment of Thaddeus Stevens," the "role of the Negro in the Reconstructed South," and the "causes for the rise of the Ku Klux Klan" (p. 25). Hutchins's thesis is well-organized and useful (despite his evaluation procedures), but since he treats all responses as of the same time, determining patterns that might be considered historical is not possible. John Hammond Moore provides excellent information about the South Carolina press's negative reaction to Dixon's 1905 play but generally approving response for the 1915 film: "South Carolina's Reaction to the Photoplay *The Birth of a Nation*," *The Proceedings of the South Carolina Historical Association* (1963): 30–40. Russell Merritt studied the Boston events of April 1915, claiming that "most of the audience that came out of the Tremont theatre that night in 1915, for instance, believed Griffith's story was historically true, that *The Birth of a Nation* was a nostalgic, but essentially accurate description of the Civil War years and their aftermath" (p. 26). The evidence for this, however, is uncertain since certainly some Bostonians vehemently protested the film. (See below.) Merritt continues his essay, arguing that in comparison with

Dixon, Griffith's representation of blacks is toned down. This approach to the film repeats one associated since 1915 with defenders of the film. "Dixon, Griffith, and the Southern Legend," *Cinema Journal* 12, no. 1 (Fall 1972): 26–45.

In chronological order, the period articles and reviews that I studied are: D. W. Griffith, "The Motion Picture and Witch Burners," n.d. (numerous papers in "Flickerings from Film Land by Kitty Kell" column), rpt. in *Focus*, pp. 16–99; D. W. Griffith, "The Future of the Two-Dollar Movie," n.d. (numerous papers), rpt. in *Focus*, pp. 99–101; Rev. Dr. Charles H. Parkhurst, "'The Birth of a Nation,'" n.d. (review in numerous papers), rpt. in *Focus*, pp. 102–3; "'The Birth of a Nation,'" *New York Times*, 4 March 1915, 9; Hector Turnbull, "A Stirring Drama Shown," *New York Tribune*, 4 March 1915, 9; "Negroes Object to Film," *New York Times*, 7 March 1915, n.p.; "W," "The Birth of a Nation," *The New York Dramatic Mirror* 73, no. 1890 (10 March 1915): 28; Mark Vance, "The Birth of a Nation," *Variety*, 12 March 1915, rpt. in *Focus*, pp. 22–25; George D. Proctor, "The Birth of a Nation," *Motion Picture News* 11, no. 10 (13 March 1915): 40–50; W. Stephen Bush, "The Birth of a Nation," *Moving Picture World* 23 (13 March 1915): 1586–87, rpt. in *Focus*, pp. 25–28; Francis Hackett, "Brotherly Love," *New Republic* 2, no. 20 (20 March 1915): 185–86, rpt. in *Focus*, pp. 84–86; "A Reconstruction Story," *New York Times*, 21 March 1915, n.p.; "Moving Picture Justly Denounced by Jane Adams [sic]," *New York Evening Post*, 25 March 1915, n.p. (in D. W. Griffith Papers); "Protests on Photo Play," *New York Times*, 31 March 1915, n.p.; "Promise to Tone Down Two Scenes of Vicious Photo Play," *New York Age*, 1 April 1915, 1; James W. Johnson, "Views and Reviews," *New York Age*, 1 April 1915, 4; "Films and Births and Censorship," *Survey*, 3 April 1915, 4–5; "Capitalizing Race Hatred," *New York Globe*, 6 April 1915, n.p., rpt. in *Focus*, pp. 73–75; Thomas Dixon, "Reply to the *New York Globe*," *New York Globe*, 10 April 1915, n.p., rpt. in *Focus*, pp. 75–77; D. W. Griffith, "Reply to the *New York Globe*," *New York Globe*, 10 April 1915, n.p., rpt. in *Focus*, pp. 77–79; "Dixon on His Motive" (editorial), *New York Globe*, 8 April 1915 (in D. W. Griffith Papers); "What Some Globe Readers Have to Say," *New York Globe*, 9 April 1915 (in D. W. Griffith Papers); National Board of Review, "Censoring Motion Pictures," *New Republic* 2, no. 23 (10 April 1915): 262–63; "'The Birth of a Nation,'" *Outlook*, 14 April 1915, 854; "Egg Negro Scenes in Liberty Film Play," *New York Times*, 15 April 1915, n.p.; "Negroes Mob Photo Play," *New York Times*, 18 April 1915, n.p.; "Mass. Protests Vicious Movie," *New York Age*, 22 April 1915, 1; W. James Johnson; "Views and Reviews," *New York Age*, 22 April 1915, 4; "Censorship: The Curse of a Nation," *Boston Evening Transcript*, 23 April 1915, n.p., rpt. in *Focus*, pp. 87–88; Thomas Dixon, "Fair Play for *The Birth of a Nation*," *Boston Journal*, 26 April 1915, n.p., rpt. in *Focus*, pp. 90–95; D. W. Griffith, "Defense of *The Birth of A Nation* and Attack on the Sullivan Bill," *Boston Journal*, 26 April 1915, n.p., rpt. in *Focus*, pp. 88–90; "Tom Dixon's 'Clansman,'" *Crisis* 10, no. 1 (May 1915): 19–20; "The Clansman," *Crisis* 10, no. 1 (May 1915): 33, rpt. as "'The Birth of a Nation': An Editorial," in *Focus*, pp. 64–66; "Fighting Race Calumny," *Crisis* 10, no. 1 (May–June 1915): 40–42, 87–88, rpt. in *Focus*, pp. 66–73; "Chicago Prepares to Forestall 'Birth of a Nation,'" *Chicago Defender*, 1 May 1915, 3; "The Death of a Movie," *Chicago Defender*, 1 May 1915, 8; "Regulation of Films," *Nation* 100, no. 2601 (6 May 1915): 486–87; James

W. Johnson, "Views and Reviews," *New York Age*, 6 May 1915, 4; "Mayor Thompson Bars 'Birth of Nation' from Chicago," *Chicago Defender*, 15 May 1915, 2; Rolfe Cobleigh, ["Why I Oppose *The Birth of a Nation*"], [26 May 1915], rpt. in *Fighting a Vicious Film: Protest against "The Birth of a Nation"* (Boston: Boston Branch of the National Association for the Advancement of Colored People, 1915), rpt. in *Focus*, pp. 80–83; "*Birth of a Nation* Case Dismissed," *New York Age*, 27 May 1915, 4; "'The Birth of a Nation,'" *Crisis* 10, no. 2 (June 1915): 69–71; Helen Duey (?), *Woman's Home Companion*, 1 June 1915 (D. W. Griffith Papers); Charlotte Rumbold, "Against 'The Birth of a Nation,'" *New Republic* 3, no. 31 (5 June 1915): 125; "Progressive Protest Against Anti-Negro Film," *Survey*, 5 June 1915, 209–10; "The Dirt of a Nation," *Chicago Defender*, 5 June 1915, 8; Henry MacMahon, "The Art of the Movies," *New York Times*, 6 June 1915, sect. 6, p. 8; "Meetings," *Crisis* 10, no. 3 (July 1915): 148–49; "'Wid,'" Films and Film Folk" (ca. 13 July 1915) (D. W. Griffith Papers); Harlow Hare, *Boston American*, 18 July 1915, n.p., rpt. in *Focus*, pp. 36–40; "'The Birth of a Nation,'" *Gazette* (Cleveland, Ohio), 11 September 1915, 2; "'The Birth of a Nation,'" *Gazette*, 2 October 1915, [2]; Ward Greene, *Atlanta Journal*, 7 December 1915, n.p., rpt. in *Focus*, pp. 30–33; Ned McIntosh, *Atlanta Constitution*, 7 December 1915, n.p., rpt. in *Focus*, pp. 33–36; "The Attorney General's Broadside," *Advocate* (Cleveland, Ohio), 2, no. 37 (22 January 1916): [4]; S.E.F. Rose, "The Ku Klux Klan and 'The Birth of a Nation,'" *Confederate Veteran* 24, no. 4 (April 1916): 157–59; Henry Stephen Gordon, "The Story of David Wark Griffith," *Photoplay* 10, no. 5 (October 1916): 90–94; and Vachel Lindsay, *The Art of the Moving Picture* (1915) (1922; rpt., New York: Liveright, 1970), pp. 74–77.

19. The more irate reviewiers already recognized the racism of "uncle Tom" and "Sambo" characters. "'The Clansman,'" *Crisis* 10, no. 1 (May 1915): 65.

20. "The Dirt of a Nation," *Chicago Defender*, 5 June 1915, 8; Dan Streible, "A History of the Boxing Film, 1894–1915: Social Reform and Social Control in the Progressive Era" (Unpublished seminar paper, University of Texas at Austin, Spring 1989), pp. 13–22.

21. Griffith, "The Motion Picture and Witch Burners" (1915), rpt. in *Focus*, pp. 96–99.

22. Dixon, "Fair Play for *The Birth of a Nation*," *Boston Journal*, 26 April 1915, n.p., rpt. in *Focus*, pp. 90–95.

23. Griffith, "Reply to the *New York Globe*" (10 April 1915), rpt. in *Focus*, p. 79.

24. Merritt, "Dixon, Griffith, and the Southern Legend," p. 26.

25. Dixon, "Fair Play for *The Birth of a Nation*" (26 April 1915), pp. 90–95.

26. Moore, "South Carolina's Reaction," p. 40. Williamson argues in *The Crucible of Race* that the radical-conservative attribution of bestial qualities shifted from blacks to other minorities after 1906. Moore's information suggests otherwise.

27. "Egg Negro Scenes in Liberty Film Play," *New York Times*, 15 April 1915.

28. Richard Watts, Jr., "D. W. Griffith," *New Theater and Film* (November 1936), rpt. in *New Theater and Film, 1934 to 1937*, ed. Herbert Kline (San Diego, Calif.: Harcourt-Brace-Jovanovich, 1985), p. 238; Lewis Jacobs, "D. W. Griffith: *The Birth of a Nation*" (1939, from *The Rise of the American Film*), rpt. in *Focus*, p.

159; editor's note for David Platt, "Fanning the Flames of the War," *Daily Worker* (New York City), 20 December 1939, 7. This was one of four articles on prowar filmmaking in 1914–1918 published 18–21 December 1939. Films Platt considered possibly progressive were *Juarez* and *Mr. Smith Goes to Washington*; David Platt, "Will Film World Cave In as It Did in '14?" *Daily Worker*, 21 December 1939, 7.

29. A socialist newspaper, the *New Leader*, implied in 1940 that the Communist party chose particularly to "court" blacks because of defections due to the Hitler-Stalin pact. While the pact had serious repercussions in the party, direct approaches to blacks were at least a decade old. Ted Poston, "CP Purges Ford as Scapegoat for Failure among Negroes," *New Leader*, 30 March 1940, 4; Philip Taft, "Party Organizer (New York, 1927–1938)," in *The American Radical Press, 1880–1960*, vol. 1, ed. Joseph R. Conlin (Westport, Conn.: Greenwood Press, 1974), p. 262; Cripps, *Slow Fade*, p. 68. Eugene Gordon, "'Yes, I Mean You Guys,' Barks Mr. Paglia," *Daily Worker* ca. 4 January 1940, n.p.; Seymour Stern, "Suppression of Showing Marks 25th Year of 'Birth of a Nation,'" *New Leader*, 16 March 1940, 3.

30. Daniel Aaron, *Writers on the Left* (New York: Harcourt, 1961); Richard H. Pells, *Radical Visions and American Dreams: Culture and Social Thought in the Depression Years* (Middletown, Conn.: Wesleyan University Press, 1973). Additional criticisms and defenses of *The Birth of a Nation* through the 1930s include (in chronological order): Thomas Dixon, "Civil War Truth," *New York Times*, 8 May 1921; "[Griffith] Defends Film Production," *New York Times*, 9 May 1921; "Foes of Klan Fight 'Birth of a Nation,'" *New York Times*, 3 December 1922, 5; "Movies Turn Deaf Ear to Colored Plea," *Christian Century* 47, no. 2 (24 September 1930): 1140–41; Barnet G. Braver-mann, "Griffith: The Pioneer," *Theatre Guild Magazine* 8 (February 1931): 28–31, 60–61 (Braver-mann would soon be an editor of *Experimental Cinema*; he writes: "It is thus clear that Griffith's background did not help him to develop a penetrative social outlook"); Seymour Stern, "Hollywood and Montage," *Experimental Cinema* 4 (1932): 47–52; Peterson and Thurstone, *Motion Pictures and the Social Attitudes of Children*, pp. 35–38, 60–61; Harry Alan Potamkin, *The Eyes of the Movie*, International Pamphlets, no. 38 (n.p., 1934); Seymour Stern, "Birthday of a Classic," *New York Times*, 25 March 1935; Seymour Stern, "'The Birth of a Nation': In Retrospect," *International Photographer* 7 (April 1935): 4–5, 23–24; Richard Watts, Jr., "D. W. Griffith," *New Theater and Film* (November 1936), rpt. in *New Theater and Film*, ed. Klein, pp. 237–40; Archer Winsten, "'The Birth of a Nation' Surprises Old Admirer," *New York Post*, 5 October 1937; Milton MacKaye, "The Birth of a Nation," *Scribner's Magazine* 102, no. 5 (November 1937): 40–46, 69; V. F. Calverton, "Cultural Barometer," *Current History* 49, no. 1 (September 1938): 45–47; Lewis Jacobs, "D. W. Griffith: *The Birth of a Nation*" (1939), rpt. in *Focus*, pp. 154–68.

31. David Platt, "Negroes Barred from Hollywood Jobs, Slandered in Its Films," *Daily Worker*, 20 February 1940, 7. This is the second of the series that ran from 19 to 28 February 1940. On the 1933 Payne Fund studies, see Peterson and Thurstone, *Motion Pictures and the Social Attitudes of Children*.

32. Seymour Stern, "Griffith: I. *The Birth of a Nation*," *Film Culture* 36 (Spring–Summer 1965): 36–37; Seymour Stern, "Suppression of Showing Marks

25th Year of 'Birth of a Nation,'" *New Leader*, 6 March 1940, 3. Stern's reference in 1965 is to his articles in the *New Leader* and the *New York Times*. However, the latter essay seems moderately harmless, with another essay in the *New York Herald Tribune* of possibly greater provocation. More likely, Stern's alienation from his colleagues develops from his second article in the *New Leader* in which he attacks Jay Leyda (see below). Seymour Stern, "'The Birth of a Nation' Marked an Industry's Coming of Age," *New York Herald Tribune*, 16 June 1940; Seymour Stern, "Pioneer of the Film Art," *New York Times Magazine*, 10 November 1940, 16–17.

33. "No Show," *New Leader*, 16 March 1940, 3. The following week Stern accused Jay Leyda, assistant curator at the Museum of Modern Art, of "depart[ing] from accepted canons of cinematic criticism, and substitut[ing] outright political propaganda" in Leyda's film notes for a retrospective of Soviet cinema. Seymour Stern, "Film Library Notes Build 'CP Liberators' Myth," *New Leader*, 23 March 1940, 3. Many people believe this article contributed to events that led to the request for Leyda's resignation from the museum.

34. The first issue (February 1930) of *Experimental Cinema* lists Platt and Jacobs as coeditors for the Cinema Crafters (Philadelphia), with Hollywood editor Stern and New York editor Potamkin.

35. Pells, *Radical Visions and American Dreams*, p. 34. Also see: Aaron, *Writers on the Left*; Ian H. Birchall, "Marxism and Literature," in *The Sociology of Literature*, ed. Routh and Wolff, pp. 92–108; and George Steiner, "Marxism and the Literary Critic," in *Sociology of Literature and Drama*, ed. Elizabeth and Tom Burns (Harmondsworth, England: Penguin Books, 1973), pp. 159–78.

36. Aaron, *Writers on the Left*; Pells, *Radical Visions and American Dreams*, pp. 342–46; Max Nomad, "1940 Saw Intellectuals Retreat from Leftist Traditional Orthodoxy," *New Leader*, 4 January 1941, 5. Nomad is citing Lewis Corey, in the *Nation* (1940).

37. George Amberg, "Introduction," *Experimental Cinema*, pp. iii–iv. Potamkin at least was already aligned with U.S. communists. Furthermore, as of issue number 3 (1931), *Experimental Cinema* was receiving support from the Workers Film and Photo League of America and The American Prolet-Kino. Issue 3 lists three coeditors: Jacobs, Platt, and Stern, with Potamkin dropping out because *Experimental Cinema* printed a criticism written by Samuel Brody of an essay that Potamkin had published in *Close Up*. Issue 4 (1932) has five coeditors: Jacobs, Platt, Stern, Alexander Brailovsky, and Barnet G. Braver-mann. The last issue, number 5 (1934) lists editors Jacobs, Stern, and Braver-mann, but Platt is not among the associate or corresponding editors. Platt *is* listed as teaching at the Harry Alan Potamkin Film School along with Jacobs, Brody, Ralph Steiner, Irving Lerner, and Leo Selzter (p. 54).

38. William Alexander, *Film on the Left: American Documentary Film from 1931 to 1942* (Princeton: Princeton University Press, 1981), pp. 46–47; Russell Campbell, *Cinema Strikes Back: Radical Filmmaking in the United States, 1930–1942* (Ann Arbor, Mich.: UMI Research Press, 1982), pp. 96, 329n.

39. "Eisenstein Attacks 'Birth of a Nation' / Protests Slanderous Use of His Name," *Daily Worker*, 14 January 1941, 7(?). Also see in this period: Paul Goodman, "Film Chronicle: Griffith and the Technical Innovations," *Partisan Review* 8, no. 3 (May–June 1941): 237–40; Barnet G. Bravermann, "D. W. G., The Creator of Film Form," *Theatre Arts* 29 (April 1945): 240–50.

40. Peter Noble, "A Note on an Idol," *Sight and Sound* 15, no. 59 (Autumn 1946): 81–82.

41. D. W. Griffith, *"The Birth of a Nation," Sight and Sound* 16, no. 61 (Spring 1947): 32; Seymour Stern, "Griffith Not Anti-Negro," *Sight and Sound* 16, no. 61 (Spring 1947): 32–35.

42. Italics in the original. This latter ploy comes from a 1921 defense by Griffith. "Defends Film Production," *New York Times*, 9 May 1921.

43. "Without Comment" (Museum of Modern Art pamphlet, ca. 1946, p. 3), rpt. in *Sight and Sound* 16, no. 61 (Spring 1947): 35; E. L. Cranstone, "'The Birth of a Nation' Controversy," *Sight and Sound* 16, no. 63 (Autumn 1947): 119 (Cranstone writes: "We have have heard it all before and know that red-baiting is a dangerous occupation" [p. 119]—an ironical observation given what was about to happen in the United States); Seymour Stern, "The Griffith Controversy," *Sight and Sound* 17, no. 65 (Spring 1948): 49–50; editor's note, *Sight and Sound* 17, no. 65 (Spring 148): 50; Peter Noble, "The Negro in *The Birth of a Nation*," *The Negro in Films* (London: Skelton Robinson, 1948): 33–43, rpt. in *Focus*, pp. 125–32; V. J. Jerome, *The Negro in Hollywood Films* (New York: Masses and Mainstream, 1950). Also see: James Agee, "David Wark Griffith," *Nation* 167, no. 10 (4 September 1948): 264–65; James Mason Brown, "Wishful Banning," *Saturday Review* 32, no. 11 (12 March 1949): 24–26; Dore Schary, "Censorship and Stereotypes," *Saturday Review* 32, no. 18 (30 April 1949): 9–10; Seymour Stern, "'The Birth of a Nation,'" *Cinemages*, special issue no. 1 (1955).

44. Seymour Stern, "D. W. Griffith and the Movies," *American Mercury* 68, no. 303 (March 1949): 308–19; Seymour Stern, "The Cold War against David Wark Griffith," *Films in Review* 7, no. 2 (February 1956): 49–59; Stern, "Griffith: I. The Birth of a Nation," *Film Culture* 36 (Spring–Summer 1965): 1–210. Also see Seymour Stern, "The Soviet Directors' Debt to D. W. Griffith," *Films in Review* 7, no. 5 (May 1956): 202–9. For evidence that Stern's view has its current adherents, see Herbert C. Roseman, "Why the Wacko-Liberals Hate the Late Seymour Stern: The Most Authoritative of D. W. Griffith Scholars Long Ago Exposed Communists' Filmic Distortions," *Quirk's Reviews* (May 1985): 7 (in New York Public Library Performing Arts clipping file on Seymour Stern).

45. A recent exception to this pattern of separating form and content when discussing *The Birth of a Nation* is Michael Rogin's essay, "'The Sword Became a Flashing Vision': D. W. Griffith's *The Birth of a Nation*," *Representations* 9 (Winter 1985): 150–95.

Chapter Eight
The Logic of Alternative Readings

1. Terry Beers, "Reading Reading Constraints: Conventions, Schemata, and Literary Interpretations," *Diacritics* 18, no. 4 (Winter 1988): 82–93.

2. Ibid., p. 92.

3. Ellsworth, "Illicit Pleasures," p. 46.

4. Fetterley, *The Resisting Reader*, p. xx.

5. Crawford and Chaffin, "The Reader's Construction of Meaning," p. 25.

6. Ibid.

7. Annette Kolodny, "A Map for Misreading: Or, Gender and the Interpretation of Literary Texts" (1980), rpt. in *The New Feminist Criticism*, ed. Showalter, pp. 47–48.

8. For some discussion of whether women prefer plot structures that do not emphasize the hermeneutic codes, see Kuhn, "Women's Genres," pp. 18–28; Tania Modleski, "The Search for Tomorrow in Today's Soap Operas," *Film Quarterly* 33, no. 1 (Fall 1979).

9. Richard Dyer, "Introduction," *Gays and Film*, ed. Richard Dyer, rev. ed. (London: British Film Institute, 1980), p. 4.

10. Gerald Hannon, "Throat-ramming" (1975), rpt. in *Flaunting It! A Decade of Gay Journalism from the "Body Politic,"* ed. Ed Jackson and Stan Persky (Vancouver: New Star Books; Toronto: Pink Triangle Press, 1982), p. 9.

11. Ken Popert, "Help Them See *Cruising*" (1980), rpt. in *Flaunting It!*, ed. Jackson and Persky, p. 209.

12. An instance of such a debate is among writers in *Body Politic* over representations in *Cruising*. One part of the discussion dealt with the realism of the film: that *Cruising*, despite its possible appeal to the worst in stereotyping homophobia, also had verisimilitude to gay activities. Much as feminists have questioned whether films that represent women in their oppression, and thus constitute a realism, are politically progressive or reactionary, so too the homosexual community argued the complexities of such a contradictory situation. See discussions in 1979–1980 reprinted in *Flaunting It!*, ed. Jackson and Persky, pp. 196–213.

13. Dyer and Derek Cohen emphasize that gay culture is also saturated with other variables, such as male versus female, and class. Derek Cohen and Richard Dyer, "The Politics of Gay Culture," in *Homosexuality: Power and Politics*, ed. Gay Left Collective (London: Allison and Busby, 1980), pp. 174–75.

14. Kevin B. Smith, "The Radical Faeries Take New York," *Advocate*, 1 August 1989, 39.

15. Kent Bakken, "Judy Garland's Hometown," *Advocate*, 15 August 1989, 37–40.

16. For some sense of this, see Richard Dyer, *Heavenly Bodies: Film Stars and Society* (New York: St. Martin's Press, 1986), p. 141. Similar issues surround the notion of camp; see Jack Babuscio, "Camp and the Gay Sensibility," in *Gays and Film*, ed. Dyer, pp. 40–57; Richard Dyer, "It's Being So Camp as Keeps Us Going," *Body Politic* 10 (September 1977): 11–13; Andrew Britton, "For Interpretation—Notes against Camp," *Gay Left* 7 (Winter 1978–1979): 11–14; Cohen and Dyer, "The Politics of Gay Culture," pp. 172–86.

17. Babuscio, "Camp and the Gay Sensibility," p. 46.

18. Other reading responses besides associations might occur. A good counterinstance is, of course, reading individuals from a camp perspective. Dyer makes it clear that Garland was not read as herself a camp figure (as Jeanette MacDonald was) but as a person who was camping. *Heavenly Bodies*, pp. 178–93. The dynamics for discovering people to be seen as camp are what Babuscio and others describe. Thus, Garland's case is quite different from that of many other female stars considered part of the gay male panorama of objects of interest.

19. Dyer, *Heavenly Bodies*, pp. 193–94.

20. Joe McElhaney, "Gay Spectatorship and Judy Garland" (Unpublished sem-

inar paper, New York University, Fall 1984); Dyer, *Heavenly Bodies*. McElhaney's work predates Dyer's *Heavenly Bodies*, but McElhaney also references a BFI publication by Dyer, "*A Star Is Born* and the Construction of Authenticity," in *Star Signs*, which I have not seen. Consequently, I do not know to whom to credit certain ideas and will tend to treat their works together when both offer the same point.

21. Dyer also notes that the subculture he is investigating comprises male gays who are also primarily urban and white. *Heavenly Bodies*, p. 142.

22. Ibid., pp. 142–43.

23. McElhaney, "Gay Spectatorship and Judy Garland," pp. 4, 8.

24. Dyer, *Heavenly Bodies*, p. 167.

25. This formulation has a very real historical source in period discussions of "homosexuality." I shall expand on this below.

26. Dyer, *Heavenly Bodies*, p. 146.

27. Cohen and Dyer remark about this process: "All this [appreciation of culture] was connected to being queer; indeed, it was part of being queer. Queerness brought with it artistic sensitivity—it gave you the capacity to appreciate and respond to culture. It was a compensation for having been born or made queer; it was a positive to set beside the negative of being queer, with which it was inextricably bound up." "The Politics of Gay Culture," p. 177. Also see Donald Webster Cory, *The Homosexual in America* (New York: Greenberg, 1951), p. 13. Cory is a pseudonym for the gay male author of this book; more on his view below.

28. Dyer, *Heavenly Bodies*, p. 154.

29. Kenneth Anger, *Hollywood Babylon* (1975; rpt., New York: Dell Publishing, 1981), p. 416.

30. McElhaney, "Gay Spectatorship and Judy Garland," p. 6; Dyer, *Heavenly Bodies*, p. 168.

31. McElhaney, "Gay Spectatorship and Judy Garland," p. 7. This latter notion McElhaney attributes to Dyer.

32. Dyer, *Heavenly Bodies*, p. 178.

33. In a study of female impersonators in the early 1970s, Esther Newton concludes that the women preferred as models for imitation "(1) are widely known, (2) have a highly individualistic and mannered style, and (3) are well liked by the gay community." Thus, the function of female impersonators in this area may involve camp, but those whom they impersonate are not objects of satire. Women mentioned by Newton as then currently in vogue include the following: Mae West, Sophie Tucker, Hildegarde, Hermione Gingold, Phyllis Diller, Bette Davis, Marlene Dietrich, Pearl Bailey, and Judy Garland. *Mother Camp: Female Impersonators in America* (Chicago: University of Chicago Press, 1972), p. 48.

34. McElhaney, "Gay Spectatorship and Judy Garland," p. 5.

35. M. M. Bakhtin, *Speech Genres and Other Late Essays*, trans. Vern W. McGee (Austin: University of Texas Press, 1986), pp. 46–47.

36. Dyer, *Heavenly Bodies*, pp. 142–43.

37. Thomas J. Watson and Bill Chapman, *Judy: Portrait of an American Legend* (New York: McGraw-Hill, 1986), p. 64.

38. Anne Edwards, *Judy Garland: A Biography* (New York: Simon and Schuster, 1974), p. 144.

39. Researchers have recently been emphasizing that the image of a star is significant as a potential determinant in historical events. Among the most pertinent discussions of this are the following: Stephen Heath, "Film and System: Terms of Analysis, Part II," *Screen* 16, no. 2 (Summer 1975): 101–6; Richard Dyer, *Stars* (London: British Film Institute, 1979); and Charles J. Maland, *Chaplin and American Culture: The Evolution of a Star Image* (Princeton: Princeton University Press, 1989).

40. Watson and Chapman, *Judy*, p. 11.

41. *Current Biography 1941*, ed. Maxine Block (New York: H. W. Wilson Company, 1941), pp. 317–18.

42. Sidney Skolsky, "Tintypes" (ca. July 1941; New York Public Library Clipping file on Garland—hereafter NYPL-Garland); Sheilah Graham, "Hollywood: Mickey Seems to Be Growing Up," (ca. 16 January 1943; NYPL-Garland); Jerry Mason, "Sham Dancer?" (possibly the *Sun Baltimore*, 22 August 1943; NYPL-Garland); "Judy's Symphonic Jive," *Newsweek* 22 (12 July 1943): 80–81.

43. Gerold Frank, *Judy* (1975; rpt., New York: Dell Publishing Co., 1976), pp. 209–90.

44. Elaine St. Johns, "The Truth about Judy Garland's Health," *Photoplay* 31, no. 6 (November 1947): 46–47, 85 (the quotation appears on p. 47).

45. Also see "Working Girl," *Time* 54 (14 November 1949): 101–2.

46. Maxine Arnold, "The Punch in Judy," *Photoplay* 33, no. 4 (September 1948): 41 and 98.

47. Alan Branigan, "Judy's Future at Stake" (ca. 21 June 1950; NYPL-Garland); "Judy Couldn't Relax," *Newsweek* 36 (3 July 1950): 14–15.

48. Garland's smash stage opening at the London Palladium the following spring was headlined in *Life*: "Judy Goes Boom / But gets up to go on with the show." *Life* starts its paragraph report, "Judy Garland was shaking with nerves" and uses three-quarters of its space to show two pictures of Garland slipping during a dance step, falling, and then being helped back up: an event to foreshadow perfectly the mythology of Garland. *Life* 30 (23 April 1951): 49. Also see Alan Branigan, "Like Lemon Drops: Judy's Troubles Seem to Melt Away as Palace Audience Makes Her a Star" (ca. 21 October 1951; NYPL-Garland); "Judy Comes Back," *Life* 31 (29 October 1951): 105–6; Harold Clurman, "Punch and Judy," *New Republic* 125 (26 November 1951): 21–22; Robert Kass, "Film and TV," *Catholic World* 174, no. 1041 (December 1951): 223–24; Allene Talmey, "The Judy Garland Phenomenon," *Vogue*, January 1952, 115; Nathaniel Benchley, "Offstage," *Theatre Arts* 36, no. 2 (February 1952): 18–19.

49. Clifton Fadiman, "Judy and Juan: Two High Moments" (*Holliday*, March 1952), rpt. in *Party of One: The Selected Writings of Clifton Fadiman* (Cleveland, Ohio: The World Publishing Company, 1955), p. 287 (italics in original).

50. Garland's image continues in this vein through the 1950s. See in particular A. E. Hotchner, "Judy Garland's Rainbow," *Reader's Digest* 61, no. 364 (August 1952): 73–76 (accompanied by an engraving of Garland in a suitcoat with bowtie and cropped hair); Cameron Shipp, "The Star Who Thinks Nobody Loves Her," *Saturday Evening Post* 2 (April 1955): 28–29, 94–96; Joe Hyams, "Crack-Up," *Photoplay* 51, no. 1 (January 1957): 38–41, 60–62; Judy Garland as told to Joe Hyams, "The Real Me," *McCalls*, April 1957, 78–80 +.

51. John D'Emilio, *Sexual Politics, Sexual Communities: The Making of a Homosexual Minority in the United States 1940–1970* (Chicago: University of Chicago Press, 1983), p. 4. Also see Jeffrey Weeks, *Sex, Politics and Society: The Regulation of Sexuality since 1800* (London: Longman, 1981). Weeks focuses on the international development of the term and its implications. For the post–World War II period, he concentrates on the British scene.

52. D'Emilio, *Sexual Politics, Sexual Communities*, pp. 21, 13.

53. David F. Greenberg, *The Construction of Homosexuality* (Chicago: University of Chicago Press, 1988), pp. 400–433. As with Weeks, Greenberg has little to say specifically about the 1950s, skipping from turn-of-the-century theories to gay liberation.

54. Dyer, *Heavenly Bodies*, p. 169, quoting a Mattachine Society prospectus that Dyer dates to 1950.

55. Also see Martin S. Curtler, "Homosexual Minority" (in letters column), *Saturday Review of Literature* 32, no. 23 (4 June 1949): 25; Lambert Fairchild, "Dissent over Homosexuals," *Saturday Review of Literature* 32, no. 25 (18 June 1949): 21; Vernon Albert Ward, Jr., N.S.A., and Martin S. Curtler, "Homosexual Minority," *Saturday Review of Literature* 32, no. 28 (9 July 1949): 25–26; Leonard Brown and Robert L. Bretz, "Homosexual Minority," *Saturday Review of Literature* 32, no. 31 (30 July 1949): 24.

56. Cory, *The Homosexual in America*, p. 40. The date is 1950 when ninety-one employees in the State Department were fired for being gay.

57. Vito Russo, *The Celluloid Closet: Homosexuality in the Movies* (New York: Harper & Row, 1981), p. 126.

58. Donald Vining, *A Gay Diary*, 3 vols. (New York: Pepys Press, 1979). Vining enjoyed the ballet but did not seem to go often to the movies or stage shows. Thus, he does not remark about Garland. Also see the Hall Carpenter Archives, *Walking after Midnight: Gay Men's Life Stories* (London: Routledge, 1989), pp. 78–98.

59. Cory, *The Homosexual in America*, pp. 92–94, 97, 98, 13.

60. My selection was somewhat limited by the novels available through the University of Texas at Austin. However, from my original list of twenty I was able to consider seventeen. Several of these used a gay character or gay episode as a minor feature of the plot. One hinged on the notion of latent homosexuality, ending with the individual killing his wife because she had a lover (Stuart Engstrand, *The Sling and the Arrow* [New York: Creative Age, 1947]). Some few of them must have been so coded that I could not perceive the homosexual themes. This left the nine I mention: James Barr (pseudonym for James Fugate), *Quatrefoil* (New York: Greenberg, 1950); John Horne Burns, *Lucifer with a Book* (New York: Harper & Bros., 1949); Truman Capote, *Other Voices, Other Rooms* (New York: Random House, 1948); Michael DeForrest, *The Gay Year* (New York: Castle Books, 1949); Paul Goodman, *Parents' Day* (1951; rpt., Santa Barbara, Calif.: Black Sparrow Press, 1985); Thomas Hal Phillips, *The Bitterweed Path* (New York: Rinehart, 1949); AndrTellier, *Twilight Men* (New York: Greenberg, 1931); Ward Thomas, *Stranger in the Land* (Boston: Houghton Mifflin Co., 1949); Gore Vidal, *The City and the Pillar* (New York: E. P. Dutton, 1948).

61. Samuel M. Steward, "Introduction," *Quatrefoil*, p. x.

62. Thomas, *Stranger in the Land*, p. 44.

63. Capote, *Other Voices, Other Rooms*, p. 78. Capote's novel has a high literary reputation, but in terms of this discussion, the book offers distressing stereotypes.

64. DeForrest, *The Gay Year*, pp. xvi, 116, 250, 267.

65. "Abel," "A Star Is Born," *Variety*, 29 September 1954, 6; Bennett Cerf, "Trade Winds: Babes in Hollywood," *Saturday Review* 37 (23 October 1954): 8; Bosley Crowther, "A Star Is Born," *New York Times*, 12 October 1954, 23; "Film Reviews: A Star Is Born," *Films in Review* 5 (November 1954): 479–81; Philip T. Hartung, "The Screen: Home Is the Star," *Commonweal* 61, no. 3 (22 October 1954): 60–61; Robert Kass, "Film and TV," *Catholic World* 180, no. 1077 (December 1954): 221–22; Arthur Knight, "SR Goes to the Movies: Saying It with Music," *Saturday Review* 37 (30 October 1954): 28–29; John McCarten, "The Current Cinema: Boy, Girl, and General," *New Yorker* 30 (23 October 1954): 145; "The Month's Best . . . ," *Coronet* 36, no. 3 (July 1954): 6; "New Day for Judy," *Life* 37 (13 September 1954): 163–66, 168, 170; "The New Pictures," *Time* 64 (25 October 1954): 86–87; "A Star Is Born," *Harrison's Reports* 36, no. 40 (2 October 1954): 156; "Triumph for Hollywood," *Newsweek* 44 (1 November 1954): 86; Moira Walsh, "Films," *America* 92, no. 3 (16 October 1954): 83; Jesse Zunser, "Judy Garland in a One-Woman, 3-Hour Show," *Cue*, 23 October 1954, 17.

66. Some of this information also comes from casual conversations with friends of mine.

67. Walsh, "Films," p. 83.

68. Dyer, *Heavenly Bodies*, p. 180.

69. For comparison, see Robert Scholes's description of his encounter with a videotape of Garland singing "Over the Rainbow" in her later 1950s career: *Protocols of Reading* (New Haven: Yale University Press, 1989), pp. 125–34.

70. Cohen and Dyer, "The Politics of Gay Culture," pp. 179–82.

71. Three additional studies of the alteration of denotative material for identification or pleasure by gay men and women are the following: Richard Goldstein, "Pornography and Its Discontents," *Village Voice*, 16 October 1984, 19–22, 44; Chris Straayer, "Redressing the 'Natural'" (Paper delivered at the Ohio University Film Conference, Athens, Ohio, Fall 1984); Bonnie Zimmerman, "What Has Never Been: An Overview of Lesbian Feminist Literary Criticism" (1981), rpt. in *The New Feminist Criticism*, ed. Showalter, pp. 200–224.

Chapter Nine
With the Compliments of the Auteur

1. Peter Wollen, "Godard and Counter-Cinema: Vent d'Est" (1972), rpt. in *Readings and Writings: Semiotic Counter-Strategies* (London: Verso, 1982), pp. 79–91. Wollen schematizes his list for "Hollywood-Mosfilm"/revolutionary counter-cinema: (1) narrative transitivity/narrative intransitivity; (2) identification/estrangement; (3) transparency/foregrounding; (4) single diegesis/multiple diegesis; (5) closure/aperture; (6) pleasure/un-pleasure; (7) fiction/reality (p. 79).

2. Steve Neale, "'New Hollywood Cinema,'" *Screen* 17, no. 2 (Summer 1976): 117–22. Neale refers to an Elsaesser essay in *Monogram* 6, and to Robin Wood,

"Smart-Ass and Cutie Pie: Notes toward an Evaluation of Altman," *Movie* 21 (Autumn 1975): 1–17.

3. Neale, "'New Hollywood Cinema,'" pp. 117–18.

4. Ibid., p. 118.

5. Ibid., p. 120.

6. David Bordwell, "The Art Cinema as a Mode of Film Practice," *Film Criticism* 4, no. 1 (Fall 1979): 56. Bordwell updates the essay in his *Narration in the Fiction Film*.

7. Bordwell, "The Art Cinema," pp. 58–59.

8. Steve Neale, "Art Cinema as Institution," *Screen* 22, no. 1 (1981): 11–39.

9. Ibid., p. 36.

10. Bordwell, *Narration in the Fiction Film*, p. 231.

11. Bordwell, *Making Meaning*, pp. 44–50.

12. Ibid., pp. 48–49.

13. Dwight Macdonald, *On Movies* (New York: Berkley Medallion Books, 1969), p. 344 (italics in original).

14. "Mosk," "The Connection," *Variety*, 10 May 1961, 6.

15. "Importers Seek Theatre Outlets: Mushrooming of New 'Art' Houses Is Foreseen to Give Playing Time," *Motion Picture Herald* 166, no. 6 (8 February 1947): 50.

16. For a more extensive discussion of these changes, see Janet Staiger, "Individualism versus Collectivism: The Shift to Independent Production in the U.S. Film Industry," *Screen* 24, no. 4–5 (July–October 1983): 68–79.

17. Noel Meadow, "French Pictures Gain in Popularity," *New York Times*, 8 June 1947; "Runs, Hits, No Errors," *New York Times*, 29 June 1947; Thomas M. Pryor, "Foreign Films Become Big Business," *New York Times*, 8 February 1948.

18. Handel, *Hollywood Looks at Its Audience*; William R. Weaver, "Studios Use Audience Research to Learn What Pleases Customers," *Motion Picture Herald* 164, no. 3 (20 July 1946): 37; William R. Weaver, "Audience Research Has Hollywood Renaissance," *Motion Picture Herald* 175, no. 6 (7 May 1949): 29.

19. Handel, *Hollywood Looks at Its Audience*, p. 99.

20. Thomas M. Pryor, "Extending a Helping Hand to Foreign Pictures, *New York Times*, 5 March 1950. Independent distributors were, quite understandably, distressed about the Motion Picture Association of America's proposal, seeing it as an insidious threat to their business. They responded, organizing among themselves. Thomas M. Pryor, "Foreign Film Distributors Organize," *New York Times*, 18 March 1950. As others have noted, the Hollywood majors and the MPAA also invested directly in foreign cinemas, partially because of foreign trade restrictions but also, obviously, for general profit potentials. See, for instance, Michael Silverman, "Italian Film and American Capital, 1947–1951," in *Cinema Histories, Cinema Practices*, ed. Patricia Mellencamp and Philip Rosen (Frederick, Md.: University Publications of America, 1984), pp. 44–46.

21. Paul A. Baran and Paul M. Sweezy, *Monopoly Capital: An Essay on the American Economic and Social Order* (New York: Monthly Review Press, 1966). For a further discussion of this as it relates to the history of the U.S. film industry, see Janet Staiger, "'Announcing Wares, Winning Patrons, Voicing Ideals': Thinking

about the History and Theory of Film Advertising," *Cinema Journal* 29, no. 3 (Spring 1990): 3–31.

22. William Appleman Williams, *The Contours of American History* (1961; rpt., New York: Franklin Watts, 1973), pp. 451–78; Baran and Sweezy, *Monopoly Capital*.

23. Chaim I. Waxman, "Perspectives on Poverty in Early American Sociology," in *Ethnicity, Identity, and History: Essays in Memory of Werner J. Cahnman*, ed. Joseph B. Maier and Chaim I. Waxman (New Brunswick, N.J.: Transaction Books, 1983), p. 194.

24. Sidney J. Levy, "Symbols for Sale," *Harvard Business Review* 37, no. 4 (July–August 1959): 117.

25. "High-Brow, Low-Brow, Middle-Brow," pp. 99–101. See chapter 4 above at n. 29.

26. Dallas W. Smythe, Parker B. Lusk, and Charles A. Lewis, "Portrait of an Art-Theater Audience," *Quarterly of Film, Radio and Television* 8 (Fall 1953): 28–50.

27. Smythe reports figures in the following categories. Qualities of pictures most important: acting—40 percent; story—33 percent; stars—7 percent. Reasons for liking foreign films: realism—30.7 percent; "generally better"—17.4 percent; "better acting"—13.0 percent. Pp. 41 and 43.

28. Handel, *Hollywood Looks at Its Audience*, pp. 127, 124.

29. Kenneth P. Adler, "Art Films and Eggheads," *Studies in Public Communication* 2 (Summer 1959): 10, 9, 11. Also see John E. Twomey, "Some Considerations on the Rise of the Art-Film Theater," *Quarterly of Film, Radio and Television* 10 (Spring 1956): 239–47.

30. Bosley Crowther, "The 'Ten Best,'" *New York Times*, 29 December 1946, sect. 2, p. 1.

31. Paul Moor, "The Upset at Cannes," *Theatre Arts* 35, no. 8 (August 1951): 22–23, 95–96. Once the festival circuit becomes more important for selling films abroad, U.S. manufacturers become more sensitive to its judgments. This obviously is starting at about this time.

32. "John Mason Brown, "A Tale of One City," *Saturday Review* 29 (6 April 1946): 16; "Italy's Bitter Tale," *Newsweek* 27 (4 March 1946): 86; Manny Farber, "'Open City,'" *New Republic* 115 (15 July 1946): 46; Bosley Crowther, "How Italy Resisted," *New York Times*, 26 February 1946, 21; "The New Pictures," *Time* 47 (4 March 1946) 96.

33. "Italy's Bitter Tale," p. 86; John McCarten, "The Current Cinema," *New Yorker*, 2 March 1946, 81; Farber, "'Open City,'" p. 46; Crowther, "How Italy Resisted," p. 21; "Movie of the Week: *Open City*," *Life* 20 (4 March 1946): 111.

34. Brown, "A Tale of One City," p. 17; Crowther, "How Italy Resisted," p. 21.

35. John Simon, "Why Do They Rave So over Rohmer?" *New York Times*, 29 October 1972, sect. 2, p. 1.

36. In *Making Meaning*, Bordwell implies that strict auteurist readings of the sort he wishes to explain are those in which critics attempt to unify all aspects of the film (narrative, narration, and subject matter) through the source of the director-as-author. These he argues appear in the mid-1950s. The authorship strategy

I am pointing out is much more informal at this historical point, although I shall return to this below.

37. Robert Hatch, "Movies: Director's Picture," *New Republic* 118 (29 March 1948): 31.

38. Besides Hatch: Bosley Crowther, "'Paisan,'" *New York Times*, 30 March 1948, 26; "Herb," "'Paisan,'" *Variety*, 11 February 1948, 14; Gen't, "Letter from Rome," *New Yorker* 11 (9 November 1946): 73–74; "Movie of the Week: *Paisan*," *Life* 25 (19 July 1948): 41–44; "Episodes in Italy," *Newsweek* 31 (12 April 1948): 87–88; "The New Pictures," *Time* 51 (19 April 1948): 92, 95–96.

39. Michael Budd, "*The Cabinet of Dr. Caligari*: Conditions of Reception," *Cin–Tracts* 12 (Winter 1981): 41–59, and "The National Board of Review and the Early Art Cinema in New York: *The Cabinet of Dr. Caligari* as Affirmative Culture," *Cinema Journal* 26, no. 1 (Fall 1986): 3–18.

40. Howard Thompson Lewis, *Cases on the Motion Picture Industry* (New York: McGraw-Hill Book Company, 1930), p. 543.

41. I surveyed the *New York Times* by scanning its reprints of film-related articles in its *Encyclopedia of Film*. The article appears 23 January 1949. Jean Cocteau garners one article for his *Blood of a Poet*. This begins prior to Rossellini's affair with Ingrid Bergman, although that event surely reinforced attention to him. Of course, articles often detail Hollywood personnel's activities but as extraneous or separate from any overt authorial influence they may have on textual messages. This is not the case for these early articles on Rossellini where the writers try to connect Rossellini's biography and personal views about the world and about making films to the subject matter and style of his films.

42. Gertrude Samuels, "The Director—Hollywood's Leading Man," *New York Times*, 26 October 1952. This situation changes in the mid- and late 1950s. But I would argue that the causes also relate to the simultaneous development of the package-unit system of production in which Hollywood directors also began seeking brand-name recognition. It is this economic factor that would, as Neale suggests, eventually participate in producing the "new Hollywood" cinema. Also see chapter 4 on Hitchcock as an author.

43. Twomey, "Some Considerations," p. 241; Bernard Friend, "The Cinema Club Flourishes Again in France," *New York Times*, 27 March 1949; Thomas M. Pryor, "Film Society Movement Catches On," *New York Times*, 18 September 1949.

44. I stressed major films up to 1960 but only two or three per director. The films sampled were: *Open City* (1945, reviewed primarily in spring 1946); *Paisan* (1946, spring 1948); *Shoeshine* (1946, fall 1947); *Bicycle Thief* (1948, winter 1949); *Day of Wrath* (1943, spring 1948); *Bitter Rice* (1948, winter 1950); *The Miracle* (1948, winter 1950–1951); *Miracle in Milan* (1951, winter 1951); *Rashomon* (1950, winter 1951–1952); *Diary of a Country Priest* (1950, spring 1954); *Umberto D* (1952, fall 1955); *The White Sheik* (1952, spring 1956); *La Strada* (1954, summer 1956); *Seventh Seal* (1956, fall 1958); *Wild Strawberries* (1957, summer 1959); *The 400 Blows* (1959, fall 1959); *Hiroshima, mon amour* (1959, spring 1960); *Breathless* (1959, spring 1961); *L'Avventura* (1959, spring 1961); *La Dolce Vita* (1959, spring 1961); *Rocco and His Brothers* (1960, summer

1961); *Last Year at Marienbad* (1961, spring 1962); *Cloe from 5 to 7* (1961, fall 1962); *L'Ecclisse* (1962, fall 1962); *Repulsion* (1965, fall 1965); *Accident* (1967, spring 1967); *Teorema* (1968, spring 1969); *My Night at Maud's* (1969, spring 1970); *Love and Anarchy* (1973, spring 1974); *Scenes from a Marriage* (1973, fall 1974).

45. Given that art films were said to appeal to highbrows, I wanted to determine what reading directions art film audiences might be receiving from their publications. Surprisingly, the eight review sources were moderately erratic. At times the most penetrating and complex remarks were in *Variety*. Some trends may be discerned in these publications, but they are not apparent from this study. Because the total number of reviews approximates 240, I am referencing only those from which I directly quote.

46. "T.M.P.," "Shoe-Shine," *New York Times*, 27 August 1947, 19.

47. Bosley Crowther, "The Bicycle Thief," *New York Times*, 13 December 1949, 44.

48. Bosley Crowther, "Bitter Rice," *New York Times*, 19 September 1950, 39; "New Films," *Newsweek*, 36 (18 September 1950): 92.

49. A. H. Weiler, "La Strada," *New York Times*, 17 July 1956, p. 19; "The Strong Grow Weak," *Newsweek* 48 (16 July 1956): 84; Arthur Knight, "Italian Realism Refreshed," *Saturday Review* 39 (30 June 1956): 23; "The New Pictures," *Time* 68 (23 July 1956): 84.

50. James Reichley, "The Beauty and the Beast," *New Republic* 135 (31 December 1956): 22.

51. Bosley Crowther, "Rosho-Mon [*sic*]," *New York Times*, 27 December 1951, 18; "New Films," *Newsweek* 39 (7 January 1952): 59; Ray Falk, "Japan's 'Rasho Mon' [*sic*] Rings the Bell," *New York Times*, 21 October 1951.

52. *Rashomon* is an early non-European import. Shown in an art house in New York after winning the Venice Film Festival's grand prize, it was treated much as were European films, with the exception that some of its strangeness was attributed to cultural differences. Akira Kurosawa is always mentioned in the reviews as the director.

53. Bosley Crowther, "Diary of a Country Priest," *New York Times*, 6 April 1954, 35; John McCarten, "The Current Cinema," *New Yorker* 30 (17 April 1954): 113; Hollis Alpert, "Classics from France and England," *Saturday Review* 37 (27 March 1954): 25. "Mosk" in *Variety* seemed to comprehend it; 12 September 1951, 18.

54. Stanley Kauffmann, "Swedish Rhapsody," *New Republic* 140 (27 April 1959): 20.

55. Bosley Crowther, "Wild Strawberries," *New York Times*, 23 June 1959, 37; "Mosk," "Smultronstallet," *Variety*, 24 September 1958, 6; "The New Pictures," *Time* 75 (13 July 1959): 68.

56. "Love in a Mass Grave," *Time* 75 (16 May 1960): 88.

57. Bosley Crowther, "Breathless," *New York Times*, 8 February 1961, 26; "Mosk," "A Bout De Souffle," *Variety*, 27 January 1960, 6; Stanley Kauffmann, "Adventures of an Anti-Hero," *New Republic* 144 (13 February 1961): 20.

58. "Cubistic Crime," *Time* 77 (17 February 1961): 62.

59. "Rhythm of the Times," *Newsweek* 57 (17 April 1961): 108.

Chapter Ten
Chameleon in the Film, Chameleons in the Audience

1. The epigraph is drawn from Rob Edelman, "Zelig," in *Magill's Cinema Annual 1984*, ed. Frank N. Magill (Englewood Cliffs, N.J.: Salem Press, 1984), p. 475.

2. As defined in chapter 2, significance is "'designating a relation to facts and ideas outside [the text's] system'"; it refers to what an individual values about a text. The term is used in distinction from meaning.

3. The thirty-two reviews were read for their comments about the significance (not meaning) of the film; i.e., what the film was implying about extratextual conditions. If the reviewer indicated several points of significance, each one was noted. In a few instances the reviews did not include significance statements. I did not, however, consider the headlines because headlines are often written by someone other than the reviewer. The reviews covered were the following: Robert Asahina, "Hyping Mediocrity," *The New Leader* 66, no. 17 (19 September 1983): 19; Sheila Benson, "The Human Chameleon Named Zelig," *Los Angeles Times*, 29 July 1983, sect. 6, pp. 1, 4, and 6; Richard A. Blake, "Thalia," *America* 149, no. 4 (6 August 1983): 73; Vincent Canby, "Film View: Celebrity Isn't Much to Celebrate in These Movies," *New York Times*, 27 November 1983, sect. 2, pp. 17 and 22, and "Film: 'Zelig,' Woody Allen's Story about a 'Chameleon Man," *New York Times*, 15 July 1983, sect. 3, p. 8; Harry Cheney, "Zelig," *Christianity Today* 27, no. 13 (2 September 1983): 81; John Coleman, "Films: Here Comes Everybody," *New Statesman* 106, no. 2742 (7 October 1983): 27–28; Richard Combs, "Zelig," *Monthly Film Bulletin* 50, no. 597 (November 1983): 293–94; David Denby, "The Past Revisited," *New York* 16, no. 28 (18 July 1983): 51–52; Samuel Dresner, "Film: Woody Allen, Theologian," *Midstream* 31, no. 3 (March 1985): 45–50; Edelman, "Zelig," pp. 473–78; Richard Feldstein, "The Dissolution of the Self in 'Zelig,'" *Literature/Film Quarterly* 13, no. 3 (1985): 155–60; Aryeh L. Gotlieb, "Troubled Jew?" *Midstream* 31, no. 3 (March 1985): 51–53; Richard Grenier, "Woody Allen on the American Character," *Commentary* 76, no. 5 (November 1983): 61–65; Robert Hatch, "Zelig," *Nation* 237, no. 7 (17 September 1983): 220; Pauline Kael, "The Current Cinema: Anyone Home?" *New Yorker* 49, no. 25 (8 August 1983), 84, 78–89; Stanley Kauffmann, "Stanley Kauffmann on Films: One Character in Search of an Author," *New Republic* 189, no. 3 (15 and 22 August 1983): 24–25; Bill Krohn, "Zelig," *Boxoffice* 119 (September 1983): 160–61; Jack Kroll, "Happiness Is a Single Self," *Newsweek* 102, no. 3 (18 July 1983): 72; Mark Le Fanu, "Zelig," *Films and Filming* 349 (October 1983): 42–43; Lawrence O'Toole, "Changing with the Times," *Maclean's* 96, no. 31 (1 August 1983): 50; John Pym, "Duke Ellington's Brother: *Zelig*," *Sight and Sound* 52, no. 4 (Autumn 1983): 283; Leonard Quart, "Zelig," *Cineaste* 13, no. 2 (1984): 42–43; Margaret Ronan, "Zelig," *Scholastic Update*, 116, no. 6 (11 November 1983): 11; Andrew Sarris, "Films in Focus: Woody Allen at the Peak of Parody," *Village Voice* 28, no. 29 (19 July 1983): 39; Richard Schickel, "Meditations on Celebrity," *Time* 122, no. 2 (11 July 1983): 67; John Simon, "Surfaces Mostly," *National Review* 35, no. 15 (5 August 1983): 950; "Step" [S. Klain], "Zelig," *Variety* 311, no. 11 (13 July 1983): 15; J. M. Wall, "Zelig," *Christian*

Century 100, no. 24 (17–24 August 1983): 752; Wendy Weinstein, "Zelig," *Film Journal* 86 (19 August 1983): 22–23; Colin L. Westerbeck, Jr., "The Invisible Man: You Are What You Meet," *Commonweal* 110, no. 15 (9 September 1983): 468–69; R. Richard Williams, "Zelig," *Cinefantastique* 14, no. 2 (1983/84): 53; and Vernon Young, "Parental Guidance Suggested: 'Moscow on the Hudson,'" *Hudson Review* 37, no. 3 (Autumn 1984): 457–60.

Additional responses not counted in the above collection include two essays by Robert Stam: "A Tale of Two Cities: Cultural Polyphony and Ethnic Transformation," *East-West Film Journal* 3, no. 1 (December 1933): 105–116, and Stam and Ella Shohat, "*Zelig* and Contemporary Theory: Meditation on the Chameleon Text," *enclitic* 9, nos. 1–2 (1987): 76–93, reprinted in substantially the same version in *Subversive Pleasures: Bakhtin, Cultural Criticism, and Film* (Baltimore: The Johns Hopkins University Press, 1989), pp. 198–218. Stam (and Shohat) use *Zelig* as an application of Bakhtin's notions to which I will refer below. Also see Nancy Pogel, *Woody Allen* (Boston: Twayne, 1987), pp. 171–186, which was called to my attention after I completed the study. Pogel is quite typical in her critical reading.

By "theme": celebrities (Asahina, Benson, Canby, Hatch, Kael, O'Toole, Sarris, Schickel, Simon, Step, Westerbeck, Young); "capricious social opinion" (Feldstein, Simon, Step); insanity (Krohn, Kroll, Simon); insignificance (Kael); proof of existence (Kauffmann); conformism (Asahina, Cheney, Coleman, Dresner, Grenier, Kael, Kauffmann, Quart, Ronan); being one's self/self-identity (O'Toole, Ronan); modern man (Blake, Canby, Kael, Quart); Everyman (Cheney, Coleman, Westerbeck); a nonhero (Combs); identification and Lacanian mirror stage (Feldstein); being liked (Kauffmann); being a success (Quart); redemption through love (Le Fanu, Weinstein); being or not being Jewish (Combs, Dresner, Gotlieb); being Woody Allen auteur-celebrity (Combs, Denby, Edelman, Kroll, O'Toole, Quart, Schickel, Simon, Westerbeck).

4. Documentaries (Asahina, Benson, Blake, Canby, Coleman, Combs, Denby, Grenier, Hatch, Kael, Kauffmann, Krohn, Kroll, Pym, Quart, Sarris, Schickel, Simon, Step, Weinstein, Westerbeck, Williams, and Young). Of those twenty-three, only Denby, Krohn, and Schickel did not mention *Reds*. Several of the writers mentioned that Warren Beatty (director of *Reds*) was then having an affair with Allen's former girlfriend, Diane Keaton, also starring in *Reds*, thus in part motivating the connection. For the other parodies and allusions: *Citizen Kane* (Canby, Combs, Kroll, Le Fanu, Pym, Sarris, Weinstein, Williams); the Elephant Man (Combs, Kael, Krohn, Step); Melville's confidence man (Kael, Kauffmann); Stephen Jacob Weinberg (Grenier); the interviewees (Kauffmann, Kroll); commercialism (Coleman); life in the 1920s (Pym, Quart, Wall); psychoanalysis (Kroll, Step); and interpretation (Blake).

5. David Bennett, "Parody, Postmodernism and the Politics of Reading," *Critical Quarterly* 27, no. 4 (Winter 1985): 27–43.

6. Stam and Shohat, "*Zelig* and Contemporary Theory," pp. 176–77.

7. Such arguments include to what degree he authored books signed or co-signed by P. N. Medvedev or V. N. Vološinov. The debates also involve Bakhtin's religious beliefs and the influence of those beliefs on his theoretical perspectives. Specifically, since his notion of dialogue is connected to an ideal discussion be-

tween man and God, whatever hinders dialogue is bad. Another issue is the attraction of Bakhtin's ideas to groups in contention: marxists, Christians, liberal humanists. Some of these disagreements will show up in my synopsis of Bakhtin. However, since my remarks do not require coming to conclusions about any of these issues and since I have no ability to contribute to these discussions, I would simply refer to several useful books and essays: Tzvetan Todorov, *Mikhail Bakhtin: The Dialogical Principle* (1981), trans. Wlad Godzich (Minneapolis: University of Minnesota Press, 1984); Katrina Clark and Michael Holquist, *Mikhail Bakhtin* (Cambridge: Harvard University Press, 1984); Ken Hirschkop, "A Response to the Forum on Mikhail Bakhtin," *Critical Inquiry* 11, no. 4 (June 1985): 672–78; Gary Saul Morson, "Dialogue, Monologue, and the Social: A Reply to Ken Hirschkop," *Critical Inquiry* 11, no. 4 (June 1985): 679–86; Denis Donoghue, "Reading Bakhtin," *Raritan* 5, no. 2 (Fall 1985): 107–19; Robert Young, "Back to Bakhtin," *Cultural Critique* 2 (Winter 1985–1986): 71–92; Ken Hirschkop, "The Domestication of M. M. Bakhtin," *Essays in Poetics* 11, no. 1 (April 1986): 76–87; Joseph Frank, "The Voices of Mikhail Bakhtin," *New York Review of Books*, 23 October 1986, 56–60; Michael Sprinker, "Boundless Context: Problems in Bakhtin's Linguistics," *Poetics Today* 7, no. 1 (1986): 117–28; David Lodge, "After Bakhtin," in *The Linguistics of Writing: Arguments between Language and Literature*, ed. Derek Attridge, Alan Durant, and Colin MacCabe (New York: Methuen, 1987): pp. 91–102; Graham Pechey, "On the Borders of Bakhtin: Dialogization, Decolonization," *Oxford Literary Review* 9, nos. 1–2 (1987): 59–84; Allon White, "The Struggle over Bakhtin: Fraternal Reply to Robert Young," *Cultural Critique* 8 (Winter 1987–1988): 217–41. Also useful on Bakhtin's translinguistic theory besides further citations below are: Caryl Emerson, "The Outer Word and Inner Speech: Bakhtin, Vygotsky, and the Internalization of Language," *Critical Inquiry* 10, no. 2 (December 1983): 245–64; Caryl Emerson and Gary Saul Morson, "Penultimate Words," in *The Current in Criticism: Essays on the Present and Future in Literary Theory*, ed. Clayton Koelb and Virgil Lokke (West Lafayette, Ind.: Purdue University Press, 1987), pp. 43–64; David Patterson, *Literature and Spirit: Essays on Bakhtin and His Contemporaries* (Lexington: University of Kentucky Press, 1988); Graham Pechey, "Bakhtin, Marxism, and Post-Structuralism," in *The Poetics of Theory*, ed. Francis Barker, Peter Hulme, Margaret Iverson, and Diana Loxley (Colchester, England: University of Essex Press, 1983), pp. 234–47; Paul Thibault, "Narrative Discourse as a Multi-Level System of Communication: Some Theoretical Proposals concerning Bakhtin's Dialogic Principle," *Studies in Twentieth Century Literature* 9, no. 1 (Fall 1984): 89–117.

8. White, "The Struggle Over Bakhtin," pp. 228–29.

9. Michael Holquist, "Answering as Authoring: Mikhail Bakhtin's Trans-Linguistics," *Critical Inquiry* 10, no. 2 (December 1983): 313.

10. Todorov, *Mikhail Bakhtin*, pp. 41, 41–42 (italics in original).

11. Roman Jakobson, "Linguistics and Poetics" (1960), rpt. in *The Structuralists from Marx to Lévi-Strauss*, ed. Richard and Fernande DeGeorge (Garden City, N.Y.: Doubleday & Company, 1972), p. 89.

12. Todorov, *Mikhail Bakhtin*, p. 54.

13. M. M. Bakhtin, "The Problem of Speech Genres" (1952–1953), in *Speech Genres and Other Late Essays*, pp. 68, 69.

14. Critics underline that the notion of "dialogue" in Bakhtin should not be confused with the Hegelian or Marxist notions of "dialectics." See Morson, "Dialogue, Monologue, and the Social," p. 684, and Young, "Back to Bakhtin," p. 76. Young writes: "Bakhtin, on the other hand, makes it very clear in those texts signed with his own name that dialogism cannot be confused with dialectics. Dialogism cannot be resolved; it has no teleology. It is unfinalized and open ended. Dialectics, according to Bakhtin, are monological."

While I believe that the opposition of Self and Other is sundered in the use of a socially based language system, I do have trouble with the idea that any individual utterance is dialogical. The theory, as I understand it, has the speaker constructing his or her image of the listener's response. Constructing an "image" or "representation" is, however, not the same as actually taking in the Other's dialogue. Thus, it is questionable to me whether the speaker is really speaking the Other's words, or just a representation of what they might be. The difference is significant ontologically. For the purposes of this discussion, however, I shall let the dialogical stand.

15. Holquist, "Answering as Authoring," p. 311 (italics in original).

16. Todorov, *Mikhail Bakhtin*, p. 42.

17. Charles I. Schuster, "Mikhail Bakhtin as Rhetorical Theorist," *College English* 47, no. 6 (October 1985): 594–607. Also see Frank, "The Voices of Mikhail Bakhtin," p. 59.

18. Wayne C. Booth, "Freedom of Interpretation: Bakhtin and the Challenge of Feminist Criticism" (1982), rpt. in *The Politics of Interpretation*, ed. W.J.T. Mitchell (Chicago: University of Chicago Press, 1983), p. 57.

19. David Carroll, "The Alterity of Discourse Form, History, and the Question of the Political in M. M. Bakhtin," *Diacritics* 13, no. 2 (Summer 1983): 65–83.

20. In this usage, for Bakhtin, "languages" are ideological languages, not English, French, and so on. Heteroglossia is Bakhtin's term for "other-languagedness"; polyphonia refers to "many-voicedness." See Linda M. Park-Fuller, "Voices: Bakhtin's Heteroglossia and Polyphony, and the Performance of Narrative Literature," *Literature in Performance* 7, no. 1 (November 1986): 2.

21. Mikhail Bakhtin, "Discourse in the Novel" (1934–1935), in *The Dialogic Imagination*, p. 272.

22. Hirschkop, "The Domestication," p. 79.

23. *Skaz* refers to representations of verbal speech, particularly speech with accents or dialects.

24. Bakhtin, "From the Prehistory of Novelistic Discourse" (1940), in *The Dialogic Imagination*, p. 49 (italics mine). Bakhtin privileges the novel, and particularly Dostoevsky's work, as dialogical rather than monological. However, since he also speaks of utterances as so constructed, his thesis about the specificity of the novelistic genre cannot hold. This has been noted by other writers including Todorov, *Mikhail Bakhtin*, pp. 63–64, and Carroll, "The Alterity of Discourse," p. 71.

25. Mikhail Bakhtin, *Problems of Dostoevsky's Poetics* (1929, orig. pub. 1963), trans. R. W. Rotsel (Ann Arbor, Mich.: Ardis, 1973), p. 153 (italics in original).

26. Bakhtin, "From the Prehistory of Novelistic Discourse," p. 75.

27. Ibid., pp. 75–76.

28. Linda Hutcheon, *A Theory of Parody: The Teachings of Twentieth-Century Art Forms* (London: Methuen, 1985), p. 23.

29. Todorov, *Mikhail Bakhtin*, pp. 41–42 (italics in original).

30. Bakhtin, "Discourse in the Novel," pp. 281–82. That Bakhtin believes this to be locally possible is similarly implied in M. M. Bakhtin, "Toward a Methodology for the Human Sciences" (1930s–1940s), in *Speech Genres*, p. 159. Also see Ronald Schleifer, "Enunciation and Genre: Mikhail Bakhtin and the 'Double-Voiced Narration' of 'The Rape of the Lock,'" *New Orleans Review* 15, no. 4 (Winter 1988): 33.

31. Sprinker, "Boundless Context," 124.

32. Bakhtin, "Toward a Methodology for the Human Sciences," p. 170.

33. Bakhtin, "Discourse in the Novel," p. 419.

34. Even if the speaker does not vocalize an utterance regarding *Zelig*, for Bakhtin and Vološinov, inner speech functions from the same sources and model as external speech. The Self is talking to the Self.

35. *Magill's Cinema Annual* quotes the *New York Times*, so it also might be said to mention *Kane*.

36. Stam and Shohat, "*Zelig* and Contemporary Theory," pp. 191, 179–80.

37. Stam and Shohat come close to this observation when they write, "The film *Zelig*, like the Zelig phenomenon, becomes an object-text of critical discourse and of cultural and psychoanalytic speculation. Within a kind of hermeneutic ludism, both film and character become a text open to diverse interpretative grids" (ibid., p. 184). They then proceed, however, by referencing Lacanian psychoanalytical theory, to suggest that viewers position themselves to become each of the characters: "Zelig's transformations, in this sense, can be seen as literalizing the psychic chameleonism of spectatorship" (p. 186). Assuming as it does the passive taking in of the utterance, such a thesis of communication is not that of Bakhtin's notion of the dialogic.

THIS BIBLIOGRAPHY includes most of the sources used in Part One but only the more general articles and books in Part Two.

Aaron, Daniel. *Writers on the Left*. New York: Harcourt, 1961.

Alexander, William. *Film on the Left: American Documentary Film from 1931 to 1942*. Princeton: Princeton University Press, 1981.

Allor, Martin. "Relocating the Site of the Audience." *Critical Studies in Mass Communication* 5 (1988): 217–33.

Althusser, Louis. *Lenin and Philosophy and Other Essays*. Trans. Ben Brewster. New York: Monthly Review Press, 1971.

Altman, Rick. "Television Sound." 1985. Rpt. in *Television*, ed. Newcomb. Pp. 566–84.

Anderson, Howard. "*Tristram Shandy* and the Reader's Imagination." *PMLA* 86 (October 1971): 966–73.

Andrew, J. Dudley. "Film and Society: Public Rituals and Private Space." *East-West Film Journal* 1, no. 1 (December 1986): 7–22.

———. *The Major Film Theories: An Introduction*. New York: Oxford University Press, 1976.

Ang, Ien. *Watching Dallas: Soap Opera and the Melodramatic Imagination*. 1982. Trans. Della Couling. London: Methuen, 1985.

Babuscio, Jack. "Camp and the Gay Sensibility." In *Gays and Film*, ed. Dyer. Pp. 40–57.

Bakhtin, M. M. *The Dialogic Imagination: Four Essays*. Trans. Caryl Emerson and Michael Holquist. Austin: University of Texas Press, 1981.

———. *Problems of Dostoevsky's Poetics*. 1929. Orig. pub. 1963. Trans. R. W. Rotsel. Ann Arbor, Mich.: Ardis, 1973.

———. *Speech Genres and Other Late Essays*. Trans. Vern W. McGee. Austin: University of Texas Press, 1986.

Barnouw, Dagmar. "Review of *The Act of Reading* and *The Implied Reader* by Wolfgang Iser." *Modern Language Notes* 94 (December 1979): 1207–13.

Barthes, Roland. "The Death of the Author." 1968. In *Image, Music, Text*, trans. Stephen Heath. New York: Hill and Wang, 1977. Pp. 142–48.

———. *The Pleasure of the Text*. 1973. Trans. Richard Miller. New York: Hill and Wang, 1975.

———. *S/Z*. 1970. Trans. Richard Miller. New York: Hill and Wang, 1974.

Baxandall, Michael. *Patterns of Intentions: On the Historical Explanation of Pictures*. New Haven: Yale University Press, 1985.

Beaujour, Michel. "Exemplary Pornography: Barres, Loyola and the Novel." In *The Reader in the Text*, ed. Suleiman and Crosman. Pp. 325–49.

Becker, Samuel L. "Marxist Approaches to Media Studies: The British Experience." *Critical Studies in Mass Communication* 1 (1984): 66–80.

Beers, Terry. "Reading Reading Constraints: Conventions, Schemata, and Literary Interpretation." *Diacritics* 18, no. 4 (Winter 1988): 82–93.

Benjamin, Walter. "Theses on the Philosophy of History." In *Illuminations*, ed. Hannah Arendt, trans. Harry Zohn. New York: Schocken Books, 1969. Pp. 253–64.

Bennett, Tony. "Text and Social Process: The Case of James Bond." *Screen Education* 41 (Winter/Spring 1982): 3–14.

Bennett, Tony, and Janet Woollacott. *Bond and Beyond: The Political Career of a Popular Hero*. London: Methuen, 1987.

Bergstrom, Janet, and Mary Ann Doane. "The Female Spectator: Contexts and Directions." *Camera obscura* 20–21 (May–September 1989): 5–27.

Birchall, Ian H. "Marxism and Literature." In *The Sociology of Literature: Theoretical Approaches*, ed. Routh and Wolff. Pp. 92–108.

Bobo, Jacqueline. "*The Color Purple*: Black Women's Responses." *Jump Cut* 33 (1988): 43–51.

Booth, Wayne C. "'Preserving the Exemplar': Or, How Not to Dig Our Own Graves." *Critical Inquiry* 3 (Spring 1977): 407–23.

Bordwell, David. "The Art Cinema as a Mode of Film Practice." *Film Criticism* 4, no. 1 (Fall 1979): 56–64.

———. *Making Meaning: Inference and Rhetoric in the Interpretation of Cinema*. Cambridge: Harvard University Press, 1989.

———. *Narration in the Fiction Film*. Madison: University of Wisconsin Press, 1985.

Branigan, Edward. *Point of View in the Cinema: A Theory of Narration and Subjectivity in Classical Film*. Berlin: Mouton Publishers, 1984.

Britton, Andrew. "For Interpretation—Notes against Camp." *Gay Left* 7 (Winter 1978–1979): 11–14.

Brooke-Rose, Christine. "The Readerhood of Man." In *The Reader in the Text*, ed. Suleiman and Crosman. Pp. 120–48.

Browne, Nick. "The Political Economy of the Television (Super) Text." 1984. Rpt. in *Television*, ed. Newcomb. Pp. 585–99.

Brunsdon, Charlotte, and David Morley. *Everyday Television: "Nationwide."* London: British Film Institute, 1978.

Budd, Michael. "*The Cabinet of Dr. Caligari*: Conditions of Reception." *Ciné-Tracts* 12 (Winter 1981): 41–59.

———. "The National Board of Review and the Early Art Cinema in New York: *The Cabinet of Dr. Caligari* as Affirmative Culture." *Cinema Journal* 26, no. 1 (Fall 1986): 3–18.

Bürger, Peter. "The Institution of 'Art' as a Category in the Sociology of Literature." *Cultural Critique* 2 (Winter 1985–1986): 5–33.

Campbell, Russell. *Cinema Strikes Back: Radical Filmmaking in the United States, 1930–1942*. Ann Arbor, Mich.: UMI Research Press, 1982.

Carey, James W. "A Cultural Approach to Communication." *Communications* 2 (1975): 1–22.

Carroll, David. "The Alterity of Discourse Form, History, and the Question of the Political in M. M. Bakhtin." *Diacritics* 13, no. 2 (Summer 1983): 65–83.

Carroll, Noël. "The Power of Movies." *Daedalus* 114, no. 4 (Fall 1985): 79–103.

————. "Toward a Theory of Film Editing." *Millennium Film Journal* 3 (1978): 79–99.

Chabot, C. Barry. "Three Studies of Reading." *College English* 37 (December 1975): 425–31.

Chambers, Iain, John Clarke, Ian Connell, Lidia Curti, Stuart Hall, and Tony Jefferson. "Marxism and Culture." *Screen* 18, no. 4 (Winter 1977/78): 109–19.

Chartier, Roger. "Intellectual History or Sociocultural History? The French Trajectories." Trans. Jane P. Kaplan. In *Modern European Intellectual History: Reappraisals and New Perspectives*, ed. Dominick LaCapra and Steven L. Kaplan. Ithaca: Cornell University Press, 1982. Pp. 13–46.

Clark, Timothy J. "Preliminaries to a Possible Treatment of 'Olympia' in 1865." *Screen* 21, no. 1 (Spring 1980): 18–41.

Cohen, Derek, and Richard Dyer. "The Politics of Gay Culture." In *Homosexuality: Power and Politics*, ed. Gay Left Collective. London: Allison and Busby, 1980. Pp. 172–186.

Cory, Donald Webster. *The Homosexual in America*. New York: Greenberg, 1951.

Coste, Didier. "Three Concepts of the Reader and Their Contribution to a Theory of the Literary Text." *Orbis Litterarum* 34, no. 4 (1979): 271–86.

Coward, David. "The Sociology of Literary Response." In *The Sociology of Literature*, ed. Routh and Wolff. Pp. 8–17.

Crawford, Mary, and Roger Chaffin. "The Reader's Construction of Meaning: Cognitive Research on Gender and Comprehension." In *Gender and Reading: Essays on Readers, Texts, and Contexts*, ed. Elizabeth A. Flynn and Patrocinio P. Schweickart. Baltimore: The Johns Hopkins University Press, 1986. Pp. 3–30.

Cripps, Thomas. *Slow Fade to Black: The Negro in American Film, 1900–1942*. London: Oxford University Press, 1977.

Crosman, Robert. "Do Readers Make Meaning?" In *The Reader in the Text*, ed. Suleiman and Crosman. Pp. 149–64.

————. "Some Doubts about 'The Reader of *Paradise Lost*.'" *College English* 37 (December 1975): 372–82.

Culler, Jonathan. *On Deconstruction: Theory and Criticism after Structuralism*. Ithaca: Cornell University Press, 1982.

————. "Prolegomena to a Theory of Reading." In *The Reader in the Text*, ed. Suleiman and Crosman. Pp. 46–66.

————. *The Pursuit of Signs: Semiotics, Literature, Deconstruction*. Ithaca: Cornell University Press, 1981.

————. *Structuralist Poetics: Structuralism, Linguistics, and the Study of Literature*. Ithaca: Cornell University Press, 1975.

Danto, Arthur. "The Artworld." *Journal of Philosophy* 61 (1968): 571–84.

Darnton, Robert. "Danton and Double-Entendre." *New York Review of Books*, 16 February 1984, 19–24.

————. *The Great Cat Massacre and Other Episodes in French Cultural History*. New York: Vintage Books, 1984.

DeMaria, Robert, Jr. "The Ideal Reader: A Critical Fiction." *PMLA* 93 (May 1978): 463–74.

D'Emilio, John. *Sexual Politics, Sexual Communities: The Making of a Homosexual*

Minority in the United States 1940–1970. Chicago: University of Chicago Press, 1983.

de Saussure, Ferdinand. *Course in General Linguistics*. 1915. Trans. Wade Baskin. New York: McGraw-Hill Book Company, 1966.

Dillon, George L. *Language Processing and the Reading of Literature: Toward a Model of Comprehension*. Bloomington: Indiana University Press, 1978.

Dyer, Richard. *Heavenly Bodies: Film Stars and Society*. New York: St. Martin's Press, 1986.

———. "It's Being So Camp as Keeps Us Going." *Body Politic* 10 (September 1977): 11–13.

———, ed. *Gays and Film*. Rev. ed. London: British Film Institute, 1980.

Eagleton, Terry. *Criticism and Ideology: A Study in Marxist Literary Theory*. 1976. London: Verso, 1978.

———. *Literary Theory: An Introduction*. Minneapolis: University of Minnesota Press, 1983.

Eco, Umberto. *The Role of the Reader: Explorations in the Semiotics of Texts*. Bloomington: Indiana University Press, 1979.

Ellsworth, Elizabeth. "Illicit Pleasures: Feminist Spectators and *Personal Best*." *Wide Angle* 8, no. 2 (1986): 45–56.

Estes, W. K., ed. *Handbook of Learning and Cognitive Processes*. vol. 4: *Attention and Memory*. Hillsdale, N.J.: Lawrence Erlbaum Associates, 1976.

Fell, John L., ed. *Film before Griffith*. Berkeley: University of California Press, 1983.

Fetterley, Judith. *The Resisting Reader: A Feminist Approach to American Fiction*. Bloomington: Indiana University Press, 1978.

Fish, Stanley. "Interpreting 'Interpreting the *Variorum*.'" 1976. Rpt. in *Is There a Text in this Class?* Cambridge: Harvard University Press, 1980. Pp. 174–80.

———. "Interpreting the *Variorum*." *Critical Inquiry* 2 (Spring 1976): 465–85. Rpt. in *Reader-Response Criticism*, ed. Tompkins. Pp. 164–84.

———. "Literature in the Reader: Affective Stylistics." *New Literary History* 2, no. 1 (Autumn 1970): 123–62. Rpt. in *Reader-Response Criticism*, ed. Tompkins. Pp. 70–100.

———. "Normal Circumstances, Literal Language, Direct Speech Acts, the Ordinary, the Everyday, the Obvious, What Goes without Saying, and Other Special Cases." *Critical Inquiry* 4 (Summer 1978): 625–44.

Fiske, John. "British Cultural Studies and Television." In *Channels of Discourse*, ed. Robert C. Allen. Chapel Hill: University of North Carolina Press, 1987. Pp. 254–89.

———. *Television Culture*. London: Methuen, 1987.

———. *Understanding Popular Culture*. Boston: Unwin Hyman, 1989.

Fleener-Marzec, Nickieann. *D. W. Griffith's "The Birth of a Nation": Controversy, Suppression, and the First Amendment as It Applies to Filmic Expression, 1915–1973*. New York: Arno Press, 1980.

Garnham, Alan. *Psycholinguistics: Central Topics*. London: Methuen, 1985.

Garnham, Nicholas. "Contribution to a Political Economy of Mass-communication." In *Media, Culture and Society*, ed. Richard Collins, James Curran, Nicholas Garnham, Paddy Scannell, Philip Schlesinger, and Colin Sparks. London: Sage Publications, 1986. Pp. 9–32.

Gassett, Thomas F. *Uncle Tom's Cabin and American Culture*. Dallas: Southern Methodist University Press, 1985.

Geertz, Clifford. *The Interpretation of Cultures*. New York: Basic Books, 1973.

Genette, Gerard. *Narrative Discourse: An Essay in Method*. 1972. Trans. Jane E. Lewin. Ithaca: Cornell University Press, 1980.

Gibson, Walker. "Authors, Speakers, Readers, and Mock Readers." 1950. Rpt. in *Reader-Response Criticism*, ed. Tompkins. Pp. 1–6.

Graff, Gerald. "The Genesis of Secrecy: On the Interpretation of Narrative by Frank Kermode." *New Republic*, 9 June 1979, 27–32.

Griswald, Wendy. "The Fabrication of Meaning: Literary Interpretation in the United States, Great Britain, and the West Indies." *American Journal of Sociology* 92, no. 5 (March 1987): 1077–1117.

Gurevitch, Michael, Tony Bennett, James Curran, and Janet Woollacott, eds. *Culture, Society and the Media*. London: Methuen, 1982.

Hall, Stuart. "Cultural Studies: Two Paradigms." *Media, Culture and Society* 2 (1980): 57–72.

Hall, Stuart, Dorothy Hobson, Andrew Loew, and Paul Willis, eds. *Culture, Media, Language: Working Papers in Cultural Studies, 1972–79*. London: Hutchinson, 1980.

Handel, Leo A. *Hollywood Looks at Its Audience: A Report of Film Audience Research*. Urbana: University of Illinois Press, 1950.

Hansen, Miriam. "Pleasure, Ambivalence, Identification: Valentino and Female Spectatorship." *Cinema Journal* 25, no. 4 (Summer 1986): 6–32.

Hebdige, Dick. *Subculture: The Meaning of Style*. London: Methuen, 1979.

Heller, Terry. *The Delights of Terror: An Aesthetics of the Tale of Terror*. Urbana: University of Illinois Press, 1987.

Hirschkop, Ken. "The Domestication of M. M. Bakhtin." *Essays in Poetics* 11, no. 1 (April 1986): 76–87.

———. "A Response to the Forum on Mikhail Bakhtin." *Critical Inquiry* 11, no. 4 (June 1985): 672–78.

Hohendahl, Peter Uwe. "Introduction to Reception Aesthetics." Trans. Marc Silberman. *New German Critique* 10 (Winter 1977): 29–63.

———. "Prolegomena to a History of Literary Criticism." Trans. Jeannine Blackwell. *New German Critique* 11 (Spring 1977): 151–63.

Holland, Norman N. "Recovering 'The Purloined Letter': Reading as a Personal Transaction." In *The Reader in the Text*, ed. Suleiman and Crosman. Pp. 350–70.

———. "Stanley Fish, Stanley Fish." *Genre* 10 (Fall 1977): 433–41.

———. "UNITY IDENTITY TEXT SELF." 1975. Rpt. in *Reader-Response Criticism*, ed. Tompkins. Pp. 118–33.

Holquist, Michael. "Answering as Authoring: Mikhail Bakhtin's Trans-Linguistics." *Critical Inquiry* 10, no. 2 (December 1983): 307–19.

Holub, Robert C. *Reception Theory: A Critical Introduction*. New York: Methuen, 1984.

Hutcheon, Linda. *A Theory of Parody: The Teachings of Twentieth-Century Art Forms.* London: Methuen, 1985.

Hutchins, Charles L. "A Critical Evaluation of the Controversies Engendered by D. W. Griffith's *The Birth of a Nation.*" Master's thesis, University of Iowa, 1961.

Iser, Wolfgang. *The Implied Reader: Patterns of Communication in Prose Fiction from Bunyan to Beckett.* Baltimore: The Johns Hopkins University Press, 1974.

Jakobson, Roman. "Linguistics and Poetics." 1960. Rpt. in *The Structuralists from Marx to Lévi-Strauss*, ed. Richard and Fernande DeGeorge. Garden City, N.Y.: Doubleday & Company, 1972. Pp. 85–122.

Jauss, Hans Robert. *Toward an Aesthetics of Reception.* Trans. Timothy Bahti. Minneapolis: University of Minnesota Press, 1982.

Johnson, Richard. "Culture and the Historians." "Three Problematics: Elements of a Theory of Working-Class Culture." In *Working-Class Culture*, ed. John Clarke, Chas. Critcher, and Richard Johnson. London: Hutchinson, 1979. Pp. 41–71 and 201–37.

Kahn, Victoria. "The Figure of the Reader in Petrarch's *Secretum.*" *PMLA* 100, no. 2 (March 1985): 154–66.

Kapsis, Robert T. "Hollywood Filmmaking and Reputation Building: Hitchock's 'The Birds.'" *Journal of Popular Film and Television* 15, no. 1 (Spring 1987): 4–15.

Kincaid, James R. "Coherent Readers, Incoherent Texts." *Critical Inquiry* 3 (Summer 1977): 781–802.

Kline, Herbert, ed. *New Theatre and Film, 1934 to 1937.* San Diego, Calif.: Harcourt-Brace-Jovanovich, 1985.

Klinger, Barbara. "Digressions at the Cinema: Reception and Mass Culture." *Cinema Journal* 28, no. 4 (Summer 1989): 3–19.

———. "In Retrospect: Film Studies Today." *Yale Journal of Criticism* 2, no. 1 (1988): 129–51.

———. "Much Ado about Excess: Genre, Mise-en-Scene, and the Woman in *Written on the Wind.*" *Wide Angle* 11, no. 4 (1989): 4–22.

Kolodny, Annette. "A Map for Misreading: Or, Gender and the Interpretation of Literary Texts." 1980. Rpt. in *The New Feminist Criticism: Essays on Women, Literature and Theory*, ed. Showalter. Pp. 46–62.

Kuentz, Pierre. "A Reading of Ideology or an Ideology of Reading." Trans. Wayne Gymon. *Sub-stance* 15 (1976): 82–93.

Kuhn, Annette. "Women's Genres." *Screen* 25, no. 1 (January–February 1984): 18–28.

Kuhn, Thomas S. *The Structure of Scientific Revolutions.* 2d ed. Chicago: University of Chicago Press, 1970.

Lakoff, George, and Mark Johnson. *Metaphors We Live By.* Chicago: University of Chicago Press, 1980.

Lange, Victor. "The Reader in the Strategy of Fiction." In *Expression, Communication and Experience in Literature and Language*, ed. Ronald G. Popperwell. London: The Modern Humanities Research Association, 1973. Pp. 86–102.

Leenhardt, Jacques. "Toward a Sociology of Reading." Trans. Brigitte Navelet and Susan R. Suleiman. In *The Reader in the Text*, ed. Suleiman and Crosman. Pp. 205–24.

Livingston, Sonia M. "Interpreting a Television Narrative: How Different Viewers See a Story." *Journal of Communication* 40, no. 1 (Winter 1990): 72–85.

Lovell, Terry. "Marxism and Cultural Studies." *Film Reader* 5 (1982): 184–91.

McElhaney, Joe. "Gay Spectatorship and Judy Garland." Unpublished seminar paper, New York University, Fall 1984.

Mailloux, Steven. *Interpretative Conventions: The Reader in the Study of American Fiction*. Ithaca: Cornell University Press, 1982.

———. "Reader-Response Criticism?" *Genre* 10 (Fall 1977): 413–31.

Merritt, Russell. "Dixon, Griffith, and the Southern Legend." *Cinema Journal* 12, no. 1 (Fall 1972): 26–45.

Metz, Christian. *Film Language: A Semiotics of the Cinema*. 1971. Trans. Michael Taylor. New York: Oxford University Press, 1974.

———. *Language and Cinema*. 1971. Trans. Donna Jean Umiker-Sebeok. The Hague: Mouton, 1974.

Michaels, Walter Benn. "The Interpreter's Self: Peirce on the Cartesian 'Subject.'" 1977. Rpt. in *Reader-Response Criticism*, ed. Tompkins. Pp. 185–200.

Modleski, Tania. "The Search for Tomorrow in Today's Soap Operas." *Film Quarterly* 33, no. 1 (Fall 1979).

———. *The Women Who Knew Too Much: Hitchcock and Feminist Theory*. New York: Methuen, 1988.

Moore, John Hammond. "South Carolina's Reaction to the Photoplay *The Birth of a Nation*." *The Proceedings of the South Carolina Historical Association* (1963): 30–40.

Morley, David. *Family Television*. London: Comedia, 1986.

———. *The "Nationwide" Audience: Structure and Decoding*. London: British Film Institute, 1980.

———. "Texts, Readers, Subjects." In *Culture, Media, Language*, ed. Hall et al. Pp. 163–73.

Mukařovský, Jan. "Detail as the Basic Semantic Unit in Folk Art." 1942. "On Poetic Language." 1940. In *The Word and Verbal Art*, trans. John Burbank and Peter Steiner. New Haven: Yale University Press, 1977. Pp. 180–204 and 1–64.

Mulvey, Laura. "Visual Pleasure and Narrative Cinema." *Screen* 16, no. 3 (Autumn 1975): 6–18.

Musser, Charles. "Archeology of the Cinema: 8." *Framework* 22/23 (1983): 4–11.

———. *Before the Nickelodeon*. USA, Films for Thought, 1983.

Naumann, Manfred. "Literary Production and Reception." 1973. Trans. Peter Heath. *New Literary History* 8 (Autumn 1976): 107–26.

Neale, Steve. "Art Cinema as Institution." *Screen* 22, no. 1 (1981): 11–39.

———. "'New Hollywood Cinema.'" *Screen* 17, no. 2 (Summer 1976): 117–22.

Neisser, Ulric. *Cognitive Psychology*. New York: Appleton-Century-Crofts, 1967.

Nelson, Katherine. "Social Cognition in a Script Framework." In *Social Cognitive Development*, ed. J. H. Flavell and L. Ross. Cambridge: Cambridge University Press, 1981. Pp. 97–118.

Newcomb, Horace, ed. *Television: The Critical View*. 4th ed. New York: Oxford University Press, 1987.

Newcomb, Horace M., and Paul M. Hirsch. "Television as a Cultural Forum: Implications for Research." *Quarterly Review of Film Studies* 8, no. 3 (Summer 1983): 45–55.

Newton, Judith. "History as Usual? Feminism and the 'New Historicism.'" *Cultural Critique* 9 (Spring 1988): 87–121.

Pechey, Graham. "Bakhtin, Marxism, and Post-Structuralism." In *The Poetics of Theory*, ed. Francis Barker, Peter Hulme, Margaret Iverson, and Diana Loxley. Colchester, England: University of Essex Press, 1983. Pp. 234–47.

———. "On the Borders of Bakhtin: Dialogization, Decolonization." *Oxford Literary Review* 9, nos. 1–2 (1987): 59–84.

Pells, Richard H. *Radical Visions and American Dreams: Culture and Social Thought in the Depression Years*. Middletown, Conn.: Wesleyan University Press, 1973.

Petro, Patrice. "Mass Culture and the Feminine: The 'Place' of Television in Film Studies." *Cinema Journal* 25, no. 3 (Spring 1986): 5–21.

Phelan, James. "Data, Danda, and Disagreement." *Diacritics* 13, no. 2 (Summer 1983): 39–50.

Prince, Gerald. "Introduction to the Study of the Narratee." 1973. Trans. Francis Mariner. Rpt. in *Reader-Response Criticism*, ed. Tompkins. Pp. 7–25.

———. "Notes on the Text as Reader. In *The Reader in the Text*, ed. Suleiman and Crosman. Pp. 225–40.

Rabinowitz, Peter. "Truth in Fiction: A Reexamination of Audiences." *Critical Inquiry* 4 (Autumn 1977): 121–41.

Radway, Janice. *Reading the Romance: Women, Patriarchy, and Popular Literature*. Chapel Hill: University of North Carolina Press, 1984.

Ray, William. "Recognizing Recognition: The Intra-Textual and Extra-Textual Critical Persona." *Diacritics* 7, no. 4 (Winter 1977): 20–33.

Rendall, Steven. "The Critical *We*." *Orbis Litterarum* 35, no. 2 (1980): 97–114.

Richards, I. A. *Practical Criticism: A Study of Literary Judgment*. New York: Harcourt, Brace & World, 1929.

Riffaterre, Michael. "Describing Poetic Structures: Two Approaches to Baudelaire's 'Les Chats.'" 1966. Rpt. in *Reader-Response Criticism*, ed. Tompkins. Pp. 26–40.

———. "The Referential Fallacy." *Columbia Review* 57, no. 2 (Winter 1978): 21–35.

Rosenfield, Israel. "A Hero of the Brain." *New York Review of Books*, 21 November 1985, 49–55.

———. "The New Brain." *New York Review of Books*, 14 March 1985, 34–38.

Ross, James F. "On the Concepts of Reading." *Philosophical Forum* 6, no. 1 (Fall 1974): 93–141.

Routh, Jane, and Janet Wolff, eds. *The Sociology of Literature: Theoretical Approaches*. Keele, England: University of Keele Press, 1977.

Russo, John Paul. "I. A. Richards in Retrospect." *Critical Inquiry* 8, no. 4 (Summer 1982): 743–60.

Russo, Vito. *The Celluloid Closet: Homosexuality in the Movies*. New York: Harper & Row, 1981.

Rutherford, John. "Structuralism." In *Sociology of Literature*, ed. Routh and Wolff. Pp. 43–55.

Schleiermacher, Fr. D. E. *"The Hermeneutics*: Outline of the 1819 Lectures." 1974. Trans. Jan Wojcik and Roland Haas. *New Literary History* 10, no. 1 (Autumn 1978): 1–16.

Schmidt, Henry J. "'Text-Adequate Concretizations' and Real Readers: Reception Theory and Its Applications." *New German Critique* 17 (Spring 1979): 157–69.

Scholes, Robert. *Protocols of Reading*. New Haven: Yale University Press, 1989.

Schor, Naomi. "Fiction as Interpretation/Interpretation as Fiction." In *The Reader in the Text*, ed. Suleiman and Crosman. Pp. 165–82.

Schuster, Charles I. "Mikhail Bakhtin as Rhetorical Theorist." *College English* 47, no. 6 (October 1985): 594–607.

Sherwood, Richard. "Victor Shklovsky and the Development of Early Formalist Theory on Prose Literature." *Twentieth Century Studies* 7/8 (December 1972): 26–40.

Showalter, Elaine, ed. *The New Feminist Criticism: Essays on Women, Literature and Theory*. New York: Pantheon Books, 1985.

Silberman, Marc. Review of "Holub's *Reception Theory*." *New German Critique* 33 (Fall 1984): 249–54.

Silva, Fred, ed. *Focus on "The Birth of a Nation."* Englewood Cliffs, N.J.: Prentice Hall, 1971.

Singer, Harry, and Ruddell, Robert B., ed. *Theoretical Models and Processes of Reading*. Newark, Del.: International Reading Association, 1976.

Smith, Barbara Herrnstein. "Contingencies of Value." *Critical Inquiry* 10, no. 1 (September 1983): 1–35.

Sprinker, Michael. "Boundless Context: Problems in Bakhtin's Linguistics." *Poetics Today* 7, no. 1 (1986): 117–28.

Staiger, Janet. "The Politics of Film Canons." *Cinema Journal* 24, no. 3 (Spring 1985): 4–23.

Stam, Robert. "Film and Language: From Metz to Bakhtin." In *The Cinematic Text: Methods and Approaches*, ed. R. Barton Palmer. New York: AMS Press, 1989. Pp. 277–301.

———. *Subversive Pleasures: Bakhtin, Cultural Criticism, and Film*. Baltimore: The Johns Hopkins University Press, 1989.

Stam, Robert, and Roberta Pearson. "Hitchcock's *Rear Window*: Reflexivity and the Critique of Voyeurism." *enclitic* 7, no. 1 (Spring 1983): 136–45.

Stam, Robert, and Ella Shohat. *"Zelig* and Contemporary Theory: Meditation on the Chameleon Text." *enclitic* 9, nos. 1–2 (1987): 176–93.

Steinberg, Danny D. *Psycholinguistics: Language, Mind and World*. London: Longman, 1982.

Steiner, George. "Marxism and the Literary Critic." In *Sociology of Literature and Drama*, ed. Elizabeth and Tom Burns. Harmondsworth, Middlesex, England: Penguin Books, 1973. Pp. 159–78.

Steiner, Linda. "Oppositional Decoding as an Act of Resistance." *Critical Studies in Mass Communication* 5, no. 1 (March 1988): 1–15.

Sternberg, Meir. *Expositional Modes and Temporal Ordering in Fiction.* Baltimore: The Johns Hopkins University Press, 1978.

Stierle, Karlheinz. "The Reading of Fictional Texts." Trans. Inge Crosman and Thekla Zachrau. In *The Reader in the Text*, ed. Suleiman and Crosman. Pp. 83–105.

Suleiman, Susan R. *Authoritarian Fictions: The Ideological Novel as a Literary Genre.* New York: Columbia University Press, 1983.

———. "Introduction: Varieties of Audience-Oriented Criticism." In *The Reader in the Text*, ed. Suleiman and Crosman. Pp. 3–45.

———. "Redundancy and the 'Readable' Text." *Poetics Today* 1, no. 3 (Spring 1980): 119–42.

Suleiman, Susan R., and Crosman, Inge, ed. *The Reader in the Text: Essays on Audience and Interpretation.* Princeton: Princeton University Press, 1980.

Thibault, Paul. "Narrative Discourse as a Multi-Level System of Communication: Some Theoretical Proposals concerning Bakhtin's Dialogic Principle." *Studies in Twentieth Century Literature* 9, no. 1 (Fall 1984): 89–117.

Todorov, Tzvetan. *Mikhail Bakhtin: The Dialogical Principle.* 1981. Trans. Wlad Godzich. Minneapolis: University of Minnesota Press, 1984.

Tompkins, Jane P. "An Introduction to Reader-Response Criticism." In *Reader-Response Criticism*, ed. Tompkins. Pp. ix–xxvi.

———. "The Reader in History: The Changing Shape of Literary Response." In *Reader-Response Criticism*, ed. Tompkins. Pp. 201–32.

———, ed. *Reader-Response Criticism: From Formalism to Post-Structuralism.* Baltimore: The Johns Hopkins University Press, 1980.

———. "Sentimental Power: *Uncle Tom's Cabin* and the Politics of Literary History." 1978. Rpt. in *New Feminist Criticism*, ed. Showalter. Pp. 81–104.

Tracy, David. "Creativity in the Interpretation of Religion: The Question of Radical Pluralism." *New Literary History* 15, no. 2 (Winter 1984): 289–309.

Trommler, Frank. "Working-Class Culture and Mass Culture before World War I." *New German Critique* 29 (Spring/Summer 1983): 57–70.

Vološinov, V. N. *Marxism and the Philosophy of Language.* 1929. Trans. Ladislav Matejka and I. R. Titunik. New York: Seminar Press, 1973.

Weimann, Robert. "'Reception Aesthetics' and the Crisis of Literary History." Trans. Charles Spencer. *Clio* 5, no. 1 (1975): 3–33.

Wertsch, James V., ed. *Culture, Communication, and Cognition: Vygotskian Perspectives.* Cambridge: Cambridge University Press, 1985.

White, Allon. "The Struggle over Bakhtin: Fraternal Reply to Robert Young." *Cultural Critique* 8 (Winter 1987–1988): 217–41.

Williamson, Joel. *The Crucible of Race: Black-White Relations in the American South since Emancipation.* New York: Oxford University Press, 1984.

Wimsatt, W. K., Jr. "Genesis: A Fallacy Revisited." In *The Disciplines of Criticism: Essays in Literary Theory, Interpretation, and History*, ed. Peter Demetz, Thomas Greene, and Lowry Nelson, Jr. New Haven: Yale University Press, 1968. Pp. 193–225.

Wimsatt, W. K., Jr., and M. C. Beardsley. "The Intentional Fallacy." *Sewanee Review* 54 (1946): 468–88.

Wolff, Janet. "The Interpretation of Literature in Society: The Hermeneutic Approach." In *Sociology of Literature*, ed. Routh and Wolff. Pp. 18–31.

Wollen, Peter. "Manet: Modernism and Avant Garde." *Screen* 21, no. 2 (Summer 1980): 15–25.

Young, Robert. "Back to Bakhtin." *Cultural Critique* 2 (Winter 1985–1986): 71–92.

Zimmerman, Bonnie. "What Has Never Been: An Overview of Lesbian Feminist Literary Criticism." 1981. Rpt. in *The New Feminist Criticism*, ed. Showalter. Pp. 200–224.

Index

Abrams, M. H., 22–23, 28
address, 92–95, 125, 131–35. *See also* subject positioning
Adorno, Theodor, 33
affective response, 39, 41–43, 65–67, 71, 76–78, 85, 91, 94, 118–19, 175–76. *See also* pleasure
allegorical reading, 5, 150–51, 191–92, 207
Allen, Robert C., 102–3
Allen, Woody, 197
alternative reading, 154–77
Althusser, Louis, 69–75
ambiguities, 192. *See also* gaps
Andrew, Dudley, 50–51, 223n.5
Annales School, 213n.12
art cinema, 178–95
attention, 55–57, 64
audiences, 49, 62, 121–23. *See also* readers
auteurism, 95, 179, 181, 188–95, 251–52n.36
author's intent, 19–20, 22–24, 31, 217n.19. *See also* meaning; referentiality
authorship, 3–4, 8, 22–24, 82, 89–92, 178–95, 206, 212
avant-garde film, 223n.1

Babuscio, Jack, 159–60, 162
background set, 126
Bakhtin, Mikhail, 71–72, 164, 197–209, 255–56n.7
Barnouw, Dagmar, 31
Barthes, Roland, 36–37, 46, 72, 77–78, 110
Baxandall, Michael, 20–21
Beardsley, M. C., 23–24
behavioral effects, 10
Bennett, Tony, 46–48
Bergstrom, Janet, 62
binary oppositions, 135–38, 162, 167
Birth of a Nation, The, 139–53, 238–39n.13
blanks. *See* gaps
Bleich, David, 43–45, 74
Booth, Wayne C., 28
Bordwell, David, 63–68, 81–95, 180–82, 190–95, 220n.70, 223n.5, 224n.6, 228n.65

Bourdieu, Pierre, 76
Branigan, Edward, 227–28n.50
Breathless (1959), 189
Brecht, Bertolt, 17
British cultural studies, 68–78, 81–95
Brooke-Rose, Christine, 38
Brunsdon, Charlotte, 72
Budd, Michael, 188

camp, 159, 163, 175, 245n.18, 246n. 33
canons, 14, 27, 96, 210, 233n.32. *See also* evaluating
Carey, James, 68
Carroll, Noël, 227n.50
censorship, 142, 145–46, 152
Challenger, 101, 109, 118–19, 123
Cinema 16, 189
class, 72, 92, 101–23, 127, 184, 211
codes, 19, 36–38, 60–61, 64, 72; cultural, 36, 38, 66, 109, 128; hermeneutic, 36, 38, 44, 66, 117, 173, 245n.8; proairetic, 36, 38, 44, 66, 88, 117; semic, 36, 38, 58, 110, 117; symbolic, 36, 38, 66
coherence, 12, 27–30, 37–38
Coleridge, Samuel Taylor, 25
communication theory, 45–47, 68–69, 199–204
competency, 30–34, 37–38, 44, 48
comprehending, 18–22, 216n.16
Constance School, 17
constitutivism, 63
contradictory reading, 223n.111
convention, 19, 220n.70
Crosman, Robert, 24
crosscutting, 110–11, 117–18
Culler, Jonathan, 9, 31–34, 43–45, 74, 128, 220n.65
cults, 164–65
cultural forum, 68

Danto, Arthur, 4
Danton, 4–8, 210
Darnton, Robert, 4–8, 16, 210
deconstructionism, 27–29, 32, 76, 81, 93–94, 204
defamiliarization, 28

DeMaria, Robert, Jr., 25–26
descriptionist, 63
dialogism, 200–205, 255–56n.7, 257n.14
Dillon, George, 19
Dixon, Thomas, 140–53
Doane, Mary Ann, 62
documentary cinema, 187, 190, 197, 223n.1
dominant reading, 72–78, 87–88, 155–56
double-voiced texts, 198, 202, 204
Dryden, John, 85
Dyer, Richard, 155, 157–77

Eagleton, Terry, 34
Eco, Umberto, 36–37, 110, 220n.66
Eisenstein, Sergei, 52–54, 149–50, 225n.14
Ellsworth, Elizabeth, 57, 128, 154, 174
encrustation, 46, 93, 152
ethnography, 47
evaluating, 21, 26, 30–34, 78, 90–91, 121–22, 139, 152, 174, 186. *See also* canons
Experimental Cinema, 148–49, 243n.37

fallacy: affective, 217n.28; coherence-inference, 12–13, 31–32; free-reader, 12–13, 31–32; ideal-spectator, 12–13, 31–32; intentional, 23–24; referential, 32–33
fantasy, 68, 77, 172
feminism, 51, 62, 92, 94, 156, 228n.64
Fish, Stanley, 20, 38, 40, 46, 154, 221n.79
Fiske, John, 77–78
Foolish Wives, 124–38
form and content, 142–43, 152, 193–94, 212
frame, 19
Freud, Sigmund, 61–62, 70–71
Frye, Northrop, 25

game metaphor, 28–29, 41–42, 66–67, 78, 174, 192. *See also* play
gaps, 27, 40–42, 109–10, 174
Garland, Judy, 155–77
gay politics in U.S., 158–59, 245n.13
Gay Year, The, 171–72
Genette, Gerard, 40–41, 65
genre, 39, 87–90, 95, 117, 119, 174, 185
Godard, Jean-Luc, 190
Gramsci, Antonio, 71
Griffith, D. W., 141–53

Hall, Stuart, 72–73
Hansen, Miriam, 133–37

hegemony, 69, 71, 73, 125, 210
hermeneutics, 17, 174
heteroglossia, 201, 205
high-brow/low-brow, 91–93, 184–87, 190
Hiroshima, mon amour, 189, 193
Hirsch, Paul, 68
Hitchcock, Alfred, 81–95, 189
Holland, Norman, 20, 43, 74
homologous image structures, 159–61, 172, 174, 176
homosexuality, 75, 136, 157–77
horizons of expectation, 46, 125–26
hypotheses, 41–42, 65, 173

identification, 62, 76, 88, 91, 137–38, 156, 159–60, 175–76, 232n.23
ideological state apparatuses, 69–73, 120, 127
ideology, 60, 68–73, 76, 80, 120, 127
imaginary community, 95
information processing, 63
intentional hybrid, 202–3
interpellation, 70
interpreting, 18–22; holistic, 37–39; order of, 18–22; sequential, 37, 39–42; unification of, 22–23, 29–30, 44, 58, 128, 180, 192–95, 208. *See also* reading
interpretive community, 154
intertextuality, 38, 89–95, 109, 119, 121, 128–31, 197, 201
Iser, Wolfgang, 27, 42

Jacobs, Lewis, 148–51
Jauss, Hans Robert, 46
Johnson, Richard, 74
Johnson, Sam, 25
jump cut, 193–94

Kapsis, Robert E., 90
Kincaid, James R., 28–30
Kuhn, Annette, 49

Lacan, Jacques, 61–62, 70–71, 197
Leenhardt, Jacques, 46–47
leftist politics in U.S., 139–53
Leyda, Jay, 243n.33
Life of an American Fireman, 118
life-styles, 185
linguistic theory, 53–54, 61, 63, 67, 72, 197–202; contemporary, 59–63, 78, 81–95, 197–202

McElhaney, Joe, 155, 160–77
Mailloux, Steven, 20–21, 220nn. 65 and 70
Marx, Karl, 3–4, 96–97
meaning, 18–24. *See also* author's intent;
    significance
memory, 56, 80
mentalités, 16, 140–41, 144
Metz, Christian, 60–61, 226n.36
misreading, 32–34
modernism as a reading strategy, 122, 190–
    95, 212
Morley, David, 71–75
motivation, 40–41
Mukařovský, Jan, 40–42, 65
Münsterberg, Hugo, 55–57, 64
Museum of Modern Art, 189
Musser, Charles, 102–4, 121
muted group theory, 156

narrative continuity and clarity, 102–23
narrational style, 190–95
national cinemas, 95
"Nationwide," 71–73, 88
naturalization, 37–38, 193
Neale, Steve, 179–82, 190
negative hermeneutics, 216n.9
negotiated reading, 72–78, 87–88, 155–56.
    See also alternative reading
New Criticism, 22–24, 181
new historicism, 13, 26–27, 219n.42
new Hollywood cinema, 178–79, 252n.42
Newcomb, Horace, 68
Niesser, Ulric, 67
Noble, Peter, 150–51
nonfictional cinema, 96. *See also* documen-
    tary cinema

Open City, 183, 187–88, 190
overdetermination, 236n.10

parody, 109, 121, 129, 196–209
patriarchy, 70, 77, 168
Pearson, Roberta, 81–84
perceiving, 18–22, 60, 63–65, 216n.16,
    228n.61
Personal Best, 57–58
Petro, Patrice, 49
pictorialism, 63, 227n.49
Picture Idol, The, 133
Platt, David, 146–49
play, 77–78
pleasure, 61–62, 76–78, 125

plot (*sujet*), 41–42, 65, 117
polyphony, 201
polysemy, 71–73
positivism, 73–74
poststructuralism, 47–48, 197
"primitive" cinema, 101–23
Prince, Gerald, 18–19
protocols, 65, 122, 128, 135
psychology, 43–45, 61–62, 70–71, 77,
    231n.12; cognitive, 43, 55–57, 63–68,
    78, 81–95, 154; as a reading strategy,
    81–95

Quatrefoil, 170

racism, 139–53. *See also* xenophobia
Radway, Janice, 47
readers, 24–32, 49, 215n.8; active, 55; co-
    herent, 24, 27–30, 74; competent, 24,
    30–32, 55, 60–61, 65–68, 121, 154, 156,
    173, 177, 180; cooperative, 65; empiri-
    cal, 79; female, 27, 47, 245n.8; free, 10,
    12; gay, 155–77; gendered, 88–89, 126–
    38, 156; great, 10; historical, 56; ideal, 8,
    12, 24–27, 33, 51, 55, 73–74, 91, 138,
    218n.37; lesbian feminist, 57–59; norma-
    tive, 154; passive, 51; resisting, 34, 57–
    58, 60, 138, 155–56; tabula rasa, 22–23,
    42, 71
reading, 18–24, 63–64. *See also* allegorical
    reading; alternative reading; authorship;
    contradictory reading; dominant reading;
    genre; modernism as a reading strategy;
    naturalization; negotiated reading; psy-
    chology: as a reading strategy; reflexivity;
    resisting reading; textual criticism: as a
    reading strategy
reading formations, 34, 90
reading theories, 19, 63, 93, 156, 216n.14;
    context-activated, 35, 45–58, 56, 67–68,
    75, 78, 89–95; reader-activated, 35, 43–
    45, 55–56, 74; text-activated, 35–42, 51,
    64, 73, 204. *See also* interpreting
realism, 182–95, 245n.12
Rear Window, 81–95
Red-baiting, 147–51
redundancy, 38–39, 119
referentiality, 83, 89, 93–94, 119, 126,
    131, 143, 176, 181, 185, 191, 192, 196–
    209. *See also* significance
reflexivity, 81–84, 93–95, 212
representativism, 63, 227n.49

DATE DUE

GAYLORD

PRINTED IN U.S.A.

resisting re———, 221n.80
 See also ————117
retardation————225–26n.33
Richards, ————0, 198
Riffaterre, ————, 75, 93, 96, 122,
Rossellini,————
Russian fo————
Russo, Joh————–39, 126

sadomaso————*also* evaluating
San Franci————
satire, 133
schemata, ————story of, 9, 44; as
self-identit————5; roles of, 9
 127, 15————3
 200, 20————5
semiotics, ————
sexual desi————
sexuality, 1————*ture Show,* 104
Shklovsky, ————1d play), 105–23
significanc————m), 104–23
 tiality————
signs, ideo————
 68, 125————38
social form————, 175–76, 180
social scien————, 71, 125, 197,
 89, 142, ————
sociology o————128–29, 137–38
spectators.————61, 67, 68,
spectatrix, ————
Stam, Robe——, — ——, ———, ———, ———,
 258n.37
star image, 165, 247n.39
Star Is Born, A (1954), 173–77
stereotypes, 39, 126, 132, 169
Stern, Seymour, 147–51

Wimsatt, W. K., 23–24

xenophobia, 126–38

Zelig, 196–209